TAKING AMERICA BACK

DAVID AUSTIN WALSH

Taking America Back

THE CONSERVATIVE MOVEMENT

AND THE FAR RIGHT

Yale UNIVERSITY PRESS   NEW HAVEN AND LONDON

Published with assistance from the foundation established in memory of William McKean Brown.

Yale University Press books may be purchased in quantity for educational, business, or promotional use. For information, please e-mail sales.press@yale.edu (U.S. office) or sales@yaleup.co.uk (U.K. office).

Set in Scala type by IDS Infotech Ltd.
Printed in the United States of America.

Library of Congress Control Number: 2023944621
ISBN 978-0-300-26097-7 (hardcover : alk. paper)

A catalogue record for this book is available from the British Library.

10 9 8 7 6 5 4 3 2 1

For Mom, Dad, Scott, and Claire

CONTENTS

ACKNOWLEDGMENTS

This book has had a lengthy gestation. The beginning of this project can be traced to 2010, when I was the features editor for a roundtable at History News Network on Jonah Goldberg's *Liberal Fascism: The Secret History of the American Left, from Mussolini to the Politics of Meaning,* which consisted mostly of David Neiwart, Robert Paxton, Roger Griffin, and Chip Berlet eviscerating that deeply flawed book. Goldberg was not happy about the feature—I distinctly recall him sending me a series of angry emails demanding space for rebuttal—and the entire exchange led to me writing my senior thesis at the University of Minnesota on Revilo Oliver, the work my attempt to answer the question "If American liberals are the *real* fascists, why was an avowed white nationalist and antisemite palling around with William F. Buckley Jr. at the *National Review?*" I am tremendously grateful to the former publisher of History News Network, Rick Shenkman, for taking a chance and hiring a wet-behind-the-ears college student to be the editor.

I began the project in earnest in 2017, as my dissertation project at Princeton University. I owe a tremendous debt to my dissertation advisor, Julian Zelizer. Without him, this project would not have possible. Kevin Kruse has also been a wonderful mentor and teacher—and without him I would not have the social media profile I do today! Kimberly Phillips-Fein's work, in particular *Invisible Hands,* has been tremendously influential on my own. And thank you to Leah Boustan, both for her own invaluable work and for agreeing to serve on the committee on short notice. I'd also like to thank Joe Fronczak for his feedback and guidance—his pathbreaking *Journal of American History* article on the transnational right in the 1930s was a critical influence. Thanks also to my fellow graduate students Richard Anderson, William Schultz, and Olivier Burtin for their advice and guidance on the dissertation, book manuscript, and all aspects of grad school. I'd also like to thank Richard Spiegel, Felice Physioc, Robert Decker, Kimia Shahi, Elaine Ayers, and Ezelle Sanford III for their friendship and support throughout my time at Princeton. I also want to acknowledge the incredible work my colleagues and comrades in Princeton Graduate Students United have done for graduate student workers at Princeton and around the country. I have been proud to work with all of you to fight for a better future for all of us.

I want to take a moment to acknowledge all of the people who read and commented on various stages of this manuscript. Elizabeth Tandy Shermer provided excellent feedback on the earliest version of what eventually became this work, way back in 2016. Colin Reynolds and Darren Mulloy also provided notes. Thanks also to Kathryn Olmsted, who not only was a close reader of early versions of the manuscript, but whose research path crossed mine (through the guestbook) at the Cantigny Museum in Wheaton, Illinois. I owe Jennifer Burns the title and basic conceptual framework of the book— it was on her suggestion that I developed the "right-wing popular front" framework. I also want to thank the innumerable people I've met at conferences who have provided feedback about my work and been gracious enough to share their own: John Huntington, Anna Duensing—who has become a close colleague and friend at the University of Virginia—Anton Jäger, Tim Lacy, Elizabeth Sanders, Timothy Lombardo, Nicole Hemmer, Ted Miller, and Michelle Nickerson, the late Leo Ribuffo, John Judis, Sam Tanenhaus, Walter Nugent, Heather Hendershot, Rick Perlstein, Leah Wright Rigueur, and Kathryn Brownell, to name only a few.

While I began this book at Princeton, I finished it at the University of Virginia. I have been blessed with wonderful students and colleagues as a postdoctoral fellow in the Engagements Experience program. Thank you to Joshua Mound for recruiting me, Chad Wellmon and Sarah Betzer for hiring me, and Jim Coan and Janet Spittler for being wonderful and supportive program leaders. Thanks also to my postdoctoral colleagues Swayam Bagaria, Alex Wolfson, John Handel, Sarah Teets, Liza Flood, Wendy Smith, and Laura Goldblatt for their generosity and support. I have been particularly lucky that a friend and colleague from my graduate school cohort, Benjamin Bernard, is also part of the Engagements Experience program, and I am tremendously grateful for his friendship. And I particularly want to thank Andrew Ferguson, with whom I have taught a course on conspiracy theories, paranoia, and fake news for three years. Andrew is a great friend and brilliant English scholar, and teaching with him has been the pedagogical high point of my career. I have also been overwhelmed by the community I have encountered in Charlottesville—I want to single out in particular Claire Payton and Jonathan Katz for being so kind and welcoming to my wife and me when we moved to town at the height of the COVID-19 pandemic. I also want to thank Ellen Schrecker and Michael Koncewicz for the thrill of a lifetime: their invitation to present a paper at the Tamiment Library at New York University in September 2018.

Twitter is very much a double-edged sword, but I have been blessed to find a truly remarkable community of scholars, writers, and activists online who have been a tremendous source of support and intellectual inspiration. Lawrence Glickman, Joshua Tait, Seth Cotler, Calvin TerBeek, John Ganz, Joshua Mound, John Jackson, Marshall Steinbaum, Varsha Venkatasubramanian, Greg Brew, Chad Frazier, and Josh Sheppard have all provided valuable feedback on this project.

I also want to acknowledge a number of editors at newspapers and magazines whom I have had the pleasure of working with throughout grad school. They have improved my journalistic and academic writing. Thank you to Jane Carr, Gilad Edelman, Michelle Legro, and Brian Rosenwald.

No book is possible without the generous support of archivists. I want to thank the staff at the MacArthur Memorial in Norfolk, Virginia; the special collections departments at Gettysburg College, Yale University, and the University of Oregon—in particular Patience L. Collier—as well as the Hoover Institution and Stanford University—in particular Simon Ertz—the Center for Jewish History, and the McCormick Research Center at the First Division Museum in Cantigny Park in Wheaton, Illinois—where I spent many an hour researching and climbing on war-surplus Sherman tanks. Thank you also to the Anti-Defamation League, especially Miriam Spectre. I also want to thank the Minnesota Historical Society and the special collections department at the University of Northwestern in Saint Paul, Minnesota—I ended up cutting the material from those archives in the manuscript, but they were important resources in putting me on the path to this final product. Most of all, I am incredibly grateful for the generous support from the Center for Jewish History, where I was awarded a short-term research fellowship in 2019, long delayed thanks to the COVID pandemic, that I was finally able to take advantage of in the spring of 2022.

Some personal thank-yous to my family: much love and respect to my wife Claire Denton-Spalding, without whom I quite literally could not have finished my PhD. Thank you also to her parents Will Denton and Rose Spalding, as well as Rosemarie Zagarri, for guiding me through the ins and outs of what being an academic is all about. Thank you to my brother Scott and his wife Arissa for their support.

And finally, while I promised my wife I would not dedicate this book to all the haters and losers out there, I do want to acknowledge them, because this book could not have been written without their vociferous opposition. I am proud to have such enemies.

Introduction

COMMON WISDOM AMONG mainstream pundits in 2016 held that Donald Trump had engineered a "hostile takeover" of the Republican Party and the conservative movement. Trump and Trumpism were, therefore, wholly alien to the authentic American conservative political tradition and such luminaries as Ronald Reagan and William F. Buckley Jr.[1] But this was a highly selective and misleading analysis of American politics and political history. The essential political story of MAGAism in 2016 was the displacement of a dominant conservative coalition that had broadly tolerated and in some cases even cultivated far-right support with a dominant far-right coalition that tolerated and in some cases even cultivated conservative support. Conservative political opposition to the newly ascendant far right—the so-called "Never Trump" conservatives—was rooted as much in anxieties about political backlash as in principled commitments. Many—though not all—"Never Trump" conservatives in 2016 came to grudgingly support Trump during his administration—*National Review* dedicated an entire issue to "Never Trump" in March 2016 but promptly reversed itself once Trump won the election.[2] The Republican Party establishment, though wary of Trump, has continued to be largely deferential to the former president even after the January 6, 2021 Capitol insurrection.[3] The insurrection itself was a moment so nakedly fascistic that even longtime skeptics of using the "f-word" to describe Trump and Trumpism, like acclaimed scholar of fascism Robert Paxton, concluded that the label could be fairly affixed to Trump.[4] Despite the violent spectacle of January 6, and the prospect in that month of a break with the disgraced soon-to-be-former president, the Republican Party and the conservative movement overwhelming closed ranks behind Trump. Calls for the release of the "political prisoners" of January 6 became a standard talking point in right-wing media and even among members of Congress.[5]

Little of this should have been surprising. American conservatism and the far right enjoyed a long and deeply intertwined relationship across the twentieth century, featuring a blizzarding array of schisms, alliances, antagonisms, and solidarities. Modern conservatism emerged out of opposition to the New Deal in the 1930s and 1940s, forming a right-wing popular front—a term coined by William F. Buckley Jr. in his private correspondence—with the openly racist, antisemitic, and pro-fascist far right. This coalition proved to be remarkably durable until the 1960s, when the popular front began to unravel as some conservatives proved to be unwilling to make even modest concessions to the demands of the civil rights movement and jettison explicit racism and antisemitism. These apostate conservatives would form the basis of modern white nationalism—and the boundaries between where "responsible" conservatism ended and the far right began were usually blurred. Trump's statement after the deadly Unite the Right rally in Charlottesville, Virginia—that there were "very fine people on both sides," both fascists and anti-fascists—was not an outlier.[6] Twentieth-century American conservatism did not equal fascism, but it evolved out of a right-wing popular front that included fascist and quasi-fascist elements. This is the key to understanding how American conservatism embraced MAGAism in the twenty-first century. When Richard Spencer, one of the primary architects of Unite the Right, organized a victory conference celebrating Trump's election at the Ronald Reagan Building and International Trade Center in Washington, DC, he was careful to adopt the trappings of institutional conservatism. Reporters were baffled. Spencer looked "like many young staffers on Capitol Hill," sporting a closely cropped haircut and wearing a suit and tie.[7]

Here was someone who, by all appearances, should be a member of the conservative establishment in America. He looked the part! But the notion that that the far right cannot be a faction of the responsible and respectable conservative establishment remains a deeply pernicious myth—and raises questions about why liberals expect a "responsible right" in the first place. Far-right extremism in America has always worn a suit and tie.

To be clear, there have always been significant tensions within the American right. Richard Spencer, for his part, deeply resented what he called "the purge" of apostates from "the boundaries of the official Right."[8] People like him represented the authentic soul of the American right, and had for too long been unfairly shut out of the centers of power. None loomed larger in his demonology than William F. Buckley Jr. and *National Review*. And it was true: William F. Buckley Jr. hated being called a Nazi. His political opponents took malicious glee in labeling him a Nazi, fascist, or extremist, knowing it was a surefire way to get a rise out of him. More often than not, Buckley took the bait. In May 1955, after Buckley spoke at Haverford College, a small liberal arts school just outside Philadelphia, an unofficial printing of the *Haverford News* student newspaper published a satirical article featuring a photograph of Adolf Hitler captioned "William Buckley." Buckley threatened to sue. In the spring of 1956, the newsletter of the International Typographical Union called Buckley a "fascist apologist." Buckley again threatened to sue. Most infamously, after Gore Vidal called Buckley a "crypto-Nazi" live on national television during the chaos of the 1968 Democratic National Convention in Chicago, Buckley replied that he would "sock you in the goddamn face and you'll stay plastered"—and, inevitably, threatened to sue Vidal for libel.[9]

Buckley, the Yale-educated son of a multimillionaire who emerged on the scene as a conservative *wunderkind* in the early 1950s, intensely resented being lumped in with the most radical elements of the American right. In his later years, Buckley prided himself as being first among equals of the "responsible" conservatives who set the boundaries between the "respectable" right and the radical far right. The "responsible" right consisted of people who largely thought, looked, and acted like Buckley: affluent, cultured, and sophisticated conservatives who could have marvelously witty conversations over martinis at the Yale Club. They hated communism, socialism, and New Deal liberalism, opposed labor unions and the civil rights movement, and thought Generalissimo Francisco Franco was unfairly treated by the American press. But they weren't "kooks." That label belonged to the "irresponsible" lunatic fringe, a motley assortment of Nazis, fascists, states' righters, and members of the John Birch Society who saw treasonous communist plots everywhere. Writing to John Birch Society founder Robert

Welch in 1960, Buckley averred that "the differences between us are grave indeed. You have a popular front attitude towards conservatism I do not share."[10]

But the truth was more complicated. The relationship between the far right and the "respectable" conservatives was far more intertwined than Buckley would later suggest. Not only were Welch and Buckley once friends—Buckley had approached Welch in 1955 for seed funding for the magazine that would become *National Review*—but many of the men in Buckley's orbit blurred the boundaries between the respectable and radical right. Buckley's own father, William F. Buckley Sr., who made a fortune as an oilman in Mexico in the early twentieth century, was close friends with Merwin K. Hart, the Harvard-educated head of the National Economic Council who urged his followers to stockpile guns in anticipation of a communist revolution and blamed the New Deal on the Jews. The first book review editor for *National Review*, Revilo Oliver, was a professor of classics at the University of Illinois who believed that communists and Jews were behind the civil rights movement and that the ultimate goal was the genocide of white people. Oliver would eventually become a major figure in the American neo-Nazi movement. Buckley even briefly employed George Lincoln Rockwell, the future head of the American Nazi Party, as a traveling salesman for *National Review*. Even after breaking with Buckley and explicitly embracing Nazism, Rockwell peppered his onetime boss with letters, taking the tone of a protégé disappointed by his mentor. "Our publications grow closer every day," Rockwell wrote to Buckley in January 1964, "even though you personally persist on pretending we ain't kinfolk."[11]

In his letter to Robert Welch, Buckley repudiated a "popular front" approach to the American right. The term was a loaded one: the original Popular Front was a form of big-tent left-wing politics that brought together communists, socialists, and liberals in the 1930s under the banner of antifascism. The intense, often fratricidal differences between these factions were—temporarily—put aside due to the overriding danger from the right. But the same dynamics existed on the right as well. Buckley may have denounced a right-wing popular front in 1960, but his own political career emerged out of a very real right-wing popular front that emerged in the 1930s based around shared opposition to communism, socialism, and New Deal liberalism—and a sense that these were existential threats. Unlike the left's Popular Front, which imploded after the signing of the Nazi-Soviet pact in August 1939, the right-wing popular front continued to be a viable force in American politics through the 1960s. Revilo Oliver cheekily called it "One Big Union" of conservatives, riffing off the old Industrial Workers of the World slogan.[12] Buckley may have denounced the right-wing popular front to Welch, but he was denouncing something real.

The story of the unraveling of this right-wing coalition is far more complicated than the traditional story of Buckley and *National Review* purging American conservatism of the crazies.[13] There are three basic flaws in this narrative. One, it suggests that the purge was a singular event instead of an ongoing process that did not simply end in 1965, when Buckley declared the John Birch Society persona non grata in his magazine. Two, it underrates the continued political influence of the far right and its complex relationship with conservatism into at least the 1990s. Three, perhaps most importantly, it does not take in account the actions of far rightists themselves. The modern white power movement in America was born from apostate conservatives who left the ranks of the movement because they felt it was insufficiently committed to defending white supremacy from the challenges of the Black freedom struggle. Whereas most conservatives were willing to make superficial concessions to the civil rights revolution through embracing the language of colorblindness (while also seeking to reinforce existing racial hierarchies), for the nascent white power movement even these concessions were unacceptable. And in the 1980s and 1990s—well after Buckley's "purge" in the 1960s—mainline conservatives who strayed from the reigning conservative orthodoxy on race and racism and made their views explicitly known found a home among the white nationalist movement. Richard Spencer was, in many respects, their direct heir.

Since the mid-1990s, there has been an explosion of scholarly interest in the American conservative movement. The days in which Alan Brinkley could call the study of American conservatism a historiographical problem are long over. The past twenty-five years have seen the growth of an incredibly diverse literature on post–World War II American conservatism from a multitude of different focuses and methodological aspects.[14] At the same time, there has been a smaller, albeit also robust, literature on what is variously described as the "lunatic fringe," "radical," or "extremist" wing of the American political right.[15] Even within the context of literature on the relationship between the far right and American conservatism, however, most emphasis has been placed on the relationship between conservatives and the John Birch Society in the 1960s, when the far right was (supposedly) expelled from the "responsible" conservative movement. But that story is deeply misleading. For one, it suggests that the far right and American conservatism were essentially two distinct and separate political phenomena. A closer examination of the historical record, going back to the 1930s, reveals the opposite. The modern American right arose in the 1930s as a broad coalition opposed to the New Deal, which rightists believed to be fundamentally illegitimate and a threat to American identity.

Most rightists understood New Deal liberalism, socialism, and communism to be fundamentally the same thing, and many believed the New Deal was an "alien" agenda imposed upon the United States by communists, immigrants, and above all Jews. These attitudes remained remarkably consistent from the 1930s through the 1950s and colored right-wing hostility to American entry into World War II. Relatively few on the right openly spoke in favor of Hitler and the Nazis, but most expressed the belief, publicly or privately, that Soviet communism and its New Deal domestic ally were by far more threatening to America. Rightists also took a narrow view of Americanism that only gradually—and often begrudgingly—expanded to immigrants and Jews in the 1950s and 1960s. (Provided, of course, that they embraced the right politics.) The American far right—broadly defined as sympathetic to fascism or outright fascistic, nativist, antisemitic, skeptical of democracy, anti-labor, and fiercely anti-communist—was a key constitutive component of this popular front. And crucially, late twentieth-century American conservatism evolved out of this popular front. There was no firm wall of separation between the "kooks" and "responsible" conservatism, and individual activists as well as organized groups could move fluidly from one political camp to another.

The use of the term *popular front* to describe this conservative coalition opens up analytical space to understand both the underlying unity of the American right during the mid-twentieth century and its factional differences and conflicts. This utility derives from the extensive scholarship on the left-wing popular front in the 1930s. Broadly speaking, this was an uneasy international political coalition between various factions of communists, socialists, and liberals aimed at resisting fascism. The various popular fronts in Europe and North America were not "united" in any meaningful sense—the factions of the left remained extant and very much at odds with one another—but what the popular front *did* mean in substantive political terms was the decline of bitter and vitriolic public attacks, particularly from communists, on other elements of the left.[16]

Although most far-right elements of the right-wing popular front would publicly disavow explicit Nazism, conspiratorial antisemitism—the belief in a global Jewish conspiracy, usually connected to international communism, to subvert and destroy America—was widespread in the American right from the 1930s through the 1960s. Conspiratorial antisemitism offered an explanation for the political reversals of the New Deal. Crude antisemitism held that secret Judeo-Bolshevik conspirators in the White House pushed forward the socialist "Jew Deal," but a more sophisticated version—articulated by many rightists using dog whistles and code words and the occasional explicit claim—held that Jewish political power, buttressed by Jewish immigration to the United States, was responsible for creating the conditions that allowed for the New Deal in the first place. This is why the conspiratorial antisemitism of the far right was so closely tied to support for immigration restrictions—providing opportunities for political alliances with other restrictionists. Limiting Jewish immigration to the United States was a major goal. What united more muted conspiratorial antisemites with the crudest of the Jew-baiters, particularly after World War II, was a shared anti-Zionism and opposition to the U.S. recognition of Israel. This was not rooted in any particular concern for the Arab population of Palestine, but rather fear that the international Judeo-Bolshevik-Zionist conspiracy would embroil America in a war, weakening the U.S. and allowing for the victory of international Jewish communism. Right-wing antisemitism would plague the popular front throughout its existence and would eventually help lead to its decline in the 1960s. Conspiratorial antisemitism, however, remained present, if muted, in "respectable" conservative circles throughout the rest of the century and has seen a resurgence in the new millennium.

All of the principal protagonists in this book—Merwin K. Hart, Russell Maguire, George Lincoln Rockwell, Revilo Oliver, Pat Buchanan, and Joe Sobran—have something in common. They were all connected in some way to William F. Buckley Jr. They were all figures who, at one time or another in their careers, identified themselves as conservatives. Many were liminal figures. Merwin Hart's lengthy political career—which extended from the early 1930s to his death in 1962—put him in the same social and political circles as "respectable" conservative figures as well as avowed fascist sympathizers. They were also connected to one another: one of Hart's protégés was Russell Maguire, who while owner of the *American Mercury* published articles by George Lincoln Rockwell and even—according to Rockwell—entertained the idea of financing Rockwell's American Nazi Party. Oliver was an outspoken antisemite and close collaborator with Buckley in the early days of *National Review*, after an agonizing break with Buckley and being forced out of the John Birch Society, Oliver became an influential figure in American neo-Nazi circles, including an alliance with Rockwell's successor in American Nazi politics, William Luther Pierce. Pat Buchanan was a former speechwriter for Richard Nixon, long-standing conservative pundit, and press secretary in the Reagan White House who became embroiled in controversy for flirting with Holocaust denial in the early 1990s and claiming that American foreign policy was largely controlled by Jews. Joe Sobran, a protégé of Buckley's who was on the masthead of *National Review* for years, drew fire in the 1980s and 1990s for making statements similar to Buchanan's; after finally breaking with *National Review* in 1993, Sobran made occasional appearances at Holocaust denial conferences alongside neo-Nazis and assorted white supremacists. Taken together, these men underscore the fluid, dynamic, and deeply intertwined relationship between conservatism and the far right.

They all shared something else: they were white men of social distinction, affluence, and privilege as befitting their place in the social, racial, and gender hierarchies in the United States in the first half of the twentieth century. Most were native-born; most were Christian, albeit with varying degrees of commitment to their faiths; most attained, either through birth or through wheeling and dealing, material success. Most were easterners or midwesterners, but none were what might be termed "old money"; Hart came the closest, as a Harvard classmate of Franklin Delano Roosevelt, but as the scion of an affluent family from the Mohawk Valley in upstate New York, Hart could not claim, in the context of the early twentieth century, to truly come from the *crème de la crème* of American society.

But neither were radical right-wing politics solely the province of the petit bourgeois—a product of America being, as the writer Hunter S. Thompson put it, "a nation of 220 million used car salesmen."[17] William F. Buckley in the 1960s famously dismissed the most radical elements of the far right as "kooks," publicly insinuating a kind of coarse vulgarity to his onetime political allies. But Hart was a Harvard man; Oliver had a PhD in classics and was renowned as a Sanskrit scholar; Maguire held a degree from the Massachusetts Institute of Technology and, at the height of his political activism, owned an apartment on Park Avenue in Manhattan. Even Rockwell, who went further than anyone had dared after World War II into explicit neo-Nazism, had a highly respectable background; he attended Brown University and served for nearly two decades in the U.S. Navy, attaining the rank of commander—the equivalent of a lieutenant colonel in the army—before being forced out when the full extent of his political activities was revealed. There have been many studies of grassroots right-wing organizing in the mid-twentieth-century United States; that the American right has always worn its Sunday best is not surprising. But the most radical elements of the American right that have long been stereotyped as the "lunatic fringe" have been no exception to that rule.

Ironically enough, the term *lunatic fringe* itself has been used freely as a pejorative for a variety of movements across the political, social, and cultural spectrum in the United States, almost always to characterize them as in some sense abnormal, atypical, or abhorrent. Former U.S. president Theodore Roosevelt was an early popularizer of the phrase—he wrote of his distaste for the Armory Show, a major modern art exhibition in New York City in 1913, saying sadly that there "is apt to be a lunatic fringe among the votaries of any forward movement." The term subsequently entered widespread use in the 1910s as a pejorative largely used by progressive elements to castigate rivals further to the left. In general, "lunatic fringe" had progressive or left-wing connotations until the mid-1920s, when American newspapers began to use the term, by then already a cliché, to describe far-right parties in Germany. By the mid-1930s "lunatic fringe," although it still carried some degree of anti-leftist baggage, increasingly came to include the more radical elements of the American right and its opposition to the Roosevelt administration. Buckley's use of "popular front" to describe the right may sound unusual or even absurd to liberals and leftists, but it draws on a long tradition of the fluidity of political terms and concepts in American political discourse.[18]

What bound the right-wing popular front together? Shared opposition to communism, socialism, and New Deal liberalism—and a tendency to conflate three very distinct strains of leftism and liberalism as synonymous—were the key constitutive components.[19] But opposition to these political ideologies alone is an insufficient explanation for the durability of the right-wing popular front and the vitality of right-wing political culture from the 1930s to the 1960s. There were other material and cultural factors that formed the substructure of the American right during this period and linked it with a larger international far right.

One overriding concern, linked to anticommunism but also distinct from it, was a ferocious opposition to organized labor and the ceding of any meaningful control over the workplace on the part of business owners and management. Section 7(a) of the National Industrial Recovery Act of 1933, which established federal protections for collective bargaining, and the subsequent 1935 Wagner Act affirming labor rights were loathed by broad swaths of businessmen in the United States. Merwin Hart, who before 1933 had dedicated his political and business career to a variety of anti–public spending and taxpayers' rights lobbying campaigns, became radicalized. Unions, to Hart and other members of the nascent right-wing popular front in the 1930s, were both evidence of an international communist plot and, just as maliciously, a check on the rights and prerogatives of capital. Even as it became apparent, by the end of the 1930s, that a communist revolution through the trade unions was not imminent, the American right remained militantly hostile to organized labor.

This hostility did not imply there was nothing to learn from labor. The far right, in particular, often attempted to borrow or adapt tactics from organized labor in order to oppose such groups. In the 1930s, this meant organizing local elites in quasi-fascist vigilante groups to break the power of the Congress for Industrial Organization in small towns in Ohio, Pennsylvania, and upstate New York. In the 1940s, it meant borrowing from the CIO's playbook and creating a political action committee, American Action, to oppose the CIO's own CIO-PAC in the 1946 midterm elections. This was the first right-wing political action committee established in the United States. It solicited donations from local and national businesses and disbursed campaign contributions to right-wing House and Senate candidates across the country. Its national staff featured a who's who of far-right activists and business lobbyists. Although by the 1950s it was increasingly difficult—in an era when nearly a third of Americans belonged to a union—to argue that organized labor was simply a communist front, anti-unionism remained a major theme of right-wing and far-right organizing. Opposition to the basic legitimacy of collective bargaining was remarkably consistent.

The *American Mercury* magazine, Russell Maguire's publication, retained, even as it flirted with open neo-Nazism, advertising and subscription support from several major steel companies because of the magazine's militant anti-unionism.

The American right-wing popular front understood itself as part of a broader international right. Francisco Franco's regime in Spain had particular appeal—Madrid as much as Moscow held the American right together. Why? Because Franco appealed to the disparate elements of the right-wing popular front in America, serving as a kind of Rorschach test, a psychological space where the ambitions and fantasies of the right-wing popular front could be enacted. Merwin Hart could look at Spain and see in Franco a strongman who properly disciplined labor in his country and brought the trade unions to heel. William F. Buckley could look at Franco and see a committed defender of Western Christendom. Both could look at Franco and see a dedicated anti-communist. Francoism was especially attractive to the American right because Franco occupied a liminal space in the global right: he was fascistic but his fascism could be plausibly denied. Such views were not simply products of the Cold War; these were the terms of the debate in the United States over the Spanish Civil War in the 1930s. Franco was a way for American rightists to embrace the global right without the messy baggage of Benito Mussolini or Adolf Hitler.

Far-right antisemites bitterly resented what they perceived to be "smears" about their politics, and this shared sense of victimization became a key ingredient forging the right-wing popular front together into a common coalition. Right-wingers particularly begrudged the accusations, often trotted out by liberals and leftists, that they had been sympathetic to fascism before and during World War II. They were maddened that they were being smeared as fascists and agents of foreign powers for supporting American values—Christianity (as opposed to Judaism), free enterprise, white supremacy, anticommunism, anti-liberalism, and opposition to labor—by political opponents supposedly in thrall to international communism. Indeed, there was a considerable degree of *schadenfreude* on the American right in the early 1950s, as Senator Joseph McCarthy and other anti-communist activists turned the political tables on the liberal and anti-fascist "smear artists" of the 1940s. But although sometimes the attacks from the left and the liberals were hyperbolic—while the right had its global dimensions, there was no fascist analogue to the Comintern—there were core elements of truth to the left/liberal critique of the American right as fascist-adjacent, and not just at the moment of fascism's apparent global ascendency in the 1930s. Buckley deeply resented the fascist smear, as did members of the John Birch Society, but there really *were* racists, antisemites, and Nazi sympathizers in the ranks of conservatism in the 1950s and 1960s. Conservative resentment about the fascism "smear" was so bitter precisely because the claim was not groundless.

Even before Donald Trump's election in 2016, debate raged over whether or not Trump and/or Trumpism could be characterized as fascist. Some were open to the label early on, pointing to Trump's demagoguery, calls for national renewal, and the fervor of the political mobilization behind him. (President Barack Obama reportedly called Trump a fascist in private during the 2016 campaign.) Others were more circumspect; the historian Robert Paxton said in an interview in February 2016 that there were "echoes" of fascism in Trumpism but he was reluctant to classify Trump himself as a fascist.[20] While many other voices during the Trump administration emphasized its fascistic dimensions—in particular the work of journalist John Ganz—Paxton remained on the fence.[21] But the chaos and political violence of January 6, 2021 were enough to convince Paxton, as well as other long-standing critics on the left of the Trump-as-fascist thesis, like political scientist Adolph Reed, that there was merit to the analysis.[22] Still, there remain outspoken left-wing critics of the fascism thesis, in particular historians Daniel Bessner and Sam Moyn.[23] This book will not resolve the debate nor satisfy critics of the fascism thesis, but it does seek to rethink what twentieth-century American political history looks like when the question of fascism is taken soberly and seriously as part of the American political tradition.

PART ONE THE RIGHT-WING POPULAR FRONT, 1933–53

CHAPTER ONE

"It Is Time to Brush aside This Word 'Democracy'"

WAR WAS ON THE MIND of most Americans when Secretary of the Interior Harold Ickes took the stage at New York's town hall on the morning of November 20, 1940. World War II continued to rage in Europe. Only two months earlier, President Franklin D. Roosevelt signed into law America's first peacetime draft, signaling that the United States was gearing up for potential entry into the conflict. Ickes's speech at the town hall was not about the threat overseas, but rather the danger of "native fascist groups" at home, which he described as a potential fifth column. These groups included the usual suspects of American fascism in the 1930s. The Ku Klux Klan, the German American Bund, and the Silver Shirts were all castigated by the secretary. But Ickes also named individuals. Charles Lindbergh was a "busy appeaser who would voluntarily surrender his sword even before it is demanded." Father Charles Coughlin, the infamously antisemitic radio priest, "gets his propaganda from German sources." But not everyone whom Ickes singled out as a fascist sympathizer would have been immediately familiar to a national audience. Ickes berated Merwin K. Hart, the head of the New York State Economic Council and a longtime opponent of President Roosevelt, as a man who "misses few occasions to sneer at democracy." When asked for comment by the *New York Herald Tribune*, Hart responded, "The last five years any one who has fallen for the collectivist philosophy has called every one who differed from him a Fascist. If I'm a Fascist, Ickes is the proverbial Chinaman."[1]

Ickes was right, though—Hart had repeatedly demeaned the term *democracy*. On September 20, Hart gave a speech at the elite Union League Club on East Thirty-Seventh Street and Park Avenue in which he told an assembled audience of 150 businessmen that "it is time to brush aside this word 'democracy' with its connotations." Hart's comments were provocative enough to earn a riposte from the *New York Times,* which published an editorial the next day decrying that democracy had in fact been "brushed aside nearly everywhere east of the English channel . . . [and] to brush it out of the United States would require a reversal of nearly everything that has happened in our political life since the Declaration of Independence."[2] Never a man to allow someone the last word, Hart wrote a letter to the *Times* that very day irately noting that the "editorial fails to quote my next sentence. 'It is time to return to the conception of the republic—a conception so clear that all can understand.' " Hart also insisted that the *Times* reprint his speech in full—a request with which the paper duly complied. In his remarks to the Union League Club, Hart argued that the Founding Fathers rejected the conception of democracy but instead formed a republic—after all, "Julia Ward Howe did not write the Battle Hymn of Democracy." America was a republic, not a democracy.

So why, then, did the Roosevelt administration and its political allies insist on calling America a "democracy"? Governor Herbert Lehman used the word *democracy* twenty-five times in his annual address to the New York legislature in 1939, and thirty-three times in 1940, Hart noted. "So far as I can see, the great impetus to the use of this word appeared after the meeting of the Communist International in 1935."

Democracy was, in fact, a communist plot.

Throughout his lengthy career as a professional political activist— which spanned from the 1930s to the early 1960s—Merwin K. Hart was a liminal figure on the American right. Not quite a member of the conservative establishment, and not quite an unreconstructed far right activist, Hart flitted from pole to pole within the big tent of the American right. He was, in many respects, a true popular front man, equally at home socializing with elites like senators, congressmen, and the Buckleys as well as appearing on the stump with notorious extremists like Elizabeth Dilling. An arch opponent of American intervention in World War II and so outspokenly antisemitic that the America First Committee maintained its distance from him, Hart was also careful never to explicitly endorse Nazism or fascism, and—like subsequent generations of conservatives—bitterly resented "smears" that he harbored fascist sympathies. And yet Hart was also an unrepentant admirer of Francisco Franco, even declaring at the height of the Spanish Civil War that his fight against organized labor and the New Deal in America was simply another front in the war against international communism that Franco was waging in Spain. Hart has been long ignored by historians as a marginal figure, but his lengthy career illustrates just how central the far right was in the development of modern American conservatism. Throughout his life, in speeches, newsletters, and talking to reporters, Hart decried the "alien" influence of the New Deal on American life and argued for the importance of taking America back to its authentic values and identity. For Hart, this meant rejecting communism, socialism, and New Deal liberalism . . . and there was little distinction between the three.

Hart had been a fixture in New York state politics for over thirty years before his spat with Ickes in 1940. Hart was born in Utica, in the heart of the Mohawk Valley, in 1881 to an old Anglo-Saxon Protestant family. Hart attended St. Paul's School and Harvard University, where one of his classmates was Franklin Delano Roosevelt, his future nemesis. After graduating in 1904, he returned to Utica, where he went to work for his father's manufacturing firm, building boilers and radiators for use in homes, offices, and factories. His early life trajectory was a thoroughly unremarkable story of an upper-middle-class businessman, right down to his marriage to the daughter of his father's business partner in 1909.

Hart, however, harbored political aspirations. He was elected as a Republican to the New York state legislature representing his home Oneida County from 1906 through 1910. Hart was in many ways a typical Republican backbencher of the Progressive Era—he was a staunch supporter of both President Theodore Roosevelt and New York governor Charles Evans Hughes. His legislative accomplishments were modest—his most noteworthy was co-sponsoring anti-gambling legislation signed into law by Hughes in 1908. There were, however, early signs of Hart's unease regarding democracy and its implied limitations on the power of capital and management. In 1907 he penned an article for the *Outlook* magazine criticizing William Jennings Bryan for declaring that elected officials are "selected by the people to give legislative expression to their thoughts and their will." Bryan "really advocates weakness and inefficiency," Hart wrote, in arguing that elected officials ought to be guided by concerns about the views of their constituents. Rather, the proper role of officeholders was analogous to management of a corporation. "If the manager is worthy of the place he holds, he will have free hand in the conduct of all ordinary matters." Hart framed this as a sensible, pragmatic philosophy rooted in the best practices of the "modern business corporation."[3]

How did a Progressive in 1910 move firmly into the camp of the right by the 1930s? Part of the answer lies in the very nature of Progressivism itself. The Progressive movement in the early part of the twentieth century was not a single, tightly organized political movement or even a coherently defined ideology; it was a variety of different intertwining movements and ideologies that tried to answer how best to govern a modern, industrialized society.

Modernity demanded new reforms and governmental regulation. When he became president, for example, Theodore Roosevelt instructed the Justice Department to begin to aggressively prosecute anti-trust cases and spearheaded broad health and safety regulations. But there were limits to Progressives' zeal. While many Progressives could speak the language of radicalism, they were not socialists. Roosevelt, in his first message to Congress, declared that the "mechanism of modern business is so delicate that extreme care must be taken not to interfere with it in a spirit of rashness or ignorance." Too much regulation, let alone nationalization, was off the table. In a later speech, Roosevelt also warned that "class consciousness" along the lines of the labor movement would do "far-reaching damage" to American society. Modernizing the business and regulatory environment was one thing; empowering labor was quite another.[4]

Many Progressives were also unabashed xenophobes and white supremacists. Theodore Roosevelt was an outspoken believer in the providential destiny of the Anglo-Saxon race. Madison Grant, one of Roosevelt's close personal friends in the cloistered world of New York Progressivism, was a prominent eugenicist and the author of the 1916 book *The Passing of the Great Race,* the most influential work of scientific racism of the twentieth century. (Upon reading the German translation for the first time, Adolf Hitler is reported to have described the book as "my Bible.") John B. Trevor, a law school classmate of Franklin Roosevelt and friend of Madison Grant (and, later in life, Merwin Hart), was one of the architects of the 1924 Immigration Act levying discriminatory quotas against racially undesirable immigrants from southern and eastern Europe. And Woodrow Wilson, who, although a Democrat and Roosevelt's eventual political nemesis, was also widely recognized as a Progressive leader, was a viciously anti-Black racist who segregated the federal civil service and screened the 1915 epic white supremacist film *The Birth of a Nation* at the White House.[5]

There was nothing incompatible between Progressivism and an unwavering belief in America for (white, preferably Anglo-Saxon) Americans. Indeed, while urban reform work dedicated to providing aid to immigrants in the new urban metropolises in America was one of the most noteworthy Progressive causes of the era, Progressive reformers were at best paternalistic in their attitudes to immigrants, who had to be instilled with "100 percent American" values. (Others, like Trevor, preferred to keep new immigrants out of the country altogether.) And although many Progressives had a dynamic relationship with intellectual currents on the other side of the Atlantic—many Progressive urban reformers looked to European cities for ideas on how best to govern the American cities—there was also a profoundly xenophobic streak. Woodrow Wilson even went so far as to suggest that Thomas Jefferson was not truly a "great American" because of the influence of radical French philosophy on his thinking. Keeping America American, and free from radical foreign influences, was a key component of Progressivism.[6]

Some of these Progressives would, albeit grudgingly, embrace the New Deal coalition in the 1930s. Others saw it as the harbinger of unacceptable social and political change leading to socialism or even communism. Merwin Hart was one of the latter. Hart abandoned his political career after an unsuccessful state senate bid in 1910, and settled down to practice law in Utica. Despite his age and nearsightedness, Hart served in World War I, even appealing to his old Harvard classmate Franklin D. Roosevelt—then the assistant secretary of the navy—to obtain a commission. His postwar career was unremarkable until 1926, when Hart was named the employers' representative to the New York State Industrial Survey Commission.[7] The commission was one of dozens of state investigative bodies formed in New York under Progressive Democratic governor Al Smith's tenure from 1923 through 1929. Other commissions and inquiries focused on public healthcare, public land use, public ownership of utilities, and administrative service reform. In fact, Smith's Republican opponent in the 1926 race for governor, Manhattan congressman Ogden Mills, repeatedly attacked the governor's reform agenda as "Socialism." (Smith, with characteristic bluntness, replied that "the Congressman's talk about Socialism is, using a mild term, stupid.")[8] Unlike Smith's reform commissions, however, the Industrial Survey Commission was created by the Republican legislature. The Democratic house minority leader in Albany called it an attempt by conservative Republicans to stifle a proposed law to limit the workweek for women textile workers to forty-eight hours. In addition to Hart, members of the commission also included state legislators and a representative from organized labor. Hart, for his part, functioned as a kind of grand inquisitor of pro-labor witnesses. He challenged, for example, the claims of the secretary of the boot and shoe workers' union in Rochester that prison labor from Indiana, Maryland, and Kentucky was driving manufacturing losses in the Genesee River valley, instead pointing to the "restrictive" proposed forty-eight-hour workweek bill and unionized workers' higher wages.[9]

Hart's presence on the committee, however, was not enough to prevent the group from recommending in its report to the legislature in 1927 that the bill be passed. In an attached dissent, Hart dismissed the commission's recommendation as "not predicated upon either economic or legal grounds" and feared that the end result would be to drive smaller firms out of business. (Hart was hardly a corporate titan; his business interests through his legal practice, family manufacturing company, and insurance firm ensured him affluence and a degree of local prominence, but he did not have the resources of a Carnegie or a Rockefeller.) A forty-eight-hour workweek, he wrote, "has been a mere plank in a political platform. It has become a fetish" for labor activists, who ignored "widespread evidence that the economic tendency is toward shorter hours in industry" compelled by market forces. Hart's dissent in the Industrial Survey Commission's report touched on what would become common themes in his subsequent political activism: organized labor and other outside interests were engaged in a spurious political war against employers and management.[10]

There is no explicit indication in the 1927 report that Hart considered the demands of the garment workers to be motivated by "aliens" or "Communists," but the International Ladies' Garment Workers' Union, the largest and most important union of women workers in New York State, was both heavily Jewish *and* had been wracked by bruising internal battles between socialists and social democrats on the one hand and members of the Communist Party on the other. Additionally, Emanuel Koveleski, the labor representative on the commission and a vice president of the New York State Federation of Labor, was Jewish, although hardly a radical (the communist *Daily Worker* described his work on the commission as "rather timid"). If Hart did indeed harbor a belief that communists and Jews were responsible for the commission's endorsement of the forty-eight-hour workweek bill, he kept it to himself.[11]

Franklin D. Roosevelt's election to the governorship of New York in 1928 did not appear to signal, at least initially, anything more than a continuation of Al Smith's program of moderate reforms. Roosevelt's election was an opportunity for Hart, since he had personally known FDR in college and had served as the Oneida County chair of Theodore Roosevelt's 1912 election campaign. But it quickly became clear that the new governor would embark on a much more aggressive reform agenda. FDR's appointment of Frances Perkins as New York's industrial commissioner was an ominous sign to the business interests in the state that had opposed efforts under Smith to pass forty-eight-hour workweek legislation. Perkins assailed the conclusion of the commission that Hart endorsed most strongly—that high taxes and a rising public debt were discouraging business development—at a statewide economic conference at the Hotel Astor in Times Square in April 1929.[12] In response, the manufacturers at the conference successfully proposed to create a "Committee of Twenty-Five" to further examine the economic conditions in the state from the perspective of capital. There was little hope of enacting a comprehensive pro-business agenda with Roosevelt in the governor's mansion and Perkins as industrial commissioner, but Hart and his allies hoped to keep the issue alive into 1930 when, hopefully, there would be a change in government.[13]

But the ground was shifting under their feet. The basic assumptions that governed the Harding-Coolidge-Hoover years—that the purpose of government was to provide a nourishing environment for free enterprise, thereby ensuring mass prosperity—had been called into question (to put it mildly) by the economic collapse in 1929. Roosevelt, already eyeing the presidency even before the onset of the Great Depression, set to work capitalizing on the political opportunities presented by the economic crisis, and pushed for a robust agenda in Albany emphasizing pro-labor legislation, unemployment relief, and aid to the state's farmers. Roosevelt's proto–New Deal in Albany was the antithesis of what Hart advocated for on the Industrial Survey Commission.[14]

Hart's "Committee of Twenty-Five" was made up of businessmen from around the state, including Magnus Alexander, the president of the National

Industrial Conference Board; Elon Hooker, the president of a chemical manufacturing concern; and James H. McGraw, the publishing tycoon.[15] Unlike the
Survey Commission, there was no official state sanction for the committee—
it was in essence a pro-business pressure group. The political orientation of
the committee can be gleaned by Hooker's speech to the New York Women's
Forum in December 1929, in which he blamed high taxes for the economic
downturn. (Hooker added that "the great prosperity of this country is due to a
great extent to . . . restricted immigration," and that "absolute prohibition of
immigration is needed to maintain the high standard of living in America.")
Hart launched a campaign against the public development of the St. Lawrence
Seaway the following January, since it would have to be financed by a "heavy
and growing burden of taxation."[16] In mid-June, the "Committee of 25" was
redubbed the New York State Economic Council. In a press release accompanying the rebranding, Hart declared that "we believe the present drifting
tendency in government in its relation to the economic life of the people can
be arrested."[17] Events over the next two years would prove him to be mistaken.

It is impossible to exaggerate the impact of the Great Depression on the
history of the twentieth century. "But for it," wrote historian Eric Hobsbawm,
"there would certainly have been no Hitler. There would certainly have been
no Roosevelt." It was not simply that there had been no previous economic
downturns in industrialized capitalist economies. The nineteenth century
was replete with examples of depressions, recessions, and crises. What
made the Depression unique was that it was a sustained *global* downturn
that appeared to threaten the very foundations of liberal capitalism, already
substantially weakened by the strains of the First World War. In Europe,
communism and fascism offered alternative visions of industrial modernity—and both ideologies had their American admirers.[18]

   Merwin Hart's initial vision for the business response to the economic
crisis of the Depression was certainly bold. In a speech to an assembly of
forty executives in Glens Falls on June 23, he told the gathering that New
York's economic leadership "must take a controlling part in government as
it affects business" instead of leaving it to "muddling and trimming politicians." He blamed New York's onerous regulatory environment, which had
grown ever heavier under Smith and now under Roosevelt, for the
Depression. He even went so far as to blame FDR for the explosion in unemployment. Hart's speech was short on specifics as to how businessmen

ought to "take control" of the legislative process, but the implication was clear. If a majority of voters elected into office politicians who sought to expand programs and labor protections, then business ought to treat those politicians—and, by extension, their voters—as illegitimate. Hart was, in essence, rejecting a basic principle of liberal democracy. "Politics," he sneered, "had her heyday."[19]

Hart's call for corporate leaders to take control of government made little sense, as businessmen from all walks of industry already exercised outsized power over American public life. Herbert Hoover was a proverbial self-made businessman who had built his fortune as a mining engineer and his reputation as a humanitarian before serving in the Harding and Coolidge administrations. Hoover's secretary of the treasury, Andrew Mellon, was a prominent banker and financier in Pittsburgh who owned or had a major interest in dozens of the largest companies in the United States. Hart sat on Governor Franklin Roosevelt's Budget Advisory Committee in New York, along with his fellow Economic Council member Alexander Falck, chairman of the board of Corning Glass Works.[20] However, the real issue was not that businessmen did not have enough political influence, but that the economic crisis of the Great Depression *threatened* the massive political, social, and economic influence business leaders had hitherto enjoyed. The creation of the New York State Economic Council was a preemptive move to block a challenge to the power of business over policy in New York and the rest of the country.

Hart and the other members of the Economic Council quickly ran into a major obstacle, however. Their views were incredibly unpopular.

Franklin D. Roosevelt was reelected as governor in November 1930 by a margin of over twenty points. The Democratic ticket captured every state-wide office, putting a significant dent in the GOP's control over the State Assembly.[21] The Economic Council's reputation was not helped by the public statements of James W. Gerard, Woodrow Wilson's ambassador to Germany, who sparked widespread outrage in the summer of 1930 by claiming that fifty-nine people—all businessmen—were the true rulers of America by dint of the "virtue of their ability." Although Gerard apparently meant his remark as a compliment, to detractors it suggested that businessmen both could and should effectively control local, state, and federal government through a behind-the-scenes exercise of political power.[22]

Hart was apparently undeterred by the widespread ridicule heaped upon Gerard or the punishing losses the Republican Party suffered in

Albany—less than a month after the election, he wrote several open letters to Governor Roosevelt protesting his public-works programs as "an injustice . . . to people not in the building trades."[23] The following spring, he told the New York State Bankers' Association that "only a strong, virile policy against excessive taxation" would pull the country out of the Depression, maintaining that in New York high taxes were driving job-producing businesses out of the state. Hart suggested that slashing school funding would provide the requisite savings to cut taxes, adding that for too long "we have been permitting experts to run education"—a theme that Hart would return to later in the decade.[24] Even as Republicans in the State Assembly embraced the necessity of public relief—a proposed GOP plan in September 1931 differed from Roosevelt's relief program only in the distributive mechanism of some $20 million allocated for public relief, not the amount itself—Hart steadfastly maintained that government spending caused and exacerbated the economic collapse.[25]

Although the New York State Economic Council's legislative influence on the policy process in Albany was limited, Hart's speeches were frequently broadcast on the radio, and meetings of the Economic Council were reported by major newspapers, which generally framed the group as expert businessmen seeking good-faith solutions to the Depression. Press criticism was generally muted, prompted only by errors council members made, like Gerard's much-maligned list. Given both Roosevelt's popularity in New York State and the degree to which even the Republican Party had embraced elements of his agenda, Hart served as a voice of "balance" in the state's newspapers. No matter what, Hart and the Economic Council could be relied upon to give a quote opposing the entirety of the relief agenda. An article in the *New York Times* detailing the battles in the state legislature over Roosevelt's relief plan in September 1931 closed by quoting Hart's opposition to, among other things, the payment of unemployment benefits, additional income taxes, and both the GOP *and* Roosevelt's plans to disperse aid through state agencies (if aid must be disbursed, Hart preferred that it be done at the discretion of local officials). Given the relative unanimity among state officials about the necessity of state intervention, the Economic Council's unyielding opposition at least provided good copy.[26]

Throughout the rest of 1931 and into 1932, the Economic Council continued its crusade to slash the state budget. Roosevelt openly rebuked Hart's demands in a speech to the Albany chamber of commerce in January

1932, ridiculing the council's call to slash the wages of state employees and retrench on public-works projects. The construction of state highways alone, Roosevelt told his audience, employed nearly ten thousand workers. The governor also dismissed another of Hart's long-standing demands—to slash the state parks budget—by arguing that park spending provided recreation for the poorest New Yorkers, who could not afford other recreations. Hart's grim insistence on fiscal austerity was no match for Roosevelt's sunny economic populism. Frances Perkins scoffed at the council's demands for aid cuts—"I am struck with the great amount of poverty and panhandling on the street," she told state aid workers in the winter of 1932—"[and] if we were to cut off the social services" per the council's agenda, the results would be disastrous.[27]

Still, the New York State Economic Council could claim some limited successes in its anti-spending advocacy. In February 1932 the state legislature, still controlled by the Republican Party, slashed $20 million from Roosevelt's proposed $320 million executive budget—with half the budget reductions coming from cutting highway funding, long a target of the Economic Council's ire.[28] But the 1932 budget was still larger than the 1931 budget by some $10 million, a far cry from Hart's professed goal of cutting state expenditures by 25 percent. Even cutting the budget by a quarter from fiscal year 1931 to fiscal year 1932 would have meant that the state budget was nearly $85 million larger than in 1926. Roosevelt's budget plans were in response to a massive economic emergency—the state's unemployment rate was approaching 20 percent by 1931—*and* were limited by both state statute and Roosevelt's own fiscal beliefs. Roosevelt never fully embraced deficit spending even during his presidency—federal budget cuts in 1937 were a major factor in sliding the economy back into recession—and in any event in New York the state government was constitutionally unable to engage in deficit spending. The budget had to be balanced, which meant, among other things, that taxes had to go up.

The council correspondingly served a useful political purpose for the Roosevelt administration, which fought pressure for budget cuts at every possible opportunity. Roosevelt consistently opposed regressive tax measures like a sales tax during his time in Albany; what was the point, he argued, in shifting the tax burden to people who were already unemployed? Social welfare liberals could use austerity hawks like Hart to paint opponents of relief schemes as unreasonable ideologues clinging to tired old ideas instead of adapting to the new circumstances of the Depression.

Meanwhile, the political situation in the United States continued to worsen. In June 1932 tens of thousands of unemployed World War I veterans descended on Washington, DC, to demonstrate for the early redemption of the "adjusted compensation certificates" they were to receive for their service during the war, which were worth about $1,000 and scheduled to be paid in 1945. Approximately twenty-two thousand marchers gathered in Washington by the end of June, assembling a shantytown on the banks of the Anacostia River about ten blocks from the Capitol. General Douglas MacArthur was sufficiently concerned by the possibility that the Bonus Army demonstration was a prelude to communist revolution that he instructed his subordinates to compile the names of marchers with "known communistic leanings" and ordered the War Department's "Plan White," a contingency plan dealing with a communist uprising, to be revised in light of the situation. When President Herbert Hoover ordered the U.S. Army to assist DC police in clearing the Bonus Army marchers from their encampment on July 28, MacArthur personally led the detachment, telling his deputy, Major Dwight D. Eisenhower, that "incipient revolution [was] in the air." President Franklin D. Roosevelt later privately described MacArthur as one of the most dangerous men in the country.[29]

Hart, apparently frustrated by the council's continued ineffectiveness in Albany, began seeking out national allies. He secured a meeting with President Herbert Hoover at the White House in May 1932, at which he urged the president to immediately slash the federal budget to 1926 spending levels, a demand that won Hart a ringing endorsement from conservative Chicago newspaperman Colonel Robert McCormick and his *Chicago Tribune,* one of the most widely read newspapers in the country.[30] Hart went even further than most austerity hawks when he warned the president that continued federal profligacy would cut into Hoover's support in traditional Republican strongholds like upstate New York.[31] McCormick's paper applauded the council as a necessary crusader against the "unscrupulous politicians within the District of Columbia" determined to effect the "destruction of private enterprise and the creation in its place of a collectivist society." In June McCormick traveled to New York to attend the annual meeting of the Economic Council, where speakers inveighed against federal and state taxation and spending at every level. McCormick went even further: "Congress is composed," he told the conference, "of a large majority of confused men who are led, dominated and driven by a handful of

Communists, who in turn are ably seconded by a crowd of morons calling themselves Progressives and Liberals."[32]

Red-baiting was a tried-and-true tactic against liberal reformers; even Al Smith—who had by 1932 embraced an austerity program and was attempting to block Roosevelt's nomination—had been smeared as a socialist by his Republican opponent in the 1926 New York governor's race and again in the 1928 presidential race.[33] But McCormick's suggestion— that progressives and liberals were themselves dupes of a shadowy commu- nist conspiracy—was a new public talking point. Suggesting that progressives and liberals were taking their marching orders from the Communist Party, even if unwittingly, implied that the entire political project of liberalism was somehow alien or un-American. These themes would eventually dominate the life of Hart and his organization.

Roosevelt's landslide election to the presidency in 1932—and a similar crushing victory by Democrat Herbert Lehman in the New York state gover- nor's race—demonstrated yet again that the general political tide of both New York State and the country had turned decisively against Republican politics of austerity. Hart continued, however, to press for dramatic budget cuts in New York, even going so far as to accuse Lehman of deliberately mis- citing figures to mask the state's $150 million budget deficit and demanding that state aid to education be cut by some 20 percent.[34] Education spending became the major political football in the debates over the 1933 budget; Hart found an ally in William Randolph Hearst's New York Herald Tribune, which opined that "a deep cut should be made temporarily in the state's aid to education" and commended Hart's "telling factual arguments" about the budget crisis. But Hart continued to overreach. By any reasonable measure Lehman's final $200 million budget—$100 million less than Roosevelt's a year earlier—was a massive victory for anti–government spending advo- cates in New York State. But Hart still found these cuts to be inadequate. He called for an additional $30 million in spending reductions.[35]

Despite Hart's disappointment with the continued glut of spending in Albany, his group expanded dramatically. The New York State Economic Council was, in the 1930s, a mass-membership organization. Fifty county chapters and affiliates formed across New York State, and in many instances these were actually able to substantively affect county and municipal spending. The local Economic Council branch in Westchester County organized for tax relief, claiming that financial hardships made it impossible to comply with the tax code. In Ulster County, the local chapter of the council managed to cut the county budget by 57 percent. According to Hart, the state council and its affiliates had a combined membership of more than fifty thousand taxpayers across the state.[36]

The council also enjoyed increasing national prominence. Robert McCormick maintained his ties with the group, frequently sending letters to Economic Council meetings in Manhattan and occasionally making a personal appearance. McCormick's *Chicago Tribune* began covering the council more frequently and more favorably in 1933, writing glowingly of the organization's successful efforts to reduce Roosevelt's budget in 1932 and of its grassroots organizing efforts at the county level. In a message read aloud by Hart at a council meeting in 1933, McCormick urged the group to continue to organize at the county and district level and "procure the election of . . . men who are . . . sound in their conceptions of public affairs and economics."[37]

Hart and the Economic Council were opposed to most of Roosevelt's New Deal agenda in Washington. In an op-ed published two months into FDR's presidency, Hart savaged the president for his support of minimum-wage laws, development plans for the Tennessee River valley, and the ballooning federal debt. But the council, reading the political winds, made at least an attempt to render their anti-tax, anti-spending, and anti-regulation views palatable to the public. In the same op-ed, Hart conceded that wages did in fact need be raised across the board *and* that infrastructure development could be an important mechanism to solve the unemployment crisis, but maintained that these problems would solve themselves if a way could be found to "make private business profitable." Hart's proposed solution was to relax anti-trust laws and allow for trade associations to run entire industries—"to fix prices, decide upon the volume of production, divide territory, agree upon minimum wages, set up unemployment reserves, etc."[38] Hart's proposed solution to boosting industrial productivity was industrial cartelization—*precisely* the approach the Roosevelt administration took with the National Industrial Recovery Act and the National Recovery Administration (NRA). Intimates in Roosevelt's inner circle, from Bernard Baruch to Raymond Moley, had been pressing for a kind of "cooperative government-business planning" since before the election. Even hardened anti-regulation groups—including the National Association of Manufacturers and the Chamber of Commerce—accepted in broad terms the private-partnership aspect of the NRA. Hart even joined the New York Bar Association's NRA committee. The NRA's underwriting of corporate industrial organization was entirely in keeping with the New York State Economic Council's raison d'être—to allow for businessmen to set national business policy. The problem, however, was organized labor.[39]

Under section 7(a) of the National Industrial Recovery Act (NIRA), the participation of companies in industrial cartelization—a major component of which was the long-sought relaxation of anti-trust laws—was contingent upon accepting the right of workers to organize unions and bargain collectively free of company coercion. So-called yellow-dog contracts, which banned workers from participating in labor organizing on pain of termination, were outlawed. This was too far for the business lobby—the National Association of Manufacturers and the Chamber of Commerce both unsuccessfully fought for section 7(a) to be torpedoed during congressional debates in May.[40] Hart declared in an editorial that business should not have to swallow the poison pill of labor law in order for anti-trust laws to be relaxed. It was time, he wrote, "for the American people, and especially the workers, to wake up to what is going on": section 7(a) was a scheme to promote the un-American philosophy of a "closed shop" that required union membership as a condition of employment, a usurpation of the free-labor right of contract. This had long been a talking point of anti-union management—as well as the argument that the American Federation of Labor (AFL), which Hart singled out for particular vitriol, represented a third-party "purely private organization" that served its own interests, not those of its members. (This focus on the AFL was rather odd, considering that the federation was far more conservative than its rival industrial trade unions.) According to Hart, section 7(a), the AFL, and the very concept of labor organization itself were un-American. "We recognize no classes in America. We have no working class, in the sense they use in Europe. Half the men in overalls are on their way up. They will be foremen, superintendents, vice-presidents, and presidents tomorrow." Hart argued it was vital to allow those with God-given natural talent to rise to the top. "The closed shop recognizes classes. It bars the way for the better man."[41]

Hart was enraged by the wave of labor organizing and strikes triggered by the passage of the NRA—he complained in a column in the *New York Herald Tribune* that the sidewalks on his daily commute to his office in Manhattan were now clogged with union pickets, and, falling back on anti-union bromides, charged that unions were an "outside organization" that "have not the slightest interest or responsibility in the successful conduct of business." But already by October of 1933 Hart's language had taken a turn toward the conspiratorial, at least as far as labor was concerned. The closed shop was not just un-American, it was "autocratic [and] tyrannical" because, contrary to public opinion, "unions are not . . . democratic organizations." Labor unions, from national organizations like the AFL to the local construction unions in New York, were rather "almost entirely under control of an inner ring of officers." Hart refrained, for the moment, from insinuating that all labor officials were communists or somehow under the sway of Moscow, but the implication was clear: trade unionism was in effect a conspiracy. Just who was pulling the strings, however, remained unclear in Hart's public statements.[42]

In February 1934 the council began publishing a weekly newsletter written by Hart summarizing its positions and lobbying efforts in Albany. Initially limited to the legislative season in New York State, this newsletter would within a few years become Hart's signature mouthpiece. Framed as a charitable service "to tax payers over the State," the letter urged its readers to write to their assemblymen to vote down the latest rounds of pro-labor bills under consideration. The tone of Hart's missives grew increasingly strident—he described the Tennessee Valley Authority as a "fanciful communistic plan" in March 1934, openly worrying "what other socialistic projects are pending[?]" The newsletter also turned its attention to goings-on in Washington—Hart described proposed legislation by Senator Robert Wagner that would eventually become the National Labor Relations Act as "part of the plan of a handful of men who . . . are seeking to bring about a revolution—bloodless, maybe—but a revolution that will bring liberty in the United States to an end."[43] Hart did not specify just who these men or their masters were, but the implication was clear: New Deal legislation, *particularly* labor legislation, was the product of a massive conspiracy to transform the United States into something alien.

The Economic Council was hardly the only pro-business group that believed the New Deal was un-American. The American Liberty League, founded in 1934 by a group of businessmen largely affiliated with chemical giant DuPont and automobile manufacturer General Motors, served essentially as the national analogue to Hart's more modest state organization. Concerns over labor power dominated the agenda of the Liberty League; its very founding can be traced back to a March 1934 letter from R.R.M. Carpenter, a former DuPont executive, to John Raskob, another former DuPont executive, in which Carpenter complained that his African American labor force on his South Carolina estate had proven to be truculent ever since Roosevelt's public-works program began. "Five negroes on my place in South Carolina refused work this spring," Carpenter wrote, "after I had taken care of them and given them house rent free and work for three years during bad times, saying they had easy jobs with the government." (It is unclear whether or not Carpenter sought to *deliberately* evoke the rhetoric of antebellum slave owners in his complaint, but certainly his next sentence—"Planters in our vicinity were unable to get enough labor to harvest crops in the Fall, due to [Civilian Conservation Corps] employment"—did not make the comparison any less glaring.) If wealthy South Carolinians were having these kinds of problems disciplining their Black laborers, Carpenter went on, "how many thousands of men are leaving employment to accept easy jobs with the government, paid for with the taxpayers' money and under the guise of relief[?]"[44]

Losing managerial control over their labor force was bad enough as far as businessmen were concerned, but the prospect that an organized labor movement could propel radical, even revolutionary, political change was utterly chilling. Labor organizing had intensified with the apparent blessing of the Roosevelt administration after the passage of the National Industrial Recovery Act. In the first half of 1934 alone, three major strikes—longshoremen all along the West Coast, auto workers in Toledo, and Teamsters in Minneapolis—lead to deadly clashes between workers on the one hand and police, National Guardsmen, and paramilitaries on the other. In Ohio, Washington, and California, Communist Party members and affiliates took a leading role in organizing workers; in Minnesota, the strike was organized by members of the Trotskyist Communist League of America.[45]

Contemporary press coverage of these strikes from left-leaning journalists—as well as recent scholarship—has emphasized the reactionary, even fascistic nature of the violent opposition to worker organization. Eric Sevareid, who covered the Minneapolis strike as a cub reporter for the *Minneapolis Journal,* wrote in his memoirs that he "understood deep in my bones and blood what Fascism was" after witnessing the violence in the streets of the city's warehouse district.[46] The basis for this analysis was that employers had moved beyond merely hiring Pinkertons as strikebreakers:

they attempted to mobilize—successfully, in the case of Minneapolis—anti-union paramilitaries from the city's professional classes. Ironically, the deadly violence was only halted—and the strike partially broken—when Farmer-Labor governor Floyd Olson, himself denounced by conservatives in Minnesota as a dangerous radical, deployed the National Guard to the city.

The wave of labor agitation in 1934, along with the concomitant violence, prompted a variety of organizing strategies against the New Deal—which businessmen blamed as the catalyst for the unrest—ranging from the local anti-labor lobbying of the New York State Economic Council to the creation of national organizations like the Liberty League. There were also rumblings of a coup. In August 1934 retired Marine Corps general Smedley Butler, who had loyally served American business interests in the occupations of nearly half a dozen Caribbean and Central American countries and had recently finished a stint as the commissioner of Philadelphia's police force, was approached by bond salesman Gerald C. MacGuire with a bold proposal. Butler would lead an army of World War I veterans, modeled on far-right veterans' groups in Europe, to topple the Roosevelt administration and replace it with some form of fascistic government. But MacGuire had the wrong man in Butler, whose politics had shifted increasingly to the left after leaving the corps; he promptly informed on MacGuire to Congress. As Butler's biographer Jonathan M. Katz has written, it is unclear whether the Business Plot, as it was dubbed, was a serious attempt to overthrow the U.S. government. If there were serious plans for a coup, they were never put into action (unlike efforts in the nineteenth century to successfully topple Reconstruction state governments in the South or the unsuccessful effort by President Donald Trump to stay in power after losing the 2020 election). But even if the Business Plot did not extend beyond parlor talk, it was neverthe-less parlor talk among some of the most powerful businessmen in America about the violent overthrow of the U.S. government. And while Butler was MacGuire's first choice to lead the coup, others—whom MacGuire vaguely identified with the "Morgan interests"—preferred Douglas MacArthur.[47]

The New York State Economic Council was closely tied to these broader political currents. In late 1935 the U.S. Senate began an investigation into the financiers of the Liberty League and its sister organizations. The inquiry was led by Alabama Democrat and administration ally Hugo Black, soon to be nominated to the Supreme Court. The committee sent questionnaires to hundreds of prominent businessmen across the country in January 1936 asking for "itemized statements of all sums contributed" to, among other groups, the American Liberty League, the Crusaders, the Sentinels of the Republic, the American Taxpayers' League, and the New York State Economic Council. Subsequent hearings showed that the council did share donors with its fellow traveler organizations, including A. W. Erickson, chairman of the McCann-Erickson advertising agency; J. H. Van Alstyne, president of the Otis Elevator Company; and Alfred P. Sloan, president of General Motors. But the council was not a national organization—while it maintained offices in Manhattan, its power base and the bulk of its membership were located in industrial regions in the Mohawk Valley and western New York. Still, the Economic Council was, with some fifty thousand members, a sizeable organization. (Contemporary press estimates put the size of the national Liberty League at eighty-five thousand.)[48]

The Economic Council was certainly larger than its Massachusetts analogue, the Sentinels of the Republic. The groups were similar in many ways—the Sentinels ferociously opposed child-labor laws and welfare legislation in the 1920s and early 1930s—but the Sentinels, despite being more generously funded (J. Howard Pew, president of Sun Oil, gave the group $5,000 out of his own pocket), were considerably smaller, with around three thousand members.[49] The Sentinels were also more openly antisemitic. A letter from a supporter to Sentinels president Alexander Lincoln, a Boston lawyer, declared that America needed to wake up to the "Jewish Brigade Roosevelt took to Washington," and that "this fight for Western Christian civilization can be won; but only if we recognize that the enemy is world-wide and that it is Jewish in origin." Lincoln replied, "I think, as you say, that the Jewish threat is a real one."[50] Still, such open expressions of antisemitic bigotry from right-wing business groups were relatively rare in the mid-1930s. Code words were far more preferable—the New Deal was "un-American," inspired by "alien" influences, and/or was "communistic" and possibly directed from Moscow. Anticommunism, not explicit antisemitism, was central to this approach, but in practice the boundary between viewing the New Deal as either communistic or a "Jew Deal," a popular phrase during the 1930s, was porous.[51]

The Economic Council's newsletter echoed these themes and muddied these distinctions in its July 4, 1935 edition: the New Deal was simply "the American name for Communism"; Roosevelt had lied about his communistic political allegiances in 1932 (this was also a favorite charge in Liberty

League literature). By December the council's newsletter charged that Roosevelt's program—which had been fulfilled in New York through the passage of compulsory unemployment insurance the previous year—"had its origin with the *Felix Frankfurter type of citizen,* of alien birth and even more alien sympathy, that has been all too prominent in American law-making in recent years" (emphasis mine).[52] This was as close to unambig-uous antisemitism as one was likely to find in the public statements of organizations like the council, but as the private correspondence of the Sentinels proved, more vitriolic sentiments were common on the right behind closed doors.

Hart's oblique embrace of antisemitism did not harm him politically. If anything, the scope of his ambitions increased by the late 1930s, as he began working on issues of local, national, and international scope. Between 1937 and 1941, Hart was involved in three major political initiatives: the creation of the so-called Mohawk Valley formula to break union organizing, lobbying for Francisco Franco in the Spanish Civil War, and his attempts to pull "socialist" textbooks from American schools. Hart understood these causes to be part of a broader global struggle against international communism. Taken together, Hart's activities in the late 1930s rendered him an important figure in what Joseph Fronczak has called "an emergent global Right"—and Hart's anti-labor activism and his increasing interest in foreign policy would soon earn him the epithet of "fascist" by writers and politicians on the left.[53]

The Mohawk Valley formula arose out of the attempts by the American Federation of Labor to organize the Remington Rand Corporation, a busi-ness-machine manufacturer, in the spring of 1936. Remington Rand was located in Hart's native country: its plant in Ilion, New York was only ten miles or so outside of Utica. The region had long been a stronghold for the New York State Economic Council, and indeed Remington Rand president James H. Rand Jr. was one of the council's chief supporters. In May 1936 workers walked out of Remington Rand's plants in the Mohawk Valley in response to a variety of efforts by the company to undermine the campaign; a nearly year-long battle ensued between the company and the union. Remington Rand's options to break the union were constrained by the 1935 National Labor Relations Act, although the act had yet, as of the spring of 1936, to survive legal challenges—and indeed business could hitherto count on a sympathetic Supreme Court, which had already struck down a variety of

New Deal legislation. But given that the NLRA *did* provide labor protections and given that New York governor Herbert Lehman refused to use the state police to break the strike, Rand—with the assistance of Hart and the Economic Council—embarked on a novel strategy.[54]

The "Mohawk Valley formula" entered into the lexicon of the labor movement thanks to an article in the *Nation* in August 1937. Journalist Benjamin Stolberg had apparently obtained a copy of the National Association of Manufacturers' *Labor Review Bulletin* that outlined the strategy as written by Rand. It had several key components: labeling all union activists as outside "agitators" imposing their will on the majority of non-union workers; organizing a middle-class "citizens' committee" of local "bankers, real-estate owners, business men, ministers, etc." to oppose the strike; warning of violence from the strike to justify preemptive measures; organizing mass meetings to support the "citizens' committee": building a large armed force of police and/or deputized citizens; organizing a puppet "back-to-work" movement to sow dissension in the ranks of the union; organizing a public "re-opening" of the plant with the backing of the puppet workers' organization and "staging the 'opening' as theatrically as possible"; and presenting the world with a fait accompli that the strike had been broken and the strikers were merely a minority attempting to interfere with the "right to work."[55]

Rand denied that the company had engaged in either unfair labor practices or a deliberate union-busting campaign, blaming communist agitators borrowing practices from the Congress of Industrial Organizations—in particular the sit-down strike—for the labor troubles along the Mohawk. A scathing National Labor Relations Board (NLRB) decision issued on March 13, 1937, however, threatened Remington Rand's legal position. The NLRB concluded that the company had engaged in willful violations of labor law.[56] Hart, for his part, penned a lengthy letter to the *New York Herald Tribune*—later prominently featured in anti-union materials distributed by Remington Rand while its appeal of the NLRB decision to the courts was pending—defending the company in which he essentially applied the Mohawk Valley formula.[57] Hart, presenting himself as an eyewitness to the strike at Ilion, wrote that a small minority (two hundred out of twenty-three hundred workers) voted for a strike; local merchants and bankers (at least some of whom, presumably, were New York State Economic Council members) called for a conference. This culminated in "a mass meeting of 'all interested citizens' " at which it was decided to swear in three hundred deputies to supplement the police force. Local businessmen organized a group of anti-union workers. The plant reopened with an organized guard of deputized citizens "armed with rifles and shotguns . . . placed at barricades set up on all roads leading to the village" to turn back union workers. "The next day 1,800 men had returned to work . . . thus a blow was struck for the right to work—a right even more valuable to the worker than the right to strike."[58]

The key to the political success of the Mohawk Valley formula was its adaptability and its deliberate packaging by Rand, Hart, and the National Association of Manufacturers as the lynchpin for putting down communist-inspired labor unrest in other industries around the country, particularly as the 1937 strike wave intensified. The Mohawk Valley formula was most successfully applied during the brutally violent Little Steel strikes in the spring and summer of 1937.[59] Though the massacre of ten Republic Steel workers by the Chicago Police Department on Memorial Day drew the most headlines (and was immortalized in newsreels), much of the Little Steel industrial infrastructure was found in small towns in Ohio and central Pennsylvania. Bethlehem Steel's Cambria Works, the single largest plant involved in the Little Steel strike, was located in Johnstown, Pennsylvania, about seventy miles east of Pittsburgh; the plant employed thirteen thousand steelworkers.[60] In Johnstown, as in Ilion, local elites formed a citizens' committee in response to the strike; Hart wrote to its chairman offering to act as a liaison with Remington Rand officials to better coordinate the committee's actions.[61] In Johnstown, the formula worked too well: vigilante bands of mobilized middle-class men, deputized by the citizens' committee and funded by Bethlehem, violently attacked anyone suspected of CIO affiliations. (It was later revealed that the mayor of Johnstown embezzled the majority of the money Bethlehem placed at the committee's disposal.)[62]

Left-leaning journalists at the time, as well as subsequent generations of scholars, have classified the anti-union response to the Little Steel strike as a form of fascism—a popular, violent, anti-democratic, and anti-communist mass mobilization. Indeed, Hart and his allies blamed the violence during the strike on the CIO. Less than a week after the Memorial Day massacre in Chicago, Hart organized a meeting for "private enterprise" in New York that featured as speakers columnist George E. Sokolsky, a newspaperman from upstate New York; former Huey Long aide Gerald L. K. Smith; Elizabeth Dilling, author of the 1935 anti-communist tract *The Red Network;* Reginald

Boote, the chairman of Remington Rand's puppet employee association; and Michigan congressman Clare E. Hoffman, who declared that the striking steelworkers in Chicago were killed by police "because John L. Lewis sent them to their death." Hoffman also accused Lewis, infamously aggressive in labor circles, of having "adopted methods of the Red Communist."[63]

It was an irony worthy of Shakespeare that Sokolsky, Smith, and Dilling shared the stage at Hart's meeting. Sokolsky was, like Hart, from Utica; his father was a Russian Jewish immigrant to the United States who relocated to upstate New York shortly before Sokolsky was born. Smith and Dilling, by contrast, were already notorious for rabble-rousing and conspiracy theories. Gerald L. K. Smith was, by 1937, widely reviled as a demagogue and a fascist. An evangelical Protestant minister who had a congregation in Shreveport, Louisiana at the beginning of the decade, Smith had fallen under the spell of Huey Long, the populist governor of the Pelican State. In early 1934 Smith left his ministry to devote himself full-time to political organizing, accompanying Long on trips to Washington, DC (where Long introduced Smith to politically connected and influential people, including setting up a phone call with radio priest Father Charles Coughlin). When Long was assassinated in September 1935, Smith claimed his patron was murdered by a massive conspiracy that involved the highest echelons of American government, including President Roosevelt himself. In the 1936 election campaign Smith joined forces with Coughlin and Social Security advocate Francis Townsend to back a populist anti-Roosevelt ticket led by North Dakota congressman William Lemke under the banner of the Union Party; it got less than 2 percent of the vote. The whisper campaign that Smith and his allies had fascistic ambitions intensified after Smith announced a few weeks before the election that he planned to create a "vigorously nationalistic" organization to combat collectivism in America; with the defeat of the Union Party Smith reoriented to opposing the scourge of communism in organized labor.

Elizabeth Dilling, for her part, gained notoriety for writing *The Red Network*. She billed the book as a "who's who and handbook of radicalism for patriots," listing hundreds of different individuals and organizations as communists or controlled by communists—and Dilling did not readily distinguish between communists, socialists, and New Deal liberals. Her follow-up book, *The Roosevelt Red Record*, covered essentially the same ground but focused more on the alleged communistic nature of the New Deal. Both Dilling and Smith dabbled in antisemitism in the mid-1930s, and by 1937 both were poised to wholeheartedly embrace the explanation that the Jews were behind the political trends that so distressed them.[64]

More conservative analyses of the American right have long downplayed Dilling's prominence. Richard Gid Powers, in his 1995 study of anticommunism in the United States in the twentieth century, characterized Dilling as a "crackpot" who by her "outrageous activities" overshadowed the work of respectable anti-communists like Sokolsky.[65] After all, Sokolsky had come by his anticommunism honestly; a onetime radical, he went to Petrograd after the February Revolution in 1917 to cover the political tumult for American newspapers. His experience in revolutionary Russia turned him into a life-long anti-communist. When he relocated to Shanghai after the Russian Civil War, he took his newfound politics with him—Sokolsky became a representative of the National Association of Manufacturers in Asia, liaising with Chinese businesses and the Kuomintang government. (Ironically, Sokolsky was targeted by the International Anticommunist Entente, a far-right group based out of Switzerland, while overseas; the organization sent a series of letters to the Federal Bureau of Investigation denouncing Sokolsky as a Bolshevik "Mongoloid Jew.") Sokolsky was a bitter critic of the Roosevelt administration and the New Deal—he infamously called the Social Security Act a "service charge for coercion." Sokolsky may not have made as radical a break with the left as former Communist Party members and fellow travelers who decisively broke with the Soviet Union in the 1930s—like his counterpart at United Press International Eugene Lyons, who became disillusioned with Stalinist terror while a correspondent in Moscow in the 1930s and by the end of the decade had conclusively broken with the left—but Sokolsky was entirely within the mainstream of the American right and American anticommunism in 1937.[66]

Elizabeth Dilling was even more colorful than Sokolsky. "Combining burlesque humor and narratives of combat atrocity," one of her biographers wrote, "she cultivated a performance routine that many described as entertaining." She was reportedly lauded for her impression of Eleanor Roosevelt. Dilling's reputation for theatrics was so great that, when she led a mothers' group against American intervention in World War II in the early 1940s, other non-interventionists denounced her for giving the movement a bad name—and that was *before* Dilling began to refer to American intervention in World War as "the [war] for the kikes."[67] But Dilling's uncouthness was also strategic. An upper-middle-class housewife from a posh suburb of

Chicago, she played against expectations of middle-class propriety in order to dramatize her causes. More important, Dilling's embrace of anticommunism came from a similar place as Sokolsky's. Dilling was something of a world traveler in the 1920s, touring Europe and Asia extensively. In 1931, Dilling took a trip through the Soviet Union. She attributed this experience as her road-to-Damascus moment, a life-changing event that plunged her headfirst into the anti-communist struggle. She was shocked by communism's "atheism, sex degeneracy, broken homes, [and] class hatred," singling out the Soviet anti-religious campaigns and the common practice of Muscovites to bath in the city's rivers in the nude for particular revulsion. She was also alarmed by the insistence of her guides in Russia that communist revolution would soon break out in the United States.[68]

Armed with her newfound anti-communist conviction, Dilling became a prominent anti-communist activist in Chicago in the mid-1930s, even testifying as an expert witness to an Illinois state senate panel investigating charges levied by drugstore magnate Charles Walgreen that communist professors at the University of Chicago were indoctrinating his niece with communist values. To insist that activists like Dilling were ultimately distractions from the serious work of sober anti-communists who had sincere and legitimate reasons to abhor communists belies the extent to which the "kooks" *were* the fact of anticommunism in the United States in the 1930s, had similar stories of anti-communist radicalization, and were to be found alongside the sober, respectable Sokolskys of the country.

The "kooks" and the sober anti-communist conservatives found themselves agreeing on most of the pressing issues of the day, including the most significant international issue after 1936, the Spanish Civil War.

Hart increasingly viewed the struggle against organized labor and the New Deal in the United States as but one front of a global war against international communism. This was not a unique view among critics of the Roosevelt administration—Al Smith suggested at a gala banquet in 1936 that the New Deal was essentially communistic—but Hart's view that the struggle against communism was both domestic *and* international affected his activist work.[69] In 1938 Hart—purportedly on the advice of his doctor—embarked on a lengthy trip to more temperate climates than upstate New York. Hart chose to travel to Spain, then in the midst of a brutal civil war between the Spanish Republic and the Spanish Nationalists, who started the war after a failed attempted coup against the Republic after the left-wing Popular Front won the 1936 Spanish general elections.[70] Even before his return to the United States he quickly became a mouthpiece for General Francisco Franco's Nationalist regime.[71] Articles and letters by Hart then began appearing in a variety of publications over the autumn and winter of 1938 defending Franco and calling for American recognition of the Nationalist government. In November, Hart penned a column in the *New York Herald Tribune* claiming that the Spanish Republicans had firebombed Guernica while retreating from Franco's troops in a false-flag operation.[72] Hart also helped to organize, along with Catholic writer and activist John Eoghan Kelly (who was almost certainly the catalyst for Hart's trip to Spain), art deco artist Hildreth Meière, and several other prominent Manhattanites the American Union for Nationalist Spain (AUNS) in December 1938, allowing the new organization use of the New York State Economic Council's office to prepare mailers and other materials to promote Franco's cause. Hart even became chairman of the AUNS and personally received a telegram from Franco thanking him for his efforts on behalf of Spain in the United States.[73]

Hart was in some respects an outlier among pro-Franco Americans for the simple reason that he was Episcopalian, not Catholic. Most of the outspoken supporters of Franco in the United States were Catholics. The most prominent was undoubtedly radio priest Father Charles Coughlin. Coughlin, who served as a parish priest in Detroit, began broadcasting over the radio in October 1926 and built up a national audience that, at its peak in the mid-1930s, numbered over 10 million listeners. In 1930, in response to the Depression, Coughlin became increasingly fixated on the dangers of Bolshevism, which he linked to Jewish conspiracy. In testimony before Congress, he claimed that socialism derived from "the Hebrew, Karl Marx" as well as from the Illuminati. Coughlin's broadcasts became increasingly antisemitic as the decade progressed; he linked Jews to the global depression and speculative finance as well as communism. Originally a supporter of Roosevelt and the New Deal, Coughlin broke with the president in 1935 and, along with Gerald L. K. Smith, was one of the principal figures behind the Union Party in 1936. In 1938 Coughlin openly endorsed the notorious antisemitic forgery *The Protocols of the Elders of Zion*, alleged to be a blueprint for Jewish global domination but actually written by tsarist officials in Russia at the beginning of the century. Coughlin openly admired Mussolini, and almost got his program kicked off the air in November 1938 for a rabidly antisemitic broadcast after Kristallnacht in which he defended Hitler and the Nazis, and—unsurprisingly—saw the Catholic Franco as the defender of Western Christendom in Spain against godless Judeo-Bolshevism.

The American public hardly champed at the bit for aggressive U.S. intervention in Spain—although pro-Republican mail sent to the State Department during the war outnumbered pro-Nationalist mail by nearly thirty to one, opinion polls showed some 70 percent of Americans opposed relaxing the embargo on trade with the belligerents in the Spanish war. Although most American Catholics were not particularly pro-Franco or pro-fascist in the late 1930s, actively pro-Franco voices tended to be Catholic and the Catholic hierarchy was generally sympathetic to Spain.[74] Anticommunism was the primary driver of opinion on the part of both the official Church hierarchy and the Catholic laity—the Republicans were iden- tified with anarchism and communism, and American Catholics were quick to link anti-religious repression in the atheist Soviet Union to massacres of clergy by Republican troops in Spain. Christian supporters of Franco— Protestant *and* Catholic—frequently linked the anti-clerical violence in Spain with the repressions of the Christian churches in Russia that had been ongoing for over a decade. Boston's Cardinal O'Connell described Franco as "fighting the fight of Christian civilization"; Joseph Thorning, a professor of ethics at the Catholic St. Mary's College in Maryland, told a meeting of the Knights of Columbus in Brooklyn in March 1938 that there were links between Republican atrocities targeting priests and the "slaying of 'millions' of Christians" in the Soviet Union.[75] Still, there were divides between Protestants and Catholics on Spain—Thorning's comments were prompted by a statement issued by sixty-one Methodist and Episcopalian bishops urging the Catholic hierarchy to pressure Franco to cease bombing Republican-held cities—but these were also opportunities for anti-communist Catholics and Protestants to collaborate. Thorning praised the Protestant War Veterans of the United States for protesting the letter as pro-communist. Merwin Hart's leadership of the American Union for Nationalist Spain was another element of rapprochement between anti- communist Protestants and Catholics. Coughlin's magazine *Social Justice* even published an article by Hart.[76]

Hart's views on Franco, the Spanish war, and communism were expli- cated most fully in his 1939 book *America, Look at Spain,* published shortly after the Nationalists declared victory in April. Hart drew most of the material for the book from his 1938 trip to Spain—in fact, both the title and the major arguments of the book were adapted from a radio broadcast Hart made from Málaga—along with supplemental material from representatives of the Spanish government in the United States. In his introduction Hart specifically singled out for praise Juan de Cárdenas, the "duly accredited agent of General Franco in the United States" and soon-to-be Spanish ambassador, making Hart's work for all intents and purposes semi-official Francoist propaganda. The book was not simply about Spain, however—Hart wrote it to "warn the American people of a new danger": international communism. Communism had been "defeated in Italy [by Mussolini], in Germany [by Hitler], and now in Spain," but, he warned darkly, "it will probably make its last stand in the United States." Communists, per Hart, caused the civil war in Spain by destabilizing the country and seizing power through the victory of the Popular Front in the 1936 Spanish elections. Communism as an international movement also menaced the United States, both as an impediment to American interests abroad and as a potentially revolutionary force at home.[77]

Throughout the book, Hart frequently digressed from his Francoist history of Spain and the civil war to compare the communist conspiracy in Spain to conditions in the United States; for instance, he noted in one section purportedly on communist policies in the Spanish Republic from 1931 to 1936, that "in whatever countries the Communists have worked, they have favored laws . . . forbidding the people . . . to own or carry arms," before launching a lengthy diatribe against the spate of federal and state gun-control laws passed in the United States since 1919. "In view of the fact that active communism in the United States dates from the end of the World War and that many of these anti-gun laws have been passed since that time, is it entirely unlikely that the passage of these laws is due to Communist influence?" Hart didn't leave it there. He maintained that American citizens needed to "heed the clear lesson of Spain and . . . own, and, if need be . . . carry arms to protect them from the Communist menace."[78]

Three points immediately stand out from Hart's comments. First, the suggestion that gun control was a communist plot to disarm the American public is both unsupported by any contemporary evidence and presages similar claims about gun control from the American right in the latter half of the twentieth century and the first decades of the twenty-first. Second, Hart was *directly* involved in the creation of the Mohawk Valley formula three years before, a constituent element thereof being the creation of armed middle-class property owners to fight union organizers, if necessary, with deadly violence. Third, Hart understood this call for armed self-defense against communism in both an international and a class context. In fact, Hart was explicit on this point later in his book, where in his penultimate chapter he reproduced verbatim his letter to the *New York Herald Tribune* on the Remington Rand strike as an example of middle-class Americans success-fully organizing against the kind of communist-inspired disorder that neces-sitated Franco's coup in Spain. Hart also cited a letter he received during the Little Steel strike in June 1937, purportedly from the wife of a steelworker in Warren, Ohio. "They are going to try to make my husband join the C.I.O. We don't believe in Communism. Our police don't do a thing! . . . All of my people were born and raised in Warren, but I'm beginning to think we may as well go to Russia, or are we going to have what is happening in Spain?"[79]

Hart also looked to Franco's Spain for political remedies for the New Deal. Long an opponent of the prevailing rate of wage and minimum-wage laws in New York, he wrote wistfully of how Nationalist Spain "has no 'prevailing rate of wage comparable in any sense to [the United States]. Plasterers do not get two dollars an hour. . . . There are no six hour-days. There is little interruption to normal work through senseless strikes." Francoist Spain had, in sum, Hart's desired socioeconomic order. The threat of violent reprisals properly disciplined labor. Hart also admired a peculiarly regressive tax imposed by the Nationalist mayor of Seville on the population of his city. "Every man over eighteen must give one day's work a month." Those with capital could simply pay a tax to exempt themselves from the labor requirement. "The mayor doesn't go to any distant capital city and return with a grant from a 'WPA.' " . . . The labor is given, the money is paid by the people of Seville." Hart applauded the Franco government's labor charter, as well as the practices of Seville's mayor, as rightly emphasizing "the right and the duty to work." In this sense, Hart saw Franco's agenda as essen-tially synonymous with the goals of the Mohawk Valley formula: to build a middle-class alliance predicated on the explicit threat of violence to discipline labor and suppress communist activity.[80]

Not surprisingly, Hart's arguments were widely interpreted as an apologia for fascism by American liberals and the American left. The Anti-Defamation League (ADL) began monitoring Hart and his activities in response to his pro-Franco activism, noting in their reports that Hart had begun, by early 1939, to be seen in public with Fritz Kuhn, the head of the German American Bund, a prominent Nazi front organization. (The ADL also noted that Hart downplayed Kristallnacht in Germany in *America, Look at Spain,* suggesting that press reports of the violence were exaggerated in a fashion similar to reports of German atrocities in Belgium during the First World War.)[81] The press corps assailed Hart as a propagandist—even Jay Allen, the former European correspondent for the right-wing *Chicago Tribune,* dismissed Hart as a "special pleader" for Franco in November 1938.[82] The left was more direct in its criticism—the communist *Daily Worker,* which had never been supportive of Hart or his politics, described him as a "Big Business Tory" who was now working with "avowed fascists" to support Franco. (The *Daily Worker* dropped all pretenses by the following February, invariably referring to Hart as the "fascist president of the New York State Economic Council" in its editorials and reporting.)[83]

Hart's advocacy for Spain, combined with his strident anti–New Dealism and anticommunism, provided him with interesting political bedfellows. On December 8, 1938, the council hosted a luncheon in Manhattan honoring Texas representative Martin Dies, the chairman of the House Un-American Activities Committee. Dies's keynote speech denounced both the left and the right. "I detest the Communist Party and the German-American Bund alike," he told the assembled audience, a remark made somewhat awkward by Fritz Kuhn's presence in the audience. According to Dies, he had originally planned to limit his remarks to a denunciation of communism, but felt compelled to mention the Nazis in his speech when he spotted Kuhn from the dais. Hart scrambled to tell the reporters covering the meeting that anyone was free to buy a ticket to the luncheon and he was unaware of Kuhn's presence. "It is possible," he said, "that not all who have come in this way are sympathetic to what we have to say." Dies, for his part, was overheard muttering that he wished Kuhn "had brought [Earl] Browder," the head of the American Communist Party, "along too and a few others to hear what I have to say about the American doctrine." Dies singled out the bund's promotion of "class hatred" as well as racial bigotry in his remarks, apparently under the impression that National Socialism and Soviet communism were synonymous. Kuhn's presence may have been unwelcoming to Hart and Dies, but clearly something in their attacks on the New Deal and communism had attracted the Nazi leader—Dies, for example, condemned "the mistreatment of the Jews in Germany" in his speech but then almost immediately redirected to discuss the "massacre of thousands of Christians in Russia and Spain" and suggested that prominent members of the Roosevelt administration, including Interior Secretary Harold Ickes and Labor Secretary Frances Perkins, were secretly in the pocket of Moscow. (Kuhn quipped to a reporter, "[I could've] gone to a church and heard the same thing.")[84]

Hart had another encounter, of sorts, with Kuhn less than three months later. The night before Kuhn and the German American Bund organized their infamous rally at Madison Square Garden on February 20, 1939, featuring some twenty thousand attendees under banners picturing George Washington and the swastika, Hart and the General Committee for Americanism and Neutrality (a redubbed version of the AUNS) organized a rally at the Seventh Regiment Armory on Park Avenue in Manhattan. Twelve thousand people attended. The general themes of the meeting were anti-communism and the necessity of rapprochement with Franco's Spain. The Christian Front, a radical antisemitic group organized by supporters of Charles Coughlin the previous summer, disrupted the meeting.[85] An unidentified spokesperson for the front demanded that Hart read aloud to the assembled audience a telegram supposedly sent to the group personally by Franco. Hart, after briefly consulting with his fellow speakers, refused, and the Christian Front demonstrators were ejected from the meeting by police. This account, which appears in the press reporting of the event, was challenged by the historian Michael Chapman, who wrote a sympathetic study of the AUNS in 2011. Chapman claimed that the supposed Christian Front contingent were in fact staffers from Juan de Cárdenas's office who were prevented from taking the dais because of the arrangement the AUNS had with the armory to prohibit political messages from foreign govern- ments from being read aloud. Regardless of whether or not this specific contingent was, in fact, an official delegation of the Christian Front, the group's literature was nevertheless distributed at the doors of the armory, and a substantial number of the rally attendees were Coughlin supporters. Later in the evening, a speech by Alexander Hamilton Rice, a geography professor at Harvard University, was drowned out by applause for a portrait of Coughlin being paraded through the audience. (The subject of Rice's speech, the conflict of "Christianity and civilization against communism and atheism," was a common talking point with pro-Franco activists.) The very next day, Kuhn held his rally at Madison Square Garden. Although Coughlin denied rumors that he had been scheduled to speak—and indeed the Detroit radio priest did not make an appearance that day—a number of his Christian Front supporters did reportedly attend the bund meeting.[86] Hart did not have any direct connection with the bund rally. In fact, the night before he had offered oblique criticism of the domestic Nazis as "making as serious a mistake as the Communists in their activities in the United States," mirroring the statement of his political ally Martin Dies a few months earlier. And Hart's pro-Franco rally did not spark anything approaching the same level of outrage in New York City as did Kuhn's bund rally the next evening. Fifteen hundred police officers surrounded Madison Square Garden in an attempt to keep a hostile crowd, estimated at nearly fifty thousand people, from engaging in violent altercations with the Nazis.[87] There were no reports of counterdemonstrators at the Seventh Regiment Armory. Unlike Kuhn, Hart and his fellow pro-Franco speakers were implicitly accepted as legitimate by New Yorkers—or at least as an acceptable part of American political discourse—in a way that Kuhn was not. Simply from a practical political perspective, affiliation with the openly Nazi bund was toxic—even Charles Coughlin felt compelled to distance himself from the rally.[88] Still, there were some notable political commonalities between the two meetings. While Hart criticized the Nazis in the United States, he also praised Hitler and Mussolini, along with Franco, for having defeated communism in their own countries, lines that drew considerable applause from the audience.

The very presence of the Christian Front at both rallies suggests that Hart and Kuhn were speaking to a common audience. This overlap sparked a series of political attacks against Martin Dies in early 1940. Frank Hook, a liberal Democratic congressman from Michigan, accused Dies that January of having ties with radical antisemites and fascist sympathizers, citing his relationship with William Dudley Pelley, the leader of the fascistic Silver Shirts movement, and his friendship with Hart, whom Hook described as an "energetic fellow-traveler" and "Park Avenue operator" of the Christian Front. These charges were an exaggeration—the documents Hook cited as evidence of Dies's relationship with Pelley turned out to be forgeries. Hart, for his part, denied he had any direct affiliation with the Christian Front, describing Hook's allegations as "an unmitigated lie."[89] Although Hook's charges were politically motivated—part of an unsuccessful effort to terminate Dies's committee—they did reflect substantive concerns. Even the most sympathetic biographer of Hart's major collaborator in the AUNS, John Eoghan Kelly, concedes that Kelly was connected to the Christian Front and frequently gave speeches to gatherings of the group.[90] Hart may have indeed been telling the truth when he angrily told the press he'd never heard of the Christian Front before the February 19 rally at the armory, but he was surrounded at AUNS meetings by Christian Front affiliates. And though Hart may not have been a Silver Shirt or a Christian Fronter, his pro-Franco and anti-communist political activism mobilized the same supporters.

In essence, Hart was continuing to operate according to the basic premise of the Mohawk Valley formula, a form of anti-liberal and anti-democratic mass politics. Hart, James Rand, and the anti-CIO organizers in 1936 and 1937 were aware that mass mobilization might spin out of the strict control of management, but that the risks were worthwhile in order to preserve the power of employers. The question of whether or not Hart in fact was directly connected to the Christian Front is, in some respects, beside the point. So, for that matter, were debates about whether or not Hart's support for Franco in Spain made him a fascist sympathizer. Fascism was not an organized international movement in the 1930s. There was no fascist equivalent of the Communist International.[91] Hitler and Mussolini did not automatically become allies upon Hitler's seizure of power in 1933 because of their shared radical right-wing politics; nor, for that matter, did the German Nazis maintain cordial relations with the "Austrofascist" regime of Engelbert Dollfuss, who was assassinated by an Austrian Nazi in 1934.[92] At a minimum, however, all of these movements were part of a broader global right that drew its domestic support from similar groups of supporters—generally middle and professional classes, backed by capital owners—and skeptical of liberalism and democracy.

Hart continued to engage energetically in right-wing activism in 1940 and 1941. His overriding concern remained the same: to oppose communism and its sundry alien influences from gaining a foothold in American life and to advocate for the continued survival of the free-enterprise system in the United States. Although still ferociously opposed to organized labor, which he considered the prime domestic battleground in the struggle against international communism, Hart increasingly viewed education as another theater in that war. Most of Hart's domestic activist efforts in 1940 and 1941 were dedicated to building a national network to remove allegedly subversive pro-communist textbooks from America's schools. Hart and the Economic Council were by no means the only activists working on this issue, but he continued to be an important part of a dense ecosystem of conservative groups dedicated to fighting against communism, socialism, and New Deal liberalism. If the left had its anti-fascist Popular Front in the 1930s, then the right had its own popular front of activists and organizations pushing a militantly anti-communist and anti-liberal agenda.

Hart had long been concerned about cultural subversion by Communist Party front groups and communist sympathizers. He constantly complained about mainstream press coverage of the Spanish Civil War and the pro-Republican sympathies of many American intellectuals (singling out Theodore Dreiser in *America, Look at Spain* for particular ire).[93] In December 1939, in a speech in Binghamton, New York, Hart turned his ire to what he described as a " 'subtle, sugar-coated' effort to convert youth to Communism" by the Binghamton school district's use of subversive school textbooks written by Harold Rugg, a professor at Columbia University's Teachers College. Hart was hardly the first to claim that there was subversive activity afoot in America's schools. Charles Walgreen, the founder of a national drugstore chain, drew headlines in 1935 when he claimed that his niece was being indoctrinated into "free love and Communism" by her professors at the University of Chicago. (Walgreen retracted his charges after an investigation by the Illinois state senate—at which Elizabeth Dilling testified— eventually donating some half a million dollars to the university by way of apology . . . on the condition that his funds be used to promote "pro-American" views.)[94] And to be fair, Rugg's textbooks did have a political component to their pedagogy—since his earliest days as an educator, Rugg was explicit that he hoped to teach students to be skeptical of authority and conventional wisdom. As far as conservative activists were concerned, this was tantamount to communism. (It did not help matters that Rugg, although a critic of the Communist Party line himself, *was* willing to include communist writers in his pedagogical materials.) Correspondingly, Rugg found himself the subject of attacks from a variety of right-wing groups and activists in the late 1930s and early 1940s, ranging from the American Legion to Bertie Forbes, the publisher of *Forbes* magazine, to Hart and the New York State Economic Council (Hart apparently first became acquainted with the Rugg books after reading a critical article in *Forbes*). The most recent study of the Rugg textbook controversy emphasized that competing visions of

"Americanism"—respect for authority, religion, and pro-market economics versus Rugg's conception of participatory democracy—were the fundamental issues at stake. Both Rugg and most of his critics, including Forbes and the American Legion, contested "Americanism" through the term *democracy*, with Rugg insisting that he had a "deep loyalty to the historic American version of the democratic way of life" and that his textbooks would instill in students a healthy democratic skepticism that "could serve as the true implementation of democracy."[95]

For Hart, who had already come to the conclusion that the very term *democracy* was a Comintern plot to subvert the American republic, Rugg's commitment to democracy made him automatically suspect. In his speech in Binghamton, Hart relied on his continued close relationship with Martin Dies to bolster his expert anti-communist credentials—no small irony, since one of the major criticisms of Rugg's texts was that Rugg could not be trusted as an elitist "expert." Hart specifically cited Rugg's hostility to the advertising industry in the textbook *An Introduction to Problems of American Culture*, saying that the Dies committee had exposed anti-advertising "impartial private research groups" as communistic.[96] Hart's accusations set off a firestorm in Binghamton, spurring the Binghamton Teacher Association to investigate the books and conclude that Hart's concerns were "justified to a degree." The superintendent of the Binghamton school district bowed to pressure the following spring and pulled Rugg's texts out of the classroom. Hart, for his part, reveled in his role in removing Rugg's books from Binghamton, urging readers of his *Economic Council Letter* to "ascertain whether these Rugg Social Science Textbooks are in use in their schools," and promising that the Economic Council would provide guidance through "constructive suggestions" on how best to remove them.[97]

The campaign against Rugg had become in essence a soft version of the Mohawk Valley formula. Rugg was a pro-communist outside agitator who required middle-class members of the Economic Council to organize against him and his work. While there was not the same implicit threat of violence in the anti-Rugg campaign as in the organizing efforts against the CIO, Hart and his fellow anti-communist activists saw the struggles in the same terms. If labor organizing threatened to disrupt control over labor, then Rugg's textbooks threatened to disrupt control over young people and had to be dealt with accordingly. The council noted in the spring of 1940 that it had received inquiries "from states as far west as California" and that "aid is daily being asked in ferreting out such books." The council was "prepared to furnish" such aid, and would gladly "instruct parents how to proceed" in removing the Rugg books from their schools.[98] By the fall, eight school districts had removed Rugg's books from their curricula, a victory Hart attributed to the tireless activism of council members, noting that the council's committee on education was "already in communication with some sixty other communities from the Atlantic to Pacific" to fight back against Rugg's subversive texts.[99] Hart's campaign reached a crescendo on February 22, 1941, when Hart appeared alongside Rugg on a panel at the annual conference of the Progressive Teachers Association in Philadelphia. Hart reiterated that Rugg's books had a "socialistic viewpoint" that painted a negative picture of capitalism and free enterprise; Rugg, for his part, retorted that Hart was bitter that scholars were insisting that "children study *all* of the historical records" (emphasis mine). "How free shall private enterprise be? . . . We want the story of free enterprise told, but we also want the story of [the] new definition of liberty told." By this, Rugg meant the transformations in American society of conceptions of public versus private goods. Rugg pointed out that one hundred years ago, "all water supplies were privately owned, and now they are publicly owned." But this spoke to the fundamental incompatibility of Rugg's vision of American society with Hart's—a man, after all, who had spent much of the last thirty years campaigning *against* public ownership and public expenditures of all kinds. Pointing to Hart and his fellow free-enterpriser on the panel, Alfred Falk of the Advertising Federation of America, Rugg declared, "Make no mistake. These men are not friendly enemies. They're enemies. The interests Mr. Hart represents are your enemies and your children's enemies."[100] The damage had already been done, though. Rugg's textbook faded out of classrooms. Hart and his allies, coordinating with grassroots activists across the country, had won a major victory.[101]

Hart's influence peaked between 1937 and 1941. There were admittedly limits to his accomplishments. Franklin D. Roosevelt was still president. The New Deal was still the reigning paradigm in American politics. Even Hart's most important success, his work with James Rand in creating the Mohawk Valley formula, did not prevent the company from losing both its arbitration case in front of the National Labor Relations Board and a later case in federal court. Nevertheless, Hart could point to real successes over the past decade. He had organized a mass-membership organization in New

York State and had received national press coverage of his efforts—and was seen as sufficiently influential to merit a congressional investigation. The Mohawk Valley formula was used successfully in the Little Steel strike in 1937. Harold Rugg's textbooks were pulled out of classrooms around the country. And Hart had built alliances with other right-wing activists to support Francisco Franco in Spain. He enjoyed an international reputation as an anti-communist crusader—and notoriety in the United States as a fascist sympathizer, in no small part thanks to Harold Ickes's November 1940 speech publicizing Hart's belief that democracy was a Soviet plot.

Hart apparently believed that widespread circulation of his original claim would exonerate him from charges that he was hostile to the self-governance of the American people and that he harbored sympathy for the fascist powers in Europe. His critics on the left saw through him. Freda Kirchwey, the editor in chief of the *Nation,* wrote that Hart's speech contained "a slightly oblique expression of anti-Semitism." What else could Hart mean by "foreign" and "alien" influences? Kirchwey went on to list Hart's ample and well-documented ties with far-right and fascist-sympathizing groups in New York State and nationally, as well as his lobbying work for the Franco regime. And, Kirchwey concluded, Hart was no pariah among business elites for his efforts. "According to the news account of the meeting published in the columns of the *Times* itself, Mr. Hart's 'audience heard him in grim silence. Many came up to shake his hand afterward.' "[102]

Democracy, like most political concepts, has always had its meaning contested. In 1937, a few years before Hart gave his speech, W.E.B. Du Bois wrote a novella he called *A World Search for Democracy* in which a thinly fictionalized version of himself offers observations on comparative systems of government. Du Bois defined democracy, "real democracy," as "based upon the widest recognition of human equality" in which no one individual or group, by dint of their race or class position, enjoyed disproportionate political and economic power over another. "Only for a moment, in the United States of America in 1867, when four million black slaves had enfranchisement and the possibility of economic power added to their legal freedom, did the world trend set toward universal human development," that is, real democracy.[103]

The prospect of real democracy terrified Merwin K. Hart.

CHAPTER TWO

"The Super Superpatriotic Type"

AMERICA FIRST AND THE FAR RIGHT

ISOLATIONISM IS A LONG-LAMENTED term. Historians have largely rejected its usage to describe those opposed to American entry into World War II, favoring instead *non-interventionism*—Stephen Wertheim noted that the very term itself, which suggests a kind of retrograde political orientation, was coined by advocates of American intervention. Indeed, there have been recurrent waves of scholarship—ranging from the conservative Justus Doenecke to the work of leftist critiques like Wertheim and Daniel Bessner—critical of the liberal internationalism of the Roosevelt administration, arguing that the subsequent blood-soaked postwar American global empire was the direct consequence of the liberal internationalism of the Roosevelt administration.[1]

But while *isolationism* may have been a term coined by non-interventionists' political opponents, the equally charged *America First* was decidedly their own appellation. Like the overwhelming majority of advocates of non-interventionism, Merwin K. Hart and his political allies—ranging from Robert McCormick to Charles Lindbergh to Senator Robert Taft—did not describe themselves as isolationists, but rather as advocates of America's national interests, which they identified with free markets, free enterprise, and anticommunism. For them, Nazi triumph in World War II was preferable to U.S. entry into the war, which would signal the final victory of the hated New Deal in American domestic politics. And while Hart,

McCormick, and even—to a lesser extent—Lindbergh were not Nazis, they *did* have a history of engaging in right-wing mass political mobilization as well as nativism and antisemitism, placing them on the far right of the political spectrum. Hart was actually denied a leadership position with the America First Committee because leading members of that organization considered his political reputation to be too toxic to risk public affiliation.

The narrative of victimization—that right-wing critics of the administration were particularly singled out for political persecution through the prosecution of alleged fascist sympathizers in the infamous *U.S. v. McWilliams* trial in 1944—needs to be read against the much more serious incarceration of hundreds of thousands of Japanese Americans in concentration camps without trial, an action that met with a muted response from right-wing activists. Still, while the narrative of the "smear campaign" has been exaggerated, liberals did reap political dividends from portraying their right-wing critics as "crackpots." The Roosevelt administration actually *benefited* from Gerald L. K. Smith's buffoonish 1944 campaign for the presidency as the candidate of his own America First Party. By the end of the war, considerable damage had been done to the public image of Hart and his political allies on the right.

Merwin Hart's opposition to American entry into World War II was, given his earlier pro-Franco views, perhaps inevitable. In September 1939 the Economic Council's newsletter darkly warned that if the United States did declare war on Germany, "economy and free enterprise will disappear and we shall probably never see them again." Hart went on to suggest that President Roosevelt's advisors were eager to enter the European war in order to eradicate the remains of the capitalist system in America and thereby hasten "Russia's plan to communize the world." Hart urged Congress to protect the American people from their interventionist president in the White House, adding that the "Hitler-Stalin pact shows [the communists and the Nazis] possesses a common tyranny" and emphasized that the real threat to America was internal communist subversion.[2] These were common viewpoints across the political spectrum in 1939, as the Nazi-Soviet pact in August made it easy to conflate communism and fascism into a common category in American political discourse.[3]

On November 30, 1939, Merwin Hart organized what he dubbed a "MASS MEETING FOR AMERICA" at Madison Square Garden. Hart modeled his event on his pro-Franco rally at the Seventh Regiment Armory earlier in the year, and the list of co-organizers and speakers was a who's who of "respect-able" "patriotic" organizations in New York—the popular front of the right. The rally, which Hart described as "anti-Communist, anti-Fascist, and anti-Nazi," featured a speech from HUAC chairman Dies, as well as one by Jeremiah Cross, the former New York State commander of the American Legion. Some fifteen thousand rally goers turned up. The evening proceeded tranquilly, in marked contrast to Fritz Kuhn's bund rally in February. Dies extensively quoted George Washington's farewell address warning against foreign entanglements, and cheers greeted the news that Fritz Kuhn had been arrested earlier that evening on embezzlement charges. (Chants of "What about Browder?" and "Browder next!" broke out in reply to the announcement.) Hart and his fellow non-interventionists had deftly managed, for the moment, to position themselves as simultaneously antiwar, anti-fascist, anti-communist, pro-American, and committed to racial and religious tolerance—one of the speakers on the handbill was the New York commander of the Jewish War Veterans. Hart, Dies, and the other speakers were able to position themselves as defenders of peace and American democracy, opposed to fascism and communism abroad and also, more importantly, at home. But this political alignment would last only through the following spring before it encountered a fatal obstacle: the collapse of France in the spring of 1940.[4]

Like most Americans, Hart and his fellow travelers professed a desire to see France and Britain defeat Hitler's Germany. Strict neutrality in the war did not appear to offer any real downside as long as the French and the British remained in a strong strategic position. After all, France supposedly possessed the strongest army in Europe. Upon the outbreak of the conflict, most American pundits confidently predicted an Anglo-French victory, albeit one that would take years as the democracies mobilized their econo-mies for total war. The United Press's war analyst described Germany's posi-tion as "unfavorable" and its armies as "unseasoned and without the well-trained officers, non-commissioned officers, and soldiers" to be found in France.[5] Herbert Hoover boldly predicted in October that a German victory was impossible; he was convinced that British and French naval power and the economic resources from their vast empires meant that the Allied powers would inevitably triumph. But the fall of France sent shock waves across the United States. Without American support, Great Britain could soon go the same way as France, leaving Germany totally dominant in western Europe and, with an evident ally in Soviet Russia, rendering almost all of Eurasia hostile to the United States. Hart, characteristically, blamed the Popular Front government of the "Blum regime" in France for the country's collapse and suggested that "[America's] policies, too, have been influenced from foreign capitals." (Léon Blum, the Socialist prime minister of France from 1936 to 1937 and again briefly in 1938, was also the first Jew to serve in the post, a fact not lost on his opponents both in France and abroad.) "National unity," Hart went on, "is impossible unless we throw out international influences."[6] But while public opinion increasingly favored relaxing the neutrality acts of the 1930s and assisting Great Britain, opponents of intervention began to organize.[7]

In the spring of 1940, a group of Yale students organized the America First Committee (AFC) to oppose American entry into the war. America First's politics were initially moderate—early supporters at Yale included Gerald Ford, Potter Stewart, Sargent Shriver, and R. Douglas Stuart, AFC's lead organizer—but the organization quickly attracted the backing of prominent right-wingers, including veterans of the anti–New Deal right of the 1930s as well as former New Dealers. Its professed aims in September 1940 were hardly radical: the United States ought to first arm itself. The preliminary nationwide advertisements for America First in October stressed that America "needs guns. We need men. We need ships enough for a two-ocean navy independent of any other power. Let nobody take them away from us. Let nobody give them away."[8] Preparedness was the watchword, not disarmament. Aviator Charles Lindbergh, although not yet affiliated with America First, endorsed the passage of the peacetime draft that same month.

America First committed itself to forming the broadest possible political coalition against extending American involvement in the European war. The new group took pains to incorporate liberals and even socialists into its ranks as well as those on the anti–New Deal right. This actually stymied Merwin Hart's influence within America First and the broader noninterventionist movement. Hart volunteered in the autumn of 1940 to set up a New York branch of the Chicago-based organization, but his efforts were blocked by John T. Flynn, a longtime columnist with the *New Republic* who was also based in New York.[9] Flynn, like Hart, opposed American entry into the war and had been a long-standing critic of Franklin D. Roosevelt, but Flynn's politics in the 1930s were the polar opposite of Hart's. Flynn opposed the National Recovery Administration on the grounds that it had effectively suspended the Sherman Anti-Trust Act and allowed for industrial cartelization—the very feature that Hart had advocated for and the only aspect of the NRA that he and the New York State Economic Council had praised.[10] Flynn's major complaint about the NRA was that it did not go far enough in ensuring the protection of labor rights. Flynn also supported the Loyalists during the Spanish Civil War, condemning Franco's troops as "Spanish fascist legions" and claiming that fascist supporters were falsely attributing Francoist atrocities to the Spanish communists—which was, considering Hart's charges about Guernica being a false-flag operation, true.[11] And while Flynn opposed direct American intervention in the war in 1940, he was hardly pro-German; he harshly criticized Neville Chamberlain's appeasement policy in October 1938 and affirmed his support for the cash-and-carry policy advocated by Roosevelt and passed by Congress in September 1939. Cash-and-carry loosened the 1937 Neutrality Acts to allow trade in arms and ammunition with belligerent powers provided that sales were made in cash and the belligerents assumed the risks of transportation, a policy that by default favored British interests, since the Royal Navy controlled the seas.[12] Flynn wrote to Douglas Stuart in Chicago, "Hart is himself the super super-patriotic type. He has been widely accused of fascist leanings . . . and is constantly being 'exposed' [as such]." Flynn also told Stuart that Hart and his allies in Manhattan were upset that Lessing Rosenwald, the Jewish former chairman of Sears Roebuck, was on America First's national committee. Flynn became head of America First's New York chapter instead.[13]

The America First Committee, although a national organization, allowed its local chapters a considerable degree of autonomy. Flynn effectively froze Hart out of the New York chapter because of their long-standing political disagreements and because Flynn made a conscious effort to exclude the fascist-sympathetic right from his local branch. Not every America First chapter followed suit. In Chicago, the head of the National Gentile League, an antisemitic group established in Maryland in 1934, addressed an America First meeting.[14] Particularly in the Midwest, local AFC leaders leveled the old charges that the New Deal was the "Jew Deal" and that President Roosevelt was either being maneuvered into war by his Jewish advisors or was a secret Jew.[15]

These repeated scandals involving antisemitism and fascist sympathies would dog America First throughout its existence and contribute to its image as a far-right, pro-Nazi organization. But, at least initially, liberals like Flynn retained a great degree of influence, albeit in constant tension with pressure from the right. Had Flynn not been active in blocking Hart from organizing the AFC New York chapter, it is highly likely that Hart would have succeeded in the power struggle, given both his relationship with Robert McCormick, one of the major financiers of the national committee, and the high degree of tolerance AFC national leadership had for right-wing activists joining its ranks. Notably, Lessing Rosenwald, whom Hart objected to as an AFC national leader on the basis of his Jewish ethnicity, resigned from the organization after Henry Ford become a national committee member. (Mindful of bad publicity, the AFC ejected Ford by the end of 1940).[16] As a single-issue non-ideological organization, the America First Committee was not part of an anti–New Deal right-wing popular front. Ironically, outside of New York, it operated along political lines not dissimilar to Hart and the New York State Economic Council: embracing opponents of Roosevelt from all political persuasions save *explicit* Nazis and communists.

Hart did not take his political defeat by Flynn lying down. He had maintained ties with Charles Lindbergh throughout 1940 and in October Hart, along with Carl W. Ackerman, dean of the Columbia Journalism School, approached Lindbergh about the formation of a new antiwar committee on the East Coast to coordinate opposition to American entry into the war. Lindbergh demurred, apparently unaware of the political fight between Hart and Flynn and preferring instead to throw his weight behind America First as a national organization in Chicago. Lindbergh in general hated organizational work, writing in his diary after Hart's offer that "we have had more than enough of committees already. We need leaders, not [more] committees. . . . I think Hart feels like I should take over . . . but that would mean giving up the type of work that I am now doing," making speeches on the radio and being feted as a celebrity speaker.[17]

With Lindbergh having rejected a leadership role, Hart turned to an incredibly unlikely front man for a New York-based anti-interventionist group—Manhattan's answer to America First in Chicago—that was supposed to have as its remit organizing the eastern seaboard. The No Foreign War Committee almost immediately imploded, in no small part because the man Hart tapped for a leadership role, Verne Marshall, the editor in chief of a small Iowa newspaper, was completely out of his depth in

New York. In a radio debate at town hall with Dean Acheson, Marshall dared hecklers in the audience to join him onstage for fisticuffs. By April, the organization had disbanded.[18]

Hart was temporarily chastened by the No Foreign War fiasco. He did not make further efforts to form a new dedicated non-interventionist group, nor did he attempt to wrest control of the New York America First chapter from Flynn. He did, however, continue to speak out against extending American aid to Britain and potential American entry into the war as head of the New York State Economic Council. He testified in front of the Senate Foreign Relations Committee in February 1941 opposing Roosevelt's proposed Lend-Lease legislation, telling senators that while he wanted Britain to win the war, American involvement would exhaust the country's economic resources and then, "with the highly organized communistic network that has been developed in the United States," Russia could "quietly and . . . effectively take control here. That, I believe, is the great danger that lurks in the background." (Ironically, Joseph Curran, the president of the CIO's National Maritime Union, also testified against the bill the same day, on the grounds that the postposed legislation was "downright fascist." Curran reversed himself in July after the German invasion of the Soviet Union.)[19] Hart repeatedly expressed the fear that war measures would ultimately serve the interests of the Soviet Union and international communism, especially after the beginning of the German attack on Russia on June 22, 1941. Hart opposed an administration proposal in July that would allow for the seizure of industrial facilities for war production on the grounds that the war materials produced could find their way to Russia—if the bill were passed, he told the Senate Foreign Affairs Committee, it must include an amendment preventing aid to Russia.[20] He supported the extension of the draft in 1941, but called for strict prohibitions on sending draftees outside of the Americas.[21] And Hart insisted that the expansion of industrial production without coercive measures against industrial labor unions would lead to the victory of communism in the United States. In his penultimate peacetime newsletter for the Economic Council, Hart bemoaned what he considered a basic truth—that the German-Russian war had blinded Americans to the incoming "swarms of Russian agents . . ., all of them Communist," to the United States, which would inevitably "heighten Communist influence in our republic."[22] Hart wrote to Ohio senator Robert Taft in July urging that the United States shun Soviet Russia—"I hate Nazism and Fascism but godless Communism is far worse. For us to join even indirectly with Soviet Russia would probably lead to a Communist United States [even] if we won."[23]

It was no accident that Hart aired his concerns to Taft. The eldest son of former president William Howard Taft, Robert Taft shared Hart's core conviction that American entry into the war would lead inexorably to the final cementation of the New Deal and the end of the free-enterprise system in America. Taft had been elected to the Senate only recently, in 1938, but due to his political pedigree and support from former president Herbert Hoover had quickly emerged as one of the most important leaders of the anti-Roosevelt right within the Republican Party. For Taft the New Deal far outweighed any foreign adversary as his primary political enemy—indeed, Taft declared in a speech in early 1940, at the height of the Nazi-Soviet pact, that "there is a good deal more danger of the infiltration of totalitarian ideas from the New Deal circle in Washington than there will ever be from any activities of the communists or the Nazi bund." He adamantly opposed extending aid to Britain after the collapse of the Allied position on the European continent and was more or less indifferent to the prospect of German victory, which Taft did not feel significantly affected U.S. interests. "War is worse," he wrote to Hoover in early 1941, "even than a German victory." Unlike Lindbergh and Hart, however, Taft did not see the specter of Jewish conspiracy behind efforts to bring America into the war.[24]

Hart increasingly resented the "attacks" on himself and the Economic Council as pro-fascist and antisemitic. In April 1941, Congressman Joseph Clark Baldwin, a Republican from Manhattan, said in a speech at a New York State Economic Council meeting on the proposed Saint Lawrence Seaway project, "I have been informed that certain sponsors of the New York State Economic Council hold views on our American democracy and its defense completely at variance with mine. . . . Those who place race or party prejudice above patriotism; those who refuse to recognize the vital impor-tance of national unity . . . are preparing the downfall of our nation, just as the same elements prepared the downfall of France." Hart, also present at the meeting, took the podium and attempted to directly respond to Baldwin. "I am not unaware that there has been a whispering campaign that members of the Economic Council have . . . prejudice against the Jews. . . . We have many Jewish members on our board and many Jewish members of the economic council itself."[25]

Despite his professed anti-antisemitism, Hart remained an outspoken supporter of Lindbergh as the aviator courted public controversy. On April 23, 1941, Lindbergh spoke to a crowd of some ten thousand to fifteen thousand America Firsters at Madison Square Garden in Manhattan, sparking what press reports described as a "near riot" between non- and pro-interventionists. The Associated Press reported that several men and women were beaten to unconsciousness in the garden during the rally when they produced anti-Lindbergh signs; there were also skirmishes in the streets between supporters and opponents of AFC. Hart wrote a letter to the *New York Herald Tribune* the next day defending Lindbergh from the "name-calling and abuse heaped on him from certain directions," including denunciations from banker Paul Warburg, New York mayor Fiorella LaGuardia, and of course President Roosevelt.[26] (In response to Roosevelt's denunciation, Lindbergh resigned his commission in the Army Air Corps Reserve.)[27] Praise from the German press did not help Lindbergh's image—the *Hamburger Fremdenblatt* described Lindbergh as a "real American of Swedish descent out of the Middle West" who opposed war "through devoted love of his country."[28]

America First became increasingly sensitive throughout 1941 to criticism that it was pro-Nazi or antisemitic. The liberal anti-fascist group Friends of Democracy labeled AFC part of a "Nazi Transmission Belt," more dangerous than the bund because "it does not bear the stigma of an alien loyalty." John Flynn retorted that this charge was an "infamous smear."[29] But America First's public image was further damaged by the appearance of Joseph McWilliams, whom *Time* had dubbed "Mr. McNazi" for his support for Hitler, at another America First rally at Madison Square Garden in May. John T. Flynn, who gave the introductory remarks, noticed McWilliams in the crowd. Echoing Martin Dies's condemnation of Fritz Kuhn at a New York State Economic Council event two years earlier, Flynn declared from the dais that "just because some misguided fool in Manhattan who happens to be a Nazi gets a few tickets to this rally, this meeting of American citizens is called [by the press] a Nazi meeting." Both boos and cheers greeted McWilliams. Despite Flynn's protestations to the contrary, there were America First supporters in the audience who saw McWilliams as a fellow traveler, if not an outright ally.[30]

Lindbergh worsened matters for America First on September 11, 1941, when, in a speech in Des Moines, Iowa, the flier charged that the "British, the Jewish, and the Roosevelt Administration" were "the three most important groups which have been pressing this country toward war," adding that the Jews were also a "danger to this country" through "their large ownership and influence in our motion pictures, our press, our radio, and our Government."[31] North Dakota senator Gerald Nye—one of America First's prominent allies on Capitol Hill—further damaged the group's public image through his stump speeches decrying "international bankers" pushing America toward war, as well as his investigation into the pro-war content of Hollywood films in September 1941. Nye, who specifically targeted Jewish film industry leaders, was criticized for conducting an essentially antisemitic probe. Nye retorted that pro-war Jewish organizations had been the ones that injected the "anti-Semitic issue" into the proceedings. The hearings, which had been aided by an independent investigation financed by America First donors and led by Flynn, ultimately did more damage to America First than to the film industry.[32]

Hart, for his part, wrote Lindbergh several congratulatory letters about his Des Moines speech, confiding that he, too, had been smeared "as Fascist, anti-Semitic, and all the rest."[33] Lindbergh strenuously denied that his remarks were antisemitic, and received guarded support from the America First Committee, whose members were not eager to muzzle the voice of their most popular speaker. In a press statement AFC blamed pro-interventionists for "twisting and distorting what Colonel Lindbergh said at Des Moines [by] trying to label that address as antisemitic."[34] In the eyes of non-interventionists like Lindbergh and Hart, liberal and left-wing allies of the administration were unjustly smearing principled opposition to the Roosevelt White House as radical, pro-fascist, and antisemitic—a continuation of liberal attacks on New Deal opponents in the 1930s. And, in the case of Lindbergh and Hart, these smears were paradoxically proof that their analysis of undue Jewish influence in the media and in the administration was correct.

Lindbergh and Hart were not outliers. Political antisemitism—the belief that Jews had an undue influence in the Roosevelt administration and, through this influence, were subverting America's traditions and replacing them with the socialism and communism of the New Deal state—was commonplace on the American right in the 1930s and 1940s. Conservative broadcaster Fulton Lewis Jr., a pioneering Capitol Hill correspondent for the Mutual

Broadcast System whose folksy Washington, DC, commentary pioneered broadcast punditry, had dinner with Lindbergh and former diplomat William R. Castle shortly before the outbreak of war. According to Lindbergh's diary, they discussed concerns "about the effect of the Jewish influence in our press, radio, and motion pictures," with Lewis even confiding to Lindbergh that "Jewish advertising firms threatened to remove all their advertising from the Mutual system if a certain feature [Lindbergh did not specify which] were permitted to go on the air."[35] After Lindbergh's Des Moines speech, he recorded in his diary that John Flynn agreed with his point—"He feels as strong as I do that the Jews are among the major influences pushing this country toward war"—and was livid only because Lindbergh publicly expressed those sentiments.[36]

The defense of Lindbergh that the America First Committee made— that the pro-war Jewish lobby was smearing patriotic American opponents of the war with spurious charges of antisemitism to stymie dissent—itself had a long history in American politics and the history of American anti-semitism. When Henry Ford financed the creation of the antisemitic tract *The International Jew* in the 1920s, he not only strenuously denied (in public) that he harbored any particular animosity to the Jews, but claimed in the penultimate chapter of the fourth volume of the tract his prediction that good Jews will "see the truth [of the book] and act upon it." (Ford also called for the abolition of the Anti-Defamation League, "which grows frantic over innocent remarks on the part of 'Gentiles.' . . . No one can give the Jews [such] a bad reputation but the Jews themselves.")[37] Even William Dudley Pelley, the leader of the Silver Shirts, denied to the Dies Committee in 1940 that he "[held] any hatred toward any Jew in the United States," although in testimony the following day he told the committee, "I do say freely I that I am anti-Semitic." However, Pelley insisted to the committee that he had "no animus against the individual Jew" but rather "against the tactics of Jewry as a whole."[38] This qualifier did not pass the credibility test in the case of Pelley, who had built a career arguing, for example, that hubcaps produced by Chrysler Motors bore the Star of David.[39] In general, however, the rhetorical move of denying that antisemitic statements or inferences harbored any particular animus to individual Jews was tied to a specific form of *political* antisemitism. Hart trafficked in this form of political antisemitism, although he was careful to keep direct statements about Jewish influences out of his public statements in the 1930s and early 1940s. Lindbergh was less circumspect—not only did he make frequent private asides about Jewish influence in his diary, he was willing to unequivocally embrace political anti-semitism publicly in Des Moines.

These forms of political antisemitism were all the more influential precisely *because* they were not explicitly identified with fascism; Hart and Lindbergh took pains to emphasize that they were not connected with foreign fascist governments or native fascist movements. But while neither figure was an explicit fascist, their public statements, political connections, and commitment to a right-wing form of mass politics—particularly when combined with their fierce anticommunism and antisemitism—placed them both on the spectrum of fascistic politics. This was certainly the analysis of their liberal and left-wing critics. The American right consistently rejected this criticism in the 1940s as bad-faith smears, and indeed the belief that allegations of fascist sympathies and fascist politics were ultimately liberal and left-wing ad hominem attacks meant to silence dissent colored a later generation of American right-wing political culture. The origins of William F. Buckley Jr.'s later litigiousness in the 1950s and his threat to punch Gore Vidal live on national television in the 1960s ultimately lay in the political clashes of the early 1940s.

Merwin Hart and the American right continued to feel victimized by left-wing smears during the war years. Hart, like many right-wing non-interventionists, made a gesture of closing ranks behind the war effort immediately after Pearl Harbor. The New York State Economic Council offered its support to the New York government as well as the War Department and the Treasury in December, and supported Roosevelt's call for national unity. Hart, however, had conditions: "a truce on the effort to change the United States into a collectivist society." He praised the selection of former executive vice president of Sears Roebuck Donald Nelson as head of the War Production Board, who could bring the entrepreneurial spirit of American private enterprise into Washington, DC ("Everybody behind Nelson!") and conceded that "certain dictatorial powers must be exercised during this war," but warned that "we must reject the idea now being so cunningly injected into the public mind that, of course, when the war is over, we shall be a Socialist State." Hart was not alone in his misgivings; Lindbergh wrote in his diary the day that Germany and Italy declared war on the United States that "we talk about spreading freedom and democracy all over the world . . . [but] we haven't even got them here in America, and the farther we get into this war the farther we get from freedom and democracy." (Given Lindbergh's politics views on race, he was presumably referring to the New Deal state, not the American system of racial apartheid.) Calls for unity masked the reality that the bitter prewar political battles would continue.[40]

Franklin D. Roosevelt certainly harbored no illusions about that. Even before the war, state and federal officials, partly at the behest of Roosevelt, had taken a marked interest in investigating those with alleged right-wing sympathies. For all of the attacks levied against Martin Dies for his associa- tion with Hart and other activists and Dies's repeatedly stated belief that communism, not fascism, was the greater threat to American democracy, Dies's House Un-American Activities Committee launched multiple inves- tigations into various fascist organizations and sympathizers, including the German American Bund, the Silver Shirts, and Gerald L. K. Smith. The Federal Bureau of Investigation maintained open case files on hundreds of right-wingers, including Merwin Hart, Charles Lindbergh, and even U.S. senators Burton Wheeler and Gerald Nye. Roosevelt pressed his security chiefs to aggressively investigate and prosecute antiwar and right-wing opponents—he personally sought FBI files on Joseph McWilliams, the American Destiny Party leader whom John T. Flynn unsuccessfully attempted to have ejected from America First's May 1941 rally at Madison Square Garden, as well as Lawrence Dennis, the Harvard-educated writer who had been dubbed by *Life* magazine as "America's no. 1 intellectual fascist."[41] Attorney General Francis Biddle duly complied with Roosevelt's directives. In July 1942 a grand jury in Washington, DC, indicted twenty- eight right-wing activists for sedition. Pelley, McWilliams, and Dennis were among those facing charges. Father Charles Coughlin and Gerald L. K. Smith narrowly escaped charges themselves; Coughlin had by 1942 been forced by the Catholic Church to retire from public life, while neither the Justice Department nor the Treasury Department could find anything to charge against Smith despite an exhaustive investigation.

Hart also escaped prosecution, but the sedition case had a broader chilling effect on the American right. The government investigations were only a part of what historian Leo Ribuffo in *The Old Christian Right* referred to as the Brown Scare of the wartime years. Right-wing critics of the New Deal were labeled as Nazis and fascist sympathizers by liberal and left activ- ists. Hart was no exception. The communist *Daily Worker,* whenever it had

the occasion to devote column space to him, identified him as "profascist."[42]
In November 1942 Hart filed a lawsuit against the liberal anti-fascist group
Friends of Democracy, the same organization that referred to America First
as a "Nazi Transmission Belt," for defamation in New York state court for
listing Hart's name in a pamphlet as one of "200 American Quislings" who
were still active in the United States in 1942.[43] Hart sought $1 million in
damages, claiming that the charges, which his lawyer called tantamount to
declaring him a traitor, caused "great anxiety of mind, humiliation, and
mortification."[44] Friends of Democracy—whose board members included
Rex Stout, the author of the Nero Wolfe detective stories—defended its
charges on the basis that all of the people called "Quislings" had connections
with organizations mentioned in the July federal indictments. Friends of
Democracy also asserted that Hart "has been actively engaged in the dissem-
ination of pro-Franco propaganda in the United States" and that this demonstrated that he was "a pro-Nazi, pro-Axis propagandist following the Quisling
line." While the judge did not comment on the veracity of those claims in his
verdict, the court did rule in favor of Friends of Democracy, dismissing in a
sidebar Hart's contention that Friends of Democracy's allegations that he
had relationships with other alleged "American Quislings" were based on
"facts not truly stated."[45]

Hart's public reputation continued its precipitous decline with the
publication in 1943 of investigative journalist Avedis Derounian's 1943 best
seller *Under Cover: My Four Years in the Nazi Underworld of America—The
Amazing Revelation of How Axis Agents and Our Enemies Within Are Now
Plotting to Destroy the United States,* which he published under the pen name
John Roy Carlson. Both the major arguments and the overall tone of the
book can be gleaned from the title. Derounian contended that a massive fifth
column of fascist agents and pro-fascist sympathizers formed a vast, well-
organized clandestine network that had been active in the United States
since the late 1930s. It was, in many ways, the consolidation of the "Nazi
Transmission Belt" charge levied against America First by Friends of
Democracy. (The group in fact employed Derounian as their chief investigator.) The book was a massive success, selling over 1 million copies between
1943 and 1944, and earning praise from syndicated liberal columnists
Walter Winchell and Max Lerner, among others. New York congressman
Arthur G. Klein even lauded the book in the floor of the House of
Representatives. Although Hart was not the focus of the book, which related

in breathless detail Derounian's encounters with a number of right-wing activists then facing trial for sedition (Derounian, posing as an Italian American fascist sympathizer named George Pagnanelli, attended pro-fascist rallies as well as bund and Christian Front meetings in New York City), Derounian dedicated a lengthy passage to Hart, describing him as a "grave digger of democracy."[46]

Hart had not been taken in by Derounian, who repeatedly attempted to interview him in 1940 under the persona of Rudolph Eibers, a "patriotic" Detroiter, but was repeatedly rebuffed by Hart's secretary. The best Derounian/Eibers could manage was a sit-down with Archibald Stevenson, Hart's deputy at the New York State Economic Council, but Stevenson did not deliver the requisite pro-fascist material that Derounian was looking for. He called Stevenson "one of the shrewdest men I had ever interviewed" because instead of secretly confiding to Derounian/Eibers a hidden admiration for Adolf Hitler, disdain for the Jews, or belief that Francisco Franco was the greatest anti-communist fighter of the times, Stevenson actually condemned Charles Lindbergh for his racist views, denounced Hitler, Franco, and Mussolini, praised the American way of life, and assured Derounian/Eibers that some of his best friends were Jews.[47]

Derounian's interview with Stevenson did not deter him from portraying Hart and his organization in a decidedly negative light. *Under Cover* quoted freely from *America, Look at Spain,* castigating Hart as having "denounced the ideals and principles which had motivated the French and American revolutions." He savaged Hart for his leadership in the American Union for Nationalist Spain, his frequent denunciations of democracy in his public speeches, his support for America First (Derounian did not mention that Hart had actually been boxed out of America First for his right-wing political views), and his various contacts with the other far-right activists who were profiled in the book. Derounian also cited Supreme Court justice Robert H. Jackson and Interior Secretary Harold Ickes, both of whom had denounced Hart as a "pro-fascist."[48]

Hart's economic views were also cited by Derounian as evidence of his pro-fascist politics. Derounian labeled him a "professional propagandist" for corporate America and an "ultra-reactionary businessman" who had opposed the forty-hour work week, child-labor laws, labor unions, and practically every aspect of the New Deal. Although American political discourse increasingly eschewed centering economic analysis in Americans' understanding of fascism during the war, instead placing Nazism and fascism in the general category of "totalitarianism" (and many quietly putting Soviet communism, America's putative anti-fascist ally, in the same category), the left continued to center capitalism in its examination of fascism. Derounian—who was neither a communist nor a particularly sophisticated political thinker—did not center capital and right-wing political mobilization to either the same degree or with the same level of nuance as, for instance, Benjamin Stolberg, but Hart's opposition to the New Deal state at practically every level—and in particular his ferocious hostility to organized labor—was understood to be related to his support for Franco and other alleged fascist sympathies.

Derounian's claims were controversial at the time. Socialist leader Norman Thomas described Derounian's book as an outrageous smear on anti-interventionists. Those on the right were particularly livid—conservative publisher Frank Gannett, who held a senior position in the Republican National Committee and briefly entertained a bid for the Republican nomination for president in 1940, attempted unsuccessfully to suppress the sale of *Under Cover.* The *Chicago Tribune* claimed to have exposed Derounian as an antisemite for editing the *Christian Defender,* an antisemitic newspaper in New York, while undercover as a fascist sympathizer. (Although this was hardly to Derounian's credit, it was not a shattering revelation—Derounian admitted having done so in *Under Cover.*) The *Tribune* also heavily implied that the Reverend Leon M. Birkhead, one of the leaders of Derounian's employer, Friends of Democracy, was a communist. Various people mentioned in the book sued Derounian (although not Hart, who was presumably already chastened by the failure of his earlier lawsuit against Friends of Democracy), eventually receiving either apologies or settlements. Historians have been no less critical. Leo Ribuffo wrote in 1983 that Derounian had, on balance, done more harm than good with *Under Cover,* as the often unsubstantiated allegations found in the book fed into the hysteria of the wartime Brown Scare, a key prelude to the anti-communist hysteria of the postwar years. Another scholar of the period, Benjamin Alpers, described *Under Cover* as a rambling, conspiracy-fueled account that is "difficult to imagine reading . . . from start to finish."[49] Indeed, Derounian's basic argument—that there existed a vast and tightly organized fascist underground in the United States—was incorrect, and could have been better used as a description of the American Communist Party.

There were indeed fascist sympathizers in the United States in the 1930s and 1940s, and either fascist sympathies or the utilization of fascist forms of politics—in particular the harnessing of violent right-wing mass mobilization to be used against political enemies—were important components of the American right in the period. But there was a distinction between being a proponent of fascistic politics and actively taking marching orders from Rome or Berlin. Hart bitterly noted in his newsletter that "a striking fact [about *Under Cover*] is that not a Communist or a Communist fellow-traveler is characterized anywhere in the book."[50]

The Roosevelt administration sought to harness the power of the state to suppress the far right as far back as 1935, when he authorized the FBI to investigate pro-Nazi organizations and agitators. The outbreak of war in 1939 was a catalyst for additional surveillance of far-right networks, which the administration identified as a potential reservoir for foreign espionage and political opponents of Roosevelt's interventionist agenda. "American entry into the war," wrote Leo Ribuffo in his classic history of the wartime Brown Scare, "made . . . indictments virtually inevitable." In January 1944 the premier Brown Scare court case—*U.S. v. McWilliams* (Joe McWilliams was the first-named defendant)—finally made it to the courtroom.

With a handful of notable exceptions, including Lawrence Dennis, Gerald Winrod, Elizabeth Dilling, George Sylvester Viereck, and William Dudley Pelley, most of the defendants were relatively obscure figures with small followings. No elected officials faced prosecution. Neither did Hart or his old allies in the American Union for Nationalist Spain, who could have in theory faced prosecution for violating the Foreign Agents Registration Act for their lobbying work on behalf of Franco's government. But the United States was not at war with Spain, and in any event Roosevelt administration's political aims were achievable without prosecuting a man who had sat on Governor Roosevelt's economic advisory board only ten years prior.

The trial was a circus. Edward C. Eicher, the presiding judge, was a career politician and administrator who had only been appointed to the bench in 1942 and struggled to control the courtroom, an almost impossible task even for an experienced jurist considering the number of defendants. The chief prosecutor, O. John Rogge, struggled to prove his case that the defendants were a conscious part of a "worldwide Nazi movement" to establish like-minded governments in other countries, including in the United States. The problem was that, while prosecutors were amply able to demonstrate that many of the defendants, in particular Pelley, who referred to himself as the "American Hitler," held some political views in common with the German Nazis—above all with regard to Jews—there was no international conspiracy linking the defendants directly to Berlin. The courtroom antics dragged on throughout the summer and fall of 1944 until Eicher died of a heart attack at the end of November and his successor declared a mistrial.

Both the sedition trial and the runaway success of *Under Cover* need to be understood within the context of the New Deal state's larger obsession with security and questions of loyalty. The same concerns were major factors, at least at the federal level, behind the incarceration of some 112,000 Japanese Americans in concentration camps beginning in February 1942.[51] Lieutenant General John DeWitt, the commanding officer of U.S. Army troops on the West Coast, maintained in his reports justifying the concentration camps that large numbers of Japanese Americans had traveled to Japan to receive ideological indoctrination and acted as agents and lobbyists for the Japanese government on their return. "Their loyalties were unknown," he wrote in 1943, "and time was of the essence."[52] California state senator Jack B. Tenney, a Democrat who had supported Roosevelt for president in 1932 and 1936 and who headed the California Senate Factfinding Subcommittee on Un-American Activities—the California state equivalent of HUAC—expanded his focus from investigating communist subversion in the state to justifying extreme measures against the Japanese American population in California. To be fair, support for mass imprisonment of Japanese-Americans was found across the political spectrum—Earl Warren, the Republican attorney general of California, was also a key advocate. But the decision ultimately rested with President Roosevelt who, at the same time he directed his attorney general to step up the investigation and prosecution of pro-fascists on the East Coast, also signed orders to round up and incarcerate Japanese Americans on the grounds of military necessity for national defense.

The imprisonment of Japanese Americans in concentration camps was a racially targeted component of the Brown Scare. Echoes of this were to be found in Derounian, who hardly mentioned Japan in *Under Cover* but did emphasize that Japanese sympathies were common among "Negro fascists," quoting a Black nationalist speaker who told a meeting in a community basement hall in Harlem that he "felt no enmity with people of the totalitarian powers, especially Japan. The Japanese have never lynched or exploited the Negro." After the massive success of *Under Cover,* copycat books proliferated, justifying mass incarceration as a necessary measure against Japanese spies and their fascist allies in Germany and Italy. The most successful anti-Japanese Brown Scare book, *Betrayal from the East,* was even adapted into a motion picture by RKO. While overwhelmingly white right-wing opponents of the New Deal felt that their reputations had been smeared by the Brown Scare, there was a far higher human cost to the scare in the Japanese American concentration camps that dotted the landscape of the American West. Insofar as any on the far right were concerned with internment at all, it was to call for harsher measures—Gerald L. K. Smith demanded that rations for Japanese American civilians be cut in his May 1943 newsletter.[53] Hart and his organization also remained silent. Flynn, a ferocious critic of the sedition trials as a smear against patriotic Americans, was too busy preparing a book blaming communists and Jews for the government's persecution of right-wingers and suggesting that the Roosevelt administration knew about Pearl Harbor in advance and let it happen as an impetus to enter the war in Europe.[54] Right-wing solidarity against the wartime actions of the New Deal state apparently stopped at the color line.

Liberals were not exactly eager to critically examine race relations in wartime America, either. W.E.B. Du Bois wrote an essay for the *Atlantic* in December 1941 in which he argued that "Hitler's race philosophy and methods are exactly the same as ours." Edward A. Weeks, the editor in chief, rejected the essay. "You make an assertion which will antagonize literally forty-nine out of fifty readers," he said, before adding for good measure that Du Bois underestimated the "biological handicap" afflicting the American Negro.[55]

The campaigns against right-wing non-interventionists did ultimately serve a political purpose: the defense of the New Deal in American politics. By the early 1940s, many of the rising stars of the Republican Party had grudgingly accepted New Deal liberalism as the dominant paradigm in American politics and had shifted their messaging from outright opposition to a critique of its implementation. Harold Stassen had successfully campaigned on such a platform to win the governorship of Minnesota in 1938—although Stassen's victory was also aided by an antisemitic campaign to tar incumbent Farmer-Labor governor Elmer Benson as a puppet of Jewish interests in the state capitol. Wendell Willkie ran a liberal and pro-interventionist presidential campaign in 1940; Earl Warren was elected governor of California in 1942 pledging that he would support Franklin Roosevelt more closely than his Democratic opponent. But there were potentially troubling signs on the horizon; in the 1942 midterm elections, the Democratic Party lost the popular vote in the House as well as forty-five seats, retaining its majority only because the South remained solidly Democratic. The party also lost ten Senate seats. How much of the Democrats' losses reflected discontent with government policy remains debated; the fact that several million mobilized servicemen were unable to cast ballots may have explained the severity of Democratic losses.[56]

The reversals dealt to the Democratic Party in 1942, however, did not translate into the American right posing a significant electoral or political challenge to the liberal wartime state despite the complaints of Hart and other right-wingers that the administration continued to use its various wartime powers "to change America into a collectivist state," either through high taxes, the proliferation of wartime bureaus and agencies, or wage regulations that put "too much money" in the hands of consumers.[57] The right's inability to impact wartime policy was as much a product of the wartime state's embrace of business—the traditional financial and political backers of right-wing resistance to the New Deal—as it was of political disarray. Even Alfred Sloan and the du Pont family called a (tense) truce with the liberal state as wartime orders flew in.[58]

The right's weak political power was also evident in the 1944 elections. Even though the Republican Party had enjoyed a resurgence in 1942 and in local elections in 1943, to the point that Henry Luce declared "the U.S. is now a Republican country," the early Republican frontrunners in 1944 were Wendell Willkie, who ran largely on his 1940 platform, and New York governor Thomas Dewey, a moderate interventionist whom Hart had criticized for liberalism during his first unsuccessful bid for the high seat in Albany in 1938. Voices from within the party were adamant that embracing the right would be electoral suicide—Vermont governor William H. Wills, who endorsed Willkie, denounced in a radio broadcast the "four-year locusts of Republican politics," including Robert McCormick and Gerald L. K. Smith, who "clouded the . . . crops raised in recent Republican victories in States and Congressional districts" by their hard-right opposition to the administration.[59]

The only significant internal Republican challenge from the right came from General Douglas MacArthur who, despite serving overseas as a senior commander in the Pacific, was briefly a contender for the nomination. MacArthur was supported by both old anti-interventionist leaders like Robert Wood, the former America First chair and MacArthur's old West Point classmate, and anti–New Deal internationalists like Henry Luce and his wife, Connecticut congresswoman Clare Luce. MacArthur's campaign was doomed from the start—although interested in running, as a serving general MacArthur did nothing to campaign for himself and appeared on primary ballots only in Wisconsin and Illinois, coming in a distant second behind Dewey in the Wisconsin primary and effectively ending any hope of the right wing of the party making a play at the convention.[60]

The other right-wing challenge to Roosevelt came from Gerald L. K. Smith, who announced the creation of the America First Party in March 1944. "The Democratic Party seems to be beyond redemption," he told reporters, and though "we have hopes for the Republican Party . . . we are running no risks."[61] Smith's third party, which nominated him as its presidential candidate, was intended as a potential spoiler to deter Republicans from nominating Willkie. But although Smith had not been a target of the sedition trial, his political reputation as an antisemite and a fascist sympathizer had already been cemented. The Maryland House of Delegates, in response to reports that Smith's party was organizing in Baltimore, unanimously passed a resolution hoping that Smith "will imbibe some of the spirit of tolerance as practiced in Maryland during his visit to the State."[62] After Smith issued a statement that he would not object to the nomination of Dewey, MacArthur, or Ohio governor John W. Bricker, Willkie unequivocally condemned Smith and his party, telling reporters that "any candidate of the Republican Party who does not repudiate the America First Party and Gerald L. K. Smith cannot possibly be elected President of the United States."[63] Smith claimed a victory lap after Willkie's defeat in Wisconsin, but his gloating was short-lived.[64] By the beginning of May Smith was also condemning Thomas Dewey, demanding that the Republicans draft *Chicago Tribune* publisher Robert McCormick instead. Smith had by then been disavowed by several former America First Committee staffers, who made it clear that Smith had no connection with the 1940–41 organization, and even Henry Ford had publicly distanced himself from the Detroit-based activist.[65] Smith's biggest triumph came during the Republican National

Convention in Chicago in June, when he and his supporters briefly "seized" control of the ballroom at the Stevens Hotel—an act that Smith bragged was "good old tea party Americanism," proclaiming that America First had "won a beachhead for free speech."[66] Press coverage was unrelentingly hostile— Ralph McGill, a columnist for the *Atlanta Constitution,* called Smith an "old act" familiar to "any man from the South," right down to Smith's theatrical display of his suspenders.[67] By the end of the summer the America First Party barely warranted a paragraph's worth of press coverage—even Smith's theatrical selection of John Bricker as his running mate, despite Bricker also running as Thomas Dewey's running mate on the Republican ticket, failed to attract much notice. Bricker, for his part, called Smith the "cheapest of demagogues." (Smith eventually was forced to "drop" Bricker and select Harry Romer, a former organizer for Charles Coughlin, as his new running mate.)[68] Smith and his buffoonish antics ultimately served the political interests of liberals and the Roosevelt administration, who took malicious joy in confounding his campaign efforts. Interior Secretary Harold Ickes gleefully denied Smith permission to use a bison from Yellowstone National Park as the mascot for the America First Party—"In a way I regret that I cannot see my way clear to arranging for you and one of our loudest voiced bull-buffalos to be introduced to each other." Avedis Derounian attended one of Smith's press conferences in New York at the end of September, directly challenging Smith's assertions that Friends of Democracy was unfairly smearing him as an antisemite. Upon recognizing Derounian, Smith screamed that he was an "agent provocateur and racketeer," grabbed him by the neck, and threw him out of the room, fuming, "And they wonder what makes anti-Semites." (Derounian, surprisingly, did not press charges.)[69] The Office of Price Administration denied Smith's request for additional gasoline allowances for his campaign, writing tersely that "he is not a qualified candidate for President of the United States."[70] But Smith's antics were not simply laugh lines. In a speech reminiscent of his addresses condemning Charles Lindbergh and Merwin Hart as fifth columnists in 1940, Harold Ickes said in October that Smith was part of a "Trojan horse" effort by isolationists to come to power in Washington, and that if Dewey were to be elected they would "foist upon the people of this country and of the world their own destructive and vicious ideas of isolationism."[71] This was a gross exaggeration; Dewey campaigned on largely the same foreign policy as Roosevelt, and Smith had in any event condemned him earlier in the

campaign. The charge also lacked the political credibility of the 1940 allega-
tions against Hart, who at least had demonstrable ties to Nationalist Spain
and had been an active participant in right-wing mass politics in the 1930s.
Nevertheless, that the charges continued to be made in the first place
demonstrate the political effectiveness of the liberal anti-fascist campaigns.
The power of the American right in 1944 was negligible; the moderate
Dewey won the Republican nomination, Roosevelt won handily in
November, and the Democrats picked up twenty seats in the House of
Representatives and recaptured the congressional popular vote.

Hart's reaction to these political setbacks fit a common pattern: a
renewed burst of activism and organizing, but with mixed success. In 1943
Hart rebranded the New York State Economic Council as the National
Economic Council (NEC), as befitting the group's national political aspirations. In an advertisement taken out over the Fourth of July holiday, the
NEC called for a "Re-Declaration of Independence" patterned on the 1776
document, with the New Deal state taking the place of Great Britain and
"sovereign citizens" of the Continental Congress. The list of "outrages"
included the expanding size of the federal government, the Roosevelt
administration's usurpation of the courts, restrictions on press freedom,
"the employer . . . being deprived of authority," and "the wage-earner being
forced into associations"—read: trade unions—"not of his own choosing."
The organization, befitting its grand ambitions, moved into new office space
in the Empire State Building later that month.[72]

A shared sense of resentment over "smears" eventually caused Hart
and John T. Flynn to reconcile. Flynn had greatly resented the attacks on the
America First Committee as a pro-fascist group during 1939–41, and his
public identification with AFC had led to difficulty finding work as a columnist. Flynn eventually took a job with the Republican National Committee
and published *As We Go Marching* in 1943, a mass-market jeremiad that
marked Flynn as a new man of the right. Rather than contending, as he had
throughout the 1930s, that the New Deal was flawed by its insufficient
commitment to labor rights, the New Deal/wartime state was now quasi-
fascistic, marred by deficit spending and corporate-state partnership, and
reliant on mass society. It was a critique that would be familiar, in many
respects, to Friedrich Hayek, who published his similar *The Road to Serfdom*
the next year. Hart adored Flynn's book and wrote to Flynn emphasizing the
importance of his work in order to arrest the Republican Party's drift to the

left. Like Hart, Flynn was also incandescent about Derounian's *Under Cover* and *Friends of Democracy*; Flynn even went so far as to suggest to Senator Burton Wheeler that Congress launch an investigation of Derounian and others—Flynn called them "the Smear Bund"—who he believed were being secretly financed by a liberal cabal. Flynn was also increasingly embracing antisemitism; he believed the Anti-Defamation League was the lynchpin of this cabal and that attempts to expose it would be squelched by Jewish influence in publishing and the media.

Flynn would eventually publish a pamphlet in January 1947 entitled *The Smear Terror*, which claimed that he and others, including Hart, had been the victims of "private gestapos formed to terrorize citizens who differ with the objectives of the operators." Flynn's purpose was educational: "Our people do not yet understand the forces which are behind so many 'movements' and 'crusades' for tolerance and security and democracy." He identified a number of liberal and Jewish groups as the architects of the smears against non-interventionists. Among the targets of Flynn's ire were the Non-Sectarian Anti-Nazi League, formed in 1933 to promote the boycott of German goods in response to anti-Jewish violence; Hart's old nemesis the *Friends of Democracy*; and Derounian's *Under Cover*, which he denounced as a "wilderness of lies." Flynn's language now echoed Hart's from nearly a decade earlier: the Non-Sectarian Anti-Nazi League, for example, was not an American organization but was rather controlled by "recent alien refugees."[73] Flynn even defended Hart on the charge of antisemitism. The sense of persecution on the right helped to create mutual bonds, particularly when that sense of persecution, thought to emanate from Jewish organizations, comingled with already existent antisemitism. In 1945 Flynn joined Hart and the National Economic Council in the creation of American Action, Inc., a group formed to catalyze right-wing reaction against the postwar liberal order.

CHAPTER THREE

The Role of the Crackpot

THE FAR RIGHT AFTER WORLD WAR II

ON OCTOBER 15, 1947, MERWIN HART'S National Economic Council weighed in on the debate raging in the United States about whether to support the creation of a Jewish state in Palestine. Hart had hitherto kept silent on the question of Zionism, at least in the pages of his newsletter, but his choice of guest writer for his Palestine issue, New York businessman Benjamin H. Freedman, betrayed his position. Freedman, whom Hart described as "born in New York . . . a substantial industrialist and of the Jewish faith," was one of the most outspokenly anti-Zionist voices in the United States. Freedman was indeed Jewish—his parents were immigrants from Hungary—and he had been a fixture of the New York Jewish community for decades, but he had converted to Catholicism in the mid-1930s after marrying a Catholic divorcée.[1] Freedman claimed in the pages of the *Economic Council Letter* that "the influence of the Zionist organization reaches into the inner policy-making groups of nearly every government in world—particularly into the Christian West." The Zionist cabal in the United States controlled the Jewish vote, according to Freedman, in the five key states of New York, Pennsylvania, Illinois, Massachusetts, and California. He further suggested that this Zionist voting bloc was dictating U.S. policy in the Middle East. Freedman warned that American support for a Jewish state in Palestine would unify the Muslim world against the Christian West and therefore serve the purposes of "Soviet Russian Communism," the "world's leading anti-Christian force." Such an alignment would almost certainly spark another world war, he argued, and "what if in such a war the newspapers of the United States begin printing casualty lists of American soldiers, Christians, killed in Palestine to satisfy Zionist aspirations?"[2]

Freedman's article, like most of Hart's earlier statements on "alien influences" on American life, was carefully crafted to avoid *explicit* antisemitism. He deplored the existence of antisemitism as "bad enough already" in America and attempted to frame one of his primary objections to the Zionist project in Palestine as its potential to intensify antisemitism in the United States. He was not, Freedman maintained, an antisemite—his Jewish background, which Hart highlighted in an introduction to Freedman's article, made that claim ridiculous. And indeed, Freedman was one of many American Jews who were either skeptical of the Zionist project or actively anti-Zionist, including Rabbi Elmer Berger and Lessing Rosenwald, the former America First Committee board member who resigned in protest over concerns about antisemitism in the organization in 1940, both of whom shared concerns about a potential American commitment to a Jewish state in Palestine.[3] But Freedman went further: he claimed that political Zionism was a dead letter because eastern European Jews were in fact Asiatics, converts from the Khazar Kingdom in the steppes between the Black and Caspian Seas in the twelfth century. Freedman doubled down on these claims in a follow-up column in October, declaring that "Yiddish-speaking Jews" of eastern European origin have no "historic or racial connection with . . . the ancient Hebrews," and that "American-Jewish supporters of political Zionism are guilty of un-American activity" by virtue of their "contradictory political loyalty."[4]

Hart concurred with Freedman, writing in an editor's note that American Jewish Zionists like Rabbi Abba Hillel Silver, who helped lobby the United States into voting for the United Nations plan for partition in British Mandatory Palestine at the end of 1947, were un-American. "Those who forced this project through UN are Jews first," not Americans first, he argued, before pivoting to his familiar attacks on the "communist-inspired" New Deal regime. But what was once dog whistling for Hart was now stated openly: the issue was not simply that the Roosevelt and now Truman administrations had "alien" influences, they "were infested with Jewish appointees, many of them communistic" and involved in making "nigh-treasonable concessions to Soviet Russia." Hart, too, brushed away criticism that he was engaging in antisemitism, because *"the real offense is anti-Gentilism. If anti-Jewism is stronger in the United States than at any time in the past, the Zionist Jews have brought it about."* If the Zionists continued on their path of pro-Jewish state advocacy, "there will surely be a repetition here of all of the outbursts and violence against Jews that have taken place in so many other countries." But Hart was, in his own unique way, being magnanimous. "May that day never come!" he concluded.[5]

Antisemitism remained a hallmark of the far right after World War II. Hart's antipathy toward Zionism was matched by fears of a renewed wave of Jewish immigration in the aftermath of the Holocaust. While the Truman administration recognized Israeli statehood in 1948, the Displaced Persons Act passed by Congress that same year was deliberately written to exclude Jewish survivors of the Holocaust from finding refuge in America. This was linked to a renewed round of anti-communist and anti-labor activism; because radical Jews were widely understood on the right to be leading elements in the New Deal coalition, barring further Jewish immigration was a necessary precondition to rolling back the New Deal state. A new wave of political activism to "purge" the U.S. Congress in the 1946 midterm elections brought together Hart, Flynn, and a host of other right-wing popular fronters to form the first conservative political action committee in U.S. political history, American Action, Inc. Although American Action would last only a single election cycle and would ultimately fail to topple most of its political targets, it was nevertheless the first major effort at national right-wing mobilization after World War II.

Antisemitism lingered as a force in American political life after the war. A survey conducted by *Fortune* in February 1946 identified 8.8 percent of Americans as "conscious anti-Semites," meaning those who openly expressed discomfort or dislike of Jews. Implicit bias against Jews was even greater—a follow-up poll in October 1947 showed that 37 percent of the country believed that Jews "are getting more economic power anywhere in the United States than is good for the country," and 25 percent believed the same about Jewish political power. The surveys returned ambiguous results about the geographic center of antisemitism—the 1946 poll suggested that explicit antisemitism was strongest in the cities of the Northeast and Midwest, whereas the 1947 poll suggested that implicit antisemitism was stronger in rural areas outside of the Northeast—but *did* conclusively correlate antisemitic attitudes with other political beliefs. These included distrust for Great Britain and the Soviet Union, hostility to organized labor, and disapproval of government-funded public-relief programs.[6] These were the core political beliefs of the American right stretching back to the beginning of the New Deal. Antisemitism as a political force in American life in the 1930s and 1940s was intimately connected with right-wing politics.

Antisemitism did not, however, go unchallenged. One of the biggest Hollywood films of 1947, *Gentleman's Agreement,* starred Gregory Peck as a Gentile reporter who poses as a Jew in order to write a magazine exposé on antisemitism. The film won the Best Picture Oscar. Liberal writers were increasingly concerned with antisemitism as a social and political issue, a consequence both of Nazi genocide and postwar anxieties about a potential resurgence of American fascism. Among the most perceptive of these were themselves Gentiles. Bruce Bliven, the editor of the *New Republic,* wrote a seven-part series on antisemitism and discrimination in late 1947. Bliven acknowledged that anti-Blackness, not antisemitism, was the bedrock of American racism—"the burden the Negro is forced to bear is heavier, on the whole, than that of the Jew"—but argued that "racism, like every other characteristic of potential or actual fascism, must be fought on all fronts simultaneously." Indeed, Bliven's solution to antisemitism as a political problem in America—and he singled out Merwin Hart as one of its chief political proponents—was the vigorous enforcement of fair employment laws and additional civil rights legislation, as well as the conscious transformation of social norms. "We must develop active, vigorous intolerance," he concluded, "intolerance for the expression of prejudice."[7] But it was Carey McWilliams, a left-wing lawyer and journalist based in California, who made the most cogent and sophisticated link between antisemitism and American fascism in his 1948 book *A Mask for Privilege.*

McWilliams had written extensively about racial discrimination in the 1930s and 1940s. For instance, he linked labor exploitation of Chinese, Japanese, Mexican, and Filipino farm workers in California in his 1939 book *Factories in the Field.* His stance on Japanese American mass imprisonment during the war was ambiguous; on the one hand, he condemned "evacuation" as a racist act in early 1942, but by the end of the year praised the implementation of the imprisonment scheme as efficient and humane. By 1944 McWilliams had moved again to opposition to mass imprisonment as a racist and unjustified war measure. McWilliams's views on the federal government shaped his torn conscience; he argued in his 1943 book *Brothers under the Skin* that the scourge of fascism abroad and at home necessitated aggressive government action. In some sense, McWilliams's views were the inverse of the non-interventionist right, who bitterly complained about government persecution but lifted nary a finger in opposition to Japanese American imprisonment.[8]

Despite his ambivalent response to Japanese American incarceration, McWilliams remained an astute critic of American race relations and right-wing politics. In *A Mask for Privilege,* McWilliams saw American antisemitism as primarily related to capitalism and the labor market. The decisive factor in the appearance of organized antisemitism in the United States in the 1920s and 1930s, McWilliams wrote, was the "appearance, on the clerical labor market, of a new group of competitors who could be identified for the purposes of discrimination."[9] This explained both the various social restrictions placed on American Jews—housing covenants, the quota system at the top colleges and universities in the United States, job discrimination—as well as the relative absence of mass violence against Jews in America. While the analysis in *A Mask for Privilege* was predominantly economic, McWilliams acknowledged the deep origins of the antisemitic tradition in Christianity, even if Christianity as such was an inadequate explanation for the explosion of organized antisemitism in the United States and around the world in the first half of the twentieth century.

The book framed antisemitism as a strategy by elites to enlist the support of the frightened and dispossessed middle classes and to undercut socialist critiques of capitalism. "No one has ever been called a 'communist' or a 'revolutionist' for suggesting that the Jews have too much power or that restrictions should be imposed on 'Jewish' capital."[10] McWilliams identified antisemitism as a right-wing or reactionary mechanism of control, "a powerful instrument in a violent and desperate struggle for power," citing the *Fortune* surveys connecting antisemitism in America to anti-labor politics. (He also noted that the surveys showed that poor people, and above all poor Blacks, were the least likely to express antisemitic attitudes.) Who were the purveyors of antisemitism in America? According to McWilliams, the primary responsibility lay with the leaders of heavy industry—steel, automobiles, and other manufacturers—who were naturally sympathetic to the antisemitic rationalization of "productive" versus "predatory" (read: Jewish) capital. "It is not by chance, therefore, that Henry Ford, once the most influential American anti-Semite, should have been smitten with this distinction."[11] McWilliams's analysis of contemporary antisemitism as a mass form of discontent with industrial capitalism directed against opaque and shadowy agents—in this case, the Jew—shared much with Benjamin Stolberg's analysis of fascism in the United States in the late 1930s.

Still, there were weaknesses in McWilliams's account. Although political antisemitism in the United States did not develop as a major movement in the nineteenth century, American civic and religious culture had a deep reservoir of anti-Jewishness stemming from the American Christian heritage.[12] Indeed, Richard Hofstadter, in his analysis of the Populist movement in the 1890s (writing only a few years after McWilliams) identified the Populists as antisemites and proto-fascists largely on the basis of anti-Jewish imagery in their rhetoric against bankers and financiers.[13] Most historians of Populism have rightly rejected Hofstadter's arguments as unnuanced and unsupported by evidence—the Populists did not center antisemitism in their politics to anywhere near the same extent as their agrarian radical contemporaries in other countries, or for that matter to the same extent as Henry Ford three decades later—but they were drawing on a common antisemitic imaginary. This, however, was not the same as political antisemitism.[14]

McWilliams also dismissed "purely psychological" explanations for antisemitism as evidence of an aberrant or distorted personality. This is necessarily conditional to understanding antisemitism, he claimed, as a social and material phenomenon. But there was an internal contradiction to this analysis: if antisemitism was common among the professional middle classes because of status anxieties, that was a *psychological* reaction as much as a materially grounded one. The other missing factor was the relationship between political antisemitism and political failure. Leo Ribuffo, in his study of the careers of William Dudley Pelley, Gerald Winrod, and Gerald L. K. Smith in the 1930s and 1940s, emphasized how both personal psychological factors and personal and political failures helped to radicalize the three toward extreme antisemitism.[15] The same creeping radicalization can be seen with Merwin Hart, who harbored guardedly antisemitic beliefs in the 1930s and became more willing to express them after World War II, as the New Deal state continued to apparently dominate American politics even as the political winds began to shift to the right. Related to antisemitism as a coping mechanism for political failure was antisemitism in response to a sense of (unjust) political persecution. Unlike with Hart, there is little evidence that John T. Flynn harbored antisemitic beliefs before World War II, but he came to blame Jewish influences for his personal and political setbacks and what he perceived to be "smears" against him and his political allies—political setbacks and feelings of persecution were not intrinsically catalysts for antisemitic radicalization, but they were important constitutive elements *in* such radicalization.

A *Mask for Privilege* remains one of the most insightful works about anti-semitism and capitalism in the United States in the first half of the twentieth century; McWilliams's analysis is remarkably insightful. While he referred to Gerald L. K. Smith and William Dudley Pelley as "crackpots," marginal demagogues whose public personas, thanks to massive press coverage, far outweighed their political support, he took their social role seriously. "The real function of the crackpot anti-Semite . . . is to encourage the open expression of anti-Semitism on the part of the latent anti-Semite. The crackpots function vicariously for their inarticulate listeners by doing and saying what the latter would like to do and say, but either cannot or dare not."[16] The reason why the crackpots never congealed into a national movement was because of their diffuse nature and interpersonal rivalries among them—as revealed in the sedition trial—and because "armchair anti-Semites" like Hart, Flynn, and Lindbergh did not throw their full weight behind the crackpots. McWilliams's analysis could be distorted—he believed the America First Committee was "the first attempt to form an open alliance between the armchair anti-Semites and their crackpot allies," while the reality was considerably more ambig-uous.[17] Nevertheless, McWilliams's major argument—that "reactionary" politics acted as a magnet for antisemitism—was correct, and this continued to inflect right-wing political culture in America after World War II.

In July 1945 Hart, Flynn, and a number of other anti–New Deal activists and former America Firsters, including William H. Regnery, the industrialist and financier whose son, Henry Regnery, had just founded the conservative magazine *Human Events,* met in Chicago to discuss political strategy now that Roosevelt was dead and the war in Europe had ended. The assembled activists decided to embark on a new national strategy to finally roll back the most hated elements of the New Deal. The biggest priority was to defeat congressional allies of organized labor. The organization that was created at the Chicago meeting, American Action, was intended to be a right-wing analogue to the CIO's Political Action Committee.

CIO-PAC, as it was commonly referred to, was the first political action committee in the history of American politics. Founded in 1943 under the aegis of Sidney Hillman, the president of the Amalgamated Clothing Workers of America, CIO-PAC was formed in reaction to the poor showing of liberal Democrats in the 1942 midterms. Fearful that the CIO would lose its ally in the White House in 1944, CIO-PAC intended to mobilize union voters behind Roosevelt and his supporters in Congress. CIO-PAC's efforts in 1944 were largely successful—not only was Roosevelt reelected, but a CIO-backed voter-registration drive in Martin Dies's district in Texas promoted the conservative congressman's retirement. Hillman called Roosevelt's 1944 election victory labor's "Battle of Britain, our Stalingrad," the loss of which would have been disastrous, even fatal, to the labor movement. Still, the impact of CIO-PAC in 1944 was less decisive than the initial results suggested—in many of the congressional districts that CIO-PAC targeted, Roosevelt actually *underperformed* in his vote share, suggesting that at least some union voters the CIO counted on either stayed at home or voted for Republican Thomas Dewey. The same difficulties that plagued CIO-PAC in 1944—especially building organizations in targeted congressional districts—would plague American Action two years later in the 1946 midterm elections.[18]

The specific goal of American Action was to flip targeted congressional seats from pro-labor to anti-labor representatives. Hart intended to "organize the inarticulate majorities of the Right . . . to purge both major parties of opportunist leadership that sells out American principles for minorities' votes." Although American Action leaders would insist throughout 1946 that the group was nonpartisan, in every district where American Action was acknowledged to be active the group backed the Republican candidate. Hart solicited a number of old backers of the America First Committee for the new venture, including Flynn, Regnery, and Robert E. Wood, all of whom would serve on American Action's executive board. The face of the organization was to be the former national commander of the American Legion Edward A. Hayes, who would serve as American Action chairman. Hart also reportedly sought the covert support of Gerald L. K. Smith, who continued to lick his wounds from his drubbing in the 1944 presidential election, although Smith never enjoyed a formal relationship with American Action.[19]

Upton Close, a radio commentator on the Mutual Broadcasting System, was the other great public face of American Action. Close had been on the air with the National Broadcasting Company as a Far East analyst for over a decade and had long courted controversy—the British and Canadian governments criticized his broadcasts as being damaging to the war effort in early 1942 due to his harsh words on the failure of British and Canadian troops to hold Hong Kong in the opening days of the Pacific war. He was forced off of NBC in 1944 after implying that Franklin Roosevelt had had advance knowledge of the Pearl Harbor attack and, echoing Verne Marshall's old allegations, that a cabal of pro-interventionists was responsible for a series of assassinations of antiwar voices. Close insisted that he was dumped by NBC because of communist pressure; he also maintained in his broadcasts on Mutual, which continued to give him time, that the Communist Party exercised "control of the Jewish minority" and that the Jewish press "[has] become avowedly Communist."[20] Close's case became something of a cause célèbre for conservatives, who claimed the broadcaster was the latest victim of liberal suppression of free speech (although he remained on the air at Mutual). One letter writer to the *Chicago Tribune* wrote that Close was the victim of the political power of the CIO and its Political Action Committee, which had filed a number of complaints to the Federal Communications Commission that Close's broadcasts were routinely "unfair to labor." (CIO-PAC did indeed complain to the FCC about Close, but about his Mutual broadcasts, not his commentary on NBC.)[21] By 1945 Hart had become Close's primary patron, with the National Economic Council providing the sponsorship for his radio program on the Mutual network.[22]

American Action had problems from its very beginning. At the second meeting of the executive committee at the Clark Hotel in Los Angeles at the end of August 1945, Howard Emmett Rogers, the head of the right-wing Motion Picture Alliance for the Preservation of American Ideals, reportedly walked out of the board room after denouncing the group as "nothing but another antisemitic enterprise." American Action publicly announced its debut in early 1946, proclaiming that it intended to target 187 congressmen with labor and/or radical sympathies for defeat in the 1946 elections. The group was deliberately vague on specifics, seldom publicly acknowledging *which* specific congressmen it was targeting, or how it intended to participate in the campaign. Still, American Action enjoyed support from a variety of right-wing sources, particularly as the 1946 campaign heated up, raising some $300,000 in initial donations. Robert McCormick personally donated $1,000 to Hart for American Action at the end of 1945.[23] And although

American Action repeatedly denied that it was connected with the America First Committee, many of the leaders, including Regnery and Wood, had also been America First executives in 1940 and 1941. There were even links with the American Liberty League from the mid-1930s: at a gala dinner sponsored by Merwin Hart and the National Economic Council in New York on November 12, 1946 in honor of Upton Close, prominent guests included John J. Raskob and Lammot du Pont.[24] Carey McWilliams argued in *A Mask for Privilege* that the role of the National Economic Council and American Action was to bring together "respectable" right-wing financiers and businessmen with more radical activists, the patina of money in spaces like the Waldorf-Astoria Hotel washing away the ugly stain of demagoguery. It was, McWilliams wrote, a model of "an inclusive right-wing political alliance."[25]

Still, American Action could hardly be rated a success. John T. Flynn resigned from the group in March 1946, only a few months after American Action formed, again voicing concerns about Hart's politics. Although Flynn believed that many of the attacks against Hart and other opponents of the Roosevelt administration as pro-fascist or antisemitic were liberal smears, and was even prepared to suggest in private that there was a Jewish compo-nent behind the smears, he still sought to preemptively disarm those polit-ical attacks. He wrote to Robert E. Wood in February objecting to Hart's choice of Gertrude Coogan to head the Chicago office of American Action—Coogan had published a book in 1935 that blamed a Rothschild conspiracy of controlling international finance.[26] Flynn was also irritated by Gerald L. K. Smith's public support for the organization—Smith wrote throughout 1946 that he was in "sympathy" with the aims of American Action, despite having been told by Flynn in a letter that "I know of nothing that would injure [American Action] more than your endorsement."[27]

Far more damaging to American Action than Smith, however, was Hart's inept organizational leadership. Charles Lindbergh had noted in the past that Hart, although he seemed to project strong and confident leader-ship, was in fact surprisingly ineffective as an executive. Wood wrote to Flynn at the beginning of March stating, "I am very much disturbed about the whole course of the so-called American Action Committee" and expressing dissatisfaction with Hart's leadership. "His intentions are all right," Wood wrote, "but I think he is a poor organizer and a poor execu-tive."[28] Only two districts on American Action's target list had had any organizational work dedicated to them as of March, and the lead organizer in one of those districts had not actually lived within its boundaries for years.

The initial stated goal of American Action was to organize in 187 congressional districts; the group quickly abandoned this ambitious plan in order to concentrate on a handful of districts. Given the lack of internal organizational records, it is difficult to determine precisely *which* districts were targeted, but American Action leaders acknowledged that the group was active in the campaigns against New York congressman Vito Marcantonio and Washington state representative Hugh De Lacy, both among the most left-wing members of Congress.[29] The chairman of American Action, Edward A. Hayes, longtime aide to FDR's late secretary of the navy Frank Knox and former national commander of the American Legion, acknowledged in a congressional hearing on political action committee activities in October that American Action was also active in Wisconsin, Illinois, Missouri, and Oklahoma, but declined to give specifics.[30] In his testimony, Hayes stressed that the group was nonpartisan and opposed "communism, fascism, antisemitism, and all alien or un-American groups that are attempting to destroy our form of government and way of life," but his grandiose words were belied by the relative lack of political sophistication exhibited by American Action. Unlike CIO-PAC, which ran radio spots, distributed leaflets, took out ads in newspapers, engaged in targeted registration campaigns, and had canvassers constantly working in neighborhoods that had a heavy number of CIO-affiliated residents, American Action's political work was apparently limited to knocking on doors—and there is no evidence on the actual effectiveness of American Action's direct canvassing.[31]

Given that the group had a skeletal national staff and no extant statewide political organizations, and that CIO-PAC and its allies outspent American Action $665,920 to $115,000, it is doubtful that American Action played a decisive role in the districts where it was active.[32] De Lacy, one of the group's targets, was defeated in his reelection bid, but Marcantonio handily won reelection in New York. Indeed, there is evidence to suggest that American Action's activities actually backfired. The group was widely identified in the press, particular in Black and Jewish newspapers, as a fascistic continuation of the America First Committee—racist, antisemitic, and a tool of big business. Robert Segal, a columnist for the *American Israelite*, noted Gerald L. K. Smith's sympathy for American Action and suggested that "as

Herman Goering goes to the gallows, well may he salute American Action, Inc."[33] The *Chicago Defender* called American Action a "reactionary mechanism supported by right-wing business interests," and Harlem Democrat Adam Clayton Powell openly bragged about his inclusion on what he called American Action's "purge list" because of his support for the Fair Employment Practice Committee (long described by Hart as "part of the Communist program").[34] Powell handily won reelection. Marcantonio, for his part, bragged in his victory speech that he had overcome "the Pews, the du Ponts, and the American Action, Inc." in his campaign.[35]

Still, two of the Democrats on American Action's "purge list"—De Lacy and Michigan representative Frank Hook—were defeated in November, swept away in a Republican wave. Hayes claimed a victory for the group two weeks after the election, but the fundamentals of the 1946 midterm election—a postwar strike wave, a nationwide meat shortage that was popularly blamed on price controls (in actuality, the shortage was triggered by hoarding by producers), and fourteen years of Democratic control of Congress and the White House—were far more decisive than American Action's targeted door-knocking campaigns.[36] Revealingly, the organization faded away by 1947.

Although the influence of American Action was muted and it did not leave a lasting institutional legacy, the group nevertheless indicated an important political shift for the American right. If the response of Hart and others to the New Deal, and in particular the CIO-led strike wave in the 1930s, was to embrace an often violent right-wing anti-democratic mass mobilization, then American Action was an attempt by largely the same set of actors to accomplish the same political end—the defeat of organized labor and the New Deal—through an electoral approach. But 1946 was not 1937. While communists continued to be influential in the labor movement, the 1946 strike wave did not appear to the right to have the same degree of apocalyptic potential for communist revolution as had unrest in 1937. This did not mean that right-wingers like Hart and his political allies saw organized labor as legitimate, or without the taint of communism or socialism—far from it—but by 1946 labor was grudgingly understood to be engaging in institutional politics, to be fought against on those terms. American Action was ultimately a failed attempt to replicate the institutional political power of the CIO through its Political Action Committee. It was poorly managed and organized, but the form of a right-wing political action committee organizing against the administrative state would be reproduced in subsequent decades by business interests.[37] American Action therefore tells a transitional story in the evolution of right-wing political organizing, particularly among businessmen, away from the political mobilizations of the 1930s to a more hybrid, interest-based approach.

This is not to say that American Action was not also a story of attempted mass politics—as Carey McWilliams noted at the time, American Action brought together financiers, reactionaries, and crackpots in common cause, an alliance between "the extreme reaction of right-wing industrial groups" and dedicated extremists that had the capacity to spark another fascist moment in American life. "I want to make it clear," he wrote, "I do not regard American Action, Inc. as either fascist or antisemitic . . . [but] fascist movements never emerge out of thin air."[38] As an attempt at a broad anti-liberal and anti-communist right-wing mobilization that welcomed fascistic and antisemitic support without necessarily *centering* those politics, American Action resembled nothing so much as a proto–John Birch Society—and indeed Hart would join the John Birch Society shortly before his death. Like the Birchers a decade later, American Action was also deliberately modeled on an apparently successful left-wing organizational form— the Communist Party itself in the case of the Birchers, the CIO-PAC in the case of American Action. The left remained the enemy, but given that within the framework of the broader right-wing political narrative in the mid-twentieth century liberals and leftists were in the dominant political position, mimicry made sense as a political tactic.

The consequences of the 1946 election were profound for American politics and American political economy. The Taft-Hartley Act was passed in 1947, amending the Wagner Act to prohibit, among other kinds of labor actions, wildcat strikes and sympathy strikes, and allowing states to pass so-called "right-to-work" laws prohibiting closed union shops. The hated price-control regime of the Office of Price Administration was also gone.[39] But "reactionaries" like Hart remained unsatisfied. In May 1948 Hart charged the Republican majorities in Congress with "Do-Nothingism": the "great mass of New Deal socialist-tinged legislation" remained on the books, and communists and fellow travelers remained in government. Moreover, the Republicans had not fought sufficiently against proposed FEPC legislation, had supported Zionist political aspirations in Palestine, and had done nothing to prevent an "avalanche of illegal immigration of undesirable elements—some of them probably Communists."[40] Hart was speaking in dog whistles: the actual message was: keep the Jews out.

Nearly 3 million Jews, primarily from eastern Europe, had immigrated to the United States in the late nineteenth and early twentieth centuries, but Jewish immigration had been severely restricted by the passage in 1924 of the Johnson-Reed Immigration Act.[41] The law established strict admissions quotas for new immigrants, with the aim of maintaining the existing racial composition of the United States. In practice, this meant expansive quotas for immigrants from western Europe, particularly Ireland, Great Britain, and Germany, and stricter quotas for southern and eastern Europeans— Italians, Greeks, Slavs, and of course Jews. One of the key architects of the 1924 act, John B. Trevor, was an army intelligence officer during the First World War and drew plans in 1919 as part of his military duties to suppress a Judeo-Bolshevik uprising in New York City. Trevor became a conservative activist in his later years, heading a self-described coalition of American patriotic societies, and even appearing alongside Hart as a congressional hearing in 1942 to testify in opposition to expanding presidential authority to suspend tariff laws. Antisemitism and nativism had a well-defined relationship on the American right in the first half of the twentieth century.[42]

Granted, support for immigration restrictions was hardly limited to the right. Samuel Gompers, the longtime head of the American Federation of Labor, supported literacy tests as a means of restricting immigration for decades before the 1924 act, under the belief that mass immigration threatened to flood the labor market, suppress wages, and ultimately bolster the power of management. Gompers was one of the major supports of the 1924 act, which went into law shortly before his death. The AFL remained a firm supporter of immigration restrictions into the 1930s, concerned that new waves of immigration would worsen the already abysmal living standards of American workers—the union even opposed the admission of Jewish refugees from Nazi Germany. Granted, the AFL represented the conservative wing of the labor movement; the CIO, which built power through organizing first- and second-generation workers, actively advocated lifting immigration restrictions and admitting refugees, even going so far as to express solidarity with Mexican migrant workers admitted under the bracero program while opposing the program itself. Labor's response to immigration restrictions and the European refugee crisis was ambivalent: the AFL continued to support the national origins quotas throughout World War II.[43]

American Jews, too, had an ambivalent relationship with immigration restrictions. On the one hand, American Jews were overwhelmingly sympathetic to the plight of their co-religionists in Europe and were at the forefront of anti-Nazi activism across the country. On the other hand, while liberal Jewish organizations called for the increased admission of German Jewish refugees beginning in 1933, Jewish leaders were careful to avoid calling for the outright repeal of the 1924 act: Nathan Perlman, a New York jurist and politician and an immigrant from Poland, urged Congress to set up special quotas for refugees in 1933 but said point-blank that the 1924 act ought to remain law of the land.[44] Working-class Jews, like their Gentile counterparts, feared a wave of immigration from eastern Europe would suppress their wages and decrease what little bargaining power they had over employers.

There was another element, too: fear that large-scale Jewish immigration to America would lead to an intensification of antisemitism in the United States. These concerns were rarely expressed openly among American Jewish leaders or in the Jewish press, but they were a palpable source of anxiety. Relaxing the immigration quotas could save hundreds of thousands, perhaps millions, of European Jews from persecution at the hands of the Nazis, but to do so invited, in the eyes of skeptical American Jews, the same forces of reaction to intensify in America. Even Franklin Roosevelt expressed these concerns: Roosevelt told Walter White, the head of the National Association for the Advancement of Colored People, that he was "quite apprehensive of the growing anti-Semitic and Nazi sentiment in the United States."[45] Felix Frankfurter, one of Roosevelt's closest advisors and a frequent target of Hart and other far-right antisemites as the supposed leader of a Jewish cabal in the White House, warned that fears of intensifying antisemitism should not deter the administration from acting on the refugee issue, but Roosevelt continued to express concerns in meetings with Jewish leaders about intensifying antisemitism in the United States if he moved too aggressively to help Jewish refugees.[46]

Opposition to loosening immigration and refugee restrictions was a hallmark of the right during the war. Hart testified in front of Congress in November 1942 opposing the relaxing of such restrictions in a proposed war powers bill and wrote extensively about the issue in his newsletter. He avoided crude antisemitic stereotyping, but his tone was steeped in genteel white supremacy. "In 1808," Hart wrote in the tone of an affable schoolmaster, "the first immigration barrier was erected. It stopped the importation of negro slaves." He went on to provide in thumbnail form the standard nativist arguments against immigration: that even at the height of western European immigration in the nineteenth century Ireland, Great Britain, and Germany weren't sending their best, but rather "incompetents and paupers," although despite their limitations these very fine people "[merged] with our population with reasonable rapidity." Immigrants from southern and eastern Europe were different—their "cultural background made assimilation . . . more difficult." Unlike many of the nativists in earlier decades, Hart did not have a particular problem with Italians and Greeks—the issue was Russian Jews who, he strongly insinuated, as a class had communist sympathies "antagonistic to our social order."[47]

A poll in 1944 found respondents equally split, 46-46 percent, on the desirability of allowing Jewish immigration to the United States after the war—the only groups that had more negative ratings were the Japanese and the Germans. Even the Chinese, subject to strict exclusion laws since the 1882 Chinese Exclusion Act, were deemed more desirable immigrants than Jews. The apparent about-face on Chinese exclusion was at least partially attributed to China's status as a wartime ally against Japan, although even in the 1930s American attitudes were shifting thanks to popular novels and movies like Pearl Buck's *The Good Earth* and the glamorous, American-educated, and Christian wife of Chinese leader Chiang Kai-shek (Chiang converted to Methodism upon his marriage). By 1943 Congress was on its way to repealing the Chinese exclusion laws as a symbolic gesture—albeit one with important practical consequences—of wartime solidarity with an important ally. But while the Chinese benefited from the joint struggle against the Japanese—"This man is your FRIEND," read one popular poster of the time, showing a smiling Chinese soldier; "He fights for FREEDOM"—Jews did not register as "allies" in the same fashion in American culture.[48]

Rumors abounded in northern cities that American Jews were dodging the draft or using "pull"—either financial or political—to purchase officers' commissions or otherwise receive preferential treatment in the army. Whispers abounded, particularly in the Midwest, about "New York Jews" being responsible for the most hated aspects of the rationing system. (Gerald L. K. Smith blamed Jews for his inability to receive gas rations during his abortive 1944 presidential campaign.) Prewar antisemitism—the idea that Jews were pushing America toward war—transformed into wartime prejudices that Jews were shirkers and war profiteers. Unlike the treatment of China in American popular discourse as a valiant ally, European Jews were hardly mentioned at all, and when Jews *were* discussed, it was as refugees and displaced persons, not as fighting allies. The constant references by anti-immigration activists and their congressional allies to "alien" influences, a favored term of Hart's, was designed to undermine any specifically Jewish claims to exceptionality when it came to American immigration policy.[49]

Still, some measures were taken to admit Jewish refugees. The Roosevelt administration, under pressure from Jewish groups, grudgingly took steps to save European Jews from the Holocaust, but these actions were extremely limited. In 1944 the administration set up the War Refugee Board, which—working largely through neutral governments—was able to save nearly two hundred thousand Jews in the last two years of the war (considering that nearly a quarter of all Holocaust victims died in 1942 alone, this was very much too little, too late). Indeed, the question of what to do with Jewish refugees was largely academic in the early years of the war because of the German occupation of most of eastern Europe, the epicenter of the Holocaust.[50] This began to change in 1944 and 1945, as the War Refugee Board worked to bring modest numbers of refugees into the United States (conservative columnist Westbrook Pegler quickly announced his skepticism, writing in his column that Roosevelt was potentially allowing "Communists and others who don't like our way of living and doing" into the country), but the issue did not become acute until the closing days of the war, when the advancing U.S. Army found itself responsible for the care of millions of displaced persons as it entered Germany.[51]

The conditions in which the army held displaced persons in Europe were generally appalling. Not all—not even most—were Jews. Germany utilized slave labor from all over Europe, which included huge numbers of Ukrainians, Poles, Russians, French, Czechs, and virtually every other nationality that had been under German dominion during the war. In fact, Jews numbered only around 5 to 8 percent of the initial displaced persons population under the control of the army. But virtually no special provisions were made for Jews as a special category of displaced persons. The conditions in the camps were sufficiently atrocious that President Truman was forced, under pressure from Jewish organizations, to convene a special committee under the aegis of former commissioner of the Immigration and

Naturalization Service, Earl G. Harrison. Harrison's report prompted Truman to attempt a solution: pressuring the British government beginning in August 1945 to allow up to one hundred thousand European Jews into the British Mandate of Palestine.[52]

Truman's pressure on the British made a great deal of political sense. Opinion polls were still hostile to loosening immigration restrictions in the United States, but Truman also faced political pressure from Jewish organizations to solve the refugee crisis. Benjamin Freedman wrote in the *Economic Council Letter* in 1947 that Truman and the Democratic Party sought, through their immigration policy, to influence Jewish voters in the key states of New York, California, Illinois, and Ohio—although Freedman was an antisemite, a bigot, and a conspiracy theorist, his political analysis in this instance was sound.[53] Embracing Zionist aspirations in Palestine provided a solution to the Jewish refugee crisis that would avoid battle over immigration *and* help to secure Jewish voters.

Ohio senator Robert Taft, one of the archconservatives in the United States Senate, embraced such a strategy. Taft had become an unlikely pro-Zionist in 1944, when he developed a friendship with Rabbi Abba Hillel Silver, the Cleveland-based Zionist leader. Silver was instrumental in securing Taft's support for the Zionist cause in Congress, including co-sponsoring a resolution in January 1944 with Robert Wagner, who represented to a great degree the antithesis of Taft's domestic politics, to support increased Jewish immigration to Palestine. Taft and Silver were also largely responsible for the insertion in the Republican Party platform in 1944 of a "free and democratic commonwealth" in British Palestine, much to the chagrin of Gerald L. K. Smith and his merry band of antisemites at the Stevens Hotel. But Taft's motives were not wholly idealistic. He faced a tough reelection battle in 1944—he was targeted by CIO-PAC and leading members of the Roosevelt administration, who frequently cited his opposition to the war before 1941. Taft needed Jewish support—or, at the minimum, to cut losses among Jewish voters his record might otherwise precipitate. Embracing Silver and the Zionist cause did the trick. Taft eked out a narrow victory of only eighteen thousand votes over his Democratic opponent. Silver bragged to reporters that he had helped secure Taft's victory. Taft remained one of the staunchest pro-Zionists in the Senate before U.S. recognition of the State of Israel in 1948.[54]

But despite Taft's ardor for the Zionist cause, he remained an immigration restrictionist, actively fighting measures to increase refugee quotas into the United States. Taft helped maneuver the appointment of William Chapman Revercomb, his Republican colleague from West Virginia, to the head of the Senate Judiciary Committee on Immigration. Revercomb was a ferocious critic of the New Deal and a prominent advocate of "states' rights," opposing federal legislation abolishing poll taxes and objecting to a bill that sought federal oversight over wage standards.[55] Revercomb reportedly told his colleagues on the committee that "we could solve this DP [displaced persons] problem all right if we could work out some bill that would keep out the Jews."[56] Indeed, the British government felt that American support for Jewish emigration to Palestine was self-interested—British foreign secretary Ernest Bevin stirred outrage in both Britain and America when he told a Labour Party conference in June 1946 that the American government was pressing for the admission of one hundred thousand European Jews into Palestine because "they [do] not want too many of them in New York."[57] Although Bevin's remark was crude and widely condemned as antisemitic, there was an element of truth to his statement: immigration restrictionists like Taft supported opening up Palestine to Jewish settlement while they simultaneously resisted relaxing immigration restrictions in the United States.

The antisemitic far right found itself in a paradoxical position in the debates over immigration and Palestine. On the one hand, most far-right activists had long been opposed to loosening immigration restrictions, fearing a flood of foreigners with "alien" and communistic ideas. Men like Merwin Hart had long blamed the triumph of New Deal liberalism on "un-American" elements infecting the politics of the United States like some kind of virus. On the other hand, unlike Taft, Hart and his fellow travelers were ferociously anti-Zionist and saw American support for Zionism as yet further evidence of a massive Jewish conspiracy. (Smith, for his part, remained grudgingly supportive of Taft in 1948 even as he lamented that the Ohio senator was engaged in a "breakneck attempt to please the Jew vote of New York" with his support for Israel.)[58] This was tied to the belief that Zionism was essentially synonymous with communism (which itself was predicated on Judeo-Bolshevik conspiracy theories) as well as the political argument that the creation of a Jewish state in Palestine would involve the United States in a shooting war. The former attitude drew upon widespread sentiment—U.S. Army reports from 1945 suggested that soldiers had trouble distinguishing between Zionism and communism as both were stereotypically "Jewish" ideologies—and the latter was itself a relatively common analysis of the Palestinian situation on the right.

Indeed, anti-Zionism based on American national interest need not have an antisemitic edge. Felix Morley warned in the inaugural issue of the conservative foreign affairs magazine *Human Events* in January 1944 that the U.S. risked being sucked into a war in the Middle East because of America's oil interests in the region combined with the Arab-Jewish conflict.[59] Frank C. Hanighen likewise warned that rising pan-Arabism and American interests in Saudi Arabia could lead to American involvement in a Middle East war. Hanighen actually went further than most of his contemporaries. A respected foreign affairs correspondent who had been active with the America First Committee, Hanighen wrote an article published in *Human Events* in December 1946 describing Zionism as "imperialism." Hanighen's analysis of Zionism would fit comfortably within the mainstream of left-wing anti-Zionism in the twenty-first century. He characterized Zionism as essentially a European colonial project that had the misfortune to collide with awakening pan-Arab nationalism and diplomatic maneuverings between the British Empire, the United States, and the Soviet Union. Hanighen was no leftist—he wrote angrily that the World Federation of Trade Unions, the "late Sidney Hillman's brain child," had "invaded troubled Palestine" and spread like a virus throughout the Middle East, organizing workers in the Iranian oil fields and the Iraqi railways.[60] But neither was Hanighen an antisemite—not only was his tone cool and analytical, he did not equate Zionism with communism nor suggest Zionists were an avatar of an international Judeo-Bolshevik conspiracy, and he did not complain of Jewish "anti-Gentilism." There were a wide variety of positions on the American right on Zionism. Some, like Taft, were pro-Zionist. Others, like Hanighen, were anti-Zionist. And still others, like Hart, Freedman, and Gerald L. K. Smith, were antisemitic anti-Zionists.

The key markers of antisemitic anti-Zionism on the right were the embrace of conspiracy theories—particularly the Judeo-Bolshevik conspiracy theory—along with a persecution complex. There was no specific policy position that served as a litmus test for antisemitism, but rather one's choice of language and identification within the constellation of various policy preferences. Gerald L. K. Smith naturally provides a benchmark for political antisemitism and anti-Zionism; he opposed rescinding immigration quotas and the legislation that eventually became the 1948 Displaced

Persons Act while simultaneously opposing Jewish immigration to Palestine. These stances taken alone were commonplace in American politics in the late 1940s; taken together, they suggest an antisemitic political orientation but are not in and of themselves conclusive evidence. What *is* conclusive are the dozens and dozens of pages in Smith's newsletter, *The Cross and the Flag,* which posed questions like "Is Communism Jewish?" (The answer, according to Smith, was yes.) Merwin Hart's missives in his newsletter were rather more restrained than Smith's—at least in the late 1940s—but his repeated belief that if eastern European Jews were allowed to immigrate en masse into Palestine then "Zionist Palestine [would] eventually become a Soviet Republic" and his complaints that Jewish critics were smearing him with charges of antisemitism tipped him decisively into the category of far-right political antisemite.[61]

The political impact of the far right on U.S. policy in Palestine was muted—Truman successfully pressured the British government to increase immigration quotas, eventually endorsed Palestinian partition, and quickly recognized the independence of the State of Israel almost immediately after the Israeli declaration of independence in May 1948. But the political impact of the far right on U.S. policy regarding immigrants and displaced persons was far more influential. The House subcommittee on immigration called Merwin Hart as a witness to testify while considering a bill proposed by Illinois congressman William G. Stratton to admit up to four hundred thousand displaced persons into the United States in 1947; Hart insisted that allowing displaced persons into the country would permit a wave of "terrorists" trained in communist revolutionary tactics (he also, more prosaically, argued that immigration would exacerbate unemployment and housing problems). Hart had an ally on the committee in the form of Texas congressman Ed Gossett, who frequently complained on the record that displaced persons camps in Europe are "small universities of subversives and revolutionary activities." Gossett took to the House floor on July 2, 1948 to blast the Stratton bill as a product of "a number of prominent Jewish organizations."[62]

Even though the bill eventually passed, the 1948 Displaced Persons Act was designed and administered to exclude as many Jews as possible from entering the United States. Persons who entered the American zone of occupation in Germany after December 22, 1945 would not be eligible for resettlement in the United States; this excluded the vast majority of Jewish refugees, who entered the American zone after the cutoff date. In order to make the bill more palatable to midwestern congressmen, in particular North Dakota senator and old non-interventionist leader William Ernest Langer, there was one major exemption to the cutoff date: ethnic Germans expelled from Poland, Czechoslovakia, and the Baltic states qualified for admission if they entered Allied-occupied Germany by July 1948 *and* were exempt from public-charge qualifications—essentially proof that the incoming person had enough financial assets to avoid becoming a public burden—that other displaced persons needed to meet. Although President Truman signed the bill on the grounds that it was better than nothing, he castigated the legislation in a signing statement as "[discriminating] in callous fashion against displaced persons of the Jewish faith."[63] Revealingly, despite the far right's militant opposition to relaxing immigration quotas or accepting refugees, there was very little outrage from right-wing quarters upon the passage of the Stratton Act. Not even Gerald L. K. Smith, whose 1948 Christian Nationalist Crusade convention platform included a plank against immigration of Asiatics and Jews, sought fit to mention the new law in his newsletter.

The Displaced Persons Act was subject to amendment efforts almost as soon as it was passed. A new wave of Democrats took office after the 1948 elections, including future liberal giants Paul Douglas and Hubert Humphrey, who both endorsed liberalizing the act. So, too, did President Truman, who—to the surprise of nearly everyone—won his reelection bid. Efforts were stymied, however, by conservative Nevada Democrat Pat McCarran, the new chair of the Senate Judiciary Committee. Among other actions, McCarran appointed Richard Arens, an archconservative whom contemporaries described as "bitterly antisemitic," as head of the chief of staff of the immigration subcommittee. He repeatedly used delaying tactics to avoid the passage of an amended bill. The dam finally burst in June 1950, when an amended version of the Displaced Persons Act was passed into law. The net effect of the opposition from activists like Trevor and Hart, and congressional representatives like Taft, Gossett, and McCarran was, however, unambiguous: while 450,000 displaced persons were eventually admitted into the United States through 1952, fewer than 150,000 of those admitted were Jews.[64]

Ultimately, the power of right-wing political antisemitism to affect policy began to wane in the late 1940s. A decade earlier political antisemites could enter into an uneasy coalition with antiwar activists and present a united front that was able to substantively affect American policy toward the European war, although even at that early date the right was unable to arrest the foreign policy preferences of the Roosevelt administration. Throughout the war years, the right—with the support of most of the American public— was able to block any efforts to relax American immigration laws that could prove to be favorable to Jewish refugees, and limited the options of an already disinterested Roosevelt administration in aggressively responding to the humanitarian crisis of the Holocaust. But by the end of the 1940s the non-interventionist, anti-immigrant, and antisemitic wing of the conserva- tive coalition was unable to stop American recognition of the State of Israel or completely prevent the passage of the Displaced Persons Act. On an orga- nizational level, the attempt by Merwin Hart and his political allies to build a new national right-wing movement through American Action was largely a failure. But while the influence of the far right was waning, it continued to score rearguard victories and exercised influence behind the scenes— through legislative maneuvering, the Displaced Persons Act *did* manage to largely exclude Jewish refugees from admission into the United States. This trend would continue into the next decade: even as the organizational far right reached its nadir in the early 1950s, there remained surprising levels of influence in high circles. The far right remained part of the right-wing popular front, and as immediate fears of fascism faded in American political culture in the late 1940s, fears of communism intensified. The antisemitic far right would not enjoy the level of influence it had in the 1930s, but further opportunities to flex its political muscle awaited.

CHAPTER FOUR

McCarthyism and the Far Right

SENATOR JOSEPH MCCARTHY WAS a nexus figure in the right-wing popular front in the early 1950s. By dint of his demagogic anti-liberalism and anticommunism, he bound openly antisemitic far-right activists with less extreme figures, including many Jewish conservatives. Whispers of McCarthy's latent antisemitism were sufficiently politically damaging to the Wisconsin senator that he chose twenty-six-year-old Jewish lawyer Roy Cohn as the chief counsel for his Permanent Subcommittee on Investigations in 1953 in an attempt to quash the rumors. Nevertheless, McCarthy enjoyed almost universal acclaim on the American right during his heyday—McCarthy, Cohn, Merwin Hart, and William F. Buckley Jr. could and did all comfortably rub shoulders at black-tie galas. This feat was all the more remarkable considering that before Joseph McCarthy settled on anticommunism as his winning political issue, he had been an outspoken defender of Nazi war criminals.

In December 1944 Waffen-SS *Standartenführer* Joachim Peiper had already, by any reasonable definition, perpetrated innumerable war crimes. He had served in the SS for over a decade as personal assistant to SS-*Reichsführer* Heinrich Himmler, assisting the SS chief with—among other things, the logistical details of the Holocaust. Peiper commanded troops in the field in the Soviet Union in 1942 and 1943, personally ordering several villages razed, and developing a reputation for brutality to the point that his unit was dubbed "the blowtorch battalion"—on account of the number of towns and villages it burned—by other German soldiers. Peiper was given command of an armored column for Germany's last-ditch offensive in the Ardennes Forest in Belgium at the end of 1944. Peiper fought in the subsequent Battle of the Bulge in the same fashion as he had in Russia: with unrelenting brutality.[1]

The offensive began on December 16; on the afternoon of December 17, already more than sixteen hours behind schedule, Peiper's troops captured an American convoy consisting mainly of elements of the 285th Field Artillery Observation Battalion near the town of Malmedy. Peiper continued on with his tanks southwest toward his objective, the town of Ligneuville. Shortly after the German tanks departed, some 120 captured American troops were machine-gunned in an open field by their Waffen-SS guards; 84 were killed and the survivors fled into the surrounding woods.[2]

On the scale of mass death in World War II, the Malmedy massacre was a relatively minor affair. The SS murdered over 33,000 Jews in Kiev over the course of a single day and night at the end of September 1941. The U.S. fire-bombing of Tokyo in March 1945—Operation Meetinghouse—killed anywhere from 83,000 to 125,000 people over the course of a single night.[3] But because *American* servicemen were the victims of Nazi atrocities at Malmedy, and because the first reports of the massacre came trickling in from survivors who reached American lines within roughly an hour of the shooting, Malmedy quickly became a household word in the United States. As early as December 21 the first Associated Press reports of a massacre of some 150 Americans by German troops in Belgium were being published on the front pages of major American newspapers, kept out of the banner headlines only by the latest updates from the front. The *Washington Post* breathlessly crowed, "Nazis Throw in Second Powerful Wave in Wake of Initial 200,000 Man Assault" in the headline of its December 21, 1944, edition, but "Nazi Slaying of 100 Yanks Is Confirmed" was featured as the center story above the fold.[4] Press coverage would intensify in the subsequent months.

In April 1946 the U.S. Army was ready to prosecute the man whom the newspapers had dubbed the "American doughboy's number one criminal," and the trial of Peiper and seventy-two other Waffen-SS members convened at Dachau, the site of one of Nazi Germany's most infamous concentration camps, on May 16. Tried alongside Peiper was a cross-section of the

Waffen-SS, ranging from SS general Sepp Dietrich, Peiper's commanding officer, to privates in Peiper's regiment. A number of the defendants had signed confessions after extensive interrogation by U.S. Army personnel, but Peiper consistently denied all wrongdoing. He claimed, along with a handful of other defendants, that the U.S. Army had extracted confessions from his men illegally through the use of torture. The court sentenced Peiper and forty-three of his men to death. None, however, would end up facing the gallows.[5]

There were those in the U.S. Army who believed that Peiper and the SS troops under his command had been treated too harshly. None were quite so vehemently outspoken in that belief as Colonel Willis Everett, an Atlanta lawyer who served as the chief defense counsel for Peiper and his co-defendants. Everett was appalled by what he believed to be a sham trial and allegations that army interrogators tortured the German defendants to extract confessions. He considered that the army's conduct did not correspond to the liberal democratic values the United States supposedly fought for.[6]

But there was a considerably darker side to Everett's outrage. He believed that Germany was being made subject to another harsh Carthaginian peace, as it had been after World War I, because of the machinations of vengeful Jews. Everett wrote to his family during the trial that the presiding judge, Abraham Rosenfeld, was a "Jew law member," and even insulted his fellow defense counsel Herbert Strong—a German Jewish refugee who was assigned the case because of his language skills—as a "nosey-talking-arguing Jew." He frequently complained of the "Jewish occupation" of postwar Germany. Large numbers of "Morgenthau's boys"—meaning both Jewish American New Dealers and German Jewish refugees—were in positions of influence and authority in postwar Germany. Everett viewed liberals and Jews with barely concealed hostility and suspicion.[7]

Everett was not alone in his attitudes; the star witness for the defense during the Malmedy trial was Colonel Hal McCown, who commanded an infantry battalion during the Battle of the Bulge and had been briefly captured by Peiper on December 21, 1944. McCown, who told the court that he had not seen any massacres or mistreatment of American soldiers by the SS during the battle, had his credibility somewhat undermined when he admitted on the stand he had provided tactical information to Peiper that allowed him to safely retreat during the battle; Peiper had told army counter-intelligence interrogators that while McCown was his prisoner he had confided to Peiper that Soviet communism was America's *real* enemy, and that after the war Peiper should come to America and "help him hang the Jews there."[8]

The Malmedy trial *should* have been resolved with the convictions of Peiper and his co-defendants, but instead it became a political lightning rod in both the United States and Germany. Everett embarked on a lengthy letter-writing and public relations campaign after the trial to drum up interest in allegations about a miscarriage of justice, culminating in a favorable *Time* magazine story in January 1949. Shortly afterward, Senator William Langer—who had fought to give preferential treatment to *Volksdeustche* refugees in American immigration quotas and keep out eastern European Jews—demanded an investigation into the army's conduct. By the end of March the Senate Armed Services Committee convened a subcommittee to review the case. Its members included Democrats James Eastland, Lester Hunt, and Estes Kefauver, Republican Raymond Baldwin as chair, and an obscure junior Republican senator from Wisconsin, Joseph McCarthy.[9]

Why did McCarthy serve on the committee? McCarthy was hostile to communism and apparently believed that a harsh victor's justice over the defeated Germans would drive the population into the arms of the Soviets. But there was another factor: Wisconsin, like Langer's North Dakota, had a large concentration of German Americans. And while most of Wisconsin's German Americans eschewed Nazi sympathies, not all did.[10] And at least one of Wisconsin's Nazi sympathizers was one of Joseph McCarthy's major donors.

Walter Harnischfeger was a second-generation German American. His father, Henry, had immigrated to the United States in the 1870s and over the course of fifty years established himself as one of the region's leading construction equipment suppliers. When Henry died in 1930, Walter inherited the company. During the 1930s and 1940s, the Harnischfeger family developed a reputation in Wisconsin for their Nazi sympathies. One of Walter's nephews, while attending the University of Wisconsin, bragged about his family's Nazi sympathies and of his prized possession, an autographed copy of *Mein Kampf*. Nor were the Harnischfegers' politics merely idle talk; the company was cited by the Fair Employment Practice Committee for refusing to hire Blacks and Jews during World War II.[11] Walter Harnischfeger had repeatedly advocated a negotiated peace with Germany during World War II—he made a speech in 1943 urging peace as soon as possible because "the capitalistic system will not survive" the war—and shared the far right's disdain for the Nuremberg trials after the war.[12]

Harnischfeger was also a major figure in Republican politics in Wisconsin. His financial largesse was, according to newspaper accounts, primarily directed toward party committees, but he also donated to individual candidates, including to incumbent Republican governor Walter S. Goodland's reelection campaign (despite Goodland having nixed Harnischfeger's demand for a tax cut in 1943) and to the challenge against progressive stalwart Robert LaFollette Jr. by then state circuit court judge Joseph McCarthy.[13]

The relationship between Harnischfeger and McCarthy is highly suggestive, and indicative of the broader relationship between Joseph McCarthy—and McCarthyism—and the far right. McCarthy, who was often dogged by allegations of fascism and antisemitism by liberals and the left, had an ambiguous relationship with the far right: he was not a doctrinaire rightist, but he welcomed their support and served as an important bridge linking elements of what would evolve later into "mainstream" conservatism with figures later generations of conservatives would dismiss as "kooks." But in the 1950s, they were part of the same political coalition.

The most direct evidence of a link between McCarthy and Harnischfeger stems from mutual social ties. Thomas Korb, an old friend of McCarthy's from Marquette University, was Harnischfeger's corporate attorney. Korb came to Washington as McCarthy's "administrative assistant" for the Malmedy hearings, even helping to write a speech McCarthy gave on the floor of the Senate in July 1949 denouncing the conduct of the army. Harnischfeger also provided McCarthy with material financial support, putting up collateral for a loan McCarthy took from the Appleton State Bank in 1947.[14] More important, McCarthy actively provided favors for Harnischfeger on Capitol Hill. In 1947 McCarthy, as a junior senator, made his first successful legislative push torpedoing a public housing bill that would have cost Harnischfeger, who was diversifying his interests into the postwar construction boom in the suburbs, millions of dollars. McCarthy, who served on the Senate Housing Committee, managed to block the appointment of Senator Charles Tobey to the chairmanship of a joint Senate-House housing committee, which instead went to Representative Ralph A. Gamble from New York, a public housing skeptic. The mayor of Racine,

Wisconsin famously dubbed McCarthy the "water boy of the real estate lobby" for his efforts on behalf of Harnischfeger.[15]

Harnischfeger had other friends. It is unclear whether or not he was a donor to American Action, Inc. in 1946—McCarthy conditionally disavowed the organization during his 1946 campaign, saying that "if . . . this is merely the old America First Group under a new name, then I want no part of it," but that "if the organization claims that it is organized solely for the purpose of defeating Communist and Communistically inclined candidates, then I welcome its support"—but Harnischfeger certainly fit the profile of an American Action supporter.[16] He was a rock-ribbed Republican, an admirer of Herbert Hoover, *fiercely* anti-union—he testified in favor of the Taft-Hartley Act in Congress in 1948—and, most significant, was a contributor to the National Economic Council throughout the 1950s, 1960s, and into the 1970s. In a report published in 1950 by the House Select Committee on Lobbying Activities, Harnischfeger was listed as a donor to the NEC. In 1959, Merwin Hart praised a speech given by Harnischfeger on Clarence Manion's *Manion Forum* radio program, proudly noting that Harnischfeger was a member of the board of directors of the National Economic Council. And Harnischfeger remained active even after Hart's death in 1962—he emceed an NEC awards dinner for segregationist Senator Harry Byrd Jr. of Virginia in 1972. (One of the evening's featured speakers, Georgia lieutenant governor Lester Maddox, took the opportunity to declare that "Socialism and Communism have continued to spread like wildfire because their flames have been fanned with American dollars, American technology, and American apathy.")[17]

The point of noting Harnischfeger's connections and associations is not to imply, as Joe McCarthy did repeatedly throughout his career, guilt by association. It is to suggest that Harnischfeger, like McCarthy, needs to be understood as embedded in a broader right-wing network that had extreme right-wing elements, including overt fascist and Nazi sympathizers. And Harnischfeger's position, as one of McCarthy's financial backers who had direct and overt ties to the far right, helps to explain a point that has puzzled historians of McCarthy and McCarthyism over the years. The question is not simply why McCarthy maneuvered himself into a position on the Malmedy committee, but also why the junior senator from Wisconsin crossed the line into overt antisemitism during the committee hearings.

McCarthy previewed many of his later tactics against alleged communists during the Malmedy trial investigation. He browbeat witnesses, made wild and unsubstantiated statements, and showed himself to have a flair for political theatrics. McCarthy quit the committee in May 1949 in bold fashion, declaring that his colleagues had predetermined to "whitewash" the army's conduct in the trial. He constantly self-aggrandized, contrasting the clean war he fought with the Marine Corps in the Pacific to the army's conduct in Europe. McCarthy's manner toward Jewish witnesses was especially egregious. He questioned one witness as to whether Abraham Rosenfeld, the presiding judge, "felt friendly or unfriendly toward the German race as a whole?" He even went so far as to ask, "If you were a German, would you feel that you would be willing to have a matter of life and death decided by this man Rosenfeld?" William R. Perl, a lieutenant in the army and a practicing lawyer, wrote to a friend after being subjected to the McCarthy treatment that he understood McCarthy's questioning to be contextually antisemitic, that McCarthy had come to the hearings to attack "the 1939ers and the refugees"—referring to Jewish emigrés from Nazi Germany—and that the "1939ers hated the Germans and therefore tortured them." McCarthy's abrupt departure from the committee was precipitated by his demand—which his fellow senators denied—to subject Perl to a lie detector test.[18]

McCarthy was dogged by allegations of antisemitism throughout his period of notoriety in the early 1950s, allegations fueled by his conduct during the Malmedy hearings. McCarthy deliberately recruited Jewish staffers in order to rebut charges of antisemitism, and famously selected Roy Cohn over Robert F. Kennedy as his chief counsel in 1953 for his investigations subcommittee, despite the political influence of Kennedy's family and their shared Catholicism. Cohn's anti-communist credentials as the zealous prosecutor of Julius and Ethel Rosenberg in 1952—as well as his own Jewishness—were critical factors in his selection. McCarthy even went so far as to attack critics of Cohn and his fellow investigator David Schine, also Jewish, as antisemitic, earning the senator rebukes from the American Jewish Congress, the Jewish Labor Committee, and dozens of other Jewish organizations around the country.[19] There is little evidence to suggest that McCarthy was personally antisemitic, but he clearly understood that antisemites had a place in his political coalition, actively courted their support, and engaged in one of the common tactics of the antisemitic far right—he had many Jewish friends!—as a defense against concerns over antisemitism.[20]

After McCarthy resigned from the Malmedy committee, the remaining members concluded that the army had acted appropriately in its trial of the Malmedy perpetrators at Dachau, but it upheld the army's earlier commutations of the death sentences of the convicted Waffen-SS perpetrators of the massacre to life imprisonment. Most were released from prison by the mid-1950s—Peiper was paroled in 1956, and he enjoyed a lucrative career as a salesman for a variety of German automobile manufacturers, including Porsche and Volkswagen, before moving to a village in eastern France in 1972. He was gunned down there on Bastille Day by unknown assailants—probably associated with the French Communist Party—in 1976, finally facing justice for a lengthy career of war crimes.[21]

Joseph McCarthy, for his part, had a date with destiny a few short months after the Malmedy committee hearings: at a speech in Wheeling, West Virginia on February 9, 1950, he alleged that the U.S. State Department contained over two hundred members of the American Communist Party in policymaking positions, and that the department was deliberately protecting its communist infiltrators.

McCarthyism as a technique—the use of exaggerated and paranoid claims about left-wing subversive infiltration and influence in the United States, along with demagogic practices for rooting out supposed infiltrators—obviously predated Joseph McCarthy. Martin Dies practiced a variation of the technique while serving as head of the House Committee on Un-American Activities. Merwin Hart engaged in a grassroots version while organizing vigilante groups against CIO strikers in the late 1930s. Jack Tenney, a former New Deal Democrat-turned-conservative Republican in California, led the state's equivalent of the Committee on Un-American Activities in the late 1940s, providing important pressure for the implementation, at the behest of University of California president Robert G. Sproul, of the university's infamous loyalty oath program, which required all employees to swear they were not members of the Communist Party.[22] All of these initiatives predated McCarthy's Wheeling speech.

Each of these cases also included a far-right political component. Tenney, who was eventually forced out of his chairmanship of the state senate's Un-American Activities committee in 1949 in internal state Republican political wrangling, moved hard to the right after his ouster, eventually publishing a book on Zionism's "trojan horse" in the United States and throwing in his lot with Gerald L. K. Smith, running as the vice presidential nominee on Smith's Christian Nationalist Party's 1952 presidential ticket, alongside the drafted Douglas MacArthur. Tenney understood his chances were nil; he wanted to punish the Republican Party for nominating Dwight Eisenhower. "There's more to politics than just winning," he told columnist Holmes Alexander. He merely wanted to, in Alexander's words, "dramatiz[e] the right-wing fight against the socialist internationalism of the two major parties."[23]

Joseph McCarthy and McCarthyism were not political novelties in the early 1950s; they consolidated these existing right-wing political traditions in the United States. And while McCarthy the man became a punchline for generations of American liberals and McCarthyism a byword for paranoid hysteria run amok, generations of scholarship have emphasized that *McCarthyism*, as a political project, was a largely successful one. Broad swaths of the American left were frozen out of federal and state governments, universities, and other institutions, their influence replaced by zealously anti-communist Cold War liberals or out-and-out conservatives.[24]

And McCarthy the man remained an icon to subsequent generations of the American right. The defense and rehabilitation of McCarthy as perhaps overzealous but largely in the right—and, in any event, perhaps mistaken only in some of his tactics—were at the center of right-wing mythmaking for much of the remainder of the twentieth century. William F. Buckley Jr. wrote his second book in defense of Joseph McCarthy in 1954; in 1999, he returned to the subject in a novel "based on the life of Senator Joseph McCarthy." Far-right provocateur Ann Coulter's 2003 book *Treason: Liberal Treachery from the Cold War to the War on Terrorism* argued that McCarthy was completely correct and the victim of traitorous liberal smears; her book was praised by Buckley. Conservative journalist M. Stanton Evans made a similar case in his 2007 book *Blacklisted*, arguing that McCarthy's reputation had been unfairly maligned by biased historians. Evans wrote that Senate historian Donald Ritchie was "routinely stacking the deck against McCarthy" in the edited volumes containing the transcripts of McCarthy's hearings—Evans called Ritchie on the telephone and accused him of not actually reading the primary sources, offering to "sum up the relevant data" as to why McCarthy was actually right. "The historian grew irate," he recounted, and "said 'I am growing very tired of this conversation,' and abruptly ended our discussion."[25]

If McCarthyism was bigger than Joe McCarthy, than McCarthy's status as a right-wing icon means that his personal biography and his political connections demand close examination. Defenders of McCarthy, both in the 1950s and in subsequent years, have emphasized that McCarthy did not have extensive personal ties to the most extreme elements of the American right and eschewed racism and antisemitism—highlighting, among other things, McCarthy's employment of Roy Cohn and his alliance with Rabbi Benjamin Schultz, head of the American Jewish Crusade against Communism. Yet while historians have generally concluded that McCarthy did not *center* antisemitism, fascist sympathies, and other hallmarks of the far right in his politics, in fact he had direct ties to a number of far-right political organizations and donors and acted as a kind of binding agent of the American right during the height of his notoriety from 1950 through 1954. Joseph McCarthy became one of the key icons of the American right— exceeded perhaps only by Douglas MacArthur—and the lynchpin of the right-wing popular front.

McCarthy and the far right did not play a major role in the arrest and prose- cution for espionage of Julius and Ethel Rosenberg and their associates— although twenty-four-year-old prosecutor Roy Cohn came to McCarthy's attention because of the notoriety of the 1951 trial of the pair. But McCarthy— along with prominent conservative broadcaster Fulton Lewis, Benjamin Freedman, and Gerald L. K. Smith—were involved in an attempt to smear the reputation of *Anna* Rosenberg (no relation to Julius or Ethel) in 1950. Rosenberg was a Hungarian Jewish immigrant who was the Truman admin- istration's nominee for an assistant secretary of defense post—she was smeared by McCarthy and his media allies, using information fed to them by Freedman and Smith. The extent to which McCarthy and Lewis knew about the involvement of Smith and Freedman remains in question, but the allegations—which temporarily derailed Rosenberg's confirmation hear- ings in December 1950—fit a broader pattern of right-wing conduct.[26]

Anna Rosenberg should not have been a controversial appointment for a top post in the Defense Department. Her credentials placed her to the right of many New Dealers. But she was a Jewish immigrant, born in Budapest at the beginning of the century. She grew up in New York and became a reason- ably prominent New Dealer in the city in the 1930s, serving as a regional director for the National Recovery Administration. After her stint in federal service, Rosenberg became a labor and personnel consultant for various firms and corporations in New York; her clients included Nelson Rockefeller and Macy's department store. During the Second World War, she served on the War Manpower Commission and was awarded the Medal of Freedom for her efforts. George Marshall, the sitting secretary of defense, nominated Rosenberg for an assistant secretaryship on November 9, 1950, on the basis of her wartime work. Marshall cited her as the "acknowledged authority" on "labor, manpower, and public relations." As if to underline her inoffensive moderateness, Rosenberg brought up several times in her initial confirmation hearings that she had publicly opposed the universal health insurance program proposed by President Truman, and also insisted that strictly "voluntary methods" for industrial coordination were sufficient to meet the crisis of the Korean War—distancing herself, at least rhetorically, from the recent passage of the Defense Production Act that centralized industrial production authority with the administration. Rosenberg was, in sum, the very portrait of a moderate New Dealer, in the mold of financier Bernard Baruch, who zealously advocated for the interests of private industry and voluntarism as an advisor to Franklin Roosevelt.[27] Rosenberg was to the *right* of the Truman administration on labor and health issues. But she was also a Jewish immigrant and a woman who was slated to be appointed to one of the senior positions in the American military establishment. A politically uncontroversial appointment erupted into a firestorm.

On November 10 conservative radio broadcaster Fulton Lewis Jr., whose program was heard on some four hundred radio stations across the country over the Mutual Broadcasting System, alleged on his show that Rosenberg had belonged to the John Reed Club, a Communist Party front organization for writers and intellectuals in New York City in the 1930s. Lewis had made a name for himself as one of the first congressional correspondents on the airwaves. His program, which predated the establishment of the Fairness Doctrine mandating balanced coverage of news and political events, was heard by millions.[28] Lewis received this information about Rosenberg from J. B. Matthews, a former Communist Party sympathizer-turned-HUAC informer, who in turn apparently based *his* information on the name "Anna Rosenberg" appearing in a John Reed Club petition published in the *New York Times* in 1930.[29] In response to the ensuing outcry, the Senate Armed Services Committee convened a hearing on November 29. Rosenberg denied that she had ever been a member of the John Reed Club, noting that the signature on the petition was "Anna Rosenberg," whereas she had been very careful to always sign "Anna M. Rosenberg," as her name was common in New York. She told the committee that the postmaster of New York State had informed her that there were currently forty-six Anna Rosenbergs in New York City. The signature on the petition was not hers—it would have been odd, at any rate, for a professional of her sort to have joined an organization primarily intended for writers, as Rosenberg herself pointed out to the committee during her testimony.[30]

Rosenberg's responses impressed the Armed Services Committee enough to unanimously recommend that she be confirmed, but then things took a wild turn. On December 1, chair Richard Russell was approached by Texas congressman Ed Gossett and Benjamin Freedman. Freedman demanded that Russell reopen the Rosenberg hearings, claiming he had new evidence against her.

At the same time, the Reverend Wesley Swift, a Christian Identity minister based in Los Angeles, and his longtime friend and colleague Gerald L. K. Smith, met with Mississippi congressman John Rankin. Rankin has gone down in infamy as one of the most viciously outspoken racists in the U.S. Congress in the twentieth century. Rankin—leveraging his position as an influential southern Democrat—repeatedly steered legislation to reify and reinforce the Jim Crow apartheid state in the American South. He helped to quash attempts at meaningful federal election-law reform to allow mobilized soldiers to vote in 1942 and worked together with Republicans to neuter similar legislation in 1944, in order to ensure African Americans would not have easier access to the ballot. He also helped craft the 1944 GI Bill of Rights that excluded African Americans in the South from receiving access to federal benefits. Rankin was also a notorious antisemite. He had opposed relaxing immigration quotas for eastern European Jewish immigrants in the debates over the Displaced Persons Act, and repeatedly used slurs to describe his Jewish opponents. In 1944 he called Jewish columnist Walter Winchell a "little kike," an outburst widely reported by the press. Rankin condemned Albert Einstein as a "foreign-born agitator" in 1945 on the floor of the House for Einstein's temerity for criticizing calls for reconciliation with Francisco Franco in Spain.[31]

After Swift's meeting with Rankin, the congressman took to the floor of the House of Representatives to denounce Rosenberg as a "little Yiddish woman" whose nomination ought to be opposed by all right-thinking Americans.[32] After visiting Rankin's office, Swift then paid a call to Senator McCarthy. The precise nature of his solicitation is unclear, but it illustrates

how freely far-right influence peddlers circulated on Capitol Hill and eluci-
dates a key point about McCarthy. He may not have been an ideological ally
to the same degree as the openly racist and antisemitic Rankin, but he was in
a material sense understood to be on the same side.

On December 5, Swift submitted to the Armed Services Committee a
memo by Freedman alleging that a Ralph De Sola of New York City, a former
member of the Communist Party, could testify that he had seen Anna
Rosenberg attend meetings of the John Reed Club. That evening, Edward
Nellor, a reporter who worked for Fulton Lewis, and Donald Surine, a former
FBI agent turned investigator for Senator McCarthy, flew to New York to
interview De Sola. Nellor carried with him a sealed letter from Gerald L. K.
Smith to Freedman—it is unclear whether Nellor knew of the contents—in
which the gregarious Smith congratulated Freedman on the "terrific job you
are doing in helping to keep the Zionist Jew Anna M. Rosenberg from
becoming the dictator of the Pentagon." Nellor and Surine interviewed De
Sola the next day and reported on the conversation to Lewis and McCarthy,
respectively. Fulton Lewis took to the airwaves the evening of December 6
and crowed to his listeners about the investigation, even quoting from the
affidavit before it was submitted to the Armed Services Committee. With De
Sola's written testimony in hand, procured by the rather motley alliance
between McCarthy, Lewis, Smith, and Freedman, the Armed Services
Committee reconvened its hearing on December 8 to hear De Sola testify in
person.[33]

De Sola's story, however, quickly developed some glaring problems.
Freedman's involvement in the whole affair was already known to the
committee, and several senators sought to shine a light on Freedman's politics. Tennessee Democrat Estes Kefauver drew out from De Sola that the
man who had put him in touch with Freedman was Freedman's lawyer,
Hallam Richardson, whom Kefauver connected to the "famous anti-Semitic
street corner orator" Joe McWilliams, the central defendant in the 1944 anti-
fascist Smith Act trial. What was this? Explain? De Sola sheepishly replied
that he had decided that "I couldn't go along with . . . a person who was an
anti-Semite." More damningly, De Sola testified that he was under the
impression that Nellor and Surine were investigators from the Armed
Services Committee. (Florida senator Edward Gurney eventually established
from De Sola that Surine worked for McCarthy.) De Sola also admitted that
he had been invited by Surine to leave his coat in McCarthy's office while he

was testifying before the committee, and had in fact done so, as had Ben Freedman. Finally, De Sola testified that some of the allegations in Freedman's initial memo—that, for example, Rosenberg had instructed De Sola's wife to plant communists in the New York public school system—were false.[34]

Even though De Sola was adamant that Rosenberg was a Communist Party member—in a face-to-face encounter before the committee that afternoon he appealed to Rosenberg to confess for her own sake—it quickly became apparent that the case against Rosenberg was a concocted house of cards. Freedman was called before the committee on December 11 and was forced to admit, among other things, his association with Gerald L. K. Smith, his mailing to various offices on Capitol Hill some twenty-five thousand copies of an edition of the far-right magazine *Common Sense* that attacked Rosenberg, and that he had dictated the memo he had submitted to the committee in the office of Congressman John Rankin.

Nellor testified shortly afterward. He told the committee that he and Donald Surine had clearly identified themselves to De Sola, calling his testimony a "misrepresentation." He initially avowed that he had no idea that Gerald L. K. Smith had been involved at all in the affair (and that his boss had warned him to be careful about the possibility that the accusations might be coming from far-right plants), but then almost immediately contradicted himself by telling Massachusetts Republican Leverett Saltonstall that Surine had told him that Gerald L .K. Smith had "been running around the Senate Office Building with a copy of Freedman's statement regarding De Sola." It remained unclear, even after Nellor's testimony, just what Smith's role was in Nellor's and Surine's trip to New York. The committee, based on the tone of its questions, seemed concerned about a possible link between McCarthy and Smith with Surine as an intermediary—but curiously, Surine was never questioned over his role in the matter.[35]

With De Sola's testimony revealed as seriously compromised, and the full involvement of Freedman and Gerald L. K. Smith now a matter of public record, the case against Rosenberg swiftly collapsed. There were several reasons. One, the evidence against Rosenberg was practically nonexistent. Two, while Rosenberg, as a Jewish immigrant—and, importantly, a woman—was viewed with suspicion by the far right and their allies on Capitol Hill, she did not actually have a political record that indicated affinity with the left wing of the New Deal coalition, let along the actual Communist Party. If, as Landon R. Y. Storrs has argued, the Second Red Scare was primarily directed at freezing out radical and even left-liberal voices from the policymaking apparatus, Rosenberg—simply from the perspective of her own politics—hardly qualified as a meaningful target.[36] And while Smith and Freedman were able to peddle influence on Capitol Hill, their reputations were such that they did not bear close public scrutiny. Merwin Hart or, for that matter, Walter Harnischfeger may have held similar political views, but they both either still had access to financial backing from corporate donors or owned large businesses themselves. Without institutional backing, Freedman and Smith found themselves adrift.

The Senate voted on December 21 to confirm Rosenberg's nomination. She served as an assistant secretary of defense until 1953. Gerald L. K. Smith continued to denounce Rosenberg in the pages of *The Cross and the Flag*, citing her foreign birth, Jewishness, and her support of socialized medicine as reasons enough to oppose her continued public service. Merwin Hart also took potshots at Rosenberg in the pages of the *Economic Council Letter*—Hart suggested in 1957 that the Kremlin was behind her appointment.[37] Fulton Lewis, his reputation now damaged by his involvement with the affair, took to the airwaves to denounce Freedman as a "vicious anti-Semite," an act of damage control after syndicated columnist Drew Pearson challenged him, via his own radio show on ABC, to "prove that the recent attacks on Anna Rosenberg were not inspired by un-American religious prejudice."[38]

Although Lewis distanced himself publicly from Smith and other far-right activists, he received a number of letters from other such activists expressing solidarity with him. Upton Close, his former stablemate at Mutual Broadcasting, wrote to him in January congratulating him "on the way your [sic] handling things now, and what you are saying," and expressing sympathy about him being targeted by "the ADL smear-gang." The National Blue Star Mothers of America, an organization that included a platform to "outlaw Political Zionism" on its letterhead, wrote to him cordially inquiring why he had denounced Smith, given the "existence of the Marxist-Zionist conspiracy to overthrow the existing government."[39] Lewis was chastened by the Rosenberg saga. He told Mike Wallace in a 1958 TV interview that he "automatically throws away" mail from Gerald L. K. Smith. Lewis also refrained from endorsing some of the wildest claims of the John Birch

Society in the early 1960s, even going so far as to suggest in 1962 that Birch founder Robert Welch should step down as the leader of that organization.[40] But despite his repeated denunciations of the far right in the 1950s, Lewis continued to be seen *by* the far right as a fellow traveler in the struggle against communism.[41]

Senator Joseph McCarthy was largely responsible for the delay in Rosenberg's nomination and for bringing De Sola's charges to the floor of Congress. His part in the affair was, unwittingly or not, as a front man for far-right activists to pursue their political agenda in Washington, DC. Particularly given that McCarthy had engaged in barely coded antisemitism while serving on the Malmedy massacre investigation committee, one might have reasonably expected him to lose political influence—or at least be subject to open criticism from his colleagues—in response. But McCarthy remained on the ascent. The Armed Services Committee declined to subpoena Donald Surine, McCarthy's chief investigator who had been involved in the affair. A 1952 Anti-Defamation League book on far-right influence networks, *The Trouble-Makers,* singled out Freedman, Smith, Swift, and Rankin by name in their summary of the "hatemongers" and their enablers in the Rosenberg affair. McCarthy's name was conspicuous by its absence. The bulk of the report was dedicated to the influence networks of Smith and Merwin Hart, even going so far as to publish correspondence between Hart and Smith, including a letter in which Smith enclosed a "nice, fresh copy" of the *Protocols of the Elders of Zion.*[42] But McCarthy *was* sufficiently alarmed by his growing reputation for antisemitism, thanks to his conduct over the Malmedy massacre and the Rosenberg affair, to replace Donald Surine as his principal investigator, with Roy Cohn. He told his friend future Watergate judge John Sirica that his hiring of Cohn "might convince people I am not anti-Semitic."[43] There is indeed little evidence to suggest that McCarthy harbored any particular animus toward Jews or equated, as the professional antisemites did, Judaism with communism. But anti-communist politics make for strange bedfellows, and unlike Fulton Lewis or Richard Nixon, McCarthy never publicly distanced himself from his far-right supporters. McCarthy may not have been a committed anti-semite, but he was a crass political opportunist who was happy to boost the causes of committed antisemites when it suited his own interests—provided the political cost to himself was low. When Rosenberg's nomination came to the Senate floor, McCarthy ended up voting to confirm her. Gerald L. K.

Smith bore him no grudges—he continued to call McCarthy a "fearless patriot" throughout the rest of his life.[44] McCarthy remained socially and politically connected to a wide range of far-right figures, and his influence was not yet at its apotheosis.

On February 13, 1953, the right-wing popular front held its high summit. The luminaries of the American right gathered at the Waldorf-Astoria Hotel in New York City to pay homage to one of their own: professional anti-communist activist Joseph Brown "Doc" Matthews, better known as J.B., who was poised to be named as Senator Joseph McCarthy's chief research director. Matthews had once been a left-wing fellow traveler—in fact, William F. Buckley Jr. attributed the very term *fellow traveler* to Matthews. He had written for the *Daily Worker* and the *New Masses* in the 1930s, visited the Soviet Union several times, and had even briefly served as head of the American League against War and Fascism, a Communist Party front group.

Unlike other left-wingers turned conservatives who moved right in response to Stalinist repressions (like Eugene Lyons or Isaac Levine), fear of reprisals from Soviet intelligence (like Whittaker Chambers), or evolving political analysis (like James Burnham), Matthews had a much more prosaic reason for his shift: he became management.

In 1935 Matthews held a senior position at Consumers' Research, one of the first dedicated consumer advocacy groups in the United States. That September, seventy Consumers' Research employees went on strike demanding union recognition—staff had recently organized and affiliated with the Technical, Editorial, and Office Assistants' Union, itself part of the American Federation of Labor—and the reinstatement of three workers fired for union organizing. Negotiations between the union and Consumers' Research had broken down when Matthews, a member of the board of directors, accused union organizers at a firm-wide meeting of "using gangster and racketeering methods" to build the union.[45]

The strike rapidly escalated. Matthews's son was reportedly beaten up by strikers while attempting to cross the picket line.[46] The communist press, unsurprisingly, backed the union—the *Daily Worker* noted the irony of Matthews, "noted lover of labor, now being protected by three hired detectives from an agency notorious for its strike-breaking."[47] Radical New York congressman Vito Marcantonio stood in solidarity with strikers on the picket line. On October 16 picketers, aroused by a mounted policeman injuring a worker outside of the Consumers' Research facility in Washington, New Jersey, threw stones at the plant, shattering most of its windows and prompting the arrest of twelve union members.[48]

As the strike dragged on, members of the League of Women Shoppers, a progressive consumer activist group, offered to arbitrate; Matthews and the other Consumers' Research leaders refused. In fact, Consumers' Research stonewalled the league, refusing to cooperate with its investigation at all—which, unsurprisingly, placed the onus for the strike on Consumers' Research management, that is, Matthews. Another independent inquiry about the causes of the dispute led by the Reverend Reinhold Niebuhr, then a professor at Union Theological Seminary in New York, reached the same conclusion, that management at the firm was autocratic. "Authority in the hands of a few people . . . is a set-up bound to make for . . . friction." Matthews was singled out for his "unreasonable" stance in the dispute.[49]

The strike ultimately destroyed Consumers' Research. In 1936 the National Labor Relations Board ordered that the fired union organizers be reinstated, but rather than go back to work for Matthews the labor activists formed their own rival organization, Consumers' Union, which—in partnership with the League of Women Shoppers—rapidly outstripped Consumers' Research in prestige and influence. Indeed, Consumers' Union's magazine *Consumer Reports* became the leading consumer research publication in the United States for the rest of the century.[50]

Matthews did not take his defeat lying down. In 1938 he published his memoir, *Odyssey of a Fellow Traveler,* in which he decisively broke with the left and alleged that his critics in the Consumers' Research strike were either Communist Party members or dupes subject to Communist Party discipline. The League of Women Shoppers, according to Matthews, was a communist front. So was Reinhold Niebuhr's committee—though Matthews at least gave Niebuhr the courtesy of not directly labeling him a communist. In his memoir, Matthews called himself a born-again conservative, opposed not simply to socialism or communism but to "collectivism" of any kind, which he described as "invariably lethal" to a free society.[51]

Still, Matthews's political posturing would be a mere footnote in the broader history of the American right if he had not backed up his words with actions—he became a star witness for Martin Dies's House Un-American Activities Committee in 1938. Dies promptly snapped up Matthews as his research director; Matthews, taking the skills he had honed at Consumers'

Research, began amassing an incredibly vast file on suspected communists and other subversives. Matthews's greatest value to the American right in the 1940s and 1950s, as one study of his career argued, was as essentially a living compendium of communists, radicals, and their fellow travelers. Matthews worked for Dies until 1944, when he left for a position as a consultant with the Hearst Corporation, one of the largest media organizations in the country. Hearst executives used Matthews's voluminous research files—his indexed files on communist front organizations and individuals comprised nearly twenty-five hundred names at their peak—as an effective writers' blacklist. Hearst columnists, especially George Sokolsky and Westbrook Pegler, used Matthews's material in their own writings. And Matthews was sought out by activists like Alfred Kohlberg and politicians like Joseph McCarthy—to whom Matthews fed information about Anna Rosenberg—seeking targets for persecution.[52]

Matthews was dismissed by Richard Gid Powers as a "paranoid conspiracy theorist." But other historians, including Robert M. Lichtman and Landon R. Y. Storrs, have emphasized that Matthews was in fact a central figure on the American right in the late 1940s and early 1950s, binding together various elements in a shared anti-communist orientation. In this sense, Matthews was a pivotal figure in the right-wing popular front. Even Powers conceded that Matthews played a major role in "[joining] forces with far more disreputable counter-subversives [while] maintaining . . . access to mainstream politicians and journalists." Lichtman, for his part, argued that Matthews's career demonstrates that there was an "almost seamless pattern of cooperation" between what Powers labeled "responsible counter-subversives" and "red-web conspiracy theorists." This assessment is correct and reflects a deeper underlying unity on the American right in the 1940s and 1950s. There was no firm wall of separation between the far right and "responsible" conservatism.[53]

The guest list at J. B. Matthews's testimonial dinner on February 13, 1953, was a who's who of the American right. Matthews's friend and Hearst stablemate George E. Sokolsky organized the black-tie gala. Rabbi Benjamin Schultz of the American Jewish League against Communism gave the invocation. Martin Dies, Alfred Kohlberg, Sokolsky, and Senator Joseph McCarthy all appeared on the program as speakers. (Dies was prevented from attending the actual event because of a bout of flu, but his tribute to Matthews—whom he praised as "[deserving] the gratitude and thanks of everyone who realizes the transcendent threat of Communism to everything that is decent and worthwhile in the world"—was read at the meeting.) Eugene Lyons, Alfred Kohlberg, Irene Corbally Kuhn, and former assistant to Albert Jay Nock Suzanne La Follette all appeared on the program as sponsors.[54]

Tickets went for $12.50 apiece; Roy Cohn bought out an entire table, bringing along fellow McCarthy staffers David Schine and Donald Surine as well as Julius N. Cahn, chief counsel of the Senate Foreign Relations committee; Robert Morris, chief counsel for the Senate Subcommittee on Internal Security; and Paulette Ames, the niece of media baron Walter Annenberg. William F. Buckley Jr. was in attendance, as was his sister Priscilla and his brother-in-law and future collaborator L. Brent Bozell. Ayn Rand also made an appearance. Not everyone in the room that night was a staunch right-winger; Lawrence Spivak, the moderate host of NBC's *Meet the Press,* also attended the dinner. Henry Hazlitt, Willi Schlamm, and Ludwig von Mises were also present. A number of prominent personages who could not attend in person wired their tributes; in addition to Dies's message, Sokolsky read tributes from Vice President Richard Nixon, William Randolph Hearst Jr. and movie star and virulent anti-communist John Wayne.[55]

Many of Matthews's guests were Jews. Schultz, Lyons, Kohlberg, Cohn, Cahn, and Rand were all Jewish. So were Ralph de Toledano and Victor Lasky, the coauthors of *Seeds of Treason,* a book-length defense of Whittaker Chambers; Benjamin Mandel, an ex-communist turned investigator for HUAC; and Jacob Spolansky, an old self-proclaimed red-baiter from Michigan. Morrie Ryskind, a conservative activist who would later provide seed money for William F. Buckley's *National Review,* was not personally present but sent his greetings from California. It is unclear if Arnold Forster, the general counsel for the Anti-Defamation League, personally attended the dinner; regardless, he bought a ticket from Sokolsky in January.[56]

The presence of a large and influential contingent of Jewish conservatives at the Matthews testimonial dinner was all the more remarkable considering who else was there. Merwin Hart bought a ticket, as did John T. Flynn; Allen Zoll, head of the National Council for American Education, bought out an entire table. Joseph P. Kamp also made an appearance. John B. Trevor bought a ticket and was due to attend, but was hospitalized shortly before the dinner; he sent a telegram to Sokolsky conveying his regrets.

Harry Jung, the former head of the American Vigilant Intelligence Federation, also bought a ticket and appeared on the guest list but was likewise unable to attend; when Matthews learned about Jung's aborted reservation, he wrote to him, "I wish you could have been there. *I would have been honored, indeed.*"[57]

There was, in short, a sizeable contingent from the antisemitic far right at Matthews's special night, with the full knowledge and support of Matthews and Sokolsky. Only one prominent Jewish conservative, labor journalist Victor Riesel, withdrew from the event because of the presence of Hart and company; in a telegram to Riesel, Sokolsky responded, "I regard you as bigotted [*sic*], as narrow-minded. Kindly never communicate with me under any circumstances for any purpose."[58]

As the presence at an event of so many on the Jewish right alongside the antisemitic far right—and particularly Sokolsky's response to Riesel—makes clear, a sizable number of Jewish conservatives were willing to make common cause with antisemites, and vice versa.[59] How did Jewish conservatives and the antisemitic far right justify their grudging mutual alliance?

Even Henry Ford, who, through his newspaper the *Dearborn Independent,* published a serious of infamously antisemitic articles in the 1920s, compiled into a book with the provocative title *The International Jew,* made an appeal to right-thinking Jews to accept his analysis. "What the *Dearborn Independent* says [about the Jews]"—that Jews have subverted the Anglo-Saxon business ethic, that Jews control Hollywood and the stage, that Jewish "Orientalism" is sapping American strength in literature, art, politics, economics, fashion, and sport—"is true, and tens of thousands of Jews know it is true." The fervor of the *Dearborn Independent*'s antisemitism was such that it was favorably referenced by the Nazis, and yet the paper—and by extension Ford—seemed to imply that right-thinking American Jews "who have given [the Jewish Question] a thought will agree" with the publication's conclusions. Ford was incredulous when his friend and neighbor the Reform Rabbi Leo Franklin objected to *The International Jew.* Ford assured Franklin that he considered him one of the "good" Jews.[60] This distinction between "good Jews"—sober, respectable, assimilated, and above all embracing right-wing politics—and "bad Jews"—devious, untrustworthy, supportive of the New Deal, socialism, or communism—is critical to understanding how right-wing antisemites internally justified working together with Jewish conservatives.

It is not a coincidence that the antisemitic right was most comfortable working with George Sokolsky, Alfred Kohlberg, and Benjamin Schultz. Unlike Eugene Lyons, who was an immigrant from Byelorussia, Sokolsky and Kohlberg were both native-born Americans. Sokolsky was from Merwin Hart's hometown of Utica, New York—his father was a Russian Jewish immigrant who settled there in the late nineteenth century—and Kohlberg was born in San Francisco. Kohlberg, Sokolsky, and Benjamin Schultz were all examples of "good Jews," zealous anti-communists. But not everyone on the Jewish right welcomed the tacit support.[61]

Of all the members of the Jewish right establishment, Isaac Don Levine, the editor of *Plain Talk,* was the most uncomfortable working in coalition with the antisemitic far right. He was notably *not* in attendance at J. B. Matthews's testimonial dinner in 1953. In February 1950, Levine published a front-page broadside against Merwin Hart and his scribblings in the *Economic Council Letter* entitled "The Strange Case of Merwin K. Hart." Hart, Levine wrote, was a "Trojan Horse" who, by bringing to the "noble cause of freedom the disease-carrying elements of hate and civil strife"—in other words, injecting his anticommunism with antisemitism—"unwittingly serves the common enemy and furthers the divide and wrecking operations of Stalin's fifth column." This was one of the first uses of a rhetorical device that would be increasingly common on the right throughout the next decade: that the issue with far-right antisemites like Hart was that they were undermining the credibility of the American right more broadly.[62]

Levine, in his article, examined a number of Hart's articles over the preceding two years, but honed in in particular on his recent December 1949 issue of the *Economic Council Letter* in which Hart argued that international communism was dedicated to establishing a "WORLD FAITH," which meant, in essence, Judaism. (Hart had contemptuous words for those who "grovel in an effort to prove that [Pontius] Pilate, and not Jewish authorities, were responsible for the death of Jesus.") He went on to allege that there was a "direct attack on Christianity" by a "minority of a minority [of American Jews] (for multitudes of Jews are loyal Americans and they thank God they live here, who have received privileges in this great Christian Republic such as they have never enjoyed elsewhere, [but] who now seek to destroy the very religion and culture that have given them refuge."[63]

Who was to blame for stirring up this "minority of a minority?" Unsurprisingly, Hart blamed Zionism for encouraging dual loyalty between the United States and Israel, arguing that it was hypocritical for Zionists to condemn American Christians for supporting Arab Christians in Palestine. Elements of Hart's attack on Zionism could be found in Jewish anti-Zionist discourse—Elmer Berger and Lessing Rosenwald had both expressed concerns about Zionism as an obstacle to Jewish assimilation—but Hart also included an explicit antisemitic and conspiratorial edge. Neither Berger nor Rosenwald, in their writings and public statements, framed dual loyalty as an intentional goal of the Zionist movement, and Berger affirmed in 1946 that "there can . . . be no challenging the loyalty and patriotism of American Jews, Zionists or non-Zionists," language far different than that of Merwin Hart.[64]

Hart blamed Zionists for the size of the Soviet occupation zone in eastern Germany; the insistence of the Roosevelt administration on uncon-ditional German surrender in World War II, which he suggested was a plot by Jewish interests to inflict maximum pain on Germany *and* to extend Soviet influence in the country; and "the Nuremberg and Dachau 'war crim-inal' trials, where vital American tradition and principle were trampled into the dirt"—a reference to Joachim Peiper's death sentence. "A wealth of evidence," Hart concluded, "can be adduced to show that the Zionists have Mr. Truman's administration in the hollow of their hand. The Socialist program is their program, as it is in Britain. There the Labor [*sic*] govern-ment is controlled by them. Even some of the top conservative leaders, through financial or other favors, are Zionist-influenced." Here was uncon-cealed, unmitigated, conspiratorial antisemitism—although even here, Hart insisted that he was talking only about *bad Jews*. Good, loyal, patriotic American Jews who accepted the tenets of the "great Christian Republic" in which they lived had nothing to fear.[65]

Levine didn't buy it. "Mr. Hart," he wrote, "is shrewd enough to describe the Zionists as only a minority among the Jews of the United States, to be sure, a domineering and all-powerful minority. And yet no fair-minded person can read Mr. Hart and misinterpret his design: every Jew is a Zionist, every Zionist is a Communist, every Jew is an enemy of Christianity." And Hart's words were dangerous considering his base of supporters and past statements—Levine noted both that the National Economic Council had the support of "captains of industry, prominent members of the bar, politicians, clergymen, and educators," and that Hart had actively encouraged his readers to procure firearms in preparation for a communist insurrection in his July 1948 issue of the *Letter*.[66]

But although Levine was unrelenting in his criticism of Hart, he stopped short of making firm prescriptions about him or right-wing antisemitism more broadly. *Plain Talk* merely was "[submitting] our clinical analysis of Merwin K. Hart's record to the public judgment of all those who seek the truth in the name of Christ's precept: Know the truth and the truth shall set make ye free," a line clearly directed at Christian allies on the right. While the implication was clear—the right needed to distance itself from men like Hart—there was no explicit exhortation to banish Hart from the right-wing popular front; in fact, Levine, at the end of his article, took pains to distinguish between Hart and the supporters of the National Economic Council, which "has an impressive list of influential citizens as its officers and directors."[67]

Hart, for his part, responded churlishly to Levine; he dismissed the column as a "smear" and *Plain Talk* as "by no means unsympathetic to Socialism, the twin brother of Communism." He denied that he was anti-Jewish, insisting that the National Economic Council has "always had Jewish members and supporters." He went on to add that the basic problem with Levine, as a Russian-born Zionist, was that he was "anti-Gentile" and that he "clearly does not understand the sentiments of honorable fair-play long since practiced by true Americans. He has not resisted reverting to the fear and hatred of his youth and of his fathers."[68]

But Hart also offered an olive branch of sorts: he held "a high regard for Mr. Levine's long and effective fight against organized Communists" and "welcomed the inception of *Plain Talk*," to which he had "gladly" given "our help in obtaining subscribers." Even when calling Levine's article a smear—at one point, Hart compared it to the work of Avedis Derounian—he qualified that it was "unlike Mr. Levine's usual writing." Levine dismissed Hart's words as his "merchandising [of] anti-Semitism," "[wrapping] his contraband in packages bearing the labels of free enterprise, anti-communism, and Christian love."[69]

Levine was right—Hart did strategically camouflage his antisemitic views by appealing to more ecumenical right-wing causes. But Hart also understood himself to be part of the same anti-communist struggle as, if not Levine, then other stalwarts of the Jewish right. The *Economic Council Letter* sang the praises of George Sokolsky and Alfred Kohlberg throughout the 1950s, citing them as experts on international communism.[70] And they were part of the same right-wing social and political circles in New York.

Both Hart and Kohlberg were guests at J. B. Matthews's testimonial dinner in 1953. As late as January 1960, four representatives of the National Economic Council attended Kohlberg's seventy-third birthday party (which turned out to be his last—he died less than three months later).[71] The Jewish right and the antisemitic far right were partners—albeit tense partners—in the right-wing popular front.

Merwin Hart's influence on the right became increasingly marginal as he aged. The House Buchanan Committee, convened to investigate lobbying activities in 1950, included Hart and the National Economic Council in its dragnet. Concerned that congressional investigators would embarrass the council's deep-pocket financial benefactors—the du Pont family alone contributed $90,000 in the late 1940s—Hart and the council went on the offense, declaring the subpoenas part of a fishing expedition. But Hart was eventually forced to open his books, revealing the reliance of his fund-raising apparatus on contacts furnished to him by Lammot du Pont. Although Hart continued to enjoy the influence of wealthy backers, among them Walter Harnischfeger, he was unable to leverage these connections into his dream of building a right-wing political movement in the United States. The energy on the far right was, by the mid-1950s, coming from elsewhere.

There was one significant far-right personage who was absent from J. B. Matthews's summit meeting in February 1953. Russell Maguire, the owner of the ferociously right-wing *American Mercury* magazine, was not physically present at Matthews's testimonial dinner (although he was invited), but copies of his magazine were, according to press reports, "on every table" at the dinner.[72] Maguire, who had once been a financial backer for the Economic Council, would become one of the most controversial figures in American media before the decade was out.

PART TWO THE PURGE THAT WASN'T, 1953–91

CHAPTER FIVE

Magazine Wars

RUSSELL MAGUIRE, THE OWNER and publisher of the *American Mercury* magazine from 1952 to 1960, is a relatively obscure figure today. If Maguire and the *Mercury* are remembered at all, it is for the circumstances of their decline and fall. The *Mercury* was, for a time, one of the most important right-wing publications in America, featuring a large stable of conservative writers and access to some of the most prominent conservative politicians in America. But Maguire and the *Mercury* had a dark side. When Drew Pearson noted that the *Mercury* was on every table at J. B. Matthews's testimonial dinner in February 1953, he was making a pointed critique: Maguire, whom Pearson linked to the publication of antisemitic propaganda in the United States, was one of a broader network of far-right activists who were part of the conservative coalition being feted that evening.

Maguire had earned a public reputation for bigotry as early as 1952, and yet he continued to enjoy access and stature throughout the broader American right. It would not be until 1959, after William F. Buckley's *National Review* distanced itself from the *Mercury*—after years of antisemitism and far-right rhetoric from Maguire that often spilled over into the pages of his magazine—that Maguire would lose much of his public respectability. Even then, the effects of Buckley policing the "boundaries" of American conservatism by criticizing the *Mercury* have been exaggerated— *National Review* distanced itself from the magazine only *after* the publication had been dropped by national news distributors. And that the organ of "responsible" conservatism felt the *Mercury* had gone too far did not necessarily mean the American right's rank and file felt the same way—Buckley received hundreds of letters criticizing his decision from *Mercury* and *National Review* readers, though the amount of subscription cancellations to his own magazine was less than he feared. The *Mercury* was clearly articulating the views of a substantial number of right-wingers. The *Mercury* affair previewed, in many respects, the later battles between "responsible" conservatives and the John Birch Society, and like those battles—which have been written about extensively—it suggests that there was a broad overlapping base of support between the "kooks" and the mainstream right.

The *American Mercury* enjoyed a long and prestigious history before it was acquired by Maguire in 1952. Founded by H. L. Mencken in the mid-1920s, the magazine changed hands a number of times in the subsequent decades. In 1950 freelance reporter William Bradford Huie became the editor and took the magazine in an explicitly conservative political direction. In addition to Huie's own editorials, which called for college students to "join me in a revolt against the Democratic Party" and baldly declared in 1951 that "a Republican can't be a liberal," Huie brought conservative writers and staffers to the magazine. Among the most prominent was the twenty-seven-year-old William F. Buckley Jr., who, after the success of his first book *God and Man at Yale* accepted a job with the *Mercury* in early 1952. (Buckley lasted less than a year; he found it difficult to work under Huie.)[1] The newly conservative *American Mercury* had a problem, however—it was perennially short of money. Opportunity struck later in 1952 in the form of an unlikely financial angel. Arms manufacturer turned oil and gas executive Russell Maguire decided to purchase the *Mercury*. "I've done very well in America," Maguire told a reporter, "and now I want to start putting something back." Huie gushed, "Now it looks like the very sane and respectable people on our side are getting into the fight."[2]

Maguire was extraordinarily successful. Born in Meriden, Connecticut, in 1897, he attended Worcester Academy and graduated from MIT with a degree in electrical engineering. Maguire later became an investor on Wall Street, and by the mid-1930s owned several industrial businesses as well as a brokerage underwriting firm. But his real claim to fame was his acquisition in 1939 of the Auto-Ordnance Corporation, the patent holder and manufacturer of the Thompson submachine gun.[3] Through his control of

Auto-Ordnance, Maguire quickly built up substantial contacts within the political and military establishments of the United States and Great Britain. He poached the assistant to the president of the Columbia Broadcasting System, Frederic A. Willis, as Auto-Ordnance's new vice president in June 1940, in no small part because Willis was a former U.S. Army officer and Winston Churchill's cousin.[4] Auto-Ordnance had been worth practically nothing before 1939 and did not even have a manufacturing plant, but the war brought booming business. Maguire received so many orders for Thompsons from both the British and the Americans that he had to contract out to other firms before the completion of a dedicated Auto-Ordnance factory in Bridgeport, Connecticut. By early 1941 the company had a healthy $3 million contract with the U.S. government to produce Thompsons—the company would make nearly $16 million in net profit through 1944.[5] Drew Pearson praised Maguire in his syndicated column for his foresight in "[envisioning] the sub-machine gun as one of the outstanding weapons of modern warfare" and for his patriotic business savvy.[6]

But Maguire had an ugly side. He weathered several high-profile business scandals in the 1930s and 1940s that brought forward (fair) accusations of fraud. In 1940 the Securities and Exchange Commission revoked Maguire's license to operate as a securities broker on the basis that he had illegally manipulated stock of a company in which he had interests. His acquisition of Auto-Ordnance was also the subject of a lawsuit—the estate of Marcellus Thompson took Maguire to court in New York State in December 1940, alleging "fraud, duress, and coercion" in Maguire's takeover of the company. (The lawsuit was quietly settled out of court a few months later.) And in 1942 Auto-Ordnance—by then renamed Maguire Industries—was forced to reimburse the federal government some $7 million in excessive profits. Maguire's own attorney later told the Anti-Defamation League that Maguire was a "thoroughly unscrupulous individual"—even the establishment of the charitable Russell Maguire Foundation, which netted Maguire favorable press coverage for his donations to war relief efforts, was created primarily as a tax dodge.[7]

Despite his unsavory business practices, Maguire thrived socially and financially after the end of the war. He parlayed his tidy, but still relatively modest, fortune from arms manufacturing into the oil and gas industries in Oklahoma and Texas. By the early 1950s he was reputed to be worth nearly $100 million. Maguire and his family enjoyed the life of the social elite in

New York City. A 1945 profile of Maguire described him as a "millionaire by intuition" and praised his philanthropic work through his foundation and patronage of the arts in Manhattan.[8] Maguire's marriage in 1942 to Suzanne Saroukhanoff, the daughter of a wealthy Russian businessman who fled to Paris after the Bolshevik revolution, made the *New York Times* wedding announcements page; his daughter and stepdaughter's debutante ball at the Ritz Carlton merited a column on the society page of the *New York Herald Tribune*. His stepdaughter Natasha Boissevain, whom Maguire would later appoint as the *Mercury*'s managing editor, modeled for *Vogue*.[9] Maguire cut, in sum, the figure of a wealthy, sophisticated New York businessman and social leader, a reputation that persisted even after his death. His obituary in the *New York Times* described him as an industrialist and financier, praised him for his charity work, and pointedly did not mention the *Mercury* or his politics.[10]

Although there is little evidence that Maguire was politically engaged before World War II, the Anti-Defamation League believed him to be influenced by Merwin Hart. Maguire and Hart developed a close relationship by 1947, with Hart inviting Maguire to join the National Economic Council. (Hart was by this time widely understood by other far-right activists to be a conduit to gain access to "fat cats" with deep pockets like Maguire.)[11] In July, Hart circulated a memo introducing Maguire to his colleagues and stating that the businessman had committed to contributing as much as $10,000 to the group. Maguire attended a dinner in Hart's honor at the Union League Club in Manhattan along with other wealthy New York businessmen, and appeared on a list of the NEC executive committee in a fund-raising letter authored by Hart in November 1947. The two men had a falling-out, however, over Maguire's lack of commitment to the work of the NEC. Hart, ever interested in the prospect of popular right-wing mobilization, outlined a vision of building nearly a dozen organizations to embark on a "plan of consolidated effort" to take America back from its (unnamed) enemies. This required money and organizational commitment, and Maguire had reneged on both, promising to serve on the NEC board and to donate $5,000 but never delivering. "Frankly, I have never quite understood your attitude towards us," Hart wrote. "You became quite interested in the council at one time and agreed to come on the board and the executive committee. Then you withdrew."[12] Maguire's tight-fistedness and unreliability as a business

partner, already evident in his SEC ban, the lawsuit over his acquisition of
Auto-Ordnance, and his tax-dodge charitable foundation, crippled his association with Hart, and these toxic character traits would be common
complaints made by Maguire's fellow travelers over the next decade.

Hart was not the only far-right activist with whom Maguire was
connected. The new owner of the *Mercury* was also close to Allen Zoll, the
former Christian Fronter who was, by the 1950s, the head of the National
Council for American Education and had recently waged a successful
campaign against "progressive" educators in Pasadena, California.
Education was Zoll's bailiwick. He was the author of numerous pamphlets
warning about communist subversion in American schools through liberal
dupes and fellow travelers—one of his more popular pamphlets on the
danger of direct federal aid to schools was entitled *They Want Your Children!*
(Unsurprisingly, Zoll was denounced by the National Education Association
as a dangerous extremist.)[13] Zoll had a business relationship with the
Mercury during Maguire's early tenure at the magazine—he sold subscriptions for the magazine in 1952 and claimed to have influence over Maguire's
editorial policy.[14]

These activists constituted a loose but interlocking network of far-right
activists within a broader right-wing popular front in the 1950s that ampli-
fied the voices of their fellow travelers. Both Zoll and Maguire endorsed and
distributed the work of John O. Beaty, a professor at Southern Methodist
University whose 1951 book *Iron Curtain over America* alleged a Jewish plot to
subvert the American republic. During the Second World War Beaty was a
staff officer for army intelligence in Washington, DC, a section with a long-
standing reputation for antisemitism and far-right politics.[15] *Iron Curtain
over America* was a typical catalogue of right-wing complaints about U.S.
policy since the Roosevelt administration: FDR's recognition of the Soviet
Union in 1933; the administration's maneuverings toward war with
Germany in 1941; the harsh victor's peace over Germany in 1945; the loss of
China; and restrictions placed on Douglas MacArthur during the then raging
Korean War.[16] Beaty went further than other right-wing authors by insisting
that "Judaized Khazars" were behind these politics as part of their "quadruple
aims of international Communism, the seizure of power in Russia, Zionism,
and continued migration to America." Zoll recommended the book in his
mailings for the National Council for American Education—Beaty was one
of his vice presidents. *Iron Curtain* was endorsed by a number of prominent

generals in MacArthur's clique in the military, including MacArthur's intelligence chief, Major General Charles Willoughby, and the former commanding general of the Far East Air Forces, Lieutenant General George E. Stratemeyer.[17] William F. Buckley Sr. was a fan as well, even lobbying Henry Regnery, the publisher of his son's book *God and Man at Yale*, into assisting Buckley with his attempts to distribute the book to libraries across the country.[18] Maguire, for his part, financed repeated printings of the book and helped to circulate them around the country, particularly to churches. By 1954 the book, with Maguire's financial support, was on its ninth printing.[19]

The promotion of *Iron Curtain over America* by these various figures was all the more remarkable because it was published six years after the end of World War II. But while the war *did* damage the public reputations of many right-wing and antisemitic activists who had been prominent in the 1930s—over thirty activists were indicted for sedition by the U.S. government in 1942, although the case was eventually declared a mistrial after the death of the presiding judge—the political influence of the "old right" continued well into the 1950s.

As long as Maguire and his fellow travelers on the far right could prove financially useful and their antisemitic views were not the subject of intense scrutiny from liberals and the left, they were welcomed—albeit uneasily—within the broader right-wing popular front. William Bradford Huie resigned from the *Mercury* only in December 1952, after Maguire's far-right connections were reported by NBC and *Time* magazine. Huie admitted to *Time* that he "knew about Maguire's indiscretions and operations with the Christian Front crowd. But to me money is impersonal. If suddenly I heard Adolf Hitler was alive in South America and wanted to give a million dollars to the *American Mercury*, I would go down and get it."[20] This attitude persisted among conservative publishers well into the 1950s—William F. Buckley Jr. approached both Maguire and Beaty in 1955 (the latter on the advice of his father) for seed funding for *National Review*.[21] But this closeness came at a price. The younger Buckley was enraged by allegations and ad hominem attacks that he harbored fascist sympathies. Buckley attempted to balance these tensions throughout his early years as a right-wing activist—when an aging Merwin Hart appealed to him in 1954 to set up a meeting with Senator Joseph McCarthy, Buckley wrote to the senator's office forwarding the request, but he urged McCarthy to "plan the meeting in secret," noting that it would be advisable not to meet with Hart at all, given

that "he is now almost universally regarded in Liberal circles as a pathological anti-Semite." But even as Buckley advised McCarthy to keep his distance,
he also insisted that "90% of what has been said about [Hart] is unjust" and
he continued to have prominent and respectable businessmen on the board
of directors of the National Economic Council. Widespread public exposure
of radical right-wing politics, not those politics as such, was the key to exclusion from the right-wing popular front in the 1950s, and even here money
and influence could insulate individual activists from total banishment.
Notably, in his letter to McCarthy Buckley contrasted Hart with Gerald L. K.
Smith, the head of the Christian Nationalist Crusade, who had neither
wealth nor politically influential friends.[22]

In Russell Maguire's case, his exposure as an antisemite in 1952 crippled
neither his own political influence nor the *Mercury*'s fortunes—the magazine's best days under his ownership were still ahead. Maguire replaced
Huie with John A. Clements, the public relations director for the Hearst
Corporation, and promised Clements a free hand at the magazine. The first
post-Huie edition had a print run of 150,000 copies.[23] Clements brought in
a whole stable of Hearst contributors and alumni to the magazine—J. B.
Matthews, Howard Rushmore, Victor Riesel (ironically himself Jewish), and
Irene Corbally Kuhn, among others. The political direction of the magazine
remained unchanged; the Clements-edited *Mercury* was militantly anti-
communist and published frequent defenses of Joseph McCarthy's red-
baiting campaign. The magazine's influence peaked under Clements, and a
number prominent right-wing writers contributed to the *Mercury*—the 1953
issues featured articles and reviews from Matthews; Ralph de Toledano, a
friend and confidant of Richard Nixon; Frank Meyer; China lobby bigwig
Alfred Kohlberg; and even William F. Buckley Jr., who penned a broadside
against "the intellectuals" in June 1953. The *Mercury* under Clements
remained a monthly edition of about 150 pages and had a style and format
similar to *Reader's Digest*, but with original as opposed to syndicated content.
The magazine was by no means as influential as *Reader's Digest*, but it was
one of the most widely read conservative publications of the decade. While
National Review struggled to reach twenty thousand readers as late as 1959, at
its peak the *Mercury* boasted a circulation of over one hundred thousand.[24]

    A glance at the July 1953 issue—which was one of the most controver-
sial Clements published as editor—provides a good overview of the style and

tone of the content. The bulk of the magazine was dedicated to anti–New Deal politics to one degree or another: one article blasted Franklin D. Roosevelt as a weak old man who gave away too much to the Soviets at Yalta; another declared the Securities and Exchange Commission a "good idea gone wrong," now dominated by bureaucrats "bent on putting a straight-jacket over the vital securities industry" and sneakily promoting the New Deal program of socializing business; still another predicted that private enterprise would easily exceed the track record of socialism. Not every article was explicitly political or even intellectual; the magazine included cornpone missives on the lost art of kite flying, tongue-in-cheek remembrances about basic training in the army, and dime-novel treatments of exotic espionage. The overall tone of the magazine was sentimental, maudlin, and culturally conservative in a middlebrow sense. At least some of Buckley's later contempt for the magazine stemmed not from its antisemitism but from its petit-bourgeois appeal in contrast to his own intellectual project.

Even the general-interest articles incorporated right-wing—often far-right—analysis. Alice Widener penned an exposé on the Ford Foundation in June 1953 that decried how the foundation was dominated by former New Deal bureaucrats—a standard conservative line, but Widener also found space to minimize Henry Ford's record with the antisemitic *Dearborn Independent*. "The thought occurred to me," Widener wrote, "that Henry Ford II, misled by the Foundation brain trusters, is trying to atone for all the sins his grandfather never committed."[25] Contributors to the magazine generally conflated New Deal liberalism, socialism, and communism. Harold Lord Varney, who served as an associate editor for the *Mercury* throughout the decade, labeled the liberal Americans for Democratic Action "unquestionably the most influential political body now working for Socialist ends in America."[26] There were limits to these conflations: an article ripping Arthur Sulzberger at the *New York Times* for the tone of his paper's coverage of McCarthy compared the *Times*'s objectivity on McCarthy unfavorably with the communist *Daily Worker*, but refrained from stating outright that the *Times* had pro-communist sympathies.[27] The *Mercury*'s line on liberal opposition to McCarthyism was for all intents and purposes identical to that of William F. Buckley Jr. and Brent Bozell in their 1954 *McCarthy and His Enemies*. Buckley and Bozell did take pains to distinguish between communists and liberals (something that Buckley did not always do in his personal correspondence), but suggested that "atheistic, soft-headed anti-anti-Communist liberals" were ultimately little better than communists.[28] The *Mercury*, if anything, was slightly softer on liberal opposition. It castigated liberals for being "contemptuous of the opinions of those who disagree with them," but argued that liberal opposition was due more to their embarrassment about having been "taken in ridiculously by the Reds before and during World War II" than to real ideological sympathy with communism.[29]

Conspicuous by their absence during much of Maguire's ownership of the magazine were articles on race. The attitudes of Maguire and the *Mercury*, however, can be gleaned from general-interest articles that touch on race, like a piece from December 1954 that endorsed the idea that the ruins of Great Zimbabwe in southern Africa must have been built by pre-Dutch white colonizers. The civil rights movement was understood solely through the lens of communism, although the *Mercury* generally eschewed race-baiting for a somewhat more nuanced approach of amplifying the voices of anti-communist Black journalists like George Schulyer or Manning Johnson, who criticized the radical sympathies of civil rights leaders without endorsing segregation. The *Mercury* also published pro-apartheid pieces justifying the colonialist project in South Africa in racist and paternalistic terms—" 'Give the natives the vote!' comes the cry from across the seas. How incongruous. One might just as well toss the franchise in to the laps of seven-year-olds." Maguire's magazine also made its endorsement of segregationist candidates crystal clear. In 1936, Eugene Talmadge, then governor of Georgia, told a reporter that he had read *Mein Kampf* seven times. W.E.B. Du Bois singled out Talmadge as a particularly fascistic example of southern segregationism. In February 1958 the *Mercury* wrote a glowing cover profile of Eugene Talmadge's son Herman—who had been recently elected to the Senate—praising his opposition to communism, his steadfastness in the face of left-wing media smears, and his opposition to civil rights legislation. The elder Talmadge's political commitments in the 1930s were left unmentioned, although the cover featured a drawing of Herman Talmadge in humble military fatigues in front of a Confederate flag. Still, despite the magazine's praise for Talmadge, the New York–based magazine remained a world apart from southern politics and letters—significantly, no prominent southern politicians had articles appear under their own bylines in the *Mercury* during Maguire's tenure.[30]

Congressional conservatives saw the *Mercury* as an ally in the struggle against communism and liberalism. California Republican William

F. Knowland, the widely acknowledged leader of the conservative faction in
the Senate and Republican leader from 1953 to 1959, was friendly with a
number of conservative publications while in Congress, including both
National Review and the *Mercury*. Knowland wrote an article in the debut
issue of *National Review* in November 1955 calling on Republicans to
recommit to the policy of rolling back communism in eastern Europe. Only
a month before Knowland had made the same substantive points in an
extraordinarily friendly interview with the *Mercury*, which lobbied softball
questions like "Was the diplomatic recognition of the USSR in 1933 a
blunder?" (The answer, unsurprisingly, was yes.)[31]

Ironically, considering that Maguire brought in Clements and the Hearst
crowd to mute the controversy over his own antisemitic beliefs, it was Hearst
stalwart J. B. Matthews who wrote one of the most controversial articles the
Mercury ever published—not about Jews, but about mainline Protestants. In
the July 1953 issue Matthews—who had just been named chief investigator
for Senator Joseph McCarthy—alleged that the "single largest group
supporting the Communist apparatus in the United States today is composed
of Protestant clergymen." The clergy, according to Matthews, even
"outnumber professors two to one in supporting the Communist-front apparatus."[32] Matthews's claims elicited widespread outrage and dominated
headlines across the country, leading directly to Matthews's downfall and the
first significant dent in McCarthy's armor.[33] After a bitter—and public—
battle, McCarthy was forced to fire Matthews. McCarthy stood publicly
bloodied.[34]

The condemnation from Protestant pulpits was not, however, universal.
Fundamentalist preacher Carl McIntire, whose byline would later appear in
the *Mercury*, was one of the few clergymen to publicly defend Matthews and
McCarthy—this was all the more remarkable because McIntire was an
inveterate anti-Catholic as well as an anti-communist, and McCarthy was in
1953 the most prominent Catholic politician in America. But although
McIntire never abandoned his anti-Catholicism, he was more than willing to
cooperate with conservative Catholics to oppose more paramount
concerns—namely, communism and what he believed to be secular
modernist theology, the major targets of Matthews's article.[35] Even right-
wing Jews could find themselves in coalition with antisemites in this
ecumenical right-wing popular front; in July 1954 the *Mercury* ran an article
by Rabbi Benjamin Schultz, head of the American Jewish League against

Communism, complaining that liberals had unfairly weaponized the charge of antisemitism against the right.[36] The irony of a rabbi publishing an article in a magazine owned by a widely recognized antisemite went uncommented on in Schultz's article.

Maguire's religiosity was ambiguous. He was on the one hand an Episcopalian, but on the other his editorials for the *Mercury*—which ran monthly beginning in 1954—frequently invoked fundamentalist language and themes, particularly as Maguire began publishing more openly antisemitic content. A column from June 1956 is typical: "Christ meets the deepest needs of every soul. . . . Evil forces within our borders have brainwashed us to turn to government. . . . World Government is the Beast who will lead us to destruction. It will command that we bow down and worship the coming Anti-Christ!"[37] Maguire's use of the term *World Government* was a coded reference to an international Jewish conspiracy, but his language was typical of eschatological Protestant fundamentalism.[38] Carl McIntire had also ominously warned about the looming "World Dictator" and "World Government" that would herald the end times.

Ironically, given his predilection for fundamentalist rhetoric, Maguire would cultivate the friendship of the dashing, flaxen-haired, and much more moderate Billy Graham, already a national celebrity by 1950. Maguire had hosted Graham at his Palm Beach estate in the summer of 1952 and offered the preacher financial support—"I want to subsidize you. . . . Whatever it'll take, you tell me, and I'll finance it." Graham politely declined Maguire's offer of support at that meeting, but a year later he tapped Maguire to lead fund-raising efforts for the Glen Eyrie Endowment Fund, an attempt to build a compound for Graham's ministry in Glen Eyrie, Colorado.[39] Graham became another regular contributor to the *American Mercury* between 1954 and 1958—his debut essay, an anti-communist polemic entitled "Satan's Religion," was adapted from one of his sermons. Anticommunism formed the basis of the political alliance between Graham and Maguire. That a public figure of Graham's stature continued to publish in the *Mercury* even after Maguire had been repeatedly and publicly criticized for antisemitic politics is a testament to the enduring strength of the right-wing popular front approach even into the late 1950s.[40]

The landscape of right-wing media began to shift in the latter half of the 1950s with the debut of William F. Buckley Jr.'s *National Review*. The new magazine was framed as a disavowal of both New Deal liberals and what Buckley called "the irresponsible Right," with which, Buckley wrote, he had a "considerable stock of experience." (Buckley was being modest, since he had approached Maguire earlier that year for funds for *National Review*, and in the mid-1950s had appeared as a guest on the H. L. Hunt–funded TV program *Answers for Americans;* Buckley would condemn Hunt years later for "[giving] capitalism a bad name.")[41] The magazine was to be devoted to high-minded intellectual opposition to communism, socialism, and New Deal liberalism—unlike the *Mercury,* which took mass-market cues from *Reader's Digest, National Review* was an elitist publication. This is a theme Buckley would return to time and again in his subsequent writings—that *National Review* and his various other conservative enterprises, by dint of their elitism and intellectualism, represented a respectable alternative to the crudity of right-wing politics found in places like the *Mercury.*

Buckley was the scion of an extremely wealthy family, was acclaimed for his erudition both as a speaker and a writer, and was educated at the Millbrook School and Yale University. (The most consistently thick files in Buckley's personal papers are concerned with his yacht.) Buckley's wit, wealth, and sophistication have made him an idol among conservatives on par with his friend and longtime political ally Barry Goldwater.

Yet Buckley was not as distant from the "irresponsible Right" as he liked to portray. Buckley's father, William F. Buckley Sr., was—like Russell Maguire—an oilman; the elder Buckley's precise personal wealth is unknown, but one biographer estimated his fortune in the mid-1950s to be around $20 million.[42] Billie, as he was affectionately known by friends and family, was profoundly influenced by his father and the class position he had been born into. Both father and son firmly believed in hierarchy as the natural order of the world and considered the mass democratic nature of New Deal–era society to be coarse and vulgar. The younger Buckley wrote candidly of his father's attitudes later in life—particularly his father's anti-semitism—and this worldview influenced him as a youth.[43] The elder Buckley was a close friend of the writer Albert Jay Nock, an infamously anti-democratic and antisemitic man of letters who was later cited by Billie as a major political influence.[44] When Billie Buckley was searching for seed money to start *National Review,* he scoured the entire spectrum of the right for financial angels. Robert Welch, the future founder of the John Birch Society with whom Buckley would later have a prominent public feud in the

1960s, donated some $1,000 to the venture.[45] Buckley also reached out to Maguire and, at his father's suggestion, John O. Beaty and former Texas representative Ed Gossett.[46] Although the younger Buckley positioned his new magazine as the voice of the responsible right and wrote of his distaste for the "popular front" approach to conservative politics during his later fights with the Birchers, Buckley and *National Review* were embedded *within* this coalition during their formative years.

By 1955, however, there were significant cracks forming in the popular front. In September John A. Clements resigned from the *Mercury,* along with Clements went most of the *Mercury*'s regular contributors, including J. B. Matthews, Irene Kuhn, and Ralph de Toledano. The precise catalyst for Clements's departure is not clear, but in general it was sparked by Maguire's desire to take the magazine in a more explicitly antisemitic direction. De Toledano, writing to William F. Buckley Jr. to inform him of his departure ("You don't need a book-and-record critic, do you?") said that "indications of *The Mercury*'s future course are such that I could not, in any conscience, give it the tacit endorsement of further participation."[47] Kuhn similarly told the Associated Press, "I [couldn't] continue [at the *Mercury*] in good conscience." Maguire and the *Mercury* suffered considerable damage from the departure of Clements and the Hearst crowd. With Clements out, the *Mercury* no longer had a professional journalist running the show; Maguire instead appointed his stepdaughter Natasha Boissevain managing editor despite her lack of journalism experience. Maguire's reputation, too, was publicly maligned. He skipped a ceremony where he was to appear alongside Senator William Jenner to receive the Americanism Medal from the American Legion a week after Clements resigned. The legion itself was embarrassed to be giving recognition to Maguire—a spokesperson told the press that the organization had no knowledge of Maguire's antisemitism when it voted to award Maguire the medal (despite public reporting about his views since 1952) and hastened to add that the legion was "honoring not Mr. Maguire personally but the magazine and the staff collectively."[48] But more important, the magazine was, by the time of Clements's departure, increasingly difficult to find on newsstands. The cause of the *Mercury*'s declining influence came not from Clements's resignation or conservative disavowals, but rather from an unofficial boycott of the magazine from the distribution companies that monopolized the publishing business.

Starting in 1954, the major national distributor of magazines, the American News Company, refused to handle any more editions of the

Mercury.[49] American News's boycott was a serious blow to the magazine because the company and its subsidiaries effectively had a monopoly on the distribution of magazines in the United States. In 1955, American News serviced ninety-five thousand local news dealers across America; as a vertically integrated company, it also directly operated newsstands, restaurants, coffee shops, book shops, drug stores, and dozens of other retail outlets where books, newspapers, and magazines were sold. A contemporary study of the magazine industry found that American News sold more than half of the total value of magazines in the United States in 1954—and that did not take into account the market share of American News's subsidiaries. American News also owned the Union News Company, which itself owned and operated concessions in thirty-two states and had exclusive rights for sales and distribution in 170 different department stores, hotel chains, and transit hubs, including Grand Central and Penn Stations in New York City.[50] The company's power was immense. *National Review* itself had almost been strangled in the crib by American News, which threatened to discontinue its distribution of the magazine in 1956 due to poor sales—William F. Buckley Jr. had to personally prevail upon Roy Cohn, who included American News as a client, to intercede on his behalf.[51]

The *Mercury* could not count on Cohn as an ally, for reasons that are unclear.[52] The American News boycott crippled the *Mercury*'s circulation and revenue stream. But it was not just the American News Company that was the problem—independent vendors had little appetite for the magazine's content. William LaVarre, a former roving correspondent in Latin America for a variety of American wire services whom Maguire hired as editor in chief for the *Mercury* in the summer of 1957, recalled that during his initial interviews with Maguire he had been told the magazine was foundering because the New York–based Kable News Company, a small independent distributor that continued to vend the *Mercury* after the American News boycott, dumped the magazine after its April 1957 issue thanks to "complaints from various Jewish organizations." The catalyst was a recurring column titled "Money Made Mysterious" which trafficked in thinly disguised antisemitic language about an international financial conspiracy consisting of Jewish bankers Bernard Baruch, Henry Morgenthau, Sidney Weinberg, and Paul Warburg. The Anti-Defamation League described the column as "[using] language which to the bigot can have strong antisemitic meanings."[53] The May issue saw fewer than twelve thousand sales.[54]

Nevertheless, there remained a loyal audience for the *Mercury*'s content—the only profitable component of the magazine was the "*Mercury* Reprints" series, a direct-mailing service to subscribers that reproduced individual articles, usually in a serial digest format—from the *Mercury*'s back catalogue. (J. B. Matthews's articles were among the most popular.) Individual right-wing activists and "patriotic organizations" made up most of the bulk purchases, often in lots of one thousand or five thousand. This had the benefit, as LaVarre saw it, of amplifying the *Mercury*'s voice on the right, especially among "patriotic" grassroots activists. "A reader could obtain knowledge from an article in the *Mercury* and then get a hundred copies to mail to acquaintances who did not have the magazine each . . . month."[55] Even as the sales of the magazine plummeted in 1956 due to its distribution problems, both the sales and income of "*Mercury* Reprints" were on the uptick. One reprint, entitled "Funeral of the Constitution," had nearly one hundred thousand copies purchased. This did not mean that one hundred thousand individuals had bought reprints; the actual number was probably under one hundred, considering that most reprint sales consisted of block orders. But it did mean the *Mercury* enjoyed the dedicated patronage of well-heeled right-wing activists.[56]

LaVarre began his editorship of the *Mercury* in September 1957. As part of his contract, he retained the option to purchase the magazine after a year if he so desired; there was also a no-penalty escape clause should he choose to disassociate himself from the publication. His initial impressions of the magazine were mixed. The *Mercury* had suffered from a lack of experienced leadership ever since Clements's departure, and it showed. On his first day, LaVarre found a contract with a subscription vendor that stipulated the vendor could keep all of the money from his subscriptions himself— between this and the boycott by American News and its subsidiaries, it was no wonder the magazine was financially underwater. LaVarre promptly voided the contract. LaVarre also understood that the magazine would never recover if distributors continued to boycott the *Mercury*. Fortunately for him, the American News Company effectively dissolved its monopoly on national distribution in the spring of 1957, the victim of corporate maneuvers involving a takeover and liquidation of assets. This meant that local distributors that had hitherto been largely suppressed by American News suddenly became major distributors in their own right. LaVarre met that August with George B. Davis, the president of Kable News, in an attempt to revive their past relationship. Davis told LaVarre that antisemitic content in copies of the *Mercury* that were to be were to be distributed to newsstands, as well as the direct-mail "*Mercury* Reprints" series, was unacceptable and would have to be discontinued as a condition for Kable to consider redistributing the magazine. LaVarre relayed Davis's conditions to Maguire, who went on a lengthy tirade in his office. "I am not in any form a racist or anti-Jew! I have many Jewish associates!" Maguire's protestations were somewhat undercut, however, when he reminded LaVarre that "the Bolshevist Revolution in Russia was the work of Jewish brains, of Jewish dissatisfactions, of Jewish planning, whose goal is to now create a new order in the world."[57] Maguire did slightly back down, easinig up on coded antisemitism in the first half of 1957, but by August Maguire was back to declaring that "we must cut out the cancer of Communism, Socialism, and treason. They are financed by our only real threat—*the enemy within.*"[58] Unsurprisingly, the distribution problems continued.

Due to the antisemitic content, the *Mercury* also found it difficult to attract advertisers and corporate support, with two significant exceptions. The United States Steel Corporation cut Maguire a $2,000 check in December 1957 in response to Maguire's entreaties for financial assistance "in distributing *The American Mercury* to school, college, and public libraries." U.S. Steel gave Maguire an additional $2,000 for the same purpose several months later, in March 1958. One of U.S. Steel's major competitors, Republic Steel, was even more generous. Republic's president, Charles M. White, personally wrote Maguire a $1,500 check for the distribution of the *Mercury* to libraries, and the company underwrote an additional $3,000 for the same effort.[59] Republic Steel was also the only major corporation that, by 1958, continued to advertise in the print issues of the *American Mercury.* Charles White's own politics may have played the key role in Republic's continued support of the *Mercury,* even as Maguire's editorials castigated the "Zionist-Socialists" and their attempts to "[manipulate] us and our various States into a Socialist Federal Autocracy."[60] White had been the vice president of operations for Republic Steel during the Committee of Industrial Organization's drive to organize "Little Steel" (the major steel companies in America that were *not* U.S. Steel) in 1936–37 and was infamous for his use of violence to repress labor organizing, drawing upon the so-called Mohawk Valley formula for strikebreaking that Merwin Hart helped to develop. (Hart even offered to assist organizing grassroots resistance to the strike.)[61] As president of Republic Steel during the 1950s, White advocated for national right-to-work laws, called for the repeal of the National Labor Relations Act, and financed the distribution of literature on behalf of Senator William F. Knowland, describing Walter Reuther, the president of the United Auto Workers union, as a "cunning conspirator" and an "evil genius."[62]

The steel companies' $8,500 worth of support for the *Mercury* was modest—not even enough to pay for a single issue of the magazine—but it was nevertheless significant. It was part of a broader pattern of corporation subsidization for right-wing causes in the postwar years—the libertarian Mont Pelerin Society, for example, owed its survival to the support of sympathetic businessmen—but the steel companies went further than others in continuing to support an open antisemite. Given Little Steel's past alliances with far-right activists like Hart against labor unions two decades earlier, this was an important political continuity on the part of the steel industry's corporate management. Steel support provided a lifeline for the *Mercury*. Maguire had been publishing antisemitic content in his editorials for over a year and was already on a distributors' blacklist. The support from the steel companies allowed the *Mercury* to do a limited end-run around the boycott.[63]

It also bought content. The *Mercury* had always been anti-labor—a 1953 profile of Reuther by Ralph de Toledano portrayed him as a ruthless demagogue dedicated to "[bringing] the dictatorship of a corporate state to America"—but more and more column space was dedicated to anti-labor agitprop after the generous financial support of the steel companies. The March 1958 edition was dedicated to the "labor issue" and featured contributions from Senator Knowland, among others, urging a partial repeal of the National Labor Relations Act. (An editorial insert from LaVarre reminded readers that the "notorious Wagner Act" was "written *for* Senator Wagner . . . *by* Communists from Manhattan. Manhattan's Wagner was but the front for introducing this alien ideology and 'law' into the Congressional Record.") Even as the *Mercury* explicitly trafficked in antisemitism in Maguire's editorials—and implicitly with the reference to "alien" ideologies in LaVarre's inserts—it still enjoyed support from other elements of the right-wing popular front due to shared opposition to pillars of the New Deal state.[64]

The same year that Maguire hired LaVarre, he brought on board a thirty-nine-year-old Brown University alumnus recently discharged from active-duty service in the U.S. Navy. Commander George Lincoln Rockwell had ambitions of making a new career for himself in publishing; he had launched his own magazine, *U.S. Lady,* in 1955, targeted specifically at the wives of serving U.S. military personnel. The magazine reflected Rockwell's political interests. He idolized Senator Joseph McCarthy and General Douglas MacArthur—he adopted MacArthur's habit of smoking a corncob pipe as a self-conscious tribute to the old soldier in the early 1950s—and staunchly opposed communism. *U.S. Lady* also took a firm stand against racial integration, one of Rockwell's other pet causes. The magazine did not, however, explicitly endorse Rockwell's most cherished, albeit quietly held, political belief: that Adolf Hitler was on to something. At the same time as Rockwell publicly embraced McCarthy and MacArthur, he had privately read *Mein Kampf* and the *Protocols of the Elders of Zion* and come to the conclusion that Hitler was absolutely right. He, George Lincoln Rockwell, would do what was necessary to preserve the white race. Rockwell even honeymooned at Berchtesgaden, Hitler's Alpine retreat, in 1953. His wife, Margrét Þóra Hallgrímsson, whom he had met while on military deployment in Iceland, was the niece of Iceland's ambassador to the United States.

U.S. Lady was initially successful. Remarkably for a magazine solely supported by advertising dollars, the first four issues turned a profit, but Rockwell sold his stake in the publication after those four issues. In his memoirs, Rockwell blamed the largely female staff of *U.S. Lady* for "overwhelming" him; the magazine continued to publish under different ownership for at least a decade, promoting broadly conservative—but not fascistic—standards of behavior for military wives.[65] Rockwell subsequently bounced around a variety of right-wing publications in New York, including William F. Buckley's *National Review,* for which he worked for about six months selling subscriptions on college campuses before he moved on to the *American Mercury.*

Rockwell, with his background at *U.S. Lady,* ironically fit the gender politics of *American Mercury* better than *National Review.* Although *National Review* published a number of right-wing women in the 1950s—Freda Utley placed an article in the magazine in its second issue—entire weeks could go by without a woman writing a column. The *Mercury,* by contrast, published around half a dozen women per issue. When LaVarre became editor in 1957, three of the four editors at the *Mercury* were women.[66] Buckley's dismissal of the magazine as uncouth had more than a hint of his disdain for the housewife market, which the *Mercury* appealed to with articles like "Pity the Childless Couple" and "Tried Walking Lately?"[67]

Rockwell penned three articles for the *Mercury* in 1957, all of which expressed anxieties regarding decadence and feminization. One was a Spenglerian-like lament of Iceland's degradation thanks to Marxist influences and the impression offered by American servicemen stationed there that "America is a land of uncultured, jazzy barbarians"; another was a complaint that liberals and socialists were feminizing American soldiers by making basic training less cruel (which also managed to squeeze in a dig at "brotherly-love advocates who howled for the blood of millions of Germans and gloatingly hung the German leaders" for war crimes after World War II). Rockwell's final article for the *Mercury*—published in an issue that featured his idol Douglas MacArthur on the magazine's cover, was an ode to how the Marine Corps makes "*men*" out of boys, which is why the liberals and the communists were out to neuter the corps.[68]

Rockwell's brand of casual misogyny was hardly out of step for the *Mercury,* despite its stable of women writers and an editorial staff largely consisting of women, including Maguire's stepdaughter. This was the magazine, after all, that under Maguire's ownership published an article by Irene Corbally Kuhn declaring that "women don't belong in politics," and another article wondering "is democracy making Japanese women neurotic?" Kuhn also helpfully articulated her vision of what women in politics *should* look like in a 1955 feature profiling the wives of twelve Republican senators, ranging from Peggy Goldwater to Jean McCarthy. Doloris Bridges and Mary Mundt were described as "forceful personalities without being in the least unfeminine or personally and unpleasantly aggressive." Paeans to keeping men masculine and women feminine were a staple of the magazine, although occasionally the *Mercury* encouraged particular forms of female mobilization. One article in 1954 argued that "the better element of women must come to the aid of their country" by, among other things, forming study groups to learn the mechanics of electoral politics and master political issues in order to "contribute the utmost to your family, your husband's work-opportunity, your schools, government, and church." There were limits to this vision, however; women were to "take up the challenge of the hour and learn the things we need to know to preserve our American heritage," but once the crisis had passed, women were to return to the "home [in] which [they] breath[e] the free air of American liberty. . . . The sooner women get *into* politics in a practical way, the sooner we can get *out*."[69] Traditional female gender roles could be stretched only insofar as they underwrote anti-communist politics, and only then in the context of the immediate political crisis. As for men, anything that smacked of feminization was verboten—as Rockwell wrote, "Who wants panty-waisted Marines?"

Rockwell didn't last long at the *Mercury*. He was disgusted by what he called "left-wing sympathies in some of the editors"—particularly the women working at the magazine—and made few friends with his colleagues because he reported these heterodoxies to Maguire. But Rockwell quickly grew to dislike Maguire, who, a fellow fascist told Rockwell, was "rabid about only one thing, the *Mercury*, his pet project—and the hell with the cause itself," and was all talk, no action.

Rockwell also claimed that Maguire later met with Rockwell and his friend and ally DeWest Hooker (Frederic Willis was also allegedly present). Rockwell and Hooker "presented a complete plan for a slow, secret Nazi build-up under Hooker throughout [the country]. . . . Maguire seemed entranced with everything we presented. . . . "All right!" said Maguire, with the air of a man suddenly decided on an immense step. "I'll back it! The country doesn't have five years! We've simply got to do it! I'll put in a thousand dollars for the first year!"[70]

Rockwell and Hooker were apparently insulted by the sum, given both Maguire's vast wealth and the expenses he had already sunk into the *Mercury*. "Here was a multimillionaire with over $80 million dollars, sitting in an apartment which alone must have cost him $1,500 a month, to say nothing of his fabulous palace on the water-front in Connecticut, telling us that he was going to 'back' a national political movement of gigantic proportions to save America—WITH A THOUSAND DOLLARS A YEAR!"[71]

Rockwell's account is obviously unreliable—he also claimed Maguire had tried to hire his friends to "kill key Jews at $10,000 a head," but there is no doubt that Rockwell and Maguire were close for a brief time. In any event, Rockwell's account of the internal goings-on at the *Mercury* has the ring of truth. Maguire was in a constant pitched battle with his staff over his political views. "Three or four of Maguire's supposedly picked staff were not only violently anti-Hitler, but were actually sneaky liberals. . . . Once we caught a pro-Negro article by a black married to a White girl."[72]

According to Rockwell, the *Mercury* was Maguire's way of injecting his antisemitic and pro-fascist views into conservative discourse while simultaneously clinging to respectability for both himself and his family. His socialite stepdaughter Natasha Boissevain, in 1957 the managing editor of the magazine, felt the same way. There were certain lines they would not cross—in public, anyway. After Rockwell approached him about the "left-wing" editorial direction at the *Mercury,* Maguire told Rockwell to meet him in the men's room two floors below his office, so they wouldn't be seen talking. "He told me that his wife was giving him a hard time about me. She was a White Russian and on 'our side,' but *didn't want to jeopardize the luxurious life she had attained with her husband,* nor risk the security of her children. . . . He told me his wife had heard of my efforts to organize a 'hard-core' for him, and was 'terrified.' He whispered on and on so disgustingly about the pressure on him, and kept referring to the possibility of 'cutting the thread'—meaning my employment—that I naturally offered to resign. He accepted before I had all the words out."[73]

Rockwell despised Maguire as a soft, decadent coward who—like many conservatives—was a fickle ally too terrified of being denounced by the Anti-Defamation League to do the necessary public work of organizing against the Jews. Maguire, deeply involved in the day-to-day operations of the magazine, frequently clashed with his staffers who objected to his antisemitic and pro-fascist leanings. The *Mercury* was the right-wing popular front in a microcosm—disparate groups brought together under one roof by their shared antipathy toward communism and liberalism. If the conservative elements of the popular front were uncomfortable with the fascistic far right, they were still sufficiently comfortable to work alongside the far right so long as they did not express their antisemitic views publicly.

The year 1958 would be the *Mercury*'s swan song. LaVarre opted to leave the magazine that July, frustrated—according to his memoirs—by the continued distributors' boycott and his constant battles with Jewish organizations over the *Mercury*'s content. With LaVarre gone, the *Mercury* no longer had a professional journalist running the day-to-day operations of the magazine.[74] The political fortunes of the *Mercury*'s right-wing allies in Washington also waned. Ever since Joseph McCarthy's censure in 1954, the influence of the right in Washington appeared to be in decline. McCarthy lingered in the Senate for two and a half years until his death, a staggering, alcoholic punchline who found himself persona non grata at Republican campaign events. The results of the 1958 election were a new low. William Knowland, George

Malone, and William Jenner were all defeated in their election bids. (The one bright spot was Barry Goldwater, who crushed his Democratic opponent in Arizona.) The conservative wing of the Republican Party in the Senate had lost many of its most outspoken leaders—of the twenty-two Republicans who had voted against McCarthy's censure in December 1954, only eleven were still serving by the beginning of 1959 (and North Dakota's William Langer would die at the end of the year, leaving only ten). Maguire had lost most of his allies on Capitol Hill.

The political blows to conservatism in 1958 were a catalyst for further radicalization in order to "save" America. Robert Welch founded the John Birch Society a mere month after the 1958 election. Maguire, for his part, began abandoning all pretense of restraint and doubled down on the antisemitic rhetoric in the *Mercury*. Maguire ran a column in December 1958 entitled "The *Mercury* Warned You" insinuating that a Jewish conspiracy was behind the passage of the Seventeenth Amendment establishing direct election of U.S. senators. In January 1959, with his stepdaughter Natasha once again serving as managing editor of the *Mercury*, Maguire published an editorial in which he declared that "International Zionists" were seeking to enslave the world, and that "documents are available to prove [this]," alluding to the *Protocols of the Elders of Zion*.[75] The editorial was only slightly less blatant than the usual fare in Gerald L. K. Smith's newsletter.

Maguire's column was the final catalyst that precipitated an open break between the *American Mercury* and *National Review*, the first great crack in the postwar right-wing popular front. Buckley had been expressing increasing misgivings about the *Mercury* since 1957, when he wrote to Karl Hess, an occasional contributor to *National Review* who also appeared on the masthead of the *American Mercury*, expressing "mounting alarm and horror" about the direction the *Mercury* was going under Maguire and said that the board at *National Review* was debating the question as to whether *National Review* and the *Mercury* "could . . . afford to have any regular personnel in common." Buckley's major concern was that the *Mercury*'s growing antisemitism would open *National Review*'s right flank to attack. "I am . . . astonished the left hasn't pounced," he told Hess in April. "Was there ever so exposed a target as the incumbent *Mercury*?" But Buckley confided to Hess that *National Review* would "not . . . do anything of a public nature" about the *Mercury*.[76] So long as left-wing critics did not seize on Maguire's relationship with Buckley's faction on the right, Maguire's increasingly blatant antisemitism in his columns did not warrant an open attack. In any event, it was the *Mercury*'s apparent crudity that repelled Buckley as opposed to anti-semitism per se, because he made exceptions in his personal associations for refined and polished antisemites. He maintained a close friendship with Revilo Oliver, a classics professor at the University of Illinois, throughout the 1950s despite acknowledging to Brent Bozell that Oliver had demonstrably antisemitic views. Buckley even wrote to Senator William Knowland in February 1958 appealing to him to pressure the president to pardon Ezra Pound for his collaboration with the Italian Fascist government during World War II. "Nobody takes Pound's anti-Semitism seriously."[77]

There were also significant potential risks for Buckley if he publicly criti-cized fellow travelers on the right. Charles Willoughby was on the *Mercury*'s masthead as well as that of *National Review*. Most *National Review* contribu-tors had bylines in the Maguire-run *Mercury*, and even Maguire's latest turn toward undisguised antisemitism had not triggered a right-wing backlash. Ralph de Toledano, who had resigned from the *Mercury*'s masthead in 1955 due to Maguire's antisemitism, continued to write for the magazine, publishing a feature on the dangers of communist subversion in the April 1959 issue and a glowing front-page profile of Richard Nixon in May.[78] A public attack on Maguire and the *Mercury* would expose *National Review* to charges of factionalism on the right, and could provoke a backlash from *National Review* subscribers, many of whom also read the *Mercury*. Buckley continued to opt for a moderate course. In April he decided—over the objec-tions of several of his editors and staffers, including Willoughby, William Rusher, and his public editor A. E. Bonbrake (who served essentially as the magazine's ombudsperson)—to circulate an internal memo to *National Review* contributors stating that "*National Review* will not carry on its mast-head the name of any person whose name also appears on the masthead of the *American Mercury*," but that "we will not refuse to run material submitted by persons who continue to write for the *Mercury* for the reason that to do so would be presumptuous."[79] This memo was not made public, nor was Maguire officially notified of *National Review*'s new policy.

Buckley's behind-the-scenes break with the *Mercury* was only a slight step further than his expression of private misgivings in 1957. It was not the decisive blow that crippled Maguire and his magazine. Maguire had already tried to unload the magazine to William LaVarre the previous year because of the *Mercury*'s chronic circulation problems given the unofficial boycott by the distributors. (These problems had only been compounded by LaVarre's departure.) It is exceedingly unlikely that Buckley's memo would ever have become public knowledge if Russell Maguire had not made it so. He was leaked the memo by Charles Willoughby, who shared Maguire's antisemitism and resented Buckley's "arbitrary posture"—Willoughby was one of the handful of *National Review* contributors who sided with Maguire.[80] Maguire took the dispute public in July, publishing the memo in an editorial. Maguire even bitterly noted that the *Mercury* had been in the habit of referring writers to *National Review* when their pitches better suited the needs of a weekly. "We, in fact, have tried to help feed the mouth that now nibbles at us!"[81]

Buckley and his editors were concerned that Maguire's public attacks would cripple *National Review* by prompting subscription cancellations. There were scores of angry letters, mostly concerned about the opening of a breach in the right-wing popular front. One subscriber wrote, "I am a strong conservative, and an ardent anti-socialist and anti-communist. As such, *I believe all conservatives should strive to pull together and ignore relatively minor differences.*" Another letter writer wrote that she "deplored any conflict between the two leading conservative publications which might hurt our common cause." Still another correspondent—a Catholic priest—wrote to Buckley asking, "Why can't we conservatives subordinate the secondary things to the first things?" "The common enemy is communism," wrote yet another letter writer. "Let's get with it and stop the nonsense."[82] To his credit, Buckley stood firm in the face of intra-movement criticism, but tried to emphasize the softness of his response. His standard reply to *Mercury*-inspired hate mail was to affirm that the "insidious anti-Semitism that lurks in the corners of the *Mercury* . . . has done considerable damage" to conservatism, but he emphasized that *National Review* contributors were still free to *write* for the *Mercury*—only the masthead was verboten, since it implied sympathy with Maguire's "pathological insinuations against a religious minority." This was apparently sufficient for many; Buckley later recalled that the damage to *National Review*'s brand was minimal; most conservative writers stuck with *National Review* over the *Mercury*.[83]

The *Mercury* affair was only the beginning of a bitter, protracted fight on the right that led to the splintering of the right-wing popular front in the 1960s. The John Birch Society, founded in December 1958, was the zenith of the popular front approach. The group's founding members were a veritable who's who of right-wing businessmen and political activists of the period, including founder and candy manufacturer Robert Welch, oil magnate Fred C. Koch, and University of Illinois classicist Revilo Oliver, a close personal friend of William F. Buckley Jr. and a contributor to *National Review*. Welch, who exercised a considerable degree of power over the organization, welcomed anti-communists of any political stripe and any political baggage into the organization; Merwin K. Hart became the head of the New York City chapter of the society before his death in 1962. Maguire never became a Bircher—as we shall see, he largely abandoned public life after 1960—but many of his former associates did join.[84]

Buckley's repudiation of the Birchers is a familiar story to historians of the American right: unnerved by Robert Welch's conspiracy theory–laden claims that Dwight D. Eisenhower was a dedicated communist, Buckley— partly at the behest of Barry Goldwater—penned a broadside on Welch in a February 1962 issue of *National Review*, consolidating the boundaries of "responsible conservatism." There were important resonances in the Bircher repudiation with the *Mercury* saga. Both Buckley and Goldwater were frequently assailed in the liberal press for far-right and even fascistic sympathies; disavowing the Birchers was at least in part a political tactic to nullify those attacks as Goldwater began preparing his bid for the presidency in 1964.[85] But both Buckley and Goldwater attempted, paradoxically, to hold the right together; Buckley repudiated the popular front approach in his letters to prominent Birchers while at the same time attempting to keep the public dispute confined to the person of Robert Welch, not the John Birch Society as a whole. There was a personal element in this move as well as a political one. Buckley attempted repeatedly in the early 1960s to mend his friendship with Revilo Oliver despite the latter's drift into explicit antisemitism—unlike Maguire, Oliver was witty and erudite in his approach and earned private praise from Buckley for a guardedly anti-Jewish column submitted to, but not published by, *National Review* on Jewish journalist Harry Golden.[86] Buckley's approach—specific criticism of certain leaders, as opposed to groups and organizations—was supported by Goldwater, who maintained that "you can't just [excommunicate the Birchers] in Arizona," given the prominence of their supporters. Specifically targeting Welch as irresponsible helped soften the blow; Goldwater was able to maintain support from the Birchers and other elements of the far right—he even had the support of Willis Carto, who was by the mid-1960s one of the more prominent antisemites in the United States, despite Goldwater's own partial Jewish ancestry.[87]

Russell Maguire, however, was on the sidelines during the 1964 campaign. By the mid-1960s, Maguire had disappeared from the political scene. Embittered by Buckley's repudiation, Maguire sold the magazine in 1960 to the Defenders of the Christian Faith. The *Mercury* changed hands a number of times throughout the 1960s before Willis Carto's Liberty Lobby acquired it, continuing to publish the magazine until 1981. But there is an unusual denouement in Maguire's story. After selling the *Mercury*, Maguire, using his old Hearst editor John Clements as an intermediary, began to supply information to the Anti-Defamation League on George Lincoln Rockwell, the head of the American Nazi Party, and his activities. Rockwell had briefly been a contributor to the *Mercury* in 1957, but quickly broke with Maguire. Clements told an investigator from the ADL in early 1961 that Maguire had underwritten an "intensive investigation" of Rockwell and had made the results available to the FBI. This was almost certainly motivated by the unflattering portrayal of Maguire in Rockwell's newly published autobiography, *This Time the World,* in which Maguire is portrayed as a coward unwilling to embrace the swastika because it would destroy his family's reputation among Manhattan's social elite.[88] Maguire actually began a reasonably warm correspondence with Arnold Forster, the ADL leader. Forster wrote to Maguire that his efforts against Rockwell "[contributed] to the cause of human decency and your participation in it is most heartening."[89] Forster circulated an internal memo at the end of July in which he declared, "We consider the problem of Russell Maguire to be closed," citing his professed desire to break with his past political activity and his work countering Rockwell.

Maguire's final dalliance with the Anti-Defamation League was the perfect coda to decades of duplicitous behavior. He ended his life despised by his former friends and allies in the growing conservative movement and by his contacts on the far right. The root cause of his unpopularity was not his politics, nor his bigotry and racism per se—those were common enough attitudes across the American right in the 1950s and 1960s—but his repeated untrustworthiness. Maguire made many promises of financial support to figures across the right-wing political spectrum, but rarely delivered on those promises. He made probable false claims about his charitable giving to deflect attention from his repeated practice of backstabbing his business and political partners. Even his financing of the investigation into Rockwell's American Nazi Party was motivated by petty revenge, since Maguire's correspondence with Forster suggests that he never abandoned his right-wing views. For all Maguire's importance as the publisher of the major right-wing magazine of the 1950s, his organizational incompetence and his inability to work reliably with others prevented him from ever making the kind of outsized political impact that he so desperately desired. This was probably a factor in Maguire's distance from the John Birch Society; joining the Birchers would have meant subordinating himself to a larger organization. Merwin Hart, Maguire's onetime ally and an organizational entrepreneur through the National Economic Council, was able to make this leap. Maguire was not. He died in 1966.

CHAPTER SIX

The John Birch Society and the
Second Brown Scare

ROBERT WELCH FERVENTLY believed that president Dwight David Eisenhower was a communist. In a private letter he circulated at first to close friends and eventually to hundreds of leading conservative activists and intellectuals across the country, the sixty-something retired candy manufacturer—the genius behind the Junior Mint—claimed that Eisenhower was a "dedicated, conscious agent of the Communist conspiracy." Welch went on to allege that practically every prominent member of the Eisenhower administration, with the notable exception of Vice President Richard Nixon, was also either a communist or a communist sympathizer. The notion was ludicrous—Welch's analysis was rooted less in hard evidence and more in overweening resentment that his preferred candidate, Robert Taft, had not secured the GOP nomination over Eisenhower in 1952—but it could not be easily dismissed as the rantings of an (admittedly wealthy and influential) crank. Welch was, after all, the founder and leader of the John Birch Society, the largest and most widespread right-wing mass-membership organization in a generation. Many erstwhile establishment conservatives—not the least of whom was William F. Buckley Jr.'s friend and collaborator Revilo Oliver—joined the Birchers.[1]

The John Birch Society, which made its public debut with a series of newspaper and magazine exposés in the spring of 1961, terrified liberals. A radical right-wing anti-communist organization whose leader apparently believed that moderate Republican Dwight Eisenhower was, in fact, a card-carrying Red not only raised the specter of a resurgent McCarthyism a scant four years after the Wisconsin senator finally drank himself to death, but the secrecy surrounding how the John Birch Society was organized, the support of wealthy industrialists, and its apparent mass base raised fears that the society was fascist. Ohio Democrat Stephen Young described Welch in a speech on the floor of the U.S. Senate as a "little Hitler"; the California attorney general's office opened an investigation into the society that summer to determine it if was, indeed, subversive.[2] Predictably, conservatives lashed out against Birch critics—especially those who cried fascism. Barry Goldwater blasted in his syndicated column liberal critics who were engaged in a "deliberate attempt to categorize all conservatives as fascists." "Enough of Anti-Anti Reds," wrote an irate member of the society in February 1962, tired of being accused of being a fascist "because I believe in the work that the John Birch Society is doing to save our republic." (The letter writer, James Oviatt, a Los Angeles haberdasher, was later found by the Anti-Defamation League to have been distributing copies of the *Protocols of the Elders of Zion* in Southern California.)[3]

Liberal anxieties over resurgent fascism had been a staple of American political and intellectual life since the end of World War II. But from roughly 1961 through 1964 these anxieties—centered around, but not exclusively about, the John Birch Society—reached such a crescendo that the historian Rick Perlstein dubbed it the Second Brown Scare.[4] Barry Goldwater's 1964 bid for the presidency, which cultivated and in many respects relied on the support of far-right groups like the Birchers, saw these liberal anxieties reach new heights—only to shift radically to the apparent threat of the New Left once Goldwater was defeated in a landslide by Lyndon Johnson in November 1964. The subsequent clashes between liberals and leftists in the late 1960s and 1970s—and the development of a hegemonic conservative politics during the same period—meant that the Second Brown Scare was either forgotten or ignored as liberal paranoia. Even most twenty-first-century scholars of the John Birch Society generally dismiss charges that Welch or the group was "fascist"—with the corresponding implication that most of the anxieties about the right-wing revival in the early 1960s were, at best, grossly exaggerated.[5]

But the Second Brown Scare was not simply a phantasm. Although extremists like George Lincoln Rockwell dismissed the Birchers as milquetoasts, the group had a broad tolerance of racism, antisemitism, and fascist sympathies among its grassroots membership, as attested to by extensive field reports by the Anti-Defamation League. The John Birch Society was a vehicle for political mobilization that was, in many respects, the apotheosis of the dreams of right-wing organizers like Merwin Hart for a national, mass-membership conservative organization that stretched back to the 1930s. The period also continued to see deep, albeit increasingly fraying, ties between more mainstream conservative factions and a progressively militant and violent white nationalist right. William F. Buckley Jr., Robert Welch, Revilo Oliver, and George Lincoln Rockwell, despite their political differences and frequent clashes, were nevertheless deeply intertwined figures throughout the 1960s, all part of the same right-wing mobilization that would eventually propel the American right—although not necessarily its most extreme coalition members—into a position of political hegemony within a decade.

Liberal panic over the John Birch Society led to many reporters "infiltrating" the organization, which in practice usually meant simply reading through Birch literature and attending a local chapter meeting. These "undercover" efforts at looking at the inner works of the society were the major selling point of an explosion of exposé books by journalists in the early 1960s. Gene Grove, a reporter for the *New York Post*, wrote one of the earliest examples with *Inside the John Birch Society*, which mostly rehashed the existing press coverage of Robert Welch and included excerpts from *The Politician*, but which also promised readers a detailed look at a Birch Society chapter meeting in New York. Grove had managed to finagle an invitation to the May 1961 meeting of chapter 26 in Manhattan. The chapter's leader was none other than Merwin Hart.[6]

Grove was largely unimpressed. "Recruits whose enthusiasm for the society may have been diminished by rumors of bigotry within the organization will not be reassured by the meeting place": the headquarters of the National Economic Council, in suite 1100 at 156 Fifth Avenue ("an equivocal location midway between the charm of New York's Washington Square and the splendor of uptown"). Most of the chapter leadership consisted of NEC affiliates; the assistant chapter leader was Constance G. Dall, Hart's executive vice president at the NEC, and the JBS treasurer was retired navy vice admiral Charles Freeman, another NEC associate. At the meeting Grove attended, approximately thirty people showed up, either existing members of the society or people who (like him) were invited as potential recruits. Most were men; only a third were younger than fifty. Still, Grove was impressed by the social standing of the Manhattan Birchers. This was no rag-tag bunch of lunatics. He made a point of noting that the vast majority of attendees were well dressed, with the men in neat, sharply pressed suits and the women sporting minks and pillbox hats—"if John Kennedy hadn't won the crowd, Jackie certainly had."[7]

Hart, who showed up fifteen minutes late, opened the meeting outlining the expected line of attack on the society by liberals and communists. It seemed, Hart told his audience, that a CPUSA member had infiltrated a John Birch Society meeting, and he had leaked details to CBS. But there was an upshot—CBS, afraid of being sued for libel by the JBS, was burying the story. (Grove noted sardonically that the major CBS investigative report broadcast that week was on movie censorship and did not mention the John Birch Society at all.) With the inoculation against a looming smear out of the way—"Perhaps some of you are familiar with [attacks like] that," Hart told his audience, no doubt mulling on his decades of resentment over liberal, communist, and Jewish "smears"—Hart queued up the centerpiece of most Birch Society meetings around the country: the filmstrip. In May 1961 the movie of the month was an educational program produced by Time, Inc., and ABC on the political situation in Latin America, and in particular Venezuela's diplomatic support for Cuba after the 1959 revolution. Hart labeled the film "out-and-out Communist propaganda, an attempt to lay the blame for South American poverty on the better classes in Venezuela and a plea for more foreign aid from the United States." A report from a member in charge of the letter-writing campaign in support of Major General Edwin Walker followed—"[It's] going magnificently," she said, without providing details, and claimed to be in touch with sympathizers of both Walker and the John Birch Society in army intelligence. Another young woman, whom Grove lecherously emphasized was surprisingly attractive for a Birch Society member, talked about the dangers from the American Civil Liberties Union; still another attendee went into a lengthy diatribe about communist infiltration of the Protestant churches. By this point in the meeting, the discussion had turned into a kind of greatest hits of right-wing anti-communist conspiracy theories and resentments. As the meeting adjourned, Grove leafed through an issue of Hart's *Economic Council Letter,* which he picked up from a display table; it included an article arguing that the genocide of European Jews by the Nazis was a hoax and that many of the 6 million Jews supposedly murdered by the Nazis "are right here in the United States and are now joining in the agitation for more and more support for the state of Israel—even if the American Republic goes down."[8]

Hart was never a particularly influential member of the John Birch Society—he was eighty years old in 1961 and in the last year of his life, and his chapter was small, consisted mostly of NEC sympathizers, and existed primarily to promote NEC talking points—but his membership and local leadership roles in the society are nevertheless revealing. For one, the John Birch Society was the fulfillment of Hart's long dream of a national grass-roots right-wing organization. The Manhattan chapter meeting might have been small, but hundreds if not thousands of chapters were being organized all over the country, educating members and potential members about the communist conspiracy and, most important, preparing members for political action. Hart's old political action committee American Action, Inc., an early attempt to politically organize the American right under the umbrella of a national group, had foundered because of organizational ineptitude and, crucially, because it had been created with the specific purpose of influencing the 1946 elections. The John Birch Society did not have the same narrow political remit. And for far-right activists like Hart, the Birchers offered an opportunity to bring their conspiratorial antisemitic messages to a new audience already primed to believe in fantastical conspiracy theories. If Dwight D. Eisenhower could be a covert communist, then maybe the Zionists really *did* fake the Holocaust. Anything was possible.

Other conservative leaders were threatened by the apparent scope and power of the John Birch Society, which Welch claimed had one hundred thousand members by the mid-1960s. (By contrast, Young Americans for Freedom claimed only twenty-one thousand members in 1962.)[9] William F. Buckley Jr. was, in many respects, a close ideological ally of Robert Welch. They were both zealous anti-communists, hated the New Deal state, rejected the moderate Republicanism of Dwight Eisenhower, and longed for an authentically conservative political party. Welch had even provided Buckley with (modest) financial support for the creation of *National Review* in the mid-1950s. But Buckley was wary of the blatant conspiracy theorizing of Welch, as well as Welch's closeness with the *American Mercury* and Russell Maguire, whom Buckley was now keeping at arm's length. "The differences between us are grave indeed," he wrote to Welch in October 1960. "You have a popular front attitude towards conservatism which I do not share."[10] This was rather an exaggeration on Buckley's part, considering his markedly ambivalent condemnation of the *American Mercury* in 1959. Nor was it entirely fair to Welch, who did have limits on just whom he would collaborate with in the broad spectrum of the American right. When Gerald L. K. Smith wrote to Welch fifteen months later suggesting collaboration, Welch politely declined: "In this fight against the Communist conspiracy, Mr. Smith, it is not possible for us to cooperate with you—as we try so hard to do with most other anti-Communist groups or leaders . . . because of a basic disagreement between us as to the main sources of strength of the conspiracy."[11] Concerns about the scope of the conservative coalition were rather less important than the prospect that Welch might jeopardize the enfant terrible editor's status as one of the most influential figures within the growing conservative movement. *American Opinion*, Welch's magazine, which had become the unofficial journal of the John Birch Society, had nearly as many subscribers as Buckley's *National Review*, and—like the *American Mercury*—was written in a considerably more accessible middle-brow style. If *National Review* attempted to be a conservative version of *Harper's*, the *New Yorker*, or the *New Republic*, appealing to an urbane, sophisticated, and well-educated audience, *American Opinion* strove to be a tribune for the common man.

Well, not the common man, precisely. John Birch Society members tended to be relatively affluent professionals and small-business owners, and many of the contributors to *American Opinion*, at least before the mid-1960s, were also to be found in the pages of *National Review*.[12] The paradox of the Buckley/Welch dispute, and their eventual public split, was that it was predicated on class tensions as much as ideological disagreement, but both Buckley and Welch were, by any objective standard, part of the American aristocracy: Buckley, the Yale graduate son of a multimillionaire, and Welch the soft-spoken North Carolinian who grew up on the family plantation and briefly attended Harvard Law School before making millions as a candy manufacturer. But crucially, Welch actually made his fortune as an industrialist—in contrast to Buckley, who inherited his wealth from his oil tycoon father and owed his national reputation to his journalism. Welch—and by extension the John Birch Society as a whole—was every bit as committed to the free-market and free-enterprise system as *National Review* was, but embedded in the Welch's politics was a crude form of producerism—the sense that "productive" capital derived from hard work and production was superior and more authentically American than parasitical speculative capital. This did not mean that the John Birch Society was critical of *capitalism* or, God forbid, supportive of *organized labor*—articles in *American Opinion* were ferociously hostile to labor leaders, with even conservative AFL-CIO leader George Meany singled out for criticism—but that there were tensions between the more elitist vision for the conservative movement that Buckley pioneered and the more populist Birch Society.[13]

Buckley was nervous that Welch's increasing political influence would sideline him among leading conservatives. In May 1959 Welch founded a new group—for all intents and purposes a front organization for the John Birch Society—called the Committee against Summit Entanglements (CASE). Its purpose was to pressure Eisenhower to rebuff Soviet attempts to convene a summit meeting between Eisenhower and Soviet leader Nikita Khrushchev—conservatives would eventually go apoplectic when Eisenhower not only agreed to meet with Khrushchev but allowed Khrushchev to make a twelve-day goodwill tour of the United States in September. (Presumably Welch, who believed that Dwight Eisenhower was a secretly a communist, thought that Khrushchev was to deliver to Ike his instructions on how to destroy America.) The masthead of CASE was a who's who of prominent conservatives, including Welch, Clarence Manion, Alfred Kohlberg, T. Coleman Andrews, and Fred C. Koch—all members of the John Birch Society.[14] Buckley feared he was being shut out and reached out to his old friend Revilo Oliver, the University of Illinois classicist and a contributor to *National Review* who was also a founding member of the John Birch Society. Buckley was concerned there was a boycott against himself and other *National Review* contributors and that CASE was a power move by Welch. "I undertake to say this to prove I have a nose for conspiracy, the impression to the contrary notwithstanding." He asked Oliver to talk to Welch for him. Oliver declined, but solicitously, also reassuring Buckley that there was no "boycott" of *National Review* in CASE and pointing out that none of the associate or contributing editors at Welch's magazine *American Opinion* were included on the masthead, either.[15]

But Oliver was irritated by what he perceived to be Buckley's sectarianism. "I strongly and emphatically deprecate the fissiparous tendencies of American conservatives. . . . I am dismayed by the amount of energy and emotion that conservatives in this country devote to internecine warfare." Oliver was, at heart, a popular fronter. He recognized that there were real divides on the American right, but that these were "and will remain irrelevant so long as conservatives, in both numbers and in influence, [are] a minority." The only way forward was unity—or at least, in popular front terms, a tacit agreement to avoid public feuding "until [the right is] in a position to dominate and reform the political life of the United States."[16] This was almost certainly a not-too-subtle jab at Buckley's recent memo on the *American Mercury*, which had been circulated at the beginning of April to *National Review* contributors, including Oliver.

William F. Buckley Jr. and Revilo Oliver were unlikely friends. The dour, curmudgeonly Oliver, whose pencil mustache and rumpled, bloated appearance gave him the aura of Clark Gable suffering from late-stage alcoholism, was a marked visual contrast to the young, handsome, and clean-cut Buckley. One acquaintance of Oliver in the 1950s wrote that "he gave me the creeps. His long face was exaggerated by black hair glistening back with pomade, bushy eyebrows, and beady eyes. When he smiled, his lip curled into a snarl."[17] The unpleasant and querulous University of Illinois classicist and the *National Review* publisher may have been unlikely friends, but friends they were. For a time, anyway.

Born in Corpus Christi, Texas, in 1908, Oliver—whose sinister-sounding palindromic name was a family tradition dating back at least six generations—was a renowned scholar of Sanskrit, having taught himself the language with the help of a Hindu missionary while an undergraduate at Pomona College in Los Angeles in the mid-1920s. He earned his doctoral degree at the University of Illinois in 1940, the bulk of his work being based on a new translation of the fifth-century Sanskrit drama *Mrcchakatika*. The thirty-three-year-old Oliver, as a trained philologist, was recruited by the War Department as a cryptanalyst in 1941 and served in Washington, DC, during World War II.[18] Ironically, considering Oliver's intense antisemitism, he was close during his wartime service with William F. Friedman, a Russian Jewish immigrant and the head of the Army Signal Intelligence Service.[19] After the war, he returned to the University of Illinois and settled into his academic career. Oliver won a Guggenheim Fellowship in 1945 and a Fulbright in 1953 and was respected among his classicist peers as an erudite, if pompous and long-winded, academic talent.[20] He was also notorious for his extreme anticommunist views. Oliver, writing his memoirs in 1980, recounted that he had been content to sit on the sidelines politically until 1954, when he had an "intellectual jolt" that Senator Joseph McCarthy was doomed to be pulled

down by the liberal and communistic "wolf-pack." He weighed his options—
one was to simply continue to teach Greco-Roman history and classics in the
belief that this would encourage "the best minds" to understand, through
"historical and philological research," the full scope of the crisis facing
America. But Oliver opted for the career of a public intellectual.[21]

An erudite anti-communist academic was a natural fit for *National
Review* magazine in the 1950s. Willmoore Kendall, Buckley's mentor in
college and an iconoclastic conservative presence at Yale, tapped Oliver as a
contributor to the nascent magazine in 1955 and introduced him to
Buckley.[22] Just what the enfant terrible of the American right saw in Oliver is
a mystery, although according to Kendall *National Review,* which was
intended to be a serious intellectual magazine, was having a devil of a time
attracting academic writers. Oliver was one of a handful of conservative
scholars, along with folks like Kendall, Russell Kirk, and Richard Weaver,
who was enthusiastic about contributing to the magazine. In April 1956,
after publishing a few book reviews, Oliver was formally named an "associate and contributor" to the magazine (ironically Oliver shared the
announcement of his formal relationship with *National Review* with Charles
Willoughby, also named an "associate and contributor" in the same issue).[23]

Oliver and Buckley got on famously. Both were pretentious, verbose,
and full of snobbery. Oliver, too, shared Buckley's low opinion of the
American Mercury in the 1950s—not because of the magazine's antisemitism, but because it contained "a good deal of trash" in its selection of articles. Not only did Oliver fervently back *National Review* upon its launch in
1955, he also urged Buckley and the other editors to further distance the new
venture from the dictates of mainstream journalism. "Are those the readers
whom you really want?" he chided in a letter to Buckley.[24]

But even as Oliver began writing for the magazine in earnest, he was
uneasy about the venture. Part of this was pure intellectual snobbery.
Throughout his life, Oliver was prone in his private correspondence to puns
in classical languages and allusions to obscure literary figures. No doubt his
overriding arrogance and elitism formed the basis of his friendship with
Buckley. Both had high opinions of themselves as intellectuals and wits.
Buckley, however, was a much more talented, disciplined, and modern writer;
raw Revilo Oliver prose had a turgid, overwrought quality akin to that of H. P.
Lovecraft (with similar levels of racism but considerably less imagination). "I
have noted with increasing misgivings and sorrow," Oliver commented, "a

failure to retain the intellectual finish and stylistic polish that I regard as requisite to success." While Buckley was also a snob, he, at least, had practical experience in journalism and writing for a nonacademic audience. "If the magazine dies, Revilo," he responded, "it will be precisely because it was not sufficiently 'journalistic in manner' to attract a large readership.[25]

There were signs of a more substantive disagreement between the two. Oliver, purportedly simply sharing criticisms made by friends of his but probably using his "friends" as sock puppets, attacked *National Review* for being insufficiently conservative. "It is critical, but it is a dull, apathetic, listless criticism which at times seems only the reverse of the criticism the liberals have so long applied to our society." It was also—crucially— insufficiently aggressive. "I can't help feeling that the journal is too defensive, that it waits to make up it [sic] mind on most issues, that it doesn't carry the battle to the enemy." Here Buckley took issue. "On the matter of foreign policy we are like a beacon, I feel, pointing to the fact that we are engaged in a great struggle, and that the enemy has *attributes*," contrasting this position, based on "our knowledge of history, of Communism, of diplomacy, of civilization, of original sin" with the "tergiversations" of liberalism. He also chided Oliver for missing his "principled position" on domestic policy. "Our stand on the question of desegregation, for example, entitles us, I believe, to the respect that is due those who follow principle."[26]

Oliver was, like many of *National Review*'s contributors, an unrepentant believer in the biological reality of race and the clear racial superiority of whites. Arguments to the contrary were an indicator of liberal and/or communist degeneracy. Oliver was tapped in 1957 to review the latest book of anthropologist Ashley Montagu, *Man: His First Million Years*. It is hard to imagine anyone Oliver would have loathed more—Montagu was an English Jew whose 1942 book, *Man's Most Dangerous Myth: The Fallacy of Race,* was one of the first works written—at least by a white academic—to challenge assumptions about the naturalness of racial hierarchy; he was later chosen by UNESCO to assist in drafting its landmark 1950 report "The Race Question," which rejected, with qualifications, the objective existence of racial hierarchy. Oliver accused Montagu of having "skillfully trimmed the facts of anthropology to fit the Liberal propaganda line," and had ignored "striking evidence" of the different "intellectual capacity" of different races. He even implied that Montagu was part of a plot by the United Nations to defraud and delegitimize the United States.[27]

These were not uncommon sentiments in the pages of *National Review* at the time. Just a few months before Oliver was given the Montagu assignment, Buckley penned his infamous "Why the South Must Prevail" editorial in which he declared that southern whites, as the "advanced race," were "entitled to take such measures as are necessary to prevail, politically and culturally in areas where it does not predominate numerically." Buckley added for good measure—mirroring Oliver's views—that there were ample "statistics evidencing the median cultural superiority of White over Negro; but it is a fact that obtrudes, one that cannot be hidden by ever-so-busy egalitarians and anthropologists."[28]

But while Buckley and Oliver were close through the 1950s, by the end of the decade their relationship was increasingly tense, as Oliver began to move more into the orbit of Welch and the John Birch Society. Still, despite the tension between the two, both were careful not to strain their friendship to the breaking point—at least not yet. Oliver was even a guest of Buckley's on his yacht that summer for a cruise that lasted several weeks. Indeed, Oliver was a frequent guest on Buckley's yacht, the *Panic*. Garry Wills, one of Buckley's protégés at *National Review* in the 1950s and 1960s, recalled meeting Oliver on the *Panic*—Buckley had invited him specifically to meet Wills to see if the University of Illinois classics department might be a good place for Wills to pursue a PhD. ("We can give you a first-rate education," Oliver told Wills, "but you will not have the first-rate chances at a good position you would get by coming from an Ivy League school.")[29] Oliver was still very much part of the inner circle.

But Buckley increasingly regarded him as a renegade. Oliver had delivered a speech to the Congress of Freedom, a far-right political conference that was the brainchild of Willis Carto, in Colorado Springs, Colorado, on the dimensions of the international communist conspiracy and its implications for conservative strategy. It was in many respects a boilerplate speech, a repetition of a long list of conspiratorial litanies that could have been (and often were) found in New York State Economic Council literature from the 1930s. Communists had infiltrated every dimension of American life; millions of Americans were either communists or fellow travelers, the equivalent of "some twenty combat divisions on American soil." Communism is an inherently nihilistic philosophy, one that owes as much to John Dewey as to Karl Marx. Felix Frankfurter was "the most brilliant and dangerous immigrant ever imported into this country." Buckley wrote in a private letter to Oliver that "our disagreements here are . . . not trivial; they are critical." Oliver saw communist conspiracy everywhere; Buckley believed that it is "primarily the non-Communists, indeed anti-Communists—as for instance Dwight Eisenhower is an anti-Communist—who preside over our undoing."[30]

Buckley's critique of Oliver was substantively the same as his critique of Robert Welch and the John Birch Society, although in Oliver's case it was carefully worded both to be conciliatory and to demonstrate an intellectual respect for the classicist—a respect that Buckley clearly did not have for the retired candy manufacturer. Not everything was because of a secret, all-powerful international communist conspiracy. But there was less daylight between himself and Oliver than Buckley admitted.

Oliver did not "see the formal opposition between our views. . . . So far as I know, we both attribute the evils that we most deplore primarily (i.e. by a simplification that excludes a large number of forces that we regard as secondary or incidental)" to "*two* normally distinguishable forces, Communism and the more amorphous (or polymorphic), wide-spread, and seemingly diverse thing that we call Liberalism." For Oliver, liberalism *was* theoretically distinct from communism, but "obviously the Communist conspiracy can flourish only under the cover of Liberalism in a society whose intellectual and moral resources have been sapped by Liberalism." The real difference between their analyses, according to Oliver, was that Buckley believed time was on his side. Oliver did not. He noted that Friedrich Hayek had recently estimated "it will take at least forty years" to overturn liberal hegemony in the United States—and that was clearly *National Review*'s long-term project. But Oliver did not believe that America would survive—at least in a recognizable form—for much longer. "I think of Liberalism as some-thing that, like the bacilli of tuberculosis, will be found throughout Western society; the problem is keeping it under control by building up resistance to it in individuals."[31]

It was this sensibility—that time was running out for America and extreme times called for extreme measures—more than Oliver's racism or even antisemitism that ultimately led to the rupture of Oliver and Buckley's relationship. And it would propel Oliver to seek new political allies who seemed—at least for a time—to understand the fierce urgency of the moment.

Buckley had been broadly tolerant of Oliver's antisemitism throughout the 1950s. After the imbroglio over the *American Mercury*, however, he and the other editors at *National Review* became more squeamish about Oliver's views. In December 1959 Oliver submitted a pseudonymous book review of *Only in America,* a collection of essays by Harry Golden, a prominent Jewish journalist in Charlotte, North Carolina and a cheeky critic of the Jim Crow system. Oliver, of course, hated the book. Golden, who was born in Manhattan's Lower East Side, was in his opinion an interloper to the South whose liberal bromides—"the drums for the 'United Nations,' more 'Foreign Aid,' and the rest of the 'Liberal' line"—were really just "Jewish wisdom." Buckley winced; pseudonyms were not allowed at the magazine, it was a delicate subject, and Oliver's antisemitism was impossible to miss. The editorial staff was divided; Buckley's sister Priscilla and John Leonard both wanted to scupper the piece. Frank Meyer—himself Jewish—wanted to publish it. Bozell voted to turn it down. "I think it is good enough," he told Buckley, "if anyone else had written it. But I am sure it would be unwise for us to run anything by Revilo on the Jewish question. A persuasive case of anti-Semitism could be made out against N.R. by showing that we assigned a Jewish story to a demonstrable anti-Semite." The review went unpublished.[32]

The final rupture in Buckley and Oliver's professional relationship came a few days later, again over the issue of antisemitism. A *National Review* subscriber had written to Buckley earlier in the month asking why Revilo Oliver—who was publicly associated with Buckley's magazine—had an advertisement appear featuring his name and likeness in Conde McGinley's antisemitic broadsheet *Common Sense* back in October. (The ad was for a recording of Oliver's speech to the Congress of Freedom, which was being sold as an LP by an affiliate of *Common Sense.*) Buckley again took a conciliatory approach. He wrote a cordial letter to Oliver asking him to disavow *Common Sense* in writing that could be forwarded to other readers who wrote in about the matter. Buckley framed it as a way to protect the reputation of *National Review,* similar to the *Mercury* affair, which Oliver had disagreed with but had not—unlike Charles Willoughby—sided with Russell Maguire. Oliver initially deflected—"I have no knowledge of the phonograph record of which you speak"—but Buckley insisted on a formal letter. Even if—as Oliver claimed—the speech had been bootlegged (a common enough problem in the recording industry, as a generation of pop music stars would learn in the subsequent decade), Oliver was still in a position, "through no fault of our own, to embarrass your colleagues on *National Review.*" All Buckley wanted was a letter, "which I could send out to those who inquire about the anomaly," stating that Oliver would not "willingly associate with *Common Sense* or the *American Mercury.*" If Oliver could take that step, all would be forgiven. (Buckley also enclosed a $60 check for the review of Harry Golden's book, calling it "hilarious" but rejecting it for publication on the basis of the use of a pseudonym and the business with *Common Sense.*) Oliver grudgingly complied, producing a formal letter in which he said he wrote "only for periodicals whose literary standards and editorial policies I can in general approve. . . . I have thus far written only for *National Review, American Opinion,* and *Modern Age.*" He did not mention either *Common Sense* or the *American Mercury.* But by that point it was too late. In May, after an editorial meeting, *National Review* took Oliver's name off its masthead.[33]

Still, Buckley took pains to maintain the relationship, writing as friendly a note as possible, under the circumstances, to Oliver about the editorial board's decision. He sent another friendly inquiry a few weeks later, even suggesting that they meet when Oliver was visiting the Yale campus that summer. Oliver did not answer.

By the end of the year, Buckley was taking a harder line on the size and scope of the conservative coalition. In a letter to Robert Welch that October, he reiterated many of the points that he had made to Oliver: that there was a "critical difference" in the analysis that the John Birch Society made of the state of affairs in America versus that of *National Review*—namely, that *National Review* had never claimed that the Communist Party of the United States had "operative control" of the U.S. government—and that the Birchers had done grave damage to the conservative cause as a result. Buckley also continued to be stung by his falling-out with Oliver, whom he felt had treated him shabbily despite their close and affectionate relationship. "When I ventured to disagree with him on the question whether he should publicly associate with those people . . . he immediately struck me off his list of friends. In other words, it is all right for the crackpots to disagree with him, but it is not all right for me to do so."[34]

Buckley's views had evolved, but there was more than a degree of prevarication in his comments. After all, he had distanced himself from the *American Mercury* only a year earlier despite nearly a decade of warning signs, had disavowed the *Mercury* in a calculated way that was—until Russell Maguire wrote about it—decidedly *not* meant for public consumption, and had continued to maintain a close friendship and working relationship with Oliver despite full awareness of his views. Oliver defended the popular front approach in a response to Buckley—Welch had evidently forwarded him the letter—writing that "Conservatives cannot *afford* internecine quarrels." Buckley was too worried about what liberals thought of him and not worried enough about solidarity with anti-communists. "When an association in a Conservative cause has been made public and conspicuous, so that the rupture of the association would be publicly noticed and commented upon, there is a strong moral obligation to continue the association, even at the cost of personal sacrifice." (With a characteristic classical flourish, Oliver went on to compare conservative infighting to the "pious jackasses who were fighting in the streets of Constantinople" over doctrinal disputes while the Ottomans lay siege to the city in 1453).[35]

But this was, oddly enough, unfair to Buckley. He even conceded to Oliver, "I am aware of the dangers of my position when taken too far in the direction of an exquisite aloofness." He had no problem whatsoever—quite the contrary, as a matter of fact—with forming political alliances with segregationists and white supremacists, provided they were from the right stock. Buckley was, throughout his life, an unremitting elitist who was attracted to men—and they were almost always men—who had what he perceived to be good breeding and intelligence. Men like Oliver were acceptable, for a time, provided they were learned, erudite, witty—and above all, right. Buckley shared their commitment to global white supremacy and, in the case of Oliver, tolerated or found ways to minimize their antisemitism. But Buckley also valued loyalty. And if the loyalty of someone like Oliver shifted toward the Birchers, well, that was that.

Oliver was a member of the John Birch Society inner circle in the early 1960s. Not only did he sit on the society's National Council and was personally friendly with Welch, he also maintained close ties with other senior Birch leaders, including Slobodan Draskovich, an anti-communist Yugoslav exile with an academic background (Draskovich taught economics at the University of Belgrade until 1941) and Frank Cullen Brophy, one of the most prominent members of the Birch Society in Arizona and a major local backer of Barry Goldwater. Oliver was also a regular contributor to *American Opinion* throughout the first half of the 1960s. His February 1964 article "Marxmanship in Dallas," on John F. Kennedy's assassination, however, easily dwarfed his other output for the society in terms of notoriety.

The John Birch Society initially treated the Kennedy assassination gingerly given its outspoken opposition to the administration. The

December 1963 issue of *American Opinion* even had to be pulled from the shelves because, printed before November 22, it tore into JFK with the magazine's usual gusto. But as time passed—and especially as it became apparent that the assassin was not a far-right militant but rather a self-described Marxist who had defected to the Soviet Union in 1959—the old tone quickly returned. Oliver upped the stakes in his article, proposing several outlandish hypotheses for the assassination. Oswald was, of course, acting as an agent of the international communist conspiracy, but why did the conspiracy want to assassinate Kennedy? One possibility, according to Oliver, was that Kennedy, while obviously a member of the communist conspiracy, was killed because he was planning to "turn American" and betray his communist masters. Another possibility was that JFK was killed because he had failed to keep to the communist timetable for the internal subversion of America—Oliver noted that Kennedy had failed to muscle a civil rights bill through Congress, which the professor claimed was an integral part of communist strategy to foment a race war in America. Still another possibility was that Kennedy, despite his loyalty to the bosses in the Kremlin, was killed in order to smear the American right by blaming "right-wing extremists" for the assassination to promote a national uprising by the communist underground. (Oliver also theorized that other communist-infiltrated institutions in the United States—for instance, the CIA—could have killed Kennedy as part of an internal power struggle, although he deemed this unlikely.) Every one of Oliver's theories on the assassination took for granted that Kennedy was a closet communist. Kennedy had faked the Bay of Pigs invasion to solidify Castro's control over Cuba. He had secretly collaborated with Nikita Khrushchev to manufacture the Cuban missile crisis in order to ensure Democratic victory in the 1962 midterms. He coordinated with the communist Martin Luther King Jr. to gin up a race war in America. "So long as there are Americans," he portentously intoned in his original draft of the article, "his memory will be cherished with execration and loathing." *American Opinion* as a general rule did not exercise a significant amount of editorial discretion over its contributors, but this line was slightly too inflammatory even for that publication. It was changed to "his memory will be cherished with distaste" for the print run.[36]

The outcry was immediate. On February 11 the wire services picked up the story and Oliver's charges hit almost every major newspaper in America—among smaller newspapers, especially in the Midwest, the story even made the front page. As he was a founding member of the John Birch Society, sat on the National Council, and his piece appeared in the society's magazine, Oliver's analysis of the Kennedy assassination was widely interpreted by the press to be the society's official line. Oliver even drew international headlines—the French newspaper *Le Monde* picked up on the story a few days after it hit the American press, billing it as the "the assassination of President Kennedy as seen by the John Birch Society." David D. Henry, the president of the University of Illinois, quickly issued a statement condemning Oliver's views and referred the professor's conduct to the board of trustees. Oliver was fortunate, however; not only did he have tenure, but the University of Illinois was already under sanction by the American Association of University Professors because the school had terminated a biology professor's contract in 1960 after he wrote a letter to the editor in the student newspaper that endorsed, in principle, premarital sex. Although Oliver was a headache to the administration, widely loathed by his colleagues, and had embarrassed the university on an international scale, the board of trustees not only declined to pursue firing Oliver but ultimately decided not to institute any disciplinary proceedings whatsoever other than issue a statement deploring his views.[37]

As for the John Birch Society, Robert Welch described Oliver's article in the March edition of *American Opinion* as "superb commentary" and John H. Rousselot, a former California congressman and spokesman for the society, told reporters that while Oliver's theories were not the official views of the organization, he agreed with Oliver that Kennedy was killed for failing to adhere to the communists' timetable. Only in May did Welch begin to tepidly distance himself from article, admitting at a press conference that he "did not agree with some of his premises and some of his conclusions" but that nevertheless "we think the article was worth publishing."[38]

William F. Buckley, for his part, described Oliver's theories in his syndicated column as "disastrously wrongheaded, and I say this concerning the work of a man and a scholar for whom I have the highest affection and esteem." Buckley struck an almost mournful tone, reflecting disappointment at the depths of conspiracy theorizing to which his old friend had sunk, as well as an apparent sense of responsibility for politicizing Oliver in the first place. "Ten years ago the professor, who is the single most learned man I have ever met, knew nothing about, and cared nothing for, politics. Five years or so ago we were talking in the wee hours and I chided him on the ignorant political company he was beginning to keep. He replied with a twinkle: 'Bill, just remember you got me started.' " (Buckley characteristically closed his column on a bothsides-ist note, saying that "the smear of Kennedy has been noticed and condemned" but smears against Barry Goldwater were being ignored by the liberal media.)[39]

Oliver was not the only former colleague by whom Buckley was now embarrassed. George Lincoln Rockwell and his American Nazi Party were a minute faction on the American right in the 1960s. While the John Birch Society could claim tens of thousands of members, Rockwell never had more than a few hundred followers at any given time. But what the American Nazis lacked in numbers they made up for in media notoriety. Rockwell had an almost preternatural knack for attracting press coverage, and he understood how to create public spectacle in order to amplify the spread of his message. Rockwell established his headquarters in Arlington, Virginia—just across the Potomac from the U.S. capital—and hoisted a swastika flag over his suburban compound. He toured the South with a self-described "Hate Bus," parodying the 1961 Freedom Riders protesting segregated interstate bussing. His followers shadowed and occasionally attacked prominent civil rights leaders, including Martin Luther King Jr., who was punched in the face by one of Rockwell's "stormtroopers" at a meeting in Birmingham, Alabama in September 1962. Rockwell was a popular speaker on college campuses, often invited by liberal student groups eager to prove their absolute dedication to free speech by platforming neo-Nazis. Sometimes Rockwell's campus visits didn't go according to plan. At San Diego State College in March 1962, rather than listening to and politely rejecting Rockwell's views as student organizers had hoped, one Jewish student rushed the stage and punched the Nazi leader in the face after he suggested that the Holocaust was a myth. Buckley, who was notoriously litigious about suggestions that he harbored fascist sympathies, deeply resented any suggestion that Rockwell was in any respect part of his movement. When the *New York Times* mentioned Rockwell and *National Review* in the same article in April 1961—characterizing Rockwell as a far-right activist and *National Review* as the house magazine of "the Right-Wing organizations," Buckley wrote an angry letter insisting that "to suggest that we have anything to say interesting to the membership of any organization whose heroes are . . . men who rate highly among those most despised by the editors of National Review is, well, news unfit to print."[40]

Rockwell, for his part, took malicious glee in tweaking Buckley over their past association, peppering him with letters for years after their formal relationship ended. In December 1958, about two months after Rockwell came to public notoriety for embracing Nazism due to his alleged connection with the bombing of a synagogue in Atlanta, Rockwell wrote a mash note to Buckley. "Although I know you have either chosen the path of pretended ignorance of the Jewish question, or been forced to it by circumstances, I have such unbounded respect for your genius that I cannot simply dismiss you as a 'sell-out,' as do so many of us 'extremists.' " Buckley replied that he viewed Rockwell's embrace of Nazism "with deep regret" and that he "can only hope you will fight free of its influence." Rockwell wrote a one-word reply: "Boo."[41] Buckley, who publicly referred to Rockwell as a "maniac," nevertheless kept tabs on him—National Review even requested a review copy of Rockwell's autobiography from the American Nazi Party in 1961, which was turned down on the grounds that "your publisher once worked with Rockwell and is prominently mentioned in the book."[42] Indeed, Buckley was singled out for praise by Rockwell who, in recounting his first meeting with Buckley in New York in 1958, described the offices of National Review as possessing "more pulsating brain-power and genius than any place else on earth I have ever been," despite Buckley being "extremely cagey on the Jewish question."[43]

Rockwell, ever grateful for publicity of any kind, kept tabs on what Buckley had to say about him. He wrote to Buckley that August mocking his former employer for referring to him as a "maniac," saying that he eagerly awaited the "inevitable course of events to bring you gracefully to your conservative knees." Rockwell enjoyed tweaking the National Review crowd as pampered, effeminate dilettantes who had neither the physical nor moral courage of their convictions. "The 'nice' 'Conservatives' of the National Review stripe . . . see the idiocy of the . . . left [and] propose to 'fight the menace with crushing blows from their silken gloves across the cheek of the liberals and Communists.' " Still, Rockwell offered an olive branch of sorts—he predicted that once the communists and Jews, like the big bad wolf from Little Red Riding Hood, had knocked down Buckley's house, he would be welcomed to "the barbeque" prepared for the communists by the American Nazi Party.[44]

Rockwell took glee in provoking Buckley. In a "humorous" pamphlet entitled The Diary of Ann Fink that captioned pictures of Holocaust victims with antisemitic statements, Rockwell ran a disclaimer: "William F. Buckley had nothing to do with this book." But Rockwell also slavishly sought Buckley's approval. His letters to Buckley—he wrote nearly a dozen between 1958 and 1964—were a mixture of puerile sexualized insults ("I shall . . . pull down your fancy britches and give you a spanking you won't forget" in response to a suggestion by Buckley that Rockwell was working to advance the cause of international communism) and fawning praise (in the same letter Rockwell gushes over Buckley's "intellectual brilliance").[45]

What he wanted most of all was for Buckley to admit that Rockwell was right. In January 1964 Rockwell published a fictitious teleplay of a "debate" between himself, Buckley, and John Birch Society leader Robert Welch. In Rockwell's fantasy, Buckley was far too concerned with appealing to moderates and liberals (and their Jewish backers). Rockwell did, however, certainly understand that what Buckley hated above all else was being compared to the Nazis; in his teleplay, the enfant terrible of the right was reduced to hysterics upon being compared to National Socialism. Rockwell, meanwhile, insisted that "we need ALL of us . . . —Buckley, Welch . . . and Rockwell." "Nazism," Rockwell insisted, "is the most EXTREME form of 'right-wingism,' and right-wingers should have no more terror of being connected with it than liberals have of being connected with Communists." Just as liberalism and communism were on the same side in Rockwell's Manichean worldview, so too were conservatism and Nazism. At the end of Rockwell's fantasy, he links arms with Welch and Buckley and all three shout "Sieg Heil!"[46]

Buckley did not reciprocate Rockwell's gestures, but—as with Oliver—he tried to affect, if not a reconciliation, then at least an effort to break through to Rockwell and get him to question his commitment to Nazism. As far as Buckley was concerned, this was Christian charity. In 1964 Buckley interceded with a friend of his, Father Clark, a Catholic priest in Washington, DC, to talk to Rockwell and try to convince him to renounce his political path.[47]

It didn't work.

Rockwell wrote to Buckley after the meeting. He thanked Buckley, saying that "I enjoyed the talk with Father Clark more than I am able to put into words," and that being challenged on his Nazism "cleared up a lot of hazy areas in my thinking." But the meeting also "exposed what is incontrovertibly an impassable chasm between our two worlds." According to Rockwell, the main difference between them was not antisemitism or even Nazism, but rather utilitarianism: "In a life boat sinking from overcrowding, once death was imminent for ALL and I knew I could save some thereby, I would cast out the least likely to survive. Father Clark, as I presume you would, recoiled from this in horror." Still, there were some areas of agreement. Rockwell wrote that Clark *did* agree with him when Rockwell suggested that "we shall smite the enemy hip and thigh as did our brothers in Spain, when we get our chance." (Clark, for his part, reported to Buckley that Rockwell was a "Nazi of the true, vulgar, 1937 variety.")[48]

In many respects, Buckley's attempt to intercede on behalf of Rockwell's soul only further overinflated Rockwell's ego. After all, by 1964 Rockwell was one of the most hated men in America. He lived in squalid poverty in a ramshackle "barracks" in Arlington with a handful of unstable followers. Buckley was a wealthy, influential, and respected New York journalist, editor of a major right-wing magazine and writer of a nationally syndicated newspaper column, who had taken a personal interest in engaging with Rockwell's message. For Rockwell this was vindication, and he was eager to shoulder the burden. "As I see it, I shall provide you and the Father and others like you with a great comfort. I shall eagerly perform a dirty, messy task which MUST be done, down here in the gutter, soiling my soul, suffering the lonliness [*sic*] of ostracism and loss of family and the curses of most of the world, but finally delivering to men like the Father, and, perhaps, you, a world in which 'nice' people can once again exist." Rockwell was carrying the load for Buckley. "Please don't KICK me," he concluded, "as I walk past you with the load."[49]

Buckley may not have thought that Rockwell was shouldering the heavy burden of fighting the Jews and the Blacks in the streets for him, but Rockwell did serve a useful purpose for Buckley and many other figures on the right. He was a useful contrast in claiming respectability for one's own political views—no matter how vociferously one might oppose the civil rights movement or the national liberation movements in Asia, Africa, and Latin America, or how eagerly one might embrace biological racism through the legitimating "science" of intelligence studies, one could point to Rockwell and say, "At least I'm not a Nazi." Moreover, Rockwell also served as a foil to attack opponents to the left. Buckley defended the mass arrests of civil rights protestors in Birmingham, Alabama in April 1963—including Martin Luther King Jr., who was arrested on April 12 and penned his "Letter from Birmingham Jail" during his incarceration—on the grounds that the protestors were as provocative to southern whites as Rockwell and his Nazis were to

Jewish New Yorkers. "What we need to ponder is why the Southern community . . . are as hostile to these demonstrators as New Yorkers are to Rockwell," he wrote, concluding that such hostility was entirely reasonable given the civil rights movement's sights on the "jugular vein of Southern life."[50]

William F. Buckley might have been a stalwart defender of white supremacy in America, but still, he was no fool, and he understood, unlike Rockwell, that by the mid-1960s it was unproductive to openly wear one's racism on one's sleeve. One of Buckley's regular contributors to *National Review*, James J. Kilpatrick, the editor in chief of the major daily paper in Richmond, Virginia, was one of the architects of "massive resistance" to court-ordered desegregation in the state after *Brown v. Board of Education*. Kilpatrick had no reservations about proclaiming the innate supremacy of whites. In early 1964 he participated in a debate with James Farmer, the director of the Congress of Racial Equality, in which he insisted that "Negroes as a race were not equal to whites and that Negros had made no significant contributions to Western civilization." This was too far for Buckley—he wrote to Kilpatrick that he was "very queasy . . . about the superiority bit" in his remarks at the debate—but not only did *National Review* continue to regularly publish Kilpatrick, the magazine repeatedly ran stories affirming the biological existence of race and suggesting that Black people were biologically less intelligent than whites. As historian Edward Miller has pointed out, in the early 1960s *National Review* was more explicitly racist in its editorial line than *American Opinion*, despite Revilo Oliver being a major contributor to the latter. But while Buckley repeatedly defended publishing race science in his magazine, he differentiated himself from the Rockwells and Olivers by insisting that Christian charity precluded *treating* Blacks as inferior. "My position is that whatever are the differences among the races, *and I suppose they exist*, they are utterly immaterial when put alongside . . . their unity in the brotherhood of man" (emphasis mine). Here was a conservative vision of "race relations" for the rest of the twentieth century: a move away from the crude bigotry of a Rockwell or even the more urbane scientific racism of an Oliver, but a defense of existing racial hierarchies that eschewed an *explicit* commitment to white supremacy.[51]

In 1964, the political avatar of this new conservatism was Senator Barry Goldwater. With the backing of the *National Review* crowd, as well as fervent support from the right-wing grassroots, above all from the John Birch

Society, Goldwater handily beat moderate Nelson Rockefeller for the Republican nomination. Goldwater's triumph in the primary—despite his landslide loss to Lyndon Johnson in the general election in November—is widely seen, both by historians and the conservative movement itself, as a seminal moment in American politics, the moment when the conservative movement successfully made a bid for power over one of America's two major political parties. For someone like Robert Welch—or Buckley, for that matter—Goldwater's nomination righted the historic wrong of Dwight Eisenhower's nomination in 1952. But it was not just movement conservatives who were excited about Goldwater. Despite his Jewish ancestry on his mother's side, the overwhelming majority of openly antisemitic far-rightists openly supported his campaign. An Anti-Defamation League postmortem of the campaign found that only George Lincoln Rockwell explicitly disavowed Goldwater on the grounds of his Jewish ancestry (a group of Rockwell's followers heckled Goldwater at Washington National Airport in July)—but Gerald L. K. Smith declared that Goldwater, since he had been raised as a Christian in a Christian home, was " 'cleared' of being Jewish."[52] It became a sufficient problem for Goldwater during the election that he had to disavow some of his more radical support—after Dean Burch, the new conservative Republican National Committee chairman and William Miller, Goldwater's own running mate, said that the GOP would not reject the support of the Ku Klux Klan, Goldwater hastily issued a correction repudiating them.[53] But Goldwater did *not* condemn the John Birch Society, despite his private misgivings about Welch and some of his supporters. When Goldwater told a cheering crowd at the Republican National Convention in July that "extremism in defense of liberty is no vice," there was no doubt about to whom he referred.

Like Buckley, Goldwater was savvy enough to understand that defending white supremacy in the 1960s required a new language, one based not in openly stated assumptions of white racial superiority but couched in terms of personal liberties. Goldwater was outspoken in his opposition to the Civil Rights Act, signed into law by President Johnson a few weeks before the Republican convention, on the grounds that the act—particularly its prohibitions on discrimination in public accommodations and employment opportunities—was an unconstitutional, even authoritarian, attempt to regulate private business, although he also insisted that he was "unalterably opposed to discrimination of any sort."[54]

But while Goldwater—and, for that matter, much of the conservative press—was careful to couch his hostility to civil rights in more palatable language, the upshot of Goldwaterism was not lost on political opponents. The Black press was uniformly hostile to the Goldwater campaign—the *Chicago Defender* declared that "Goldwater's extremist pronouncement is an invitation to violence and race riots," and that "Goldwaterism and fascism are now synonymous." Roy Wilkins, the head of the NAACP, compared Goldwater supporters to Hitler's brownshirts.[55] Even moderate Black Republicans loathed Goldwater—Jackie Robinson, who had by the early 1960s become one of the GOP's most prominent Black leaders, wrote in 1962 that a Goldwater candidacy would mean "farewell forever to the Negro."[56] This was not an uncommon attitude. The Goldwater campaign seemed to validate liberals' worst fears of the prospect of a new American fascism.

Ironically, the most sophisticated analysis of the fascistic potential of Goldwater came not from an American but from a Polish Marxist economist named Michał Kalecki. It was, of course, the standard line in the Soviet bloc to refer to Goldwater as a fascist or a Nazi; even Nikita Khrushchev had done so at a congress in Warsaw in July, when he compared the spectacle at the Republican National Convention to the Nuremberg rallies.[57] But Kalecki took a more sophisticated approach. He noted that the economic basis of Goldwater's support came from a "new" group of capitalists with " 'young,' 'dynamic' concerns" who rejected the New Deal regulatory state because of their naïve belief in the self-regulatory power of laissez-faire capitalism. More important, Kalecki linked the Goldwater phenomenon to the political crisis over Algeria in France, noting that what linked Goldwater and the right-wing terrorists in the Organisation armée secrète was that their "main driving force . . . is the potential emancipation of the oppressed nations, or decolonization in the broad sense." Goldwater, then, and his political allies— be they the "responsible" conservatives of *National Review* or the rightists of the John Birch Society—were unified by their fundamental commitment to preserving the global racial and political hierarchy.[58]

Goldwater lost to Johnson in one of the most lopsided elections in American history, pulling in only 38.5 percent of the vote to Johnson's 61.1 percent. But despite his landslide loss, Goldwater still managed to win fifty-two electoral votes—Arizona, of course, voted for its native son, but so too did Louisiana, Mississippi, Alabama, Georgia, and South Carolina.

Goldwater might have eschewed crude racism on the campaign trail, but white voters certainly understood that Goldwater was the man to vote for if you were for white supremacy.

Still, it was clear that while enthusiasm from the right-wing grassroots had been crucial to securing the nomination for Goldwater, groups that had been pegged as fascistic during the Second Brown Scare—above all the John Birch Society—were now a liability in expanding the conservative electoral coalition. In October 1965 *National Review* ran a special issue devoted to criticisms of the John Birch Society, ranging from its penchant for conspiracy theorizing ("Liberalism—Not Conspiracy," intoned Frank Meyer) to its initial opposition to the American escalation in Vietnam. Goldwater wrote a supportive letter to the magazine: "I hope that you will keep up what I consider to be reasonable discussions of the Birch Society." This was yet another seminal moment in the self-narrative of the American conservative movement, when principled, thoughtful, and responsible conservatives purged the "kooks" of the John Birch Society once and for all from their ranks. But the genesis of the "purge" lay less in high-minded principles and more in pragmatic calculation of the limits of a Birch-dominated political coalition. In June Neal Freeman wrote an article for *National Review* that repeated the favorite chorus of Merwin Hart and John T. Flynn from twenty years before: conservatives were being "smeared" by liberals alleging they were sympathetic to the John Birch Society. Goldwater, in his letter to *National Review,* urged Birch Society members who wished to contribute to the growing conservative movement within the Republican Party to leave Welch's organization in order to reassure nervous moderates. That the "purge" was mainly based on cold political calculation robs the purge narrative of some of its mythic power—but, more important, the John Birch Society, its members, and fellow travelers did not simply disappear because of some harsh words from Buckley's typewriter.[59]

Nor, for that matter, was the John Birch Society the only image problem American conservatism faced in 1965. In May 1965 the New Jersey State Republican Committee told its Young Republicans organization to clean house after a conservative group within the Young Republicans, who called themselves the Rat Finks, were overheard singing antisemitic and racist songs at a state convention in Wildwood, New Jersey and again at a national Young Republican conference in Miami. One song, set to the tune of "Jingle Bells," had pointedly offensive lyrics:

Riding through the Reich
In a Mercedes-Benz
Shooting all the kikes, making lots of friends
Rat-tat-tat-tat-tat
Mow the bastards down
Oh what fun it is to have the
Nazis back in town.

None of the Rat Finks were Birchers. In fact, the head of the Rat Finks, Richard Plechner, was a founding member of Young Americans for Freedom and had participated in the conference at Buckley's Sharon, Connecticut estate where the group was created. He claimed that the songs were sung in jest, poking fun at the smears of conservatives as equivalent to Nazis. Plechner lost his reelection bid as the head of the New Jersey Young Republicans as a result of the fallout of the scandal, but told reporters that the *real* reason he lost was because John Birch Society loyalists forced him out. Plechner's opponent, Clark Allen, was not a Bircher (although he did have support from some Birchers in his election bid) and in any event his political career was essentially undamaged from the episode—he later became a superior court judge.[60]

Even taking the excuses of the Rat Finks at face value—boyish all-American pranks and jocularity that simply got out of hand, the episode—and the sterling careers that most of the Rat Finks would enjoy in New Jersey Republican politics going forward—was as good an indication as any that flirting with the aesthetics of fascism was a-okay as long as you could plausibly deny that you meant it. The Anti-Defamation League, which had built a considerable apparatus in countermobilizing against the John Birch Society and other radical right-wing groups, was skeptical of Buckley's "purge" of the right. One staffer wrote in a memo analyzing the October issue of *National Review* that "the 'ideological blur' between Extreme Conservatives and the Radical Right . . . still exists and a real house-cleaning has not yet been attempted on the right. . . . It would take years of effort to separate the conservatives from the Radicals, and a lot more than articles in 'National Review,' resolutions, and mere words."[61]

CHAPTER SEVEN

The Birth of the White Power Movement

AS FAR AS WILLIAM F. BUCKLEY JR. was concerned, George Wallace was no conservative. The Alabama governor appeared on Buckley's TV program *Firing Line* on January 24, 1968 in a debate moderated by C. Dickerman Williams. Wallace was flirting with a presidential run and had been courting the support of right-wing voters. Buckley was determined to expose Wallace to conservatives as a fraud. The governor, evidently unaware that the program was meant to be a debate, appeared rattled as Buckley tore into him as a country-fried New Dealer and populist who had voted for John F. Kennedy and enthusiastically took federal dollars as governor of Alabama. Wallace was appealing to conservatives "as an imposter." Wallace was merely using the "rhetoric of conservatism" to appeal to racial grievances. Wallace's appearance on *Firing Line* followed a series of attacks on the Alabama governor in *National Review* going back nearly two years. James J. Kilpatrick, the magazine's resident southerner and arch-segregationist, wrote a profile of Wallace in 1967 dripping with condescension, although he acknowledged that his appeal "ought not to be taken lightly." Buckley was spooked enough by the Wallace movement, which even he publicly speculated might be "fascist," to dedicate another *Firing Line* program to debunking it. In April Leander Perez, a Wallace surrogate from Louisiana, made an appearance opposite Buckley, smoking a comically oversized cigar, showing every one of his seventy-six years on Earth on his face, and repeating John Birch Society talking points about the total infiltration of all elements of American society by international communism. The studio audience laughed at him.[1]

The message was clear: the Wallace movement was not only not "authentically" conservative—look at how Wallace supported Franklin D. Roosevelt!—but was for rubes, illiterates, and old people. *Real* conservatism in the United States was youthful, dynamic, well educated, and had no place for crazies, kooks, and southern-fried rednecks. Gone, evidently, was even a hint of the old popular front approach to the American right. Wallace bitterly maintained that Buckley thought of himself as the "messiah" of American conservatism, sitting in judgment on high at the *National Review* offices in New York determining who was and who was not authentically conservative.[2]

And yet Buckley, for all of his importance in conservative politics, was not the pope of American conservatism. He was not able to excommunicate renegades at will and demand they pay indulgences to be let back into the true faith. The American right was never a strictly regimented and organized hierarchy like the Catholic Church. Rather, American conservatism resembled the fragmentation of the Protestant churches, with various factions and sects vying among themselves over who was "truly" conservative. George Wallace called himself a conservative, and while many pundits on the right dismissed his self-appellation as a cynical attempt to win the votes of *their* movement, plenty on the right embraced the Alabama governor as a true brother. The John Birch Society continued to call itself a conservative group; so, too, did Willis Carto's Liberty Lobby, even as it skirted ever closer to explicit neo-Nazism by the end of the decade. Still, there were some on the right for whom the label "conservative" was increasingly a term of derision. George Lincoln Rockwell was dead—assassinated by one of his own followers in 1967—but his philosophy of militant white nationalism as the spearhead of the American right continued to influence his followers. But white nationalist leaders in the late 1960s and early 1970s—ranging from Carto to Revilo Oliver to William Luther Pierce, Rockwell's successor as head of the American Nazi movement—increasingly rejected Rockwell's fantasy of being vindicated by the conservative movement.

Instead, Oliver and Pierce collaborated together in the creation of the National Youth Alliance (NYA) from the youth wing of George Wallace's failed 1968 bid for president. The NYA sought to cultivate the next generation of white nationalist leaders, particularly by appealing to right-wing college students disgusted with the tumultuous atmosphere on campuses during the late 1960s and early 1970s. Conservatism had lost its appeal; there was little apparently left to *conserve* in the late 1960s and early 1970s, with the entire racial, sexual, and biological order in the United States being apparently overturned by communists, feminists, and Black nationalists— and the European colonial empires being rolled back by communist-backed anti-colonial movements overseas. *Conservatism* had failed because it had failed to preserve explicit white supremacy.[3] The first generation of the "white power" movement—a term coined by Rockwell in 1966—were self-consciously apostate conservatives, unwilling to make even modest concessions to the civil rights movement and committed to an understanding of whiteness that excluded American Jews.

But despite the mutual antagonisms between these various factions of the right in the late 1960s and early 1970s, and increasing differences in strategies and tactics, mainstream conservatives and the far right continued to draw from a common set of social and political assumptions and, crucially, were competing for the same common pool of support. Buckley felt it necessary to take down Wallace because, as he admitted on *Firing Line,* Wallace was "appealing to people to whom Mr. Goldwater appealed, and Mr. Reagan appeals."[4] Just who was a "conservative" remained very much contested.

One of the biggest dividing lines on the American right in the late 1960s was how to approach the question of race. There has been an explosion of scholarship since the 2000s on the centrality of white supremacy in American politics and the ways in which white supremacy undergirded liberal, conservative, and even radical politics throughout the twentieth century; the observation that the vast majority of the various factions of the American right in the late 1960s were committed to white supremacy is correspondingly banal.[5] However, there were growing fissures among conservatives between those who were committed to an *explicit* defense of white supremacy as a first principle, predicated on the biological reality of race, and those content with an *implicit* defense of white supremacy. This did not necessarily mean rejecting racial essentialism—*National Review,* for instance, continues, as of this writing in 2023, to publish defenses of race/ IQ science—but it did mean downplaying and de-emphasizing explicit racism, often by cultivating or co-opting Black conservatives as instrumental figures. The historian Heather Hendershot, who wrote the definitive history of Buckley's *Firing Line* program, noted that by contrasting his own brand of urbane, apparently race-neutral conservatism—at least to the TV audience of *Firing Line*—to the crude bigotry of caricatures like Wallace and Perez, Buckley was able to shore up his reputation as a conservative maverick, even moderate, to liberal audiences.[6] (It also helped Buckley erase the stain of the "Why the South Must Prevail" editorial.) But Buckley was not the only conservative to adopt such an approach in the late 1960s.

The John Birch Society's views on race were complicated. On the one hand, Robert Welch publicly and repeatedly disavowed anti-Black bigotry, insisting that his organization did not discriminate by color, race, or creed, so long as one was a dedicated anti-communist. And indeed, there were African American members of the John Birch Society, among both the leadership cadres (notably conservative journalist George Schuyler) and rank-and-file activists. On the other hand, large swaths of the JBS's membership were avowed racists, including people (like Oliver) in leadership positions. The John Birch Society opposed the civil rights movement as a communist plot, and correspondingly threw its weight behind segregationist politicians like George Wallace. And despite whatever proclamations Welch made about the openness of the Birch Society to Americans from all walks of life, even a cursory examination of literature and film produced by the society—and the JBS was nothing if not prolific with educational materials—clearly shows that the organization itself considered the prototypical John Birch Society member to be a middle-class white professional.[7]

Welch, like most prominent figures on the right, thought the Supreme Court's decision in *Brown v. Board of Education* was a disastrous overreach. But Welch was also *to the left* of *National Review* on segregation. His September 1956 essay in *One Man's Opinion*—the immediate precursor to *American Opinion*—entitled "A Letter to the South: On Segregation," argued that *"formal* segregation"—meaning the legal structure of the Jim Crow South—would "eventually be abandoned everywhere in the South" and that this was in fact a desirable outcome. The races would still be separate, of course, but this would be from the natural "voluntary" tendency of whites and Blacks, well within their rights as Americans, to associate with whomever they prefer.[8] Paternalistic and condescending as the future John Birch Society leader's stance was, he notably did not defend the necessity of the "advanced race" taking whatever steps might be necessary to defend its hegemonic position in the South, as Buckley did in *National Review* a year later.

Many commentators and analysts from the early 1960s who were otherwise hostile to Welch and the John Birch Society were amazed to find that the formal leadership of the organization did not, as a matter of course, explicitly center racism as part of its political program, at least initially. Scholars of the John Birch Society have agreed; one recent history of the group concluded that "the Birch Society was not formed in opposition to the desegregation process"; rather, its raison d'être stemmed from its "anticommunist, antiliberal conservatism."[9] In fact, Welch's writings on the subject in the 1950s show—in notable contrast to Buckley—a disinterest in the race question altogether, except insofar as racial tension advanced the cause of international communism. Welch blamed *Brown v. Board of Education*—which had been made possible, of course, by the communist-influenced Supreme Court under Chief Justice Earl Warren—for inflaming race relations; the civil rights movement, by pressing southern whites on political and economic rights, was tipping the South toward civil war. And this is what the communists wanted.

Because, of course, the communists secretly controlled the civil rights movement.

By the mid-1960s the JBS was making a conscious effort to highlight Black voices and Black faces in its propaganda materials. These figures were almost uniformly Black ex-communists who had turned against the party in the 1940s and 1950s. Two prominent Black speakers were featured in *Anarchy U.S.A.*, an infamous JBS filmstrip produced after the Watts uprising. The thesis of *Anarchy U.S.A.* was straightforward: the international communist conspiracy was behind the civil rights movement. Their strategy, as outlined by Vladimir Lenin, was to foment division in American society along racial lines until open warfare broke out, then use the resulting chaos to seize power and Sovietize America. Most of the leaders of the civil rights movement were in on the conspiracy; grassroots civil rights activists, although perhaps not communists themselves, were functionally serving their goals. "The civil rights movement, as we know it today," the [white] narrator solemnly intoned, "is simply part of a worldwide movement organized and directed by communists to enslave all of mankind." For good measure, the film explicitly equated the American civil rights movement to the communist revolutions in Cuba and China, and above all to the Algerian independence war, underscoring Michał Kalecki's thesis about the common features of the French and American movements.[10]

To underscore the point, *Anarchy U.S.A.* featured two Black ex-communists to assure the film's viewers that the civil rights movement was both communistic and actually harmful to Black people. Leonard Patterson joined the Communist Party USA in New York City in 1928, at the age of twenty-two. Originally from North Carolina, Patterson was selected by the CPUSA leadership in 1931 to attend the Lenin School in Moscow.[11] This was an important initiative as far as the party was concerned. Black party members had been sent to Moscow before, but hitherto had primarily studied at the Communist University of the Toilers of the East, a school comprised primarily of communists from the European colonial empires and Soviet Central Asia. Europeans (and white Americans) were sent to the more prestigious Lenin School. Patterson and the some dozen other Black communists sent on the trip were essentially there to integrate the commanding heights of the Communist International.[12] The experience was less than auspicious. The white American communists in the delegation repeatedly demeaned and humiliated their Black comrades, particularly if it was known or suspected that they had been fraternizing with Russian women, who were implicitly understood to be fellow whites (and who were also denigrated by the white American communists as whores and race traitors for fraternizing with Black men).[13] Tired of the party's racism, Patterson left the party in 1937 and by the 1950s, he was not only an eager collaborator with HUAC, he was a star witness at a hearing in Baton Rouge that sought to blame the Communist Party for the civil rights movement, even going out of his way to ingratiate himself to the arch-segregationist Louisiana state senators, saying that he opposed the Communist Party line of Black self-determination.[14]

The other Black ex-communist featured in *Anarchy U.S.A.* was Julia Brown, a self-described former FBI agent who had infiltrated the Communist Party USA at the behest of J. Edgar Hoover. In fact, Brown was not an FBI agent but rather an FBI informant. She was not, and had never been, employed by the Federal Bureau of Investigation but had taken it upon herself to infiltrate the local chapter of the Communist Party in Cleveland, passing information to the FBI on a voluntary basis. The National Association for the Advancement of Colored People denounced Brown as a fraud and huckster for misrepresenting herself, and even J. Edgar Hoover testified in front of a House subcommittee that Brown was not in fact an FBI agent and that her claims were an "improper attempt to capitalize on the name of the FBI."[15]

Nor was Brown the only Black woman affiliated with the John Birch Society to make such a claim: Lola Belle Holmes, a resident of St. Louis, Missouri, also billed herself as a former FBI agent on the John Birch speaking circuit. (Holmes, in addition to repeating the standard Birch line that the civil rights movement was a communist front, claimed that the 1963 March on Washington was originally her idea and that it had been stolen by Bayard Rustin and A. Philip Randolph.) The message from prominent Black Birchers was consistent: the civil rights movement was a communist front, and opposition to the movement by white Birchers did not make them racists. Besides, as Holmes assured an overwhelmingly white audience at a high school in New Bedford, Massachusetts in 1967, Black people "as a race have done more to retard our progress than any white man has ever done."[16] Patterson, Brown, and Holmes were featured prominently on the Birch Society's lecture circuit—not, significantly, to address Black or white southern audiences, but white northern ones. The point was not to solicit Black support for the John Birch Society, but to convince skeptical northern whites that the John Birch Society was *not* a racist organization.

The Birchers took a similar stance regarding antisemitism. From its very beginnings, the John Birch Society had been dogged by allegations that it was antisemitic, something that Robert Welch strenuously denied. Yet not only were prominent Birch leaders—not least of whom was founding member Revilo Oliver—outspoken antisemites, there were a considerable number of openly antisemitic Birchers at the local chapter level. The Anti-Defamation League, although it hesitated to label the Birch Society as an antisemitic organization outright, described the group in its publications as encouraging an atmosphere of tolerance toward antisemitism, and prominently profiled the group in its 1964 publication *Danger on the Right*. The combined weight of Goldwater's landslide loss as well as the criticism from *National Review* on the right and from the ADL on the left was sufficient to prompt Welch to opt for an image change. In February 1966 Samuel Blumenfeld, a senior Jewish Birch leader, formed, with Welch's approval, the Jewish Society of Americanists (JSA), essentially a Jewish front organization of the Birch Society. By creating an explicitly Jewish pro-Birch group, the JBS hoped to deflect some of the ADL's criticism and—as with its use of

Black Birchers to rebut charges of racism—reassure Gentile Birchers that the organization was not antisemitic.[17]

That was a tall order as long as Revilo Oliver remained a leader of the organization. In July Oliver gave a speech at the annual New England Rally for God, Family, and Country that drew widespread condemnation as antisemitic. Drawing from the ideas of the far-right political philosopher Francis Parker Yockey, Oliver obliquely criticized the foundational premise of the Birch Society—the existence of an overarching international communist conspiracy—by insisting on the biological reality of race, and darkly warning that "we, the white men of the West, who were the undisputed masters of the world a few years ago, may . . . become extinct." Oliver articulated a mid-twentieth-century version of the twenty-first-century "Great Replacement" theory—that immigration and exploding birth rates in the Third World meant that soon, European and American whites would be overwhelmed by people of color. He suggested that the civil rights movement, if it were allowed to attain real power, would end in a Haitian-style massacre of the white population, and he openly flirted with genocidal rhetoric directed toward the people of Africa and Asia. He predicted that in the near future that "wars of extermination" would be waged "on a scale and of an intensity that your mind will, at present, refuse to contemplate. The only question will be what peoples will be among the exterminated." The speech was, in and of itself, less antisemitic than committed to biological racism, but he did at one point reference a Jewish conspiracy going back to the fifth century AD—and Oliver's views on the Jews were an open secret going back to his days at *National Review*.[18]

The speech was the final straw for Oliver. For the past six months the JSA had been dedicated to attempting to disprove the ADL's charge that the Birch Society created a tolerant atmosphere for antisemitism, and Oliver's continued presence as a prominent Birch leader was more than an embarrassment. It was a political liability. As early as April Blumenfeld was pressuring Welch to expel Oliver from the organization after it came out that Oliver was scheduled to appear at a meeting of the Congress for Freedom in Shreveport, Louisiana alongside other prominent antisemites. Blumenfeld warned Welch that "when the ADL discovered Oliver's commitment to participate in the meeting, it would have disastrous consequences for both the Birch Society and the Jewish Society of Americanists." Welch demurred. A month later at a meeting in Chicago, Welch told JSA leaders that he knew

Oliver was an antisemite and had urged him repeatedly to tone down his views, but that the professor had remained recalcitrant. When Blumenfeld suggested that Oliver be expelled from the society, Welch again demurred. Oliver had "many supporters within the organization, and many Birchers were in accord with Oliver's views about the Jews." Only after Oliver's speech in New England did Welch take action, and only after the ADL publicly charged that Oliver's statements were antisemitic. Blumenfeld and other JSA leaders gave Welch an ultimatum after the ADL's public statement: either get rid of Oliver, or they would resign and the JSA would dissolve. Even then, Welch tried to defend Oliver, telling Blumenfeld "There were a lot of good patriotic Americans in the Birch Society who don't like the Jews or the Negroes and we simply can't get rid of them. . . . They are basically good people." Eventually, though, Welch succumbed to the JSA's pressure, largely because he calculated the society's public image would be harmed more by the JSA resigning than by Oliver doing so. Initially, he attempted to persuade Oliver to resign quietly, but unsurprisingly Oliver proved to be vindictive. He publicly bashed Welch as a sellout and a puppet of Jewish interests. While Oliver seldom, if ever, said anything negative in his private correspondence about William F. Buckley, he derided "the Welcher," as he dubbed him, for the rest of his life.[19]

At least some militant white nationalists saw themselves as embodying the ideals and principles upon which the John Birch Society was originally founded. Revilo Oliver, in his correspondence to his political admirers in the late 1960s and early 1970s, repeatedly expressed the belief that the original mission of the Birch Society was to organize a clandestine network of right-wing activists and supporters to mobilize in an insurgency if and when the communists seized total control of the state. Oliver wrote in 1970 that, at the 1958 meeting that established the Birch Society, he and Welch discussed contingency plans that included the "possibility that it would be necessary for the Society to go underground."[20] Perhaps unsurprisingly, Oliver was an admirer of the anonymously authored 1959 novel *The John Franklin Letters*, which envisioned a future in which the communists, under the aegis of the United Nations, abrogate American sovereignty and seize control of the country. As the communists commence a race war against the American public, with most whites in the cities and suburbs either killed outright or deported as slave labor to Africa and Asia, a small group of American patriots band together to form the Rangers, a paramilitary group that

eventually overthrows the communists through a guerrilla war that culminates in a 1956-style mass uprising against the regime.[21] The book
was popular among Birchers and favorably reviewed in *American Opinion*
(by Oliver, no less) as a chilling warning "which incidentally conveys information about techniques of survival that [the reader] may need to know
someday soon."[22]

Still, there were limits to Birch militancy. Robert DePugh, a Missouri-
based Bircher, was expelled from the society after he founded the Minutemen,
an underground militia movement (that drew, consciously or not, on the
model of the Rangers in the *John Franklin Letters*) pledged to violently oppose
the looming communist takeover of the United States.[23] But while the
Minutemen were condemned by the national office of the John Birch Society,
many rank-and-file members were sympathetic to that group's goals. An
Anti-Defamation League report from a Birch Society bookstore in New
England in January 1966 noted that customers there were openly discussing
stockpiling arms and ammunition.[24] Certainly Oliver was not the only
former Bircher who felt that the society was all talk and no action when it
came to the breakdown in social order in the tumult of the late 1960s. Donna
Allegro, a University of Denver graduate student, conservative activist (she
was a member of the Intercollegiate Studies Institute and the recipient of the
Richard M. Weaver Fellowship), and Birch Society member, wrote to Oliver
in 1970 complaining that the society's solution to "starvation, looting,
rioting, and in short the beast coming out in men" was a mere "educational
program." "Frankly if the situation is this bad then why should I send my
money to [the John Birch Society headquarters in] Belmont?"[25]

The John Birch Society did not officially endorse any candidate for president
in 1968. Certainly Hubert Humphrey was anathema, given his ties to organized labor and his support for the civil rights movement. But Richard
Nixon, the Republican candidate, had relatively lukewarm support. Many
conservatives preferred Ronald Reagan—although, notably, Buckley
endorsed Nixon in the primary as a move to block the liberal Nelson
Rockefeller from winning the nomination—but while the California
governor had run a reasonably strong primary campaign in the spring, he
was unable to overtake Nixon.[26] But, in a fear Buckley expressed on *Firing
Line* in January, George Wallace's third-party run on the American
Independent Party ticket threatened to peel off conservative voters from

Nixon in the general election, potentially keeping a liberal Democrat in the White House. Many Birchers—and those farther to the right—were sympathetic to Wallace. *American Opinion* ran back-to-back profiles of Nixon and Wallace in September 1968: Nixon was portrayed as a scheming opportunist who sold out to the liberals the moment he accepted Eisenhower's vice presidential nod in 1952. Wallace, by contrast, was *"the only candidate in the race who is genuinely, outspokenly anti-Communist"*[27] Buckley might have dismissed him as a poseur and—*quelle horreur!*—a *populist,* but Wallace's schtick could captive an audience more rapturously than Buckley's affected Ivy League mannerisms. Gonzo journalist Hunter S. Thompson would compare Wallace's charisma at rallies to a rock concert performance; Wallace's campaign appearances in 1968 were some of the most emotionally intense (and violent) of any presidential candidate in the twentieth century, not equaled until Donald Trump's 2016 run nearly fifty years later.[28]

Wallace consistently denied throughout the campaign that he was running as the candidate of segregation, extremism, or racism—rather, he was a "states' rights" man who supported law and order. Some on his campaign actually believed this—Tom Turnipseed, Wallace's campaign manager, later told an interviewer that he was attracted because Wallace was "anti-establishment . . . in a way that appealed to the average person in the South, the little guy." Turnipseed was a segregationist—he helped set up a series of segregation academies in South Carolina after *Brown v. Board*—but even he blanched at the character of Wallace supporters he met on the campaign trail. In Webster, Massachusetts, a small town on the Connecticut border, he met a bartender who asked him, "Now, when George Wallace is elected president, he's going to line up all the niggers and kill them, isn't he?" Turnipseed recalled, "It kind of got to me to know that these people really felt that way, that they wanted to kill Black people." (Turnipseed later broke with segregationism and became a civil rights lawyer.)[29]

Wallace's choice for vice president, retired U.S. Air Force general Curtis LeMay, also raised eyebrows, particularly when LeMay suggested, at the press conference in which he was introduced as Wallace's running mate, that he would support the use of nuclear weapons in Vietnam, waxing poetically in front of the cameras that if he had the choice between being stabbed by a rusty knife or dying in a nuclear blast, he'd chose the bomb. (This prompted Wallace to bring the press conference to a rapid conclusion.) But LeMay had his admirers, too. One supporter proudly wrote to the general calling him a "living legend" and opining that the vice presidency would be a "fine job for a man of your will and your efficiency." The author, Harald Friedrich, identified as a Wehrmacht veteran who had served with Rommel in the Afrika Korps.[30]

The Wallace campaign, in no small part *because* it was anarchic, chaotic, and poorly managed, appeared to offer new opportunities for right-wing organizing. Unlike more cerebral conservative groups like Young Americans for Freedom, which focused on organizing college students and professionals, particularly from elite backgrounds, Wallace appealed to working-class whites fed up with urban unrest and long-haired college hippies—the "hardhats" who would notoriously attack an antiwar protest in Manhattan in May 1970. Unlike the Humphrey or Nixon campaigns, the Wallace campaign had no dedicated student wing. Instead, there was Youth for Wallace, which sought to organize young working-class whites along with students and professionals. It was not particularly successful on either score, but it was nevertheless savvy in understanding that white working-class youths and lower-middle-class white college students shared many of the same political grievances and the same political antipathies, particularly toward the campus left.

The organizing forces behind Youth for Wallace were actual young people. John Acord, a twenty-five-year-old conservative activist with a variety of connections to Willis Carto's Liberty Lobby and affiliated groups, was the major organizational entrepreneur of the group. Acord had a lengthy background in right-wing politics. He was the titular head of the American Southern Africa Council, a lobbying group that supported aid to Ian Smith's white-minority government in Rhodesia, as well as the national field director of the American Victory Force, a pro-Vietnam War group co-organized by twenty-six-year-old Vietnam veteran Richard Barrett.[31]

Barrett was involved in American Independent Party politics—in the spring of 1968 he embarked on a speaking tour across the South in front of local Independent Party audiences—and was an outspoken Wallace supporter in his adopted hometown of Jackson, Mississippi. But Barrett was not a native of the South. Born in New York City in 1943, he served in Vietnam as an infantryman after graduating from Rutgers University, being wounded twice in combat. By his own account, his experience in Vietnam radicalized him. After returning to the U.S., Barrett became a self-identified "racist." He returned his college diploma to Rutgers in protest of the university's continued employment of the historian Eugene Genovese, at the time an outspoken Marxist and critic of the American war in Vietnam.[32] Barrett popped up on the FBI's radar after moving to Mississippi in 1966 and attempting to build connections with local Ku Klux Klan chapters—he told FBI agents sent to interview him that he had chosen to move to Mississippi specifically because he had been impressed by the commitment of Mississippi whites to racism and segregation. American Victory Force became a vanity project for Barrett after moving to Jackson. He frequently organized small pro–Vietnam War demonstrations in Jackson, drawing perhaps five dozen supporters brandishing anti-communist signs, burning Viet Cong and United Nations flags, and calling for Student Nonviolent Coordinating Committee leader Stokely Carmichael to be deported. At one such rally, Barrett led a group of supporters to the steps of the Mississippi statehouse to place a wreath to commemorate Theodore Bilbo, the late arch-segregationist senator. Barrett's ambition to build a militant, pro-war, and segregationist organization hit a wall, however, because the local Klan organizations in Mississippi considered him "a nut" who "could not keep his mouth shut."[33]

Acord, on the other hand, although a native southerner, had moved to California at an early age and, before throwing in with Wallace, was a "paid-up" member of the Young Republicans. Acord was precisely the kind of conservative whom Buckley tried to dissuade on *Firing Line* from supporting Wallace—after Nixon beat out Reagan for the GOP nomination, Acord said he would try to influence Reagan delegates to switch their support to Wallace.[34]

Youth 114 or Wallace (YFW) did not approach the political power of the Young Republicans or even Young Americans for Freedom, but it did attract right-wing dissidents on campuses across America. Acord claimed that 6,322 students had signed up for the group by September 1968, with active chapters at NYU, Ohio State, UCLA, Dartmouth, St. John's University, Creighton, Kentucky, and North Carolina State.[35] It is difficult to characterize the politics of the typical campus member of Youth for Wallace. They were overwhelmingly male and universally white, but their political backgrounds ran the gamut. The University of Maryland student newspaper profiled a number of YFW members during the campaign; the head of the YFW chapter there, a twenty-one-year-old senior named Tom Brown, blasted the Democrats and Republicans for being out of touch and undemocratic (he claimed that if there had been party plebiscites before either convention, Eugene McCarthy and Nelson Rockefeller would have been the nominees). He supported Wallace's American Independent Party because it was "the true conservative party. It is representative of the populist and American working class philosophy." Another Wallace supporter at Maryland, twenty-year-old Michael Burke, initially supported Robert F. Kennedy but switched to Wallace after RFK's assassination. (When questioned about whether or not the Wallace campaign was racist, Burke candidly admitted, "Personally, I'm prejudiced.") Youth for Wallace ran ads in at least twenty college newspapers in the run-up to the election, but—as the vice president of Youth for Wallace at the University of Kentucky admitted—it was an uphill struggle to organize college students for Wallace, especially since the governor made bashing college students one of his campaign trail standards. "Our problem is the people on campus who support Wallace and won't say anything about it. That (supporting Wallace) is not the cool thing to do in this election."[36]

Other students voiced support for Wallace with more unorthodox justifications. Charles Hopkins, one of the leaders of Duke University's Afro-American Society, wrote in an editorial in the student newspaper in early October that he would "either go fishing on election day or vote for Wallace" because, paradoxically, "perhaps a vote for Wallace would be in the best interest of black people." Hopkins was under no illusions that Wallace was friendly to Black power, but if Wallace won enough states to throw the election to the House of Representatives, the ensuing constitutional crisis would "cause a restructuring of the political system" and "demonstrate the inadequacies of the political institutions to speak to the need of all the people."[37] A vote for Wallace, in other words, was a vote to heighten the contradictions of the American political and economic system in a way that could potentially bring about revolutionary change.

Hopkins's strategy—insofar as it was a serious political statement as opposed to a provocation directed against liberal Humphrey supporters who assumed that campus radicals would cast a ballot for their candidate—was unlikely to succeed, in no small part because of the character of the Wallace coalition. One "curly-haired youth" attending a Wallace rally in Durham on October 24, 1968 told a reporter that he wished somebody would "run a knife through some of those Communists from Duke" who were protesting Wallace's speech. Wallace promised in his stump speech that he would run over protestors who blocked his car, shortly before a pro-Wallace crowd attacked an interracial group of student demonstrators, with the Wallace supporters wielding signs as clubs and throwing tear gas canisters.[38] Accelerationism was a dangerous game against these enemies.

Given that the Wallace campaign specialized in encouraging violence against college students at its rallies, it is less than surprising that Wallace supporters on campus were generally guarded in their views. The head of the Duke chapter of Youth for Wallace asked that his name be withheld before giving a quote to the *Duke Chronicle*.[39] Clearly, there was a social price to be paid for openly supporting a candidate whom other college students regularly compared to Hitler.

Youth for Wallace did not disband at the end of campaign. On November 15, 1968, Willis Carto announced at the Army and Navy Club in Washington, DC, that Youth for Wallace was being reorganized as the National Youth Alliance, an organization that would be dedicated to organizing against left-wing student groups, in particular Students for a Democratic Society (SDS). Acord later told the FBI that NYA was meant to be a "coalition of conservative youth organizations whose purpose was to counter certain campus orientated groups such as Students for a Democratic Society, which in the opinion of many of these conservatives, are fomenting chaotic conditions on American campuses." Acord and Carto already knew each other from the Wallace campaign; Carto was one of Youth for Wallace's major financial backers. NYA was the direct successor of Youth for Wallace—not only did Acord stay on as chairman, the NYA inherited YFW's mailing lists.[40]

Acord's relationship with Carto, however, quickly soured. The latter intended to take the National Youth Alliance in a more explicitly neo-Nazi direction—he distributed copies of Francis Parker Yockey's *Imperium* under the aegis of the NYA—and at the end of January held a meeting at a motel outside of Pittsburgh that Acord attended. He was disgusted by the proceedings, which resembled a meeting of the American Nazi Party, complete with swastika flags and the singing of the "Horst-Wessel-Lied," the official anthem of the NSDAP. By March, Acord had been forced out, replaced by Carto with Louis T. Byers, a former field organizer for the John Birch Society who had been ejected for his neo-Nazi views. At another NYA conference in Pittsburgh at the end of March 1969, several of Acord's allies attempted to eject Carto and the more explicit neo-Nazi elements from the organization, actually managing to win a majority of the delegates. Carto simply ignored the results of the vote and walked out of the meeting. By June there were two competing National Youth Alliances: Carto's organization based in Washington, which included Byers; Revilo Oliver; John Crommelin, a former Navy admiral and onetime vice presidential candidate for the National States' Rights Party; and retired Marine Corps general Pedro Del Valle; and a splinter faction based in Los Angeles headed by John Acord and Dennis McMahon.[41]

The Acord NYA soon launched a barrage of publicity against the Carto faction, leveraging relationships with politicians, media figures, and the conservative movement to maximize the spread of their message. Acord and McMahon received the blessing of Wallace and Turnipseed themselves, traveling to Montgomery in June 1969 to brief Wallace and his staffers on the state of the organization. "You are doing a great service to your country" in exposing Carto's neo-Nazism, Turnipseed told the pair. Even John Rarick, the Louisiana congressman described by Charles Diggs, the first chairman of the Congressional Black Caucus, as the "leading racist in Congress," disavowed Carto when questioned by reporters, claiming he had never heard of either Carto or the Liberty Lobby. There were hard limits, however, to the effectiveness of Acord's campaign. Significantly, the Acord NYA could not compete with the financial resources available to Carto and his organization. The Liberty Lobby's budget rivaled that of the John Birch Society; Acord estimated in 1969 that it was nearly $1 million a year.[42]

Initially, the Carto faction of NYA seemed poised for success. Theoretically, the organization was supposed to be militant. Byers boasted to the *Washington Post* in December 1969 that the "NYA is a fighting movement and not a talking one or a money raising one and is therefore structured like an army." He added that the NYA had not ruled out the use of violence against left-wing radicals on campus, although no plans had been made to do so.[43] Still, NYA rallies could occasionally descend into violence. An August 16, 1969 meeting at a bar in Towson, Maryland where Byers was speaking was broken up by police after a fight between organizers and a local Black man.[44]

The initial recruits to NYA were usually former Wallace supporters and members of other conservative groups—Byers was a former Bircher. What NYA offered was a much more explicitly racist and youth-oriented edge. At a meeting at the Pick-Roosevelt Hotel in Pittsburgh in September 1969, Byers and Michael D. Russell, the NYA national field director, quipped to a group of white college students that they probably didn't expect that they'd "have to fight those black savages for your girls."[45] In general, most of the NYA field organizers were young white men with explicitly racist views who felt betrayed by mainstream conservatism for accepting the language (if not the substance) of the civil rights movement and were spoiling for a fight with their left-wing classmates. James Parker Faris, a student at Berkeley, was a case in point. Faris had long been an admirer of Revilo Oliver and read his work studiously in *American Opinion,* but felt the Birch Society had not lived up to its mission. Faris was active in Youth for Wallace in California and felt delighted "when I discovered that many of the hard Right, who were coming together in the American Party, were actually secret Nationalist Socialists." But Faris was also disgusted by many of these covert Nazis, who "seemed to take delight in denouncing Hitler and National Socialism in public, and then filling their rooms with momentos [*sic*] of that era."[46] Faris would eventually be on the advisory council of the Carto NYA and a member of the National Socialist White People's Party.

Not all were as comfortable as Faris with explicit embrace of the swastika, but NYA activists were uniformly racist. John Hayes, the head of NYA's UCLA chapter, led a "Right Power Rally" at Meyerhoff Park on the UCLA campus demanding, among other things, that Ralph Bunche Hall be renamed for Douglas MacArthur; that genetics, eugenics, and ethnology be added to the science curriculum; that SDS and the Black Student Union be dissolved; and that "UCLA must provide segregated facilities for whites and non-whites."[47] (Unsurprisingly, none of Hayes's demands were met.) Many field organizers bemoaned the ineffectiveness of their demands and the harsh response from their fellow students. Stephen Lynch, the NYA chapter leader at St. John's University in New York City, complained to his student newspaper that "there is no justice for a white nationalist in the United States of America."[48]

The effectiveness of the Carto NYA was undercut by factional infighting and personality clashes. Carto, as his biographer George Michael has pointed out, had a reputation in far-right circles for alienating supporters and swindling them out of money—Revilo Oliver even accused Carto of having a Swiss bank account to protect his ill-gotten gains.[49] By the end of 1970 the Carto NYA had split into two factions—one led by Carto, the other by Byers. The Byers NYA quickly became dominated, however, by William Luther Pierce, Rockwell's former deputy, and by Revilo Oliver. Unlike Carto, who—like Russell Maguire before him—qualified his commitment to white nationalism with the desire to retain social respectability, the Byers/Pierce NYA was much more comfortable explicitly advocating violence. A 1971 editorial, "Why Revolution?", concluded that it was no longer possible to cure "the system" through constitutional methods and that revolutionary violence was in fact the answer. (Pierce also hoped that the "bold, forth-right revolutionary tone" could appeal to "young Marxist militants," who might be converted to white nationalism.) Pierce and the NYA were careful about their appeals—by 1972 their national organization apparatus had effectively ceased to exist, and in *Attack!* they encouraged supporters to organize local "action units" to create a layer of insulation between NYA and any violence.[50] Pierce advocated a prototypical version of what would become known as the strategy of "leaderless resistance," in which small independent groups, or even individuals, would commit acts of violence against the far right's litany of political enemies—communists, socialists, student radicals, Black nationalists, Jews—in pursuit of a strategy of tension. Later issues of *Attack!* called for the assassination of judges and the execution of whites deemed race traitors.

Attack! frequently published instructions on how to build or obtain weapons, especially explosives. This information in and of itself was not particularly unusual in the genre of underground literature in the early '70s—Abbie Hoffman's 1971 *Steal This Book!*, a favorite of New Left radicals, contained information on how to buy guns and build explosives, and William Powell's *Anarchist Cookbook,* which also provided detailed instructions on how to build or obtain weapons, was in Powell's own words directed to the "silent majority" of Americans to enable them to defend themselves from New Left radicals or right-wing groups like the Minutemen.[51] What was distinct about *Attack!* was that its instructions on procuring weapons were explicitly linked to fighting the race war on campuses and in the streets. Pierce's belief in the necessity of extralegal violence against radicals and agitators may have been ludicrous—from the violent police suppression of the People's Park in Berkeley, California under the orders of Governor Ronald Reagan in May 1969 to the shootings of students by National Guardsmen at Kent State a year later, the state had few qualms about unleashing violence against radicals. But that was not the point. In the pages of *Attack!* violence was an affirmative good—an expression of vitality, masculinity, and racial pride.

Most of the themes that Pierce explored in *Attack!* would resurface in his most infamous work, *The Turner Diaries,* a 1977 novel about a successful white nationalist revolution against the federal government that culminates in the total genocide of all non-whites in the United States. Pierce was inspired by Revilo Oliver in fictionalizing his political writing; Oliver gave him a copy of *The John Franklin Letters* and suggested that Pierce use the alternative future narrative device of that book for his own.[52]

Mainstream conservatives eyed the infighting over the National Youth Alliance warily. James J. Kilpatrick dedicated one of his syndicated columns to the NYA and Willis Carto, whom he described as likely to be "elevated to the position of Number One Devil" by "the Liberals' Demonology." Kilpatrick clearly disapproved of what he dubbed the "far-out right"—"These statesmen dwell in a shadow world 100 miles to the right of Robert Welch, where Americanism and anti-Semitism somehow get equated"—but his column, based largely on Acord's account, betrayed two anxieties. One—which by 1969 was already a well-worn cliché—was that liberals would use the neo-Nazi NYA to smear responsible conservatives with the charge of extremism. But the other was that the NYA and the Liberty Lobby actually represented the views of a sizable faction on the right. Louis Byers claimed that the NYA had recruited two thousand members under his tenure—an insignificant figure by the standards of national politics, but an impressive number for an explicitly neo-Nazi organization. While there was little danger that the Liberty Lobby, the National Youth Alliance, or any of their affiliate groups would rival the doyens at *National Review* in terms of raw political power, they were still very much an active and dynamic presence on the right. Other right-wingers certainly saw them as both a potential rival and a potential ally. With Young Americans for Freedom in disarray after a contentious split at its 1969 convention, a number of former YAFers found their way into the NYA.[53] At least one NYA member told the FBI that he was infiltrating the NYA on behalf of the YAF, because he believed "the NYA intended to destroy the YAF [and] currently all NYA leaders are ousted YAF members and great hostility exists between the two groups."[54] At Emory University, however, conservatives took a somewhat more ecumenical approach. D. Frank Andrews III, a conservative undergraduate, founded with the assistance of a few friends a right-wing underground newspaper on campus, the *Right Angle.* "I am the voice of conservatism at Emory," the editorial in the second issue intoned. "My writers are many: the Republican, the Y.A.F. member, the E.C.C. member, the Bircher." They were "tired of being called racists by the supporters of 'black power,' 'tired of being called fascists . . . tired of the break down of law and order." Andrews, the editor in chief, was also a member of the National Youth Alliance, joining the group in the spring of 1970, well after the Acord-Byers split. He even invited Revilo Oliver to speak on campus; he graciously declined due to a scheduling conflict and complimented Andrews: "Keep up the good fight. The important thing is to prepare a few potential leaders who will know what to do when the crash comes."[55]

In September 1971 *National Review* ran a cover story by C. H. Simonds detailing the infighting surrounding the Liberty Lobby and the National Youth Alliance. It was not complimentary. Carto was a "furtive man" who "delights in secrecy, conspiracy, and power." His brief membership in the John Birch Society in 1959 was highlighted—his prior relationship with Buckley and *National Review* went unmentioned. Most of the article was a dissection of Carto's relationship with Yockey, his promotion of *Imperium,* and an analysis of the Liberty Lobby's newsletter. But Simonds also retold Acord's version of the split between the Acord and Byers factions, making sure to highlight that "next to Jews, the most despised of all are the leaders of the legitimate Right like such as Bill Buckley Jr. . . . . They are the principal obstacles to be overcome." Ironically, Oliver was a significant factor in the story being run—he wrote a letter to Colonel Curtis B. Dall, a retired officer in the Air Force Reserve and one of Carto's closest allies, in which he described Carto as a "species that I do not have the stomach to contemplate without nausea." Oliver made sure that his former associates at *National Review* were aware of the contents of his letter.[56] Despite the far right's growing contempt for conservatives, far rightists saw no contradiction in airing their inter-factional political disputes in conservative publications. Conservatives continued to be leery of their fellow travelers on the right. And Oliver was by no means the last *National Review* contributor to make the journey from the *National Review*'s masthead to Holocaust denier.

CHAPTER EIGHT

Who Owns Conservatism?

IT WASN'T SUPPOSED TO end this way.

At the banquet celebrating *National Review*'s thirty-fifth anniversary at the Waldorf-Astoria Hotel in Manhattan in October 1990, William F. Buckley Jr. announced that he was stepping down as editor in chief. He told his friends and associates that he could look back with pride on his accomplishments over the decades at the magazine. Buckley had sought to be a "revolutionary against the present liberal political order" and to "revitalize the conservative position." He had done so, even winning the hearts and minds of many of his long-standing opponents. *National Review,* reviled by liberals in the 1950s as the vanguard of reaction, "is now recognized as a central journalistic document." And the political project to which *National Review* was dedicated had reshaped America. "We did as much as anybody," he boasted to his friends, "with the exception of himself, to shepherd into the White House Ronald Reagan."[1] At sixty-four years old, Buckley could leave *National Review* confident of its future success and enjoy a productive retirement as an *éminence grise* of American politics and culture—particularly because he had no plans to give up his TV program *Firing Line,* which is how most of the 249 million Americans who were not regular readers of his magazine were familiar with him.

Buckley should have departed *National Review* in unmitigated triumph. But ghosts from the past resurfaced. Buckley had begun his career at the magazine guardedly distancing himself from the antisemitism of the *American Mercury,* he ended it by guardedly defending prominent conservative writers, publications, and politicians from similar allegations of antisemitism. Most of Buckley's focus in his final years at the magazine revolved around Pat Buchanan, the long-standing conservative journalist and official in the Nixon and Reagan administrations, and Joe Sobran, Buckley's protégé at *National Review,* both of whom flirted with explicit racism, antisemitism, and even outright Holocaust denial in the 1980s and early 1990s. The conflict between conservative veterans like Buchanan and Sobran and the increasingly influential bloc of largely (though not exclusively) Jewish neoconservatives during the Reagan years threatened to tear the conservative coalition asunder—and illustrated how, even two decades after the "purge" of the kooks from responsible conservatism, just who was a conservative remained an open question.

The immediate catalyst was Buchanan. A frequent guest on *The McLaughlin Group*—the host, John McLaughlin, was a former *National Review* contributor—Buchanan declared on the program in August 1990 that "there are only two groups that are beating the drums for war in the Middle East"—specifically military action against Iraqi leader Saddam Hussein to remove his troops from Kuwait, which Iraq had invaded a month earlier. They were "the Israeli Defense Ministry and its amen corner in the United States."[2]

Buchanan's remarks were initially ignored by the rest of the media. The syndicated columnist and co-host of the CNN program *Crossfire* had already staked out a position opposing U.S. military intervention in the Persian Gulf, declaring that it has "quagmire written all over it." Buchanan, along with former U.N. ambassador Jeane J. Kirkpatrick and columnist Robert Novak, was widely recognized in the press as one of the leaders of "the old right," who, with the end of the Cold War, opposed further expansion of American overseas commitments. And Buchanan was not shy in identifying in his syndicated columns whom he considered his opponents to be: "neoconservatives," former Democrats or eastern Establishment types eager to spread American power at the barrel of a gun—or, as the *New York Times* more blandly put it, "assert America's primacy in the post-cold war world." Buchanan's opponents were men like former secretary of state Henry Kissinger, former assistant secretary of defense Richard Perle, and *New York Times* columnists William Safire and A. M. Rosenthal. These men shared three things in common. One, they were all influential in U.S. political and foreign policymaking circles. Two, they were all champing at the bit to go to war in the summer and fall of 1990. And three, they were all Jewish.[3]

In mid-September Rosenthal fired a broadside back at Buchanan. Writing about his remarks on *The McLaughlin Group,* Rosenthal argued that what Buchanan was really saying was "The Jews are trying to drag us into war. Only Jews want war. Israeli Jews want war to save Israel's hide. American Jews who talk of military action against Iraq want war because it would suit Israeli interests. They are willing to spill American blood for Israeli interests." What Buchanan was doing, argued Rosenthal, was invoking the same dual-loyalty charge that had been a staple of the anti-Zionist right since before the creation of the Israeli state. Nor, insisted Rosenthal, was this an isolated incident. Buchanan had repeatedly down-played and diminished the Holocaust, quipped that Congress was "Israeli-occupied territory," and sought to raise tensions between Catholics and Jews. Rosenthal highlighted Buchanan's role in Ronald Reagan's state visit to a military cemetery in Bitburg, Germany, where Waffen-SS members were interred.[4]

The pugnacious Buchanan was hardly one to back down from a fight. He blasted Rosenthal in his own column and told reporters that Rosenthal was incensed that President George H. W. Bush had not followed his advice to launch an immediate preemptive strike on Iraq. Other media figures quickly began choosing sides. Morton Kondracke, a senior editor at the liberal (but hawkish) *New Republic* and a frequent guest alongside Buchanan on *McLaughlin,* said that "calling somebody an antisemite is one of the worst things you can say" and that Rosenthal hadn't proven the charge.[5] Richard Cohen at the *Washington Post* concluded that "Buchanan had it coming" because of his claims that Rosenthal's column was prompted by a "pre-planned smear campaign" from the Anti-Defamation League.[6] The Jewish press, for its part, excoriated Buchanan, both for his comments about the ADL-led conspiracy against him and his past remarks on the Holocaust—the *Jewish Exponent* lauded Rosenthal for "affix[ing] to Buchanan the anti-Semitic label he so richly deserves."[7]

With tempers flaring over Buchanan inside and outside the ranks of the American right—and given that he called both Buchanan and Rosenthal friends—Buckley could not help but be drawn in. On September 19, he tackled the issue in his syndicated column. Buckley contended that

Rosenthal "reads Buchanan out of civilized society" by labeling him an anti-semite, and that the attack on Buchanan was "an example of Rosenthal gone ballistic"—as, he coyly suggested to the reader, Rosenthal was wont to do. Buchanan's crime was being "insensitive to those fine lines that tend publicly to define racially or ethnically offensive analysis or rhetoric." Yes, Buchanan had gone too far in suggesting that all the pro-war voices on the American right were Jewish—Buckley was a counterexample, as he supported war on Iraq. But his rhetorical excesses, while insensitive, were not substantial. Antisemitism was a sensitive issue, but "Pat Buchanan's trespasses are miles this side of the awful genocidal line in the sand."[8]

But the issue wouldn't go away. It gained momentum throughout 1990 and 1991, especially as rumors began to circulate that Buchanan would challenge President Bush in the 1992 Republican primary. Buchanan's candidacy—as well as the success at the state level of former Ku Klux Klan leader David Duke in Louisiana—sparked anxiety and outrage. Could it be that the radical right could make a comeback in 1990s America?

Buckley would eventually produce a forty-five-thousand-word essay for *National Review* entitled "In Search of Anti-Semitism," published in the December 30, 1991 issue of the magazine and a year later slightly expanded into a book of the same title. In it, Buckley defended Pat Buchanan against the charge of antisemitism, along with Buckley's friend, former protégé, and onetime *National Review* contributing editor Joseph Sobran, who had made similar comments. Buckley self-consciously invoked the political capital he had built—particularly among liberals—as the gatekeeper of reasonable, responsible, and non-bigoted big-tent conservatism. Yes, Buchanan and Sobran had gone over the line and made remarks that could be reasonably interpreted as antisemitic, Buckley insisted. But no, this did not make them antisemites on the same level as Russell Maguire.[9]

As in the 1950s and 1960s, Buckley's overriding concern was how to keep the conservative coalition together. In many respects the stakes were even higher in the 1990s. Conservatism had *won* in the 1980s. Reagan was the president. Pat Buchanan had briefly served in the Reagan White House as communications director. And while many on the right had been bitterly disappointed with the Reagan administration for not going far enough in either eradicating the hated New Deal state or rolling back the civil rights revolution, the institutional and cultural gains made by the right in the

1980s had been very real. But Reagan's successor, former vice president George H. W. Bush, had long been looked on with suspicion by conservatives. The end of the Cold War and the ongoing collapse of the Soviet Union also meant that the role of anticommunism could no longer be taken for granted in binding the right-wing coalition together.

Buckley's dilemma was heightened by the divisions on the broader right over Israel and U.S. foreign policy. There were five broad camps.

On the most extreme anti-Zionist end was the militant white power movement, which called for violent revolutionary struggle against the "Zionist Occupational Government" and saw Jews as the malevolent force behind American policy abroad as well as the civil rights revolution at home. Guardedly sympathetic to Ronald Reagan in the late '70s and early '80s, by the middle of Reagan's first term white power militants rejected the conservative revolution as insufficient to ensure white supremacy. Neo-Nazi militias like the Order declared war on the state. A spate of bombings and targeted assassinations followed.[10] As with George Lincoln Rockwell in the 1960s, these groups were easy for movement conservatives to disclaim—more often than not with barely concealed resentment that liberals had the temerity to suggest that there was any overlap between "far-right extremists" and, as *National Review* put it, "American conservatives, neoconservatives, and people who just celebrate the Fourth of July."[11]

The Liberty Lobby and its affiliates were less militant than the Order but shared the same broad assumptions about Jews, Zionism, and U.S. policy. Liberty Lobby chief Willis Carto had been writing since the 1950s about alleged Zionist control over American diplomacy, as well as Jewish control of the civil rights movement and its efforts to "pollute" the white race by promoting racial intermixing. By the late 1970s Carto had become one of the key institutional supporters of Holocaust denial through the foundation of the Institute for Historical Review, promoting among others the work of David Hoggan and the late Harry Elmer Barnes.[12] While Carto winked and nodded at the violent white power movement and frequently expressed sympathy in his writings, he was careful to avoid explicitly calling for violence.

The Liberty Lobby, too, was easy and politically useful for conservatives to disavow, in no small part because of Carto's litigiousness. In 1979 Carto sued Buckley for libel over an article published in *National Review* showing that the Liberty Lobby was one of the major financial backers of Lyndon LaRouche.[13] The case was quickly dismissed. But Buckley, no stranger to frivolous lawsuits, countersued in federal court in Washington, DC, for $16 million. The trial was, to say the least, colorful. Carto retained the services of Mark Lane, a former civil rights activist turned iconoclast author and attorney. Lane wrote several books promoting JFK assassination conspiracy theories; he also represented Peoples Temple leader Jim Jones and was present at the mass murder-suicide at Jonestown in 1979, which he survived by fleeing into the jungle. Lane's opening statement to the all-Black DC jury posited that "*National Review,* since its inception, has been a racist, pro-Nazi, pro-fascist publication" that smeared Black leaders like Adam Clayton Powell Jr. and Martin Luther King.[14] Lane's argument was dismissed by observers as cynical race-baiting on behalf of an openly pro-Nazi client, but Lane did manage to score some points. Buckley admitted that he had employed George Lincoln Rockwell at *National Review* before Rockwell's open embrace of Nazism—something he generally sought to minimize— and that he had written the infamous "Why the South Must Prevail" editorial in 1957. Buckley defended himself in court, saying that he didn't believe in universal franchise either for Blacks or for whites.[15]

Buckley's overall demeanor did little to endear him to either the jurors or Joyce Hens Green, the presiding judge, who recalled in an interview sixteen years later that Buckley turned to her at one point in his testimony to ask if he could leave court early to catch a plane. "When I said 'No,' he kept insisting that he was losing a great deal of money. The jury overheard this and did not appear impressed by his attitude." (She also found it "an odd bit of lawyering" that Buckley's own attorney walked him though his privileged background and upbringing in his questions, since District of Columbia jurors were generally not going on regular skiing holidays to Switzerland.) The jury ultimately awarded nominal damages of $1,001 to Buckley, who spent nearly $160,000 on legal fees.[16] Lane claimed a victory both for himself and for conservatism as a whole—he insisted throughout the trial that Buckley was trying to "silence a dissenting voice" in the conservative movement by smearing Carto and shutting down the *Spotlight,* which boasted 145,000 readers, and that Carto and Buckley held broadly similar views on race.[17] Judge Green, at least, was inclined to agree, describing the lawsuit in retrospect as a "libel action of one conservative opinion magazine and its principal versus another conservative opinion magazine and its principal. The men had been great friends in past years and come to a division of their ways."[18]

There was considerable overlap between the Holocaust deniers and avowed white supremacists and the libertarian faction of the right coalition. Heterodox Austrian School economist and Cato Institute co-founder Murray Rothbard, for example, was a close friend of Harry Elmer Barnes and sought to promote his work, even publishing a collected work of his essays under the aegis of the Cato Institute in 1980. Rothbard was also, despite his own Jewish background, a ferocious antisemite who referred to Jews in private correspondence as "those fucking kikes" and "cocksuckers." While Rothbard had been forced out of the Cato Institute in 1980 over disputes with Cato's funders—Rothbard held a particular animus against the Koch brothers, the major financial angels of the institute, whom Rothbard described as control freaks who sought to water down the Cato Institute's ideological purity to expand its political footprint—he nevertheless enjoyed influence in the small but zealous right-libertarian political spaces. He was an outspoken supporter of Texas congressman Ron Paul's 1988 presidential bid on the Libertarian Party ticket and, by the early 1990s, was expressing support for both Pat Buchanan and David Duke, whose platform of "lower taxes, dismantling the bureaucracy, slashing the welfare system, attacking affirmative action and racial set-asides, [and] calling for equal rights for all Americans, including whites" was something libertarians and the right more broadly could fervently embrace. While Rothbard was a particularly extreme example, more mainstream libertarian publications endorsed similar ideas—the flagship libertarian magazine *Reason* occasionally published the work of Holocaust deniers like James J. Martin under the guise of questioning Cold War militarism.[19]

Distinct from the militants, the institutionalist antisemites, and their libertarian allies was a broad faction of longtime conservative activists who harbored frustrations about the incompleteness and inadequacy of the Reagan Revolution as well as resentments toward parvenu conservatives whom they felt were mere opportunists. George H. Nash dubbed these old stalwarts "paleoconservatives," a curious self-appellation that suggested anachronism as much as tradition. These paleoconservatives bitterly resented the influence of neoconservatives—former liberals and leftists who had shifted dramatically to the right in the 1960s and 1970s, often because of explicitly racial anxieties about the Black freedom struggle.[20]

It wasn't left-wing radicalism per se that made neoconservatives such an object of suspicion—after all, the ranks of the conservative movement had long been filled with ex-communists like James Burnham, Willmoore Kendall, Frank Meyer, and Whittaker Chambers. What explained the depth of suspicion paleoconservatives felt for neoconservatives? Part of it was resentment over neoconservatives' positions of prominence in the new Reagan administration despite being relative newcomers to the right-wing political scene. As the University of Michigan historian Stephen J. Tonsor put it at a meeting of the Philadelphia Society in 1986, "It is splendid when the town whore gets religion and joins the church. Now and then she makes a good choir director, but when she begins to tell the minister what he ought to say in his Sunday sermons, matters have been carried too far."[21] Neoconservatives were not part of the movement during the wilderness years. Few had voted, let alone volunteered, for Goldwater. As late as 1975 Joseph Sobran sneered at the conservative credentials of the neoconservative magazine *Commentary*, describing it as a liberal magazine "remarkable" (among liberals) for "its willingness to take conservative views seriously," but noting that this hardly made it a "conservative" publication.[22] And now they were being showered with jobs, perks, and access, both by the Reagan administration and by a growing constellation of right-wing philanthropic foundations.

Undergirding these tensions was the identification of neoconservatives with Jews. Many of the leading neoconservatives—Irving Kristol, Norman Podhoretz, Daniel Bell, and Nathan Glazer, among others—were Jewish, and the magazine *Commentary* was so identified with neoconservatives that William F. Buckley published an editorial in *National Review* in 1971 lauding the publication for coming around to the right side. Not all neoconservatives were Jewish—Irish Catholic Daniel Patrick Moynihan being a prominent example—and though Paul Gottfried, the man who coined the term *paleoconservative*, was Jewish, the neoconservative phenomenon was almost universally understood to be a novel form of Jewish politics.[23]

Buckley and *National Review* occupied a centrist position in these factional disputes. On the one hand, *National Review* had been or was home to many of the most outspoken traditionalist conservatives, and Joseph Sobran, one of the most forceful of the paleoconservative voices, was a senior editor at *National Review* as well as Buckley's protégé. Russell Kirk continued to publish frequently for the magazine, as did Mel Bradford. On the other hand, Buckley was friendly with many of the leading lights of neoconservatism, from Norman Podhoretz to Irving Kristol, and found himself increasingly less patient with the contrarianism of the traditionalists toward the

Reagan administration. Was it not enough that conservatives finally had a foothold in Washington? After all, far more bound the right together than drove it apart.

Both neoconservatives and traditionalists were self-reflexively intellectual and often the product of advanced, if not elite, education. The liberal writer Peter Steinfels identified Irving Kristol, Daniel Patrick Moynihan, and Daniel Bell as the most important propagators of neoconservatism in the late 1970s—both Moynihan and Bell had PhDs and both Bell and Kristol were prominent academics, holding professorships at Harvard and NYU, respectively.[24] But credentialism was common among paleoconservatives, too: Melvin Bradford, for instance, held a PhD from Vanderbilt University; Gottfried earned an MA and a PhD from Yale. Even Pat Buchanan was a product of Georgetown University and later attended journalism school at Columbia. And paleoconservatives and neoconservatives shared many of the same antipathies. Both were ferociously hostile to New Left activists in the 1960s—Russell Kirk described Students for a Democratic Society as a group of "violent fanatics," while the pages of *Commentary* in the late 1960s were increasingly filled with invective against the "outrageous statements" of New Left–influenced intellectuals. Both were especially critical of the student uprisings.[25] Neither faction was as extreme as the militant far right, which believed that the revolutionary threat from left-wing students required paramilitary violence, but all shared a profound loathing for the challenge of the New Left.

Paleoconservatives and neoconservatives were also largely united around the question of race. Although Paul Gottfried, channeling the spirit of Revilo Oliver, claimed that "unlike the neoconservatives, the Old Right holds to the concept of a differentiated humanity," neoconservatives shared the same basic assumptions.[26] Even neoconservatives who generally eschewed a strict hereditarian approach reached many of the same conclusions. Daniel Patrick Moynihan's infamous 1965 report on the breakdown of the Black family in America was not based on assumptions or arguments about hereditarian or genetic difference. In fact, Moynihan took a largely historical and cultural approach, emphasizing the importance of the legacy of slavery and the "reversed roles of husband and wife," where Black women tended to dominate their husbands, leading to a breakdown in social order. Moynihan also argued that the expansion of state welfare programs was ultimately the culprit behind what he called the "tangle of pathology" of the

Black family, and that federal policy needed to be adjusted to meet this reality. Moynihan's conclusions—in large part reflecting his Catholic upbringing and broader assumptions about the proper composition of families—have been the subject of justifiably ferocious critique from feminists and African American thinkers and activists for over five decades, and a full discussion of them is beyond the scope of this chapter. What *is* pertinent is that Moynihan's conclusions about Black pathology—a point he repeatedly expanded upon in neoconservative publications like *Commentary* and the *National Interest*—were eminently compatible with concepts of a "differentiated humanity." Indeed, *National Interest* frequently published work by race/IQ proponents like Arthur Jensen and Richard J. Herrnstein.[27] Neoconservatives often differentiated themselves from paleoconservatives by their commitment to statistics and social science—as opposed to common sense, intuition, and tradition—when it came to social policy. On the critical question of race in America, however, both neoconservatives and paleoconservatives shared the same basic assumptions about Black aberrancy and degeneracy.

Even on foreign policy there were more commonalities than differences between the paleocons and the neocons, at least until the end of the Cold War. Robert Welch, himself a kind of proto-paleocon, may have initially been ambivalent about the commitment of U.S. troops to Vietnam in the 1960s, but the John Birch Society fervently believed in the necessity of victory against communism in the field and the broader Soviet menace. When Welch's successor as the head of the John Birch Society, Georgia congressman Larry McDonald, was killed when a Soviet interceptor shot down a Korean Air Lines flight that had strayed into Soviet airspace on September 1, 1983, the Birchers demanded harsh measures—*American Opinion* declared that the Soviets had assassinated McDonald, and Paul Weyrich, a frequent contributor to the magazine, urged President Reagan to close American ports to Soviet ships, cancel upcoming arms control negotiations, and expel Soviet diplomats, in addition to the administration's existing move to shut down American airspace to Soviet airlines. But neoconservatives were themselves only barely satisfied with Reagan's response to the shootdown. "The administration has always used tough words," Daniel Patrick Moynihan told reporters a few days after the incident. "What tough things have they done?" Beyond anticommunism, both paleoconservatives and neoconservatives were committed to a particular vision of swaggering, masculine American strength. Both factions derided Jimmy Carter as a weakling and a wimp, in no small part due to Carter's handling of the Iran hostage crisis and the continued decline in American prestige, already battered by the humiliating loss in Vietnam. And despite the critics of Ronald Reagan's increasingly conciliatory approach to the Soviet Union, his sunny optimism, carefully manicured cowboy image, and his record of unleashing devastating police violence against left-wing radicals appealed to the power fetishists across the right.[28]

This was the challenge conservative centrists faced in the 1980s. More bound the American right than drove it apart, but the divisions were there, and they were growing. William F. Buckley was determined to keep the right-wing popular front together.

The first major public clash between paleoconservatives and neoconservatives was over, of all things, the chairmanship of the National Endowment for the Humanities (NEH) in October 1981. Conservatives were giddy at the prospect of replacing Joseph D. Duffey, a Carter administration holdover and former head of Americans for Democratic Action who was, in the words of *Human Events,* "shoveling hundreds of thousands of dollars into the coffers of the Democratic left." (Among Duffey's sins was awarding some $800,000 in grants to organized labor.)[29] Melvin E. Bradford, an English professor at the University of Dallas, was widely thought to be the favorite for the job. Considered a Reagan loyalist, Bradford had supported Reagan's bid against Gerald Ford in 1976, helped organize the Scholars for Reagan group in 1980, and been appointed a member of Ronald Reagan's presidential transition team after Reagan's election victory. Bradford also had the support of sixteen conservative Republican senators, including Jesse Helms, John Tower, Strom Thurmond, Orrin Hatch, and Dan Quayle. But Bradford had his weaknesses. Although he had impeccably conservative political credentials dating back to his vocal support for Barry Goldwater in 1964, he was also a quintessentially southern conservative. Bradford had long been sympathetic to George Wallace and had openly supported Wallace's 1972 bid for the Democratic nomination. Bradford, a Confederate sympathizer, had also written harshly about Abraham Lincoln, whom he castigated as a tyrant and a "dangerous man" in the pages of *Modern Age* and *National Review.*[30] Nevertheless, Bradford enjoyed broad support for the position among conservative pundits and intellectuals—including Russell Kirk and William F. Buckley.

Neoconservatives, led by Irving Kristol, rallied around their own candidate—William Bennett, a political philosopher and director of the National Humanities Center in Research Triangle Park, North Carolina.[31] While both Bennett and Bradford represented a departure from Duffey, Bradford was considerably more pugnacious, vowing to cut the number and size of NEH grants and "see that conservatives [get] a better shake than they did in Duffey's regime."[32] *Human Events* noted that while Bennett had the support of neoconservatives, he was "too tight" with the existing staff of the NEH—the National Humanities Center relied on NEH grants for 15 percent of its budget—and had written a letter in defense of the NEH's grant procedures in a letter to *Harper's* in October 1980.[33]

There were regional and class dimensions at play as well. Bennett's support was primarily based among northeastern intellectuals and activists—in addition to Kristol, his major backers included the New York–based Olin Foundation. Bennett was from Brooklyn, and while he had some southern connections—in addition to his position at the NHC in North Carolina, he earned his PhD from the University of Texas in 1965—he also held a BA from Williams College in Massachusetts and a JD from Harvard Law School, and had taught at Boston College before moving to the National Humanities Center. Bradford, on the other hand, was as southern as sunshine and sweet tea, and had repeatedly told reporters that one of his major goals was to "give more [grants] to Texas and Oklahoma. . . . Not everything would go to Harvard, Yale, Princeton, and Chicago."[34]

Kristol and the Olin Foundation kept up the pressure—as did Bradford detractors like George Will, who decried Bradford's "shrill assault" on Abraham Lincoln—and in November the Reagan administration announced that Bennett, not Bradford, would get the top spot at NEH. Bradford's remaining congressional allies were incensed—Jesse Helms told reporters he would not support Bennett's confirmation until he had assurances that "scholarship from the conservative end of the spectrum as well as from the liberal end of the spectrum will be recognized."[35]

Paleoconservatives walked away from the failed Bradford nomination embittered and angry. *They* had built up conservatism into a powerful intellectual and social force, and now they were being denied the fruits of their victory. Neoconservatives were relieved that a Confederate sympathizer had been kept out of the National Endowment for the Humanities, a development that would have done nothing to defuse allegations that the Reagan administration was courting the support of former segregationists. Neither faction paid much heed to historian Eric Foner's analysis of the dispute, which hinged on the unanimity of both paleoconservatives and neoconservatives around "policies broadly perceived, whatever their initial motivation, as being anti-black."[36]

The roiling conflict between paleoconservatives and neoconservatives hit closer to home for *National Review*—and became explicitly interlaced with the question of antisemitism—in 1986, when neoconservatives accused senior editor Joseph Sobran of propagating anti-Jewish views in the magazine and in his syndicated columns. Sobran had been writing for the magazine since 1972; Buckley recruited him after Sobran engaged in a letter-writing campaign to faculty at Eastern Michigan University, where Sobran was a student, defending Buckley's right to speak on the campus. Sobran quickly became Buckley's protégé—a replacement, in many respects, for fellow Michigander Garry Wills, who had broken with Buckley due to Wills's sympathy with the New Left. (In fact, one of the first columns Sobran wrote for *National Review* was an excoriation of Wills, whose post-conservative writings he derided as crude and "dutifully vulgar." He later gently chided Wills for writing for *Playboy*.)[37] Like Wills (and Buckley), Sobran was devotedly Catholic and was dedicated to the classics—Buckley hired him away from a fellowship at Eastern Michigan where Sobran was studying Shakespeare.

Several major themes emerge from Sobran's work for *National Review*—in his twenty years with the magazine he wrote nearly four hundred stories, an output exceeded only by Buckley himself. He shared the prurient sexual obsessions common to conservative writers in the 1970s, insisting with the zeal of a deacon that sexuality needed to be properly channeled and controlled. (In this, he shared the attitudes of his patron and employer Buckley, whose commitment to the sexual enticement of conservative femininity was such that in his debut novel *Saving the Queen* CIA agent Blackford Oakes, a thinly disguised alter ego of Buckley, has a torrid affair with the queen of England.) On racial matters Sobran was typical of his fellow writers at the magazine, who had eschewed an overt commitment to white supremacy for the more nuanced colorblind ethos of conservatism in the 1970s and 1980s. But there was no mistaking Sobran's underlying commitments. He derided the Black magazines *Ebony* and *Essence* in the early 1970s for their emphasis on publishing "articles aimed at refuting theories of correlation between race and IQ"—a direct rebuttal, in many respects, to the content of *National Review* at the time—and concluded that *Ebony* and *Essence* protested too much. Sobran rarely wrote about apartheid South Africa, although when he did, he consistently downplayed the cruelty and violence of the Afrikaner regime—its "racial caste system is far milder than the tribal caste system of states like Burundi"—and insisted that South Africa was an "easy target" for American liberals that did not deserve its exalted status in "liberal demonology."[38]

On Israel, Sobran was idiosyncratic. He was emphatically not a Zionist, but neither did he embrace political anti-Zionism or, for that matter, the Palestinian cause. Yassir Arafat and the Palestinian Liberation Organization were, for Sobran as for most on the right, Soviet-backed thugs. Liberal sympathy for the Palestinians—even from liberal Jews—was simply evidence of American liberalism's deep and long-standing ties with international communism, and the condemnations of Israeli oppression by liberals were as hollow as their antipathy toward Rhodesia and even America. In 1981 Sobran even attacked Richard Cohen for taking too harsh a line on Israeli policy in the occupied Palestinian territories and in Lebanon, as well as Israel's alliances with right-wing authoritarian regimes like South Africa and Argentina. "A beleaguered nation would have to be insane to forswear the co-operation of South Africa to retain the approval of Richard Cohen."[39]

None of this necessarily meant, however, that Sobran saw Israel as a dependable American ally. Despite the Begin government's conciliatory gestures toward evangelical Christian leaders in the United States in the early 1980s—in particular Israel's cultivation of the Reverend Jerry Falwell as a political ally—Sobran insinuated that Israel was in some meaningful sense anti-Christian. (Sobran, as a Catholic, did not share Falwell's eschatological beliefs about the Jewish return to Israel as a precondition for the Second Coming of Christ.) He described Israel in one column as a "semi-theocracy that gives preferred status to one religion, Judaism, and . . . sharply discourages proselytizing by Christians" (even Falwell could not wring that concession from the Israelis)." Since Israel was dependent on American aid, "is it right . . . that Christians should be taxed to provide aid to such a society?"[40]

Sobran also flirted with the avowedly racist right. In a May 1986 syndicated column, he complained that "America has become a minority-ridden country" and blamed Blacks for skyrocketing crime rates. He framed his argument—as conservatives had approached race/IQ science for years—as simply meeting unpleasant facts head-on. "One doesn't discuss such facts in polite company. One is not supposed to notice. . . . The fact remains that white Americans live in fear of blacks," and the statistical evidence validated those fears. "That is one reason white Americans envy Europe. Two Frenchmen or two Germans, total strangers to each other, can trust each other in ways two Americans can't." Sobran's column, while undeniably racist, would almost certainly not have invited opprobrium had he not then endorsed *Instauration,* a white nationalist magazine that Sobran claimed "faces the harder facts about race." He called it an "often brilliant magazine, covering a beat nobody else will touch, and doing so with intelligence, wide-ranging observation, and bitter wit. It is openly and almost unremittingly hostile to blacks, Jews, and Mexican and Oriental immigrants." Sobran's endorsement of the magazine was not unqualified—although he called it "intellectually superior" to the liberal press, which insisted on "pure, altru-istic benevolence" between the races, he wrote that *Instauration's* "world of Hobbesian conflict at the racial level" was also unsatisfying—but he left the firm impression that he felt the magazine had an important contribution to make.[41]

That spring, Midge Decter, the executive director of the neoconservative think tank Committee for the Free World, circulated an open letter to promi-nent conservatives labeling Sobran "little more than a crude and naked anti-Semite." Decter was well connected. The Committee for the Free World included among its members Jeane Kirkpatrick, the ambassador to the United Nations; former secretary of defense under the Ford administration Donald Rumsfeld; and Irving Kristol. Decter had helped found the organiza-tion in 1981 with support from the Scaife, Olin, and Smith Richardson Foundations.[42] She was also married to *Commentary* editor Norman Podhoretz. Her opinion, in short, mattered. When such a powerful figure in American neoconservatism accused Sobran, a senior editor at *National Review,* of being an antisemite, other publications had begun to weigh in on the issue. Buckley had to respond.

Buckley's approach to the concern about Sobran was broadly similar to his reponse to the *American Mercury* issue three decades earlier; he worked behind the scenes in the gentlest possible ways to keep the right-wing coali-tion from publicly fragmenting. He wrote back privately to Decter denying that Sobran was a "crude anything. And beyond that, he is not a naked

anti-Semite, nor, in my opinion a crypto or even a latent anti-Semite."
Buckley was probably sincere in his defense of Sobran. Over the course of
Buckley's friendship with Revilo Oliver, Buckley conceded in private that
Oliver was an antisemite. He was not willing to make the same concession
over Sobran. But Buckley did write in his response to Decter that, if one did
not know Sobran as Buckley did, it would be reasonable to conclude that
some of his columns about Israel were "animated by anti-Semitism." He
would urge Sobran to tone down his rhetoric on Israel and the Jews.[43]

Buckley's attempt to keep the issue in the family, as it were, was not
successful. Decter had circulated her letter widely, and stories about the
dispute began popping up in publications ranging from *Newsweek* and the
Chicago Tribune to the *Nation*, which was enjoying more than a little schadenfreude at the expense of its conservative rivals. Buckley convened a meeting
of the editorial board—which included Sobran—at the end of May 1986.
Along with Jeffrey Hart, Richard Brookhiser, and his sister Priscilla Buckley,
he tried to convince Sobran that he had crossed the line with his columns.
Sobran rejected their criticism and "insisted that he was being victimized by
Decter, Podhoretz, and other Jews." But the members of the editorial board
held firm: while rejecting calls from columnists like Richard Cohen to fire
Sobran, they told him directly that he was *not* to write any more about Israel
or Jews, either in *National Review* or in his syndicated columns. The issue
was simply too hot, and the magazine wanted no further embarrassment
either to itself or to the broader conservative coalition. Sobran grudgingly
agreed.[44]

Although Buckley's concluding sentence—that he was confident that
Sobran would in the future "argue his positions in such a fashion as to avoid
affronting our natural allies"—could be and indeed was interpreted by
Sobran and others as a veiled threat (shut up or get in line), it was an exceedingly generous one.[45] Sobran took to the airwaves to defend himself. On a
C-SPAN special dedicated to the controversy, Sobran said he was being
targeted because he had the courage to speak out against "several ethnic
lobbies," "the black and Jewish ones in particular." He was defiant and
unapologetic, and also seemed genuinely hurt and perplexed by Buckley's
attitudes toward him and the Jewish issue. "Bill Buckley is going to give the
naïve reader the impression that he's under terrific pressure from Jews . . .
and he's not!" Sobran told host Brian Lamb. "He thinks he has to maintain a
certain kind of appearance but he really doesn't have to." Sobran went on to

dismiss the potential of a Nazi Party in the United States—despite a spate of neo-Nazi violence that had claimed the life of Jewish radio host Alan Berg in Denver only two years earlier—and said that "[we] need to stop . . . feeling guilty about the Holocaust." He added that Buckley had talked to him before he had written his *National Review* op-ed: "He was very fatherly about it, and very nice—he's a very sweet man!—and he was worried about my future more than anything else."[46] Sobran continued to write for *National Review*, although it would be several years until he wrote another cover story.

Like Joseph Sobran, Pat Buchanan was incensed by the influence of neoconservatives on the political movement he had long called home. Buchanan was, in his own words, a "from the cradle conservative." His father, William Buchanan, had briefly flirted with New Deal liberalism—even casting a vote for FDR in 1932—but, like John T. Flynn, had soured on the Roosevelt administration by the late 1930s. The younger Buchanan recalled in his memoirs that his father's favorite columnist in the 1950s was none other than Westbrook Pegler, and—like many American Catholics—he spoke glowingly about the regime of Francisco Franco in Spain. As a young man in his twenties, Pat Buchanan wrote editorials for the *St. Louis Globe-Democrat* (notably supporting Barry Goldwater's bid in 1964) and became involved in a variety of different conservative political organizations and campaigns. He was a member of Young Americans for Freedom and wrote press releases for the organization. He also worked for Richard Nixon's law office in Manhattan, parlaying his connections into a position as an advisor to Nixon's 1968 election campaign. Buchanan worked as an opposition researcher and speechwriter, and became a key policy advisor in the Nixon White House. A bridge to the conservative movement for the Nixon administration, he tried to push the president as far to the right as possible on domestic policy. (In a 1970 note to John Ehrlichman Nixon described Buchanan's views on racial issues as "segregation forever.")[47]

Buchanan, although never directly implicated in criminal activity in the Watergate scandal, advised President Nixon to take a maximalist approach against his political opponents—he played a major role in advising Nixon to conduct the infamous Saturday Night Massacre in October 1973, when Nixon fired Attorney General Elliot Richardson, Deputy Attorney General William Ruckelshaus, and Watergate Special Prosecutor Archibald Cox in an unsuccessful attempt to quash the Watergate investigation.[48] After

Nixon's resignation, White House chief of staff Alexander Haig even privately promised Buchanan the position of ambassador to South Africa (a posting Buchanan claims to have requested), but the plan was quickly squelched by President Ford, apparently conscious of the terrible political optics of handing a plum diplomatic posting to a Nixon hardliner mere days after pardoning the president.[49]

With his political career at a dead end, Buchanan returned to media, writing frequently for *Human Events* and *National Review* as well as in a nationally syndicated newspaper column in the late 1970s. Buchanan did not have the same outsized clout in conservative political circles as Buckley did in the late 1970s and early 1980s, but he was by no means marginal. In addition to his column he had his own radio program, appeared as a surrogate for Ronald Reagan in the famous 1978 debate between Reagan and Buckley on *Firing Line* over the ratification of the treaties turning over sovereignty of the Panama Canal to Panama, and, most famously, became a TV staple as the co-host of CNN's *Crossfire* in 1982, along with his frequent appearances on *The McLaughlin Group*.

To neoconservatives in the 1970s and early 1980s, Buchanan was an exemplar of the New Right. In 1977 Jeane Kirkpatrick wrote a critical review in *Commentary* of the work of Kevin Phillips, William A. Rusher, Richard J. Whalen, and Buchanan—all, according to Kirkpatrick, New Right standard-bearers—in which she characterized the New Right as "not really new at all" but rather "a strain of nativist populism whose roots are deep in American history," drawing comparisons to Richard Hofstadter's analysis of the "Radical Right" of the 1950s. For Kirkpatrick, the political prescriptions of figures like Buchanan—who urged conservatives in his 1975 book *Conservative Votes, Liberal Victories: Why the Right Has Failed* to capitalize on new class tensions between "professional bureaucrats, planners, consultants, and professors" and ordinary working- and middle-class (white) Americans in order to build a permanent conservative majority—were doomed to fail because it was inconceivable that a majority of the electorate would turn against the benefits of the welfare state. Kirkpatrick failed to appreciate the extent to which the rhetoric of "producers" versus "non-producers," in William Rusher's formulation, had already been heavily racialized. Indeed, Ronald Reagan repeatedly invoked the specter of Linda Taylor, the so-called Chicago "welfare queen," on the campaign trail in 1976—although Reagan never explicitly claimed that Taylor was African American, the implication was not lost on his audiences.[50] Buchanan, for his part, was critical of neoconservatives in the late '70s and early '80s but generally eschewed taking potshots at his fellow travelers, even defending neoconservatives as part of the right coalition. In a 1980 column attacking the NAACP's economic platform, Buchanan wrote that it was regrettable that the organization "failed to even consider the alternative held out by Republicans, conservatives, and neoconservatives who argue that, by circumscribing the federal plantation [a favorite phrase of Buchanan's] and unleashing private enterprise . . . we can pull this economy out of the ditch."[51]

In February 1985 Buchanan became White House communications director, a move widely seen as Reagan's attempt to shore up his right flank in the aftermath of his 1984 electoral victory. While Reagan had won a landslide victory, the administration had come under increasing fire from conservatives for failing to live up to its promises to shrink the size of the federal government—and traditionalist conservatives still bore considerable resentment that the spoils of the Reagan Revolution in Washington were, in their view, monopolized by opportunist neoconservatives. *Time* magazine reported that the appointment was a "concession to Reagan's right-wing supporters" and that while Buchanan had frequently been critical of the administration in the past, White House chief of staff Donald Regan insisted that Buchanan "will support the Administration's final position" on vital issues. Conservative publications—including *National Review*—applauded the appointment, contrasting the pugnacious Buchanan to his "timid, compromising" predecessor David Gergen, a holdover from the Ford administration.[52] Buckley saluted Buchanan's sacrifices for the conservative cause, noting that by relinquishing his syndicated column and TV appearances he was giving up almost 75 percent of his income for "a civil servant's pay" in the hopes of influencing policy and fulfilling the promises that Reagan had made to conservatives.[53]

Initially, Buchanan seemed poised to expand his influence at the White House. His appointment was greeted with acclaim by conservatives—Rowland Evans and Robert Novak wrote that Buchanan's appointment "represents the first legitimate conservative activist, as contrasted to inner-circle Reaganite, on Reagan's senior staff." He received a rapturous reception at the 1985 Conservative Political Action Conference (the *Washington Post* punningly reported Buchanan's "Popular Front" reception, a more revealing turn of phrase than the newspaper suspected). Inside the White House,

Buchanan was slated by mid-March to have an aide of his installed at the Office of Public Liaison. And conservatives also gloated about how angry Buchanan's appointment made mainstream journalists. Buchanan had been unremittingly hostile to the "liberal" press both in the Nixon White House and in his subsequent career, believing that the mainstream media, even more than lawyers, consultants, or the professoriate, represented the apotheosis of the antagonistic "New Class" pitted against ordinary Americans.[54] Buchanan also terrified the gay community, already suffering egregiously from the AIDS epidemic and the Reagan administration's indifference to the plague. Jeff Levi, the head of the National Gay Task Force, told the gay newspaper the *Advocate* that "Reagan is throwing a bone to the far right" with the Buchanan appointment, and that Buchanan "has done nothing but stir up homophobia and made life patently miserable for gay people, and for people with AIDS in particular."[55] But Buchanan's peak influence inside the Reagan White House lasted only a little over two months.

One factor behind Buchanan's fall from grace was the anti-communist insurgency in Nicaragua. Buchanan had long been an outspoken supporter of extending aid to the right-wing Contra rebels against the Sandinista government in Managua, and as communications director had insisted that Reagan make a nationally televised speech in April 1985 urging Congress to pass a $14 million aid package to the Contras. Reagan's other senior advisors were almost unanimously opposed to Buchanan's proposal, considering congressional support for the Contras a lost cause, and preferring to focus the president's energies on his budget proposals. Buchanan, however, would not let the issue go—and his stridency on the subject was eventually leaked to the *Washington Post,* which characterized the atmosphere as tense, with Buchanan testing his influence. The test failed—Reagan did not make the speech, and Congress did not pass funding for the Contras (leading to the Reagan administration's creative solution of illegally selling weapons to the Islamic Republic of Iran and funneling the profits to the Contras—as with Watergate, Buchanan was never directly implicated in wrongdoing in the Iran-Contra scandal).[56]

Even more damaging to Buchanan's tenure was his involvement in Reagan's controversial decision to visit a military cemetery in Bitburg, Germany, with West German chancellor Helmut Kohl in May. There were no GIs buried at the Kolmeshöhe cemetery; there were, however, several Waffen-SS members interred there. The administration intended the visit, which had been arranged by the Kohl government, to be a reciprocal gesture in exchange for Kohl's support of the deployment of Pershing II missiles to West Germany in 1983, but the Reagan administration's messaging around the event was inept. Reagan told the press in January that he did not intend to visit a concentration camp site during his state visit in order to avoid "embarrassing the Germans about their past."[57] While Buchanan's involvement in the planning of the Bitburg visit was minimal—the arrangement predated his White House appointment—he was repeatedly attacked in the press in April because of his opposition to the Office of Special Investigations (OSI), a body set up by the Justice Department in 1979 to track down Nazi war criminals living in the United States. This was a reversal of decades of U.S. policy that broadly tolerated (and, in the case of Operation Paperclip, actively recruited) former Nazis living in the United States. Since the office's inception, Buchanan had repeatedly urged that it be abolished, telling OSI head Allan Ryan in a TV interview in 1982 that it was not worth spending millions to investigate perpetrators of an atrocity that "occurred 35, 45 years ago, okay?" and also suggesting that the OSI was acting as a useful dupe for the KGB, which was eager to have the U.S. government do its dirty work in persecuting "staunch anti-Communist emigres."[58]

As the controversy over Bitburg escalated, Jewish organizations began attacking Buchanan as one of the architects of Reagan's visit, with some even holding him responsible for Reagan's failure to visit a concentration camp, despite that decision having been made months before Buchanan joined the White House staff.[59] Buchanan, however, urged the president not to back down in the face of media criticism, telling him that changing course now would be "caving in" to critics and was an unacceptable sign of weakness. Buchanan was also apparently responsible for Reagan suggesting to reporters in mid-April that the German war dead were victims of the Nazi regime "just as surely as the victims in the concentration camps."[60] Buchanan's own combative tone toward the press boomeranged against him—in May NBC reported that Buchanan "could be seen repeatedly writing the phrase 'succumbing to the pressure of the Jews' during a White House staff meeting.[61] Buchanan acknowledged that he had taken notes at the meeting, but angrily denied antisemitic intent. In this he was backed up by Kenneth Bialkin, the national chairman of the Anti-Defamation League, who sat next to Buchanan during the meeting and told the press that Buchanan had in fact written "succumb to pressure"—there was nothing about the Jews in Buchanan's notes.[62] Still, the damage to Buchanan's political influence within the Reagan administration was done. His belligerent tone had caused repeated headaches for the administration over a timeline of only a few weeks, and despite Bialkin's support Buchanan had already managed to alienate a number of major American Jewish organizations.

Buchanan's Jewish problem didn't stem just from Bitburg. For years he had been an outspoken supporter of John Demjanjuk, a Ukrainian immigrant and naturalized American citizen from suburban Cleveland who was accused in the late 1970s of being the infamously brutal guard at the Treblinka extermination camp whom inmates had dubbed Ivan the Terrible. Legal historian Lawrence Douglas has called the Demjanjuk case the "most convoluted, lengthy, and bizarre criminal case to arise from the Holocaust," one that "never reached a definitive conclusion," and if anything that is an understatement. Demjanjuk was originally accused of being a guard at the Sobibor extermination camp by Michael Hanusiak, a Ukrainian American communist who received his information from the Soviet government in 1975. The U.S. government, with relatively few legal options at its disposal to use against alleged Nazi war criminals, opted to pursue denaturalization proceedings against Demjanjuk, and it was one of the first cases prosecuted by the OSI, founded as part of an effort to standardize prosecutorial practices against alleged Nazis and Nazi collaborators. In 1981 Demjanjuk finally went to trial; a federal judge stripped him of his citizenship and a year later the Immigration and Naturalization Service (INS) initiated deportation proceedings. Before Demjanjuk's case could wend its way through the INS's procedures, however, the Israeli government requested that the United States extradite Demjanjuk to face a war crimes tribunal in Israel for his alleged actions as Ivan the Terrible. He was eventually deported to Israel in 1986 and was convicted in 1988 of war crimes after a trial that became a media sensation in Israel dwarfed only by the Eichmann case twenty-eight years earlier. But there was a problem—Demjanjuk was not, in fact, Ivan the Terrible. Material from Soviet archives showed that Ivan the Terrible was another man, Ivan Marchenko, and in 1993 the Israeli Supreme Court overturned Demjanjuk's case on appeal. But while Demjanjuk was not Ivan the Terrible, he *was* in fact a guard at the Sobibor extermination camp. To make the saga even more convoluted, an investigation by the U.S. Sixth Court of Appeals later determined that the OSI had deliberately withheld exculpatory materials from Demjanjuk's defense in the U.S. court proving that

Demjanjuk had served at Sobibor, not Treblinka, and therefore couldn't have been Ivan the Terrible. But after Demjanjuk's return from Israel to the United States, the OSI took another crack at him, this time relying on the documentary record from German and Soviet archives rather than eyewitness accounts (most eyewitnesses, by the early 2000s, were dead in any event). Demjanjuk was stripped of his citizenship again and deported to Germany in 2009, where he faced trial in a German court as an accessory to the murder of twenty-nine thousand Jewish prisoners at Sobibor. Demjanjuk was convicted in 2011, released on appeal, and finally died in a nursing home in Bavaria in 2012 at the age of ninety-one.[63]

The legal and political history of the Demjanjuk case is exceedingly complex, as it spans almost forty years across three countries, each grappling with its own historical legacy of the Holocaust. In the United States, the case involved a political and legal community eager to make amends for a history of federal immigration policy that had excluded Jewish refugees from Europe before and during World War II and limited the admission of Jewish refugees *after* World War II in favor of expanding admissions of eastern European and German refugees—many of whom were, like Demjanjuk, complicit in the Holocaust. In addition, the Demjanjuk case became a focal point for American Jewish politics in the 1970s and 1980s, part of the broader process of the historical memory of the Holocaust becoming cemented in American culture. But Demjanjuk also became a focal point for Pat Buchanan.

As far as Buchanan was concerned, the Demjanjuk case was straightforward. His earliest column on the subject, written in 1983 while Demjanjuk was facing deportation to Israel, argued that the OSI's case against Demjanjuk was weak and that Demjanjuk was not Ivan the Terrible. Buchanan was right, but he was right for the wrong reasons—he went on to claim that Demjanjuk was in fact being framed by the KGB. (The original accusation against Demjanjuk did originate from information provided by the Soviet government in 1975—and in this the political motives of Moscow were far from unblemished, as leaking information about Nazi collaborators living freely in the United States helped deflect criticism of the plight of Soviet Jewry and provided a potential weapon against Ukrainian nationalists in exile.) But Buchanan insisted that Demjanjuk was completely innocent— a clear case of a "decent and honest family man whose life has been destroyed by Soviet malice and American gullibility"—going so far as to claim, in a

1986 *Washington Post* column he penned while still serving as White House communications director, that "John Demjanjuk may be the victim of an American Dreyfus case," a rhetorical flourish designed to enrage supporters of the government's case.[64]

Buchanan's outspoken defense of Demjanjuk heightened already existing tensions over antisemitism and the paleoconservative/neoconservative divide within the conservative movement. In a sense, Buchanan was right to call Demjanjuk an American Dreyfus, because as with the Dreyfus affair in France, the question of Demjanjuk's actual guilt or innocence became secondary to the political importance of the issue, which was ultimately about Jewish political power and its relationship with the historical memory of genocide.

Avowed antisemites were explicit about this linkage. From its very first issues, the *Journal of Historical Review,* the unofficial organ of English-language Holocaust denial literature in the United States, was clear about why it sought to debunk the "myth of the six million." As contributor L. A. Rollins put it in 1983, "The Holocaust is part of a myth, comparable to earlier Jewish myths, encompassing the Holocaust, the Exodus and the Rebirth of the State of Israel and . . . this myth explains to Jews why they must support the State of Israel."[65] Holocaust deniers who wrote for the journal were deeply invested in four overlapping political projects: anti-Zionism, anticommunism, anti-liberalism, and the rehabilitation of Germany in general and the Third Reich in particular. Holocaust denial was central to each. The anti-Zionist component of the *Journal's* politics would occasionally result in articles critical of contemporary Israeli policy toward Palestinian Arabs, but these were relatively rare. Rather, most explicit anti-Zionism in the journal was expressed through Holocaust denial—the political logic being that by denying the reality of genocide against the Jews, American and European sympathy for Israel as in some sense expiation for the guilt of the Holocaust would evaporate. Anticommunism provided a useful framework to rehabilitate the Nazis—not as brutal conquerors but, mirroring Nazi propaganda from the Second World War, as valiant warriors embarked on an anti-Bolshevik crusade in defense of European civilization.

This also necessarily included a critique of New Deal liberalism—after all, the Roosevelt administration successfully waged war alongside the Soviet Union against Nazi Germany. Correspondingly, the *Journal of Historical Review* dedicated entire issues to the conspiracy theory that

Franklin Roosevelt had advance knowledge of the Japanese attack on Pearl Harbor and deliberately withheld this information from the military in order to use the attack as a back door into the European conflict. The journal even published an article in 1981 that criticized Japanese American internment, noting that "one of the most significant aspects of this act of racist repression is the fact that it was not the work of a clique of fascists and right-wing militarists. Rather, it was advocated, justified, and administered by men well known for their support of liberalism and democracy." Lest one be lured into the suspicion that the *Journal of Historical Review* was making a Horkheimerian argument about the banality of fascist processes in liberal societies, the article went on to insist that "the Germans . . . had great legal justification" for their policies against European Jews because while "the Japanese were sent to camps solely on suspicion of what they might do . . . many thousands of Jews throughout Europe had committed countless acts of murder, destruction, sabotage, arson, and theft before the Germans began their general evacuation."[66]

The *Journal of Historical Review*'s treatment of the Demjanjuk case—which was used by many far-right organizations as a cause célèbre and a fund-raising opportunity—was entirely in keeping with its broader political projects. In a review of OSI chief Alan Ryan's memoir, contributor Ted O'Keefe blasted the Demjanjuk prosecution as a politically motivated sham conducted by a "prosecutorial shyster whose mind is nimble and devious enough to carry out the duties his masters (don't worry, he tells us who they are) have entrusted him" with. Although—drawing from Buchanan's argument—much of the article castigated the OSI for falling for a KGB forgery, a significant portion was dedicated to the proposition that the death toll at Treblinka—which legitimate historians estimate at nearly 1 million—was not physically possible given various conjectured mechanics of how the gas chambers and mobile gas vans must have actually worked. Clearly—in the eyes of the *Journal*—Ryan was an Israeli puppet, and "his fawning compliance with Soviet officials might be more than enough to disqualify him for any position in American government," particularly given that the Reagan administration "at least gives lip service to American nationalism and anti-Communism."[67]

While serving in the White House, Buchanan was careful never to explicitly mirror the language of Holocaust deniers. In no small part this was because, as a senior White House official, Buchanan was able to apply political pressure on the OSI over the Demjanjuk case and other prosecutions of former Nazis. While in the White House he met with supporters of Arthur Rudolph, a former Nazi rocket scientist who had been brought to the United States under Operation Paperclip and became one of the chief designers of the Saturn V rocket for NASA in the 1960s. After an OSI investigation revealed the extensive use of primarily Jewish slave labor in the German V-2 program, Rudolph was pressured by the OSI to renounce his American citizenship and voluntarily leave the country for West Germany in 1984. Buchanan met with Rudolph's former German colleagues in October 1985 and was widely reported in the press as having given his support for restoring Rudolph's citizenship. (Buchanan denied this, telling the UPI that "he would not have any influence anyway" on the matter.)[68] Buchanan also opposed the deportation to the Soviet Union of Karl Linnas, an Estonian immigrant alleged to have been the commandant of a concentration camp outside of Tartu who had been convicted in absentia by a Soviet court in 1962. Buchanan even interceded with Attorney General Ed Meese to block Linnas's deportation shortly before he left his post as White House communications chief in February 1987.[69] At every step of the way, Buchanan emphasized—as he had with the Demjanjuk case—that his opposition to the proceedings was rooted in his anticommunism. "I think it is Orwellian and Kafkaesque," he told reporters, "to deport an American citizen to the Soviet Union to stand trial for collaboration with Adolf Hitler when the principal collaborator with Hitler in starting World War II was that self-same Soviet government."[70]

Buchanan's tone shifted, however, in an infamous March 1990 syndicated column about the Demjanjuk case. By then more questions had been raised about Demjanjuk's supposed identity as Ivan the Terrible—the CBS news program 60 Minutes aired a report that month identifying Ivan the Terrible as Ivan Marchenko, not Demjanjuk—and Buchanan reiterated his argument in the newspaper: Demjanjuk was the victim of a frame-up by the KGB. There were two novel components in Buchanan's column, however. One, he acknowledged (but did not seem especially troubled by) Demjanjuk's position as a guard at Sobibor. Two, more significantly, Buchanan repeated the talking points of Holocaust deniers about how the diesel engine used as the mechanism of death in the gas chambers at Treblinka was not actually capable of killing the 850,000 victims of the camp. "Diesel engines do not emit enough carbon monoxide to kill anybody," Buchanan insisted.[71]

Harvard law professor Alan Dershowitz penned a response later in March: "After years of flirting with the dark forces of anti-Semitism and pro-fascism," Buchanan had become "a full-fledged, card-carrying member of the so-called 'revisionist' school that denies or minimizes Hitler's murder of 6 million Jews." But the initial response from other columnists was surprisingly muted; Dershowitz's piece was the sole riposte in any major publication for nearly six months. In August Mark Lasswell wrote a profile of Buchanan for *GQ* in which he framed the column as quintessential Buchanan—good ol' Pat spewing out an uninformed opinion on a subject he knew nothing about, which is to say that Buchanan did not seem to understand that filling a specialized chamber with exhaust fumes killed not through carbon monoxide poisoning, but rather through lack of oxygen.[72]

But it was only after Abe Rosenthal's column in September 1990 that Buchanan's theories on Treblinka were widely condemned as antisemitic.[73] Why? There are three probable reasons. One, Buchanan's pattern of defending Nazi war criminals and his thoughts on Demjanjuk were already commonly known by early 1990. Two, the case against Demjanjuk as Ivan the Terrible was already falling apart. Three, unlike the Iraqi invasion of Kuwait and the looming potential of an American war in the Middle East, the potential conviction of an ex-Nazi by an Israeli court was a geopolitical nonstory. Buchanan's asinine, offensive, and antisemitic commentary on Treblinka was less a political problem than fodder for the larger issue: American policy in the Middle East and Buchanan's views on U.S.-Israel relations. This was not simply a problem for Buchanan, either. He was preparing to challenge George H. W. Bush from the right in the Republican primary in 1992, laying claim to be Ronald Reagan's legitimate successor as the high priest of American conservatism.

For conservatives, it was a time for choosing.

"In Search of Anti-Semitism" hit the newsstands in the first week of 1992, a few weeks after William F. Buckley tentatively endorsed Pat Buchanan in the 1992 Republican primary, in Buckley's reasoning as a tactical measure to underline to George H. W. Bush that he could not take conservative support for granted and to push him, as far as possible, to the right. Buckley reiterated that he would not have given Buchanan his tactical endorsement if he thought Buchanan was an antisemite—although *National Review* editor John O'Sullivan, in his introductory essay, conceded that both Sobran and

Buchanan may have inadvertently crossed a line from principled anti-Zionism into antisemitism. Both Buckley and O'Sullivan invoked the *American Mercury* saga and the "expulsion" of the Birchers from the responsible conservative movement in the 1950s and 1960s to burnish their credentials—and Buckley added for good measure that his own father's intense antisemitism gave him special insight on the subject. Buckley conceded that Joe Sobran's columns, both in 1986 and his more recent work opposing U.S. policy in the Gulf War, might be reasonably interpreted as having been "written by a writer inclined to anti-Semitism," but he also defended his friend and protégé. Buckley argued that, in the 1990s, antisemitism was a problem of the *left*, not the *right*, and while Sobran was not "blameless" he had defenders even among American Jews, citing paleoconservative political scientist Paul Gottfried, who wrote to the *New Republic* that "some neoconservatives reacted hysterically— even opportunistically—to Joe Sobran's observations about American Jews." Buchanan, for his part, was the victim of, if not a coordinated smear campaign, then a campaign of attacks triggered by the Rosenthal article in September 1990. Nevertheless, Buckley admitted that he found it "impossible to defend Patrick Buchanan from the charge that what he said and did . . . amounted to anti-Semitism, whatever it was that drove him to do or say it."[74]

One of the difficulties facing Buckley and *National Review* broadly was that, although the magazine had embraced some degree of religious ecumenicalism since its beginning, it was still very much a conservative *Catholic* magazine. Buckley had taken on the Jewish conservative writer David Brooks as an editor at *National Review* in 1984, and the young Brooks quickly became part of Buckley's inner circle. There were rumors that when Buckley stepped down from editing *National Review* he would name Brooks as his successor, but Buckley reportedly blanched because Brooks was not a Catholic (and was a Canadian to boot), opting instead for O'Sullivan. Buckley's apparent logic was that there were already conservative *Jewish* magazines in existence, notably *Commentary*, which had long since disavowed any affiliation with the left, and that the specifically Catholic character of *National Review* needed to be preserved. This colored Buckley's defense of both Buchanan and especially Sobran, who hinged his resentment of organized Jewish life in the United States on his dissatisfaction with the political power of conservative Catholicism.[75]

"In Search of Anti-Semitism" also made revealing attempts at particular forms of group solidarity. Buckley downplayed the persistence of antisemitism in Europe and North America, dismissing a poll of Austrians in 1988 that found that 20 percent of respondents were in favor of legally prohibiting Jews from owning property in Austria by commenting that "some of the questions [in the poll] were on the order of 'do you believe the experience of slavery benefitted the Negro race?' to which question 21 percent of Americans might answer Yes—reasoning, with Booker T. Washington, that slavery en route to emancipation was preferable to a continuation of the kind of life common in Africa during the 18th century." In Buckley's view, Sobran's articles on Israel and American Jews were provocative and perhaps over the line, but "on the other hand there is discussion of such questions as relative black intelligence, sexual promiscuity, and upward mobility that still gets a sober hearing in sober surroundings." Indeed, less than two years later Marty Peretz's *New Republic* would run its infamous—and since repudiated—cover story featuring the race/IQ work of Charles Murray. O'Sullivan, in his introductory essay, repeatedly emphasized the prominence of Black antisemites on the left, including Leonard Jeffries, Jesse Jackson, and Louis Farrakhan, who enjoyed the indulgence of "big-city politicians . . . respectable black organizations . . . and the willingness of the establishment media to report such matters in a context of social issues."[76] The conservative coalition—and even some liberals as well—could find common ground through anti-Black racism.

Buckley's essay provided enough political deflection for *National Review* to favorably, if guardedly, cover Buchanan's 1992 primary campaign. Senior editor Richard Brookhiser followed Buchanan around during his upset victory in the New Hampshire primary, and while Buchanan's staple talking points—the dangers of the New World Order, the rising economic threat from Asia, his opposition to a North American free-trade pact—were treated skeptically, the magazine did acknowledge that Buchanan was speaking to genuine currents on the right that had long been dormant. Murray Rothbard told *National Review's* Washington bureau chief, William McGurn, at a John Randolph Club event that "what happened to the original Right, and the cause of the present mess, was the advent and domination of the right wing by Bill Buckley and the *National Review*," but that Buchanan was here to revive it. "The original Right, and all its heresies, is back." McGurn agreed with Rothbard, writing that the "wrong turn [meant by Rothbard] is not traceable to [the Gulf War] but to Bill Buckley's purge in the mid Sixties of sundry 'non-respectables' (Birchers, Randians, anti-Zionists, etc.)," but also that Buchanan was not an orthodox paleoconservative. "After all, he is campaigning as Reagan's heir against a President who diluted that legacy." Buchanan, in the eyes of *National Review,* was an imperfect political ally who was flatly wrong about free trade, and whose vendetta against neoconservatives as "domestic liberals and thus heretics" was "simply wrong" and ultimately self-defeating to the conservative movement as it would "reduce the size and appeal of the conservative coalition and concentrate public attention on its divisions." The magazine judged him as probably unable to replicate Ronald Reagan's political magic—he lacked Reagan's sunny optimism and aura of geniality—but also understood Buchanan to be a genuine conservative.[77]

The official editorial line of the magazine—and Buckley's own stance on the Buchanan campaign—was ambivalent. An open letter to the magazine signed by Richard John Neuhaus, Robert Bork, R. Emmett Tyrrell Jr., and nearly a dozen other prominent conservatives published in the March 16, 1992 issue called Buckley and the editors "not morally consistent" for admitting Buchanan was an antisemite yet still urging conservatives to vote for him over Bush. Buckley deflected in his response—he thought that some of Buchanan's statements crossed the line and could be considered antisemitism, but Buchanan was *not* an antisemite. As for the question of voting for Buchanan, "were I resident of New Hampshire, I would vote for Buchanan in order to communicate to Mr. Bush the stamina of the protest vote, but . . . if the contest between the two were not for the nomination but for the Presidency, I would vote for Mr. Bush because of the shortcomings I find in Mr. Buchanan's policies." O'Sullivan went further in his own editorial, defending Buchanan's stance on Demjanjuk as having been vindicated and suggesting that Buchanan's intransigence in the face of his critics was attributable to his wounded "Scotch-Irish pride."[78]

For the gatekeepers of the conservative coalition, Buchanan's successes in the 1992 primary posed a challenge. On the one hand, there was little hope of Buchanan actually unseating Bush, although a strong enough showing in New Hampshire along the lines of Lyndon Johnson's surprisingly narrow seven-point victory over Eugene McCarthy in New Hampshire in 1968 might have convinced Bush to not seek reelection. Buchanan came within fifteen points of George H. W. Bush—enough to draw blood, but not enough to spook Bush out of the race (in 1976, incumbent Gerald Ford beat challenger Ronald Reagan in New Hampshire by only two points, and Ford still managed to win the primary). But while it was clear that Buchanan would neither unseat Bush nor knock him out of the race, he was positioning himself as the leader of the right wing of the Republican Party and a strong contender for 1996. O'Sullivan noted that at the 1992 Conservative Political Action Conference, "more than half the rank and file" of the conservative movement was behind Buchanan. "He probably has an even higher proportion of younger conservatives on his side." O'Sullivan was very aware of walking a political tightrope—conservative activists supported Buchanan, but Buchanan could not win against Bush. What was the solution? "My own preference would be to support Mr. Buchanan until a millisecond before he himself decides to support Mr. Bush. . . . With luck, we might then maintain the unity and integrity of the conservative movement, avoid responsibility if Mr. Bush loses the general election, and transform Mr. Buchanan from this year's Mr. Wallace into one of several respectable conservative leaders for 1996."[79]

At the end of March, the magazine took a victory lap—the Buchanan campaign prompted Bush to "[fire] the head of the National Endowment for the Arts, [embrace] voluntary school prayer, and [disavow] the 1990 budget deal." By energizing conservative voters, Buchanan "gave discontented voters a safe haven in the Republican column," and—crucially—crowded out former Ku Klux Klan leader David Duke's protest run for the nomination. "Without Mr. Buchanan in the field, Mr. Duke would have been the sole repository of protest votes. His success would have discredited conservative issues and set off a national liberal talk-in on the unregenerate racism of American society." While the magazine avowed that it differed with Buchanan on many issues—above all on the question of protectionism—"it is crucial that the debate be as fraternal as it is vigorous, as civilized as it is sharp." Intra-conservative attacks, especially if they echoed liberal criticisms (such as Buchanan being a racist or an antisemite) would "reinforce the loyalty of the conservative rank-and-file and undermine the critics, who are seen as trafficking with the enemy." In many respects, National Review's editorial stance on the Buchanan phenomenon mirrored its position on the Birchers before 1965—a widespread recognition that both Buchanan and Welch could make credible claims for being the genuine spokespersons for a national grassroots conservative movement, certainly more so than the editors at National Review. William McGurn, who followed Buchanan in the Georgia primary, wrote that "having tracked the news reports and columns,

I half-expected to find goose-stepping mobs and burning crosses. But the crowds coming out to see Pat Buchanan are not wearing white sheets or egging him on to stick it to Israel. . . . Most typical were people whose favorite radio personality is Rush Limbaugh and who refer to Buchanan as 'Pat.' "[80]

Not every contributor was impressed by the strength of the Buchanan brigades—Michael Barone dismissed the campaign as a failed attempt to "move Republican conservatism back to the isolationism, protectionism, and nativism of [Robert] Taft's time" and predicted that Buchanan was unlikely to be a strong contender in 1996. Still, Buchanan was able to translate his strength in the primary to a prime-time spot at the Republican National Convention in August, and his declaration of a "war for the soul of America"—the opening salvo of the 1990s culture wars—in his opening-night speech was infinitely more memorable than any of President Bush's bromides.[81]

National Review did not support Buchanan's 1996 run for the Republican nomination, but did not fully turn against Buchanan until his departure from the Republican Party in 1999. Ramesh Ponnuru wrote in a cover story about Buchanan that "conservative fans" of Buchanan "persist in seeing him as a comrade-in-arms" but that Buchanan—and, by extension, his political allies like right-wing writer and political theorist Samuel T. Francis—was a mere political opportunist looking to re-create Richard Nixon's "Middle American Radical" coalition. "But the Nixon coalition was not a conservative coalition, as Nixon's policies amply proved," and Buchanan was, by 1999, a tired old man "who decided at some point that exploiting cultural resentments and seeing various elites get their comeuppance mattered more than expanding freedom. . . . [Buchanan] is in no important sense a conservative anymore."[82] Ponnuru, like much of the conservative establishment in the late 1990s and early 2000s, believed that the neoconservatives had won, perhaps permanently.

Neither Buchanan nor Joseph Sobran was purged from the conservative movement because of racism, antisemitism, or even opposition to U.S. foreign policy. Buchanan was finally condemned by *National Review* only after his bid for the top slot in the Republican Party twice failed, and even then only on the grounds that Buchanan was trying to build a losing political coalition. Sobran, for his part, continued to write for *National Review* for another two years—in fact, an essay by Sobran defending himself was featured in a follow-up issue on antisemitism in March 1992. Sobran even wrote two cover stories for the magazine in 1993—one on the rise of the *Washington Post*'s style section, the other on President Bill Clinton's new appointments.[83]

The final break between Sobran and Buckley came not through the pages of *National Review,* but through Sobran's extracurricular writings. For years Sobran wrote a syndicated column in the *Wanderer,* a small traditional-istic Catholic newspaper based in St. Paul, Minnesota, which featured columns by Sobran, Pat Buchanan, and Sam Francis. And in the pages of the *Wanderer,* Sobran felt free to let loose. He compared Bill Clinton to Adolf Hitler, defended the murders of abortion doctors ("pro-abortion liberals mustn't complain about vigilante action"), and attacked the United States Holocaust Memorial Museum as dedicated to the premise that "mass murder is worse when its victims are Jews." Yet it was only after a column in which Sobran attacked Buckley personally as a social climber who turned his back on "*our* people"—meaning conservative Catholics—in order to satisfy his "social ambition" by appealing to New York Jews—"especially the Zionist apparat. He will *never* cross them"—that Buckley hit back.

Buckley was incensed. He not only fired Sobran from *National Review,* but wrote to the *Wanderer* that Sobran's column was "evidence of an inca-pacitation moral and perhaps medical," and that the article was a "breath-catching libel." Sobran, in a rebuttal, countered that "Bill's ambition has led him to play a positively malign role in conservatism . . . [muddling] his own conservatism badly, reducing it to a set of reflexive mannerisms and rendering his prose almost unreadable." As with the broadsides against the Reagan administration, these were old complaints by the far right against institutional conservatism and its leadership. And yet Sobran, despite his distaste for Bill Buckley and his social climbing—a code term not just for having too many Jewish friends, but for Buckley's softening of his archcon-servative image to appeal to moderates and liberals since the late 1960s—continued to write for *National Review* magazine until this final rupture. And Buckley, despite writing a book explicitly disavowing Sobran as an anti-semite, continued to publish him in *National Review* until Sobran's personal attack on him as a sellout.[84]

Sobran and to a lesser extent Buchanan believed themselves to be scape-goats and sacrificial lambs in the paleoconservative conflict with neoconservatism, along with such luminaries as Paul Gottfried, Sam Francis, Murray Rothbard, among others. Like Revilo Oliver and Robert Welch a generation before, they were eventually excluded from the conservative movement on the grounds of "respectability"—meaning, per Sobran, that the conservative movement *they* helped to build cast them out in order to burnish its credentials with Jewish neoconservatives and their liberal allies. Antisemitism was central to much of this narrative—even among paleoconservatives who were, like Rothbard, Jewish—but so, too, was a certain political naïveté, even incredulity, that they could face consequences for their speech and their actions, especially from other conservatives.

Sobran fell the furthest—by the early 2000s he was a frequent guest at conferences organized by the Institute of Historical Review, the publisher of the Holocaust denialist *Journal of Historical Studies,* which Sobran had allowed to reprint material from his columns and newsletters in the mid-1990s. He was persona non grata among his former colleagues at *National Review,* but when Sobran died in 2010—only two years after his former mentor William F. Buckley—he was the subject of a highly empathetic obituary by his former colleague Matthew Scully. "You know you've been around a while," Scully wrote wistfully, "when a rising conservative columnist presumes, as happened once in my company, to denigrate Joseph Sobran as if he were some old nobody—the bum who got run off for being a hatemonger." Scully called Sobran the greatest literary talent *National Review* had ever produced (perhaps overselling Sobran's literary talent compared to other *National Review* contributors like Joan Didion), and portrayed him as an essentially tragic figure. "Joe traded a friend and mentor who loved him for new company that was beneath him, *National Review* for the Institute of Historical Research."[85]

Pat Buchanan, unlike Sobran, did not openly embrace the company of the Institute for Historical Review (in fact, Buchanan's offer to Sobran to write a column for his new *American Conservative* magazine was revoked by Buchanan's editor Scott McConnell in 2001 when Sobran refused to break ties with the denialist world) and continued to enjoy prominent media positions in the 2000s—he became, after 9/11, MSNBC's in-house conservative critic of the George W. Bush administration. Buchanan's views on World War II, the Holocaust, and the question of German war guilt have remained remarkably consistent since the 1990s. It is little wonder that neo-Nazi leader Richard Spencer cut his teeth as an editor at Buchanan's *American*

Conservative in the late 2000s. In 2008 Buchanan published a book on the origins of World War II, *Churchill, Hitler, and the Unnecessary War,* in which he argued not only that British participation in World War I was a mistake (a controversial but relatively unremarkable argument that had been made by the conservative British historian Niall Ferguson a decade before in his 1998 book *The Pity of War*), but that Britain was ultimately responsible for the outbreak of World War II. Buchanan characterized German aims in 1939 as ultimately modest, aimed at creating an anti-Bolshevik alliance in Europe, and argued that Winston Churchill bore moral responsibility for the Holocaust for refusing Hitler's peace offer after the invasion of France in the summer of 1940. Criticism of the book was nearly universal—even Buchanan's own magazine published a scathing review by self-described reactionary John Lukacs, who compared Buchanan to infamous Holocaust denier David Irving.[86]

The search for antisemitism did not have to search far.

Epilogue

THE ELECTION OF DONALD TRUMP as president of the United States in 2016 precipitated an explosion of interest in reevaluating the American conservative movement. Writing in the *New York Times* a few months after the campaign ended, Rick Perlstein reflected, "The professional guardians of America's past . . . had made a mistake. We advanced a narrative of the American right that was far too constricted to anticipate the rise of a man like Trump."[1] Over the past several years, a number of historians have stepped into this void: John H. Huntington has argued convincingly that grassroots conservative activists in the latter half of the twentieth century in fact held fundamentally far-right political beliefs; Julian Zelizer has linked the radical right-wing turn in Republican electoral politics to the scorched-earth procedural tactics of Speaker of the House Newt Gingrich in the 1990s; and Nicole Hemmer has argued that the end of the Cold War fractured the Reagan Revolution and opened up space for a far-right resurgence.[2] But Trumpism remains hotly contested among scholars, especially over the question of fascism. One of the earliest pieces speculating on Trump and fascism was Isaac Chotiner's interview with the historian of fascism Robert Paxton for *Slate* in February 2016. Paxton emphasized that "there are certainly some echoes of fascism, but there are also very profound differences," especially the differing historical circumstances in Europe after World War I compared to the twenty-first-century United States. Most scholars who were pressed on this question by journalists were quick to emphasize the differences, as well as the inherent problems of historical analogizing. While most historians were circumspect about making those comparisons—at least on the record—the so-called "fascism debate" dominated both politics and historiography for most of the Trump years.[3] Was Donald Trump a fascist? Was Trump in continuity with the political traditions of American conservatism, or was he a rupture or aberration? Consensus on these questions, at least between 2017 and 2021, was elusive in no small part because of the constantly shifting political terrain.

This was before 2021.

After the January 6, 2021 insurrection, which saw the deliberate and premeditated mobilization by the Trump White House of paramilitaries to storm the U.S. Capitol Building and attempt to overturn the results of the 2020 election, Paxton no longer hesitated. "Trump's incitement of the invasion of the Capitol on January 6, 2021 removes my objection to the fascist label," he wrote in *Newsweek*. "His open encouragement of civic violence to overturn an election crosses a red line. The label now seems not just acceptable but necessary."[4] Some critics on the left have continued to insist that it is incorrect to categorize Trump and Trumpism as meaningfully fascist, either out of concerns that liberal anti-fascism could be redeployed against the left or, drawing on the work of sociologist Dylan Riley, on the grounds that authentic fascism requires a combination of robust civic associations and meaningful challenges from the left to existing power arrangements.[5] These arguments, however, have been rejected even by many Marxists— political scientist Adolph Reed, although insisting in an August 2021 editorial that he did not want to "quibble" over the fascist label, titled his essay "The Whole Country Is the *Reichstag*," and the general consensus, as of 2023, is that MAGAism is indeed a form of twenty-first-century American fascism. Even President Joe Biden called MAGA Trumpism "semi-fascism" in August 2022.[6]

What has been less precisely defined is the relationship between American conservatism and American fascism. Conservatives dating back to the 1930s bitterly resented "smears," as John T. Flynn called them, linking conservatives and conservative institutions to fascism. According to the classic conservative narrative of these political attacks, they reflect not genuine anxieties regarding the far right rooted in a fair reading of evidence from liberals and leftists, but rather cheap political attacks to discredit conservatives. This is why William F. Buckley Jr. threatened to punch Gore Vidal on national television for calling him a crypto-fascist. Conservatives crafted a deliberate political strategy to push back against liberal "smears" against conservatism by insisting that fascism and Nazism were fundamentally *left-wing* phenomena. Borrowing from early Cold War rhetoric that insisted that German Nazism and Soviet communism were two sides of the same totalitarian, statist, and collectivist coin, conservatives sought to frame themselves as the only genuine anti-fascists in American politics because of their commitment to free markets and limited government. The apotheosis of this particular argument was Jonah Goldberg's 2007 book *Liberal Fascism*, which argued that American liberalism was in fact the ideological heir of the European fascist movements of the early twentieth century. Revealingly, Goldberg's explicit motive for writing his book, as he recounts at its very beginning, is that he was tired of liberal slander that "conservatism has connections with fascism"—"the left," he maintained, "wields the term fascism like a cudgel."[7] Certainly liberalism and fascism are more closely interwoven than many liberals would like to admit, but there is an important distinction to be made between systemic critiques that implicate the practices of liberal democratic states and institutions on a global scale. Aimé Césaire made precisely this argument in his classic *Discourse on Colonialism*, astutely noting how fascism was, in many respects, the techniques of the colonialism practiced by the liberal European empires brought back to the metropole. Other thinkers—particularly from the Black radical tradition— have made apt comparisons between the liberal carceral state and fascism. Black Panther Party leader Kathleen Cleaver wrote in 1968 that what was most clearly fascist in America was "the concentration of massive police power in the ghettos of the black community across the country."[8]

This was not the same as claiming that Hillary Clinton's support for universal healthcare in the 1990s made her the heir to Mussolini.

Historians of fascism, unsurprisingly, overwhelmingly rejected Goldberg's arguments. Goldberg, wrote Robert Paxton in a critical review for *History News Network* in 2010, "wants to attach a defaming epithet to liberals and the left, to 'put the brown shirt on [your] opponents,' as he accuses the liberals of doing."[9] The "liberal fascism" trope served an important political purpose in the 2010s: to obfuscate historical and contemporary connections between the conservative movement and American fascism. It was not always effective—pundit Glenn Beck, for instance, endorsed the work of

Elizabeth Dilling on his radio show in 2010, praising her 1934 book *The Red Network* as an example of "people [in the past] who were doing what we're doing now," that is, educating Americans about the depth of liberal and communist subversion.[10] Beck caught considerable flack for praising Dilling. In general, however, "liberal fascism" suited the purposes of conservatives. It was also a politically useful inoculation against an increasingly radicalized "alternative right" that emerged from paleoconservative circles in the early part of the decade. Richard Spencer, one of the organizers of the deadly Unite the Right rally in Charlottesville, Virginia in August 2017, cut his teeth in politics as an editor at Pat Buchanan's *American Conservative* magazine. Even in the early 2010s, conservatives and the far right were synonymous. Spencer even co-edited a volume with Paul Gottfried in 2015 that bitterly lamented that Buckley's "purges" of far rightists deformed the conservative movement. But the precise boundaries between the factions remained, as had been the case over the course of the twentieth century, blurred; John Derbyshire, one of the contributors to the volume, had been a longtime contributor to *National Review* before being cashiered in 2012 after writing a racist column in *Taki's Magazine*.[11] Had Derbyshire been somewhat more circumspect about his views and avoided sparking outrage from liberals, it is entirely possible he could have continued writing for *National Review* indefinitely.

The intertwined relationship between the conservative movement and the fascistic far right has implications for the historiographical question about Trumpian aberration versus continuity with the broader history of American conservatism. From the beginning of his primary campaign in 2015, Trump was viewed with outright hostility by most members of the conservative establishment. In January 2016 the editors of *National Review* dedicated an entire issue of the magazine to attacking Trump; dozens of prominent conservative commentators proclaimed themselves "Never Trumpers," meaning that they would never vote for Donald Trump in either the primary or general election.[12] But a curious thing happened after Trump's narrow victory in November: most Never Trumpers quickly made their peace with the new political realities in the conservative movement. *National Review*, for instance, never totally repudiated its earlier criticisms of Trump, but it pivoted after he took office to an anti-anti-Trump stance.[13]

As of this writing, it is unclear what direction the Republican Party and the conservative movement will go for the rest of the decade. Donald Trump still remains influential and popular among the conservative grassroots, but MAGAism is unpopular with the general public—particularly since the January 6 uprising—and Trump-backed candidates have been repeatedly repudiated at the polls in 2018, 2020, and 2022. But even if the political hegemony of MAGAism over the Republican Party is beginning to recede—and it is far from clear that this is actually the case—the GOP remains the political home of the far right. The Republican congressional delegation in 2023 boasts among its members Marjorie Taylor Greene, who has claimed that a Jewish-controlled space laser has been setting off wildfires in the American West; George Santos, a pathological liar who, among other things, falsely claimed to be descended from Holocaust survivors and has made repeated antisemitic comments on his social media accounts; and several people who apparently coordinated with insurrectionists on January 6, 2021. Where American conservatism will go from here is an open question, but wherever it does go, the far right will be there.

NOTES

INTRODUCTION

1. See, for instance, Ryan Lizza, "Donald Trump's Hostile Takeover of the G.O.P.," *New Yorker*, January 28, 2016, https://www.newyorker.com/news/daily-comment/donald-trumps-hostile-takeover-of-the-g-o-p; and Joe Scarborough, "Donald Trump's Hostile Takeover of the Republican Party," *Washington Post*, March 1, 2016, https://www.washingtonpost.com/blogs/post-partisan/wp/2016/03/01/donald-trumps-hostile-takeover-of-the-republican-party/.

2. Ramesh Ponnnuru, "Never Trump," *National Review*, March 28, 2016, https://www.nationalreview.com/magazine/2016/03/28/never-trump/; Graham Vyse, "*National Review* in the Wilderness," *New Republic*, March 20, 2017, https://newrepublic.com/article/141411/national-review-magazine-wilderness-conservatism-age-trump.

3. For a sympathetic account of the Never Trump conservatives, see Robert P. Saldin and Steven M. Teles, *Never Trump: The Revolt of the Conservative Elites* (New York: Press, 2020).

4. Robert Paxton, "I've Hesitated to Call Donald Trump a Fascist. Until Now," *Newsweek*, January 11, 2021, https://www.newsweek.com/robert-paxton-trump-fascist-1560652.

5. Luke Broadwater, "Republicans Open Inquiry into Treatment of Jan. 6 Defendants at D.C. Jail," *New York Times*, March 9, 2023, https://www.nytimes.com/2023/03/09/us/politics/jan-6-prisoners-republican-investigation.html.

6. Rosie Gray, "Trump Defends White Nationalist Protesters: 'Some Very Fine People on Both Sides,'" *Atlantic*, August 15, 2017, https://www.theatlantic.com/politics/archive/2017/08/trump-defends-white-nationalist-protesters-some-very-fine-people-on-both-sides/537012/.

7. Lisa Mascaro, "White Nationalists Dress Up and Come to Washington in Hopes of Influencing Trump," *Los Angeles Times,* November 19, 2016, https://www. latimes.com/nation/la-na-pol-white-nationalists-thinktank-20161119-story.html.

8. Paul E. Gottfried and Richard B. Spencer, eds., *The Great Purge: The Deformation of the American Conservative Movement* (Arlington, VA: Washington Summit, 2015), ix–xviii.

9. Buckley has been the subject of multiple biographies, and his political career has been at the heart of many seminal works on the history of media and of American conservatism. See, for instance, John B. Judis, *William F. Buckley, Jr., Patron Saint of the Conservatives* (New York: Simon & Schuster, 1988); Carl T. Bogus, *Buckley: William F. Buckley, Jr. and the Rise of Conservatism* (New York: Bloomsbury, 2011); Heather Hendershot, *Open to Debate: How William F. Buckley Put Liberal America on the Firing Line* (New York: Broadside Books, 2016); Nicole Hemmer, *Messengers of the Right: Media and the Modern Conservative Movement* (Philadelphia: University of Pennsylvania Press, 2016); and Alvin S. Felzenberg, *A Man and His Presidents: The Political Odyssey of William F. Buckley, Jr.* (New Haven, CT: Yale University Press, 2017). On Buckley's lawsuits, see "Gore Vidal Is Sued by Buckley for $500,000," *Chicago Tribune,* May 8, 1969, A2; "Buckley Sues," *Atlanta Constitution,* August 15, 1969, 2A; C. Dean Reasoner to Forsythe, May 16, 1955, William F. Buckley Jr. to Morris D. Forkosch, August 13, 1957, and Morris D. Forkosch to Clarence R. Martin, September 10, 1957, all in William F. Buckley Jr. Papers (MS 576), box 2, Manuscripts and Archives, Yale University Library, New Haven, CT; "National Labor Daily to Die April 30 Unless Unions Raise $50,000," *Wall Street Journal,* March 4, 1958, 17.

10. Robert Welch to William S. Schlamm, June 30, 1955, and William F. Buckley Jr. to Robert Welch, October 21, 1960, William F. Buckley Jr. Papers (MS 576), box 2.

11. George Lincoln Rockwell to William F. Buckley Jr., January 16, 1964, William F. Buckley Jr. Papers (MS 576), box 149.

12. Revilo Oliver to William F. Buckley Jr., June 29, 1959, William F. Buckley Jr. Papers (MS 576), box 9.

13. See, for instance, George H. Nash, *The Conservative Intellectual Movement in America since 1945* (New York: Basic Books, 1976).

14. Alan Brinkley, "The Problem of American Conservatism," *American Historical Review* 99 (April 1994): 409–29. The literature on postwar conservatism is immense and growing. Postwar studies of American conservatism that emphasize political geography include Kevin M. Kruse, *White Flight: Atlanta and the Making of Modern Conservatism* (Princeton, NJ: Princeton University Press, 2005); Matthew Lassiter, *The Silent Majority: Suburban Politics in the Sunbelt South* (Princeton, NJ: Princeton University Press, 2006); Elizabeth Tandy Shermer, *Sunbelt Capitalism: Phoenix and the Transformation of American Politics* (Philadelphia: University of Pennsylvania Press, 2013); and Lisa McGirr, *Suburban Warriors: The Origins of the New American Right* (Princeton, NJ: Princeton University Press, 2001), the latter of which covers the John Birch Society. On conservatives and gender, see Michelle Nickerson, *Mothers of*

Conservatism: Women and the Postwar Right (Princeton, NJ: Princeton University Press, 2012). On media, see Hemmer, *Messengers of the Right;* Mark Major, "Objective but Not Impartial: *Human Events,* Barry Goldwater, and the Development of the 'Liberal Media' in the Conservative Counter-Sphere," *New Political Science* 34, no. 4 (2012): 455–68; and David Greenberg, "The Idea of the 'Liberal Media' and Its Roots in the Civil Rights Movement," *The Sixties: A Journal of Political History* 1, no. 2 (2008): 167–88. On Christianity and postwar conservatism, see Daniel Williams, *God's Own Party: The Making of the Christian Right* (New York: Oxford University Press, 2010); and Kevin M. Kruse, *One Nation under God: How Corporate America Invented Christian America* (New York: Basic Books, 2015).

15. On the John Birch Society, see D. J. Mulloy, *The World of the John Birch Society: Conspiracy, Conservatism, and the Cold War* (Nashville, TN: Vanderbilt University Press, 2014) as well as McGirr, *Suburban Warriors.* Most of the literature on the far right in the 1950s focuses on activists who began their careers during the Great Depression, including Leo Ribuffo, *The Old Christian Right: The Protestant Far Right from the Great Depression to the Cold War* (Philadelphia: Temple University Press, 1983); Glen Jeansonne, *Women of the Far Right: The Mothers' Movement and World War II* (Chicago: University of Chicago Press, 1996); and *Gerald L. K. Smith, Minister of Hate* (Baton Rouge: Louisiana State University Press, 1997). George Hawley's *Right-Wing Critics of American Conservatism* (Lawrence: University Press of Kansas, 2016) is a newer work that does place the postwar far right in conversation with the American conservative movement, as does Edward T. Miller's *Nut Country: Right-Wing Dallas and the Birth of the Southern Strategy* (Chicago: University of Chicago Press, 2015); and Markku Ruotisla's *Fighting Fundamentalist: Carl McIntire and the Politicization of American Fundamentalism* (New York: Oxford University Press, 2016), which covers similar ground with respect to the religious right. See also Nancy MacLean, *Democracy in Chains: The Deep History of the Radical Right's Stealth Plan for America* (New York: Viking, 2017); and especially Jennifer Burns, *Goddess of the Market: Ayn Rand and the American Right* (New York: Oxford University Press, 2009) for treatment of American libertarianism and its relationship with other elements of the U.S. right. For an excellent synthesis of recent trends in the scholarship on both libertarianism and the far right, see Larry Glickman, *Free Enterprise: An American History* (New Haven, CT: Yale University Press, 2019).

16. The vast majority of scholarship on the left popular front is national in character; there are dozens of individual histories of popular fronts in Europe and North America. Most of the English-language scholarship focuses on France, which saw a Popular Front government come to power between 1936 and 1938 under the leadership of socialist Leon Blum. The best English-language introduction to the French Popular Front is Julian Jackson, *The Popular Front in France: Defending Democracy, 1934–1938* (New York: Cambridge University Press, 1987). For Great Britain, see David Blaazer, *The Popular Front and the Progressive Tradition: Socialists, Liberals, and the Quest for Unity* (New York: Cambridge University Press, 1992). For a comparative study of two different national

popular fronts, see Martin S. Alexander and Helen Graham, eds., *The French and Spanish Popular Fronts: Comparative Perspectives* (New York: Cambridge University Press, 1989). For a cultural history of the Popular Front in the United States, see Michael Denning, *The Cultural Front: The Laboring of American Culture in the Twentieth Century* (New York: Verso, 1997). For a sympathetic analysis of the American Popular Front, see James R. Barrett, "Rethinking the Popular Front," *Rethinking Marxism* 21, no. 4 (October 2009): 531–50. Christopher Vials offers a long-term analysis from the 1930s to the 1980s centering anti-fascism as the key constitutive element of the Popular Front. See Vials, *Liberals, the Left, and the Fight against Fascism in the United States* (Amherst: University of Massachusetts Press, 2014).

17. Hunter S. Thompson, *Fear and Loathing on the Campaign Trail '72* (San Francisco: Straight Arrow, 1973), 414.

18. John H. Ferguson, "The Industrial Workers of the World," *Minneapolis Tribune*, August 31, 1913, 34; letter to the editor, "They Would Welcome the Devil, if the Devil Came as an Advocate of Votes for 'Women,'" *Baltimore Sun*, October 16, 1915, 6; "Hughes Accepts G.O.P. Nomination; Roosevelt, Named by Moose, Declines," *New-York Tribune*, June 11, 1916, 1; "The Lunatic Fringe," *New-York Tribune*, April 20, 1920, 12; "Germany's 'Lunatic Fringe,'" *New York Times*, April 30, 1924, 18. By the mid-1930s "lunatic fringe," although it still carried some degree of anti-leftist baggage, increasingly came to include the more radical elements of the American right and its opposition to the Roosevelt administration. See Dorothy Thompson, "The Lunatic Fringe," *New York Herald Tribune*, July 23, 1936, 17, which describes the "lunatic fringe" as antisemitic and pro-Nazi groups; and Walter Lippmann, "The Lunatic Fringe," *Los Angeles Times*, June 8, 1937, A4. In a commencement address at Drake University, Lippmann castigated both radicals on the left and reactionaries on the right as "lunatic fringe." Theodore Roosevelt, *History as Literature, and Other Essays* (New York: Scribner, 1913), 305.

19. See Glickman, *Free Enterprise*, especially 79–111.

20. Edward-Isaac Dovere, "Obama's 2016 Warning: Trump Is a 'Fascist,'" *Atlantic*, January 25, 2020, https://www.theatlantic.com/politics/archive/2020/01/obama-2016-trump-fascist/605488/; Isaac Chotiner, "Is Donald Trump a Fascist?" *Slate*, February 10, 2016, https://slate.com/news-and-politics/2016/02/is-donald-trump-a-fascist-an-expert-on-fascism-weighs-in.html.

21. For instance, see John Ganz, "My Fascism Problem and Yours," *Medium*, January 25, 2021, https://johnganz.medium.com/my-fascism-problem-and-yours-6b14fe6fbc74; and "What Is Trumpism?" *Unpopular Front*, January 13, 2022, https://johnganz.substack.com/p/what-is-trumpism.

22. Adolph Reed Jr., "The Whole Country Is the Reichstag," *Nonsite.org*, August 23, 2021, https://nonsite.org/the-whole-country-is-the-reichstag/.

23. Daniel Bessner, "Does American Fascism Exist?" *New Republic*, March 6, 2023, https://newrepublic.com/article/170890/does-american-fascism-exist. See also Katie Halper, interview with Jason Stanley, Jodi Dean, Sam Moyn, Daniel

Bessner, and Eugene Puryear, podcast audio, 2021, https://soundcloud.com/katie-halper/debate-is-it-fascism.

CHAPTER 1. "IT IS TIME TO BRUSH ASIDE THIS WORD 'DEMOCRACY'"

1. "Col. Lindbergh on Ickes List of 5th Columnists," *New York Herald Tribune*, November 21, 1940, 24.

2. "Union League Gets 'Americanism' Plea," *New York Times*, September 20, 1940, 13; editorial, "We, the People," *New York Times*, September 21, 1940, 11.

3. Merwin K. Hart, "The People vs. the Representative," *Outlook*, November 30, 1907, 17.

4. Walter Nugent, *Progressivism: A Very Short Introduction* (New York: Oxford University Press, 2010), 36–38, 49–50. See also Jacob Kramer, *The New Freedom and the Radicals: Woodrow Wilson, Progressive Views of Radicalism, and the Origins of Repressive Tolerance* (Philadelphia: Temple University Press, 2015).

5. On Roosevelt, see Gail Bederman, *Manliness and Civilization: A Cultural History of Gender and Race in the United States* (Chicago: University of Chicago Press, 1995). On Madison Grant, see Jonathan Peter Spiro, *Defending the Master Race: Conservation, Eugenics, and the Legacy of Madison Grant* (Burlington: University of Vermont Press, 2009). On Woodrow Wilson, see Eric Yellin, *Racism in the Nation's Service: Government Workers and the Color Line in Woodrow Wilson's America* (Chapel Hill: University of North Carolina Press, 2013).

6. David Huyssen, *Progressive Inequality: Rich and Poor in New York, 1890–1920* (Cambridge, MA: Harvard University Press, 2014). See also Daniel T. Rodgers, *Atlantic Crossings: Social Politics in a Progressive Age* (Cambridge, MA: Belknap, 1998); Woodrow Wilson, "A Calendar of Great Americans," *Forum* 16, no. 6 (February 1894): 720–21.

7. Gail Q. Unruh, "Ultraconservative Distortion: Merwin K. Hart and the National Economic Council" (MA thesis, University of Oregon, 1981), 10–11; "State Industrial Survey Read to Begin Work," *New York Herald Tribune*, July 12, 1926, 11.

8. Smith's most recent biographer argues that Smith pursued "classic, technocratic progressive reforms" during his tenure as governor, attempting to reconcile the demands of various interest groups in order provide efficient and dynamic state services. Robert Chiles, *The Revolution of '28: Al Smith, American Progressivism, and the Coming of the New Deal* (Ithaca, NY: Cornell University Press, 2018), 33–70.

9. "Survey Formed to Kill 48-Hour Bill, Says Bloch," *New York Herald Tribune*, August 20, 1926, 9.

10. New York State Industrial Survey Commission, *Report of the Industrial Survey Commission* (Albany: J. B. Lyon, 1927), 72–76.

11. "New York State Industrial Survey Report Provides for Nine-Hour Day Called Eight," *Daily Worker*, February 23, 1927, 3; Robert D. Parmet, *Master of Seventh Avenue: David Dubinsky and the American Labor Movement* (New York: New York University Press, 2005), 31–53; Daniel Katz, *All Together Different: Yiddish*

Socialists, Garment Workers, and the Labor Roots of Multiculturalism (New York: New York University Press, 2011), 98–120.

12. Hart, ironically, was the organizer of the conference, which also included a keynote by Roosevelt in which he warned of tax increases. "State Economic Congress Here to Open Today," *New York Herald Tribune*, April 15, 1929, 19; "Trade Condition Governs Taxes, Says Roosevelt," *New York Herald Tribune*, April 18, 1929.

13. Robert Dallek, *Franklin D. Roosevelt: A Political Life* (New York: Viking, 2017), 116–22.

14. Ibid., 123–29.

15. "25 Named to Aid Industry in State," *New York Times*, May 20, 1929, 7.

16. "Sees State Losing Lead in Industry," *New York Times*, December 21, 1929, 16; "Asks Legislature for Power Hearing," *New York Times*, January 17, 1930, 15.

17. "State Economic Congress Will Expand Activities," *New York Times*, June 15, 1930, 19.

18. Eric Hobsbawm, *The Age of Extremes: A History of the World, 1914–1991* (New York: Pantheon Books, 1994). On American admirers of Italian fascism, see Katy Hull, *The Machine Has a Soul: American Sympathy with Italian Fascism* (Princeton, NJ: Princeton University Press, 2021).

19. "Says Politics Blocks Advance of State," *New York Times*, June 24, 1930, 20.

20. Unruh, "Ultraconservative Distortion," 30; "Holds State Taxes Drive out Industry," *New York Times*, June 16, 1930, 5.

21. Edwin S. Mcintosh, "Roosevelt Bid for 1932 Rises on Landslide," *New York Herald Tribune*, November 6, 1930 1; James Malcolm, ed., *New York Red Book* (Albany, NY: J. B. Lyon, 1931), 21–26.

22. "59 Leaders Named by Gerard as Men Who 'Rule' America," *New York Times*, August 21, 1930, 1; "Gerard Adds Five to List of 'Rulers,' " *New York Times*, August 22, 1930, 3.

23. "Inflated Building Prompts Criticism to Roosevelt," *New York Herald Tribune*, December 8, 1930, 34.

24. "Bankers Urged to Fight Waste of State Funds," *New York Herald Tribune*, May 17, 1931, 26.

25. "Republican Relief Plan Submitted, Names State Agency to Expend Funds," *Ithaca Journal-News*, September 2, 1931, 1–2.

26. "Says Industry Tax Cuts Jobs in State," *New York Times*, March 15, 1930, 3; "Council Begins Study of Waste in Government," *New York Herald Tribune*, August 18, 1930, 15; "Republic Fight Wanes," *New York Times*, September 10, 1931, 1.

27. "State Salary Cuts Opposed by Roosevelt," *Ithaca Journal-News*, January 29, 1932, 1; "Warns against Cut in Social Services," *New York Times*, February 6, 1932, 19.

28. "Legislature Votes Budget with Cuts," *New York Times*, February 11, 1932, 1.

29. Eric Rauchway, *Why the New Deal Matters* (New Haven, CT: Yale University Press, 2021), 11–41; William M. Leahy, ed., *MacArthur and the American Century* (Lincoln: University of Nebraska Press, 2001), 33–41; Richard B. Frank, *MacArthur: A Biography* (New York: St. Martin's, 2007), 21–25.

30. Editorial, "Congress and the Rising Tide," *Chicago Tribune*, May 22, 1932, 12.

31. Ironically, upstate New York was one of only a handful of regions where Hoover retained much of his electoral support. Malcolm, *New York Red Book*.

32. "Urges Drive on Taxes," *New York Times*, May 2, 1933, 8; Unruh, "Ultraconservative Distortion," 29.

33. Chiles, *Revolution of '28*, 53–54, 90–92.

34. Merwin K. Hart, "New York State's Deficit," *New York Times*, December 24, 1932, 12.

35. "Lehman Assailed on Budget Views," *New York Times*, February 6, 1933, 6; W. A. Warn, "$30,000,000 Cut in Lehman Budget Asked," *New York Times*, February 17, 1933, 1; "State Budget Cuts Are Held Inadequate," *New York Times*, March 29, 1933, 3; "Westchester Joins Fight to Reduce Waste," *New York Herald Tribune*, July 29, 1932, 17; "Economic Council Forms County Units to Cut Taxes," *New York Herald Tribune*, April 18, 1933, 24.

36. "Westchester Joins Fight to Reduce Waste"; "Economic Council Forms County Units to Cut Taxes"; "Patriotic Societies," *Chicago Tribune*, February 4, 1936, 12.

37. Tom Pettey, "New York People Just Waking to Public Finances," *Chicago Tribune*, November 9, 1931, 5; "Launch Drives in 14 States to Curb Tax Eaters," *Chicago Tribune*, July 25, 1932, 6; "N.Y. Group Told of Tax Evils by Col. McCormick," *Chicago Tribune*, May 2, 1933, 8; "N.Y. Economic Council Accuses Roosevelt of Aiding Radicals," *Chicago Tribune*, October 24, 1934, 25.

38. Merwin K. Hart, "Control of Industry by Trade Groups Urged as a Substitute for Rigid Government Rules," *New York Herald Tribune*, April 30, 1933, A5.

39. Both business leaders and New Dealers looked to Benito Mussolini's Fascist regime in Italy as a potential model for a federal-corporate synthesis. Only after it became clear that a "corporatist" solution in the United States would involve concessions to organized labor through state intervention did corporate America sour on the Fascist example. Benjamin Alpers, *Dictators, Democracy, and American Public Culture: Envisioning the Totalitarian Enemy, 1920s–1950s* (Chapel Hill: University of North Carolina Press, 2003), 35; Arthur M. Schlesinger Jr., *The Coming of the New Deal, 1933–1935* (New York: Houghton Mifflin, 1958), 87–102; "Bar Association NRA Committee," *Wall Street Journal*, September 14, 1933, 4.

40. Schlesinger, *New Deal*, 87–102.

41. Merwin K. Hart, "Upholding the Right to the Open Shop," *New York Herald Tribune*, September 23, 1933, 10.

42. Ibid.; Merwin K. Hart, "The Heyday of the Walking Delegate," *New York Herald Tribune*, October 1, 1933, A8.

43. New York State Economic Council, *Weekly Legislative Letter*, no. 1, February 10, 1934.

44. The original letter of March 16, 1934 was published in the *New York Times* in December after it was read before the Nye Committee. "The Carpenter and Raskob Letters," December 21, 1934, 2. On the American Liberty League, see Frederick Rudolph, "The American Liberty League, 1934–1940," *American Historical Review* 56, no. 1 (October 1950): 19–33; Jared A. Goldstein, "The

American Liberty League and the Rise of Constitutional Nationalism," *Temple Law Review* 86 (2014): 287–330; and Kim Phillips-Fein, *Invisible Hands: The Businessmen's Crusade against the New Deal* (New York: Norton, 2010).

45. On the West Coast strike, see Bruce Nelson, *Workers on the Waterfront: Seamen, Longshoremen, and Unionism in the 1930s* (Urbana: University of Illinois Press, 1990). On the Minneapolis strike, see William Millikan, *A Union against Unions: The Minneapolis Citizens Alliance and Its Fight against Organized Labor, 1903–1947* (St. Paul: Minnesota Historical Society Press, 2001); and Kristoffer Smemo, "The Politics of Labor Militancy in Minneapolis, 1934–1938" (MA thesis, University of Massachusetts, Amherst), 2011. All three strikes are covered by Irving Bernstein in *The Turbulent Years: A History of the American Worker, 1933–1941* (Boston: Houghton Mifflin, 1970).

46. Eric Sevareid, *Not So Wild a Dream* (New York: Knopf, 1946), 58.

47. Jonathan M. Katz, *Gangsters of Capitalism: Smedley Butler, the Marines, and the Making and Breaking of America's Empire* (New York: St. Martin's, 2021), 319–26; Joseph Fronczak, "The Fascist Game: Transnational Political Transmissions and the Genesis of the U.S. Modern Right," *Journal of American History* 105, no. 3 (December 2018): 563–88. See also Phillips-Fein, *Invisible Hands*, 10–13. For a contemporary left-wing account, see John L. Spivak, "Wall Street's Fascist Conspiracy," *New Masses*, January 29, 1935, 9–15.

48. U.S. Senate, Special Committee to Investigate Lobby Activities, *Investigation of Lobbying Activities*, 74th Cong., 1st sess. (1950), 1770, 1772, 1796.

49. Ibid., 1771; Arthur Sears Henning, "Terror Spread among Enemies by New Dealers," *Chicago Tribune*, February 9, 1936, 1.

50. U.S. Senate, *Investigation of Lobbying Activities*, 2070–71; George Wolfskill, *The Revolt of the Conservatives: A History of the American Liberty League, 1934–1940* (Boston: Houghton Mifflin, 1962), 231, 239, 241–42.

51. Leonard Dinnerstein, *Anti-Semitism in America* (New York: Oxford University Press, 1994), 105–28.

52. *Economic Council Letter*, no. 30, July 4, 1935; no. 32, December 13, 1935.

53. Fronczak, "The Fascist Game," 566–67.

54. Marc Steven Kolopsky, "Remington Rand Workers in the Tonawandas of New York, 1927–1956" (PhD diss., State University of New York at Buffalo, 1986). See also Anson C. Smith, "The 1936 Remington Rand Strike in Middletown: A Case Study in Propaganda," *Connecticut History Review* 54, no. 1 (Spring 2015): 112–42.

55. Benjamin Stolberg, "Vigilantism, 1937," *Nation*, August 14, 1937, 166–68.

56. Remington Rand, Inc., 2 N.L.R.B. 626 (1937).

57. The 2nd Circuit Court of Appeals summarily ruled against Remington Rand the following year. *National Labor Relations Board v. Remington Rand, Inc.*, 94 F.2d 862 (2nd Cir., 1938).

58. Joint Committee of Remington Rand Employees Associations, *"Truth Will Out": Labor Board v. Remington Rand: Report* (1937), 10–11.

59. There is a robust literature on the Little Steel strike. The most comprehensive recent study—which, unlike many others, covers the entire strike throughout the Midwest as opposed to centering on Chicago, is Ahmed White, *The Last*

Great Strike: Little Steel, the CIO and the Struggle for Labor Rights in New Deal America (Oakland: University of California Press, 2016); but see also Michael J. Dennis, *The Memorial Day Massacre and the Movement for Industrial Democracy* (New York: Palgrave Macmillan, 2010) as well as Dennis, "Chicago and the Little Steel Strike," *Labor History* 53 (Spring 2012): 167–204.

60. White, *Last Great Strike*, 289.
61. Fronczak, "Fascist Game," 584. Hart's correspondence with the Johnstown citizens' committee became a matter of public record thanks to the U.S. Senate's La Follette Committee's investigation of labor law violations and labor abuses from 1936 to 1941. The committee subpoenaed the records and correspondence of a variety of Little Steel officials and local strikebreakers, including the Johnstown Citizens' Committee. Hart was not subpoenaed. U.S. Senate, Subcommittee of the Committee on Education and Labor, *Violations of Free Speech and Rights of Labor: Hearings*, 75th Cong., 2nd sess. (November 19, 1937), 7325.
62. White, *Last Great Strike*, 181–84.
63. Benjamin Stolberg, who covered labor issues for the *Nation*, characterized the anti-union forces in Johnstown as "fascist." Benjamin Stolberg, "Big Steel, Little Steel, and the C.I.O.," *Nation*, July 31, 1937, 119–23; Stolberg, "Vigilantism, Part II," *Nation*, August 21, 1937, 191–93. See also Fronczak, "Fascist Game," 585–88; "Congressman Blames C.I.O. Head for Chicago Strike Fatalities," *Globe and Mail*, June 4, 1937, 15; "Tremaine Asks Repeal of Levy on Capital Gain," *New York Herald Tribune*, June 4, 1937, 33; John Roy Carlson, *Under Cover: My Four Years in the Nazi Underworld—The Amazing Revelation of How Axis Agents and Our Enemies within Are Now Plotting to Destroy the United States* (New York: E. P. Dutton, 1943), 459–60.
64. For treatments of Dilling, see Glen Jeansonne, *Women of the Far Right: The Mothers' Movement and World War II* (Chicago: University of Chicago Press, 1996); Christine K. Erickson, " 'I Have Not Had One Fact Disproven': Elizabeth Dilling's Crusade against Communism in the 1930s," *Journal of American Studies* 36, no. 3 (2002); and Michelle Nickerson, *Mothers of Conservatism: Women and the Postwar Right* (Princeton, NJ: Princeton University Press, 2012), 19–31.
65. Richard Gid Powers, *Not without Honor: The History of American Anticommunism* (New York: Free Press, 1995), 167.
66. "The Man in the Middle," *Time*, May 24, 1954, 44–46; Th. Aubert to J. Edgar Hoover, June 24, 1930, FBI file for George Sokolsky, *The FBI: Federal Bureau of Investigation*, U.S. Department of Justice, https://archive.org/details/GeorgeSokolsky/mode/2up; "Social Security Basic Objective, Miss Perkins Says: Security Aims Benefits of Measure," *Christian Science Monitor*, December 21, 1935, 3.
67. Nickerson, *Mothers*, 25.
68. Erickson, " 'I Have Not Had One Fact Disproven,' " 474–75.
69. Chesly Manly, "New Deal Fraud: Al Smith," *Chicago Tribune*, January 26, 1936, 1; Goldstein, "The American Liberty League and the Rise of Constitutional Nationalism," 311–15.

70. There is a robust historiographical debate about the origins of the Spanish Civil War and whether or not the Franco regime can be fairly characterized as fascist. Given that recent scholarship critical of Franco has emphasized his regime as fascist and extraordinarily violent, and that several of the most prominent voices in and outside of Spain defending Franco against the charge of fascism have far-right political views, I am defining Franco for the purposes of this book as a fascist. Hugh Seton-Watson, "Fascism, Right and Left," *Journal of Contemporary History* 1, no. 1 (January 1966): 183–97; Stanley Payne, *A History of Fascism, 1914–1945* (Madison: University of Wisconsin Press, 1995); Stanley Payne, *Fascism in Spain: 1923–1977* (Madison: University of Wisconsin Press, 2000); Gutaro Gómez and Jorge Marco, *La obra del miedo. Violencia y sociedad en la España franquista* (Barcelona: Peninsula, 2011); Paul Preston, *The Spanish Holocaust: Inquisition and Extermination in Twentieth-Century Spain* (London: HarperPress, 2012); Chris Ealham, "The Emperor's New Clothes: 'Objectivity' and Revision in Spanish History," *Journal of Contemporary History* 48, no. 1 (2012): 192–202. See also Austin J. Clements, " 'The Franco Way': The American Right and the Spanish Civil War, 1936–9," *Journal of Contemporary History* 57, no. 2 (2022): 341–64.

71. Michael E. Chapman, *Arguing Americanism: Franco Lobbyists, Roosevelt's Foreign Policy, and the Spanish Civil War* (Kent, OH: Kent State University Press, 2011), 128–29. Chapman's work is the most comprehensive account of the AUNS and Hart's lobbying activities during the Spanish Civil War, but it is highly sympathetic to the point of distortion, minimizing Hart's antisemitism as well describing Hart and his allies as "conservative thinker[s]" only in the "narrow context of preserving the vitality of Depression-era America from what they judged to be the dogma of illiberal communism," which is, in fact, as both this work and many others argue, one of the defining aspects of American conservatism during the Depression and World War II and into the Cold War. See, for instance, Phillips-Fein, *Invisible Hands,* 58–60.

72. Merwin K. Hart, "Mediation Held 'Impossible' by Spanish Rebels," *New York Herald Tribune,* October 12, 1938, 1; Hart, "American in Spain Says Tonus Welcome Nationalists, for Capture Means Hot Meals," *New York Herald Tribune,* October 30, 1938, A4; Hart, "American in Franco Spain Told Besieged Guernica Was Razed by Loyalists Fleeing Bombings," *New York Herald Tribune,* November 6, 1938, A4; Hart, "Intellectuals in Spain," *New York Herald Tribune,* December 17, 1938, 12.

73. "Franco Thanks Americans," *New York Times,* February 21, 1939, 7.

74. Chapman, *Arguing Americanism,* 71, 83.

75. "Cardinal Lauds Franco's Fight," *Boston Globe,* March 19, 1938, 1; "Thorning Calls Franco Highest Type Christian," *New York Herald Tribune,* March 28, 1938, 8; Robert Wiechert, "The Nationalist Cause," *Baltimore Sun,* July 27, 1938, 8.

76. Merwin K. Hart, card index, Anti-Defamation League archives, New York. The Anti-Defamation League retains microfilm copies of its subject files at its offices in Manhattan for internal use and was kind enough to allow the author permission to view them.

77. Merwin K. Hart, *America, Look at Spain* (New York: P. J. Kenedy & Sons, 1939), viii–xi; Chapman, *Arguing Americanism*, 128–29.

78. Hart, *Look at Spain*, 74–76.

79. Ibid., 183–88.

80. Ibid., 113–15.

81. Merwin K. Hart, card index, Anti-Defamation League files.

82. "Foreign Policy Group Debates Issues in Spain," *New York Herald Tribune*, November 23, 1938, 10.

83. Editorial, "The Pastoral Letter and Democracy," *Daily Worker*, November 26, 1938, 6; "Tories Drive for State Sales Tax; Fight Budget," *Daily Worker*, February 16, 1939, 1.

84. "Leader of Bund Hears Dies Flay Nazis and Reds," *Chicago Tribune*, December 9, 1938, 20; "Bund Leader Hears Dies Denounce Body," *Boston Globe*, December 9, 1938, 28; "Nazi Leader at Dies Luncheon Hears Inquiry Head Attack Bund," *New York Times*, December 9, 1938, 10.

85. The Christian Front was also heavily active in Boston. See Charles R. Gallagher, *Nazis of Copley Square: The Forgotten Story of the Christian Front* (Cambridge, MA: Harvard University Press, 2021).

86. "12,000 at Rally Demand Strict U.S. Neutrality," *New York Herald Tribune*, February 20, 1939, 2; "Recognition of Franco Urged by New York Mass Meeting," *St. Louis Post-Dispatch*, February 20, 1939, 21; Chapman, *Arguing Americanism*, 153–55; Dinnerstein, *Anti-Semitism in America*, 122.

87. "22,000 Nazis Hold Rally in Garden," *New York Times*, February 21, 1939, 1; "Bund Rallies amid Tumult at the Garden," *New York Herald Tribune*, February 21, 1939, 1; "Fight Nazis in Big N.Y. Rally," *Chicago Tribune*, February 21, 1939, 1.

88. "Mayor Refuses to Stop Bund Rally at Garden," *New York Herald Tribune*, February 18, 1939, 5.

89. "Dies's Name Linked to 'Collaborator' of Christian Front," *Boston Globe*, January 23, 1940, 2; " 'Lie,' Hart Says of Hook's Accusation," *Boston Globe*, January 23, 1940, 2; "Dies Committee Wins House Rules Approval," *Los Angeles Times*, January 23, 1940, 2; "Hart Denies Christian Front Link," *New York Times*, January 23, 1940, 11; "House Embroiled by Mayne Letters," *New York Times*, February 2, 1940, 8.

90. Chapman, *Arguing Americanism*, 174.

91. There was an aborted attempt to organize a Fascist International in the early 1930s. See Michael Ledeen, *Universal Fascism: The Theory and Practice of the Fascist International, 1928–1936* (New York: H. Fertig, 1972). However, the actual practice of fascism across borders spread more organically, as local movements adapted elements of fascist practice to suit local conditions. See Federico Finchelstein, *Transatlantic Fascism: Ideology, Violence, and the Sacred in Argentina and Italy, 1919–1945* (Durham, NC: Duke University Press, 2010).

92. On both the fascistic nature of Austrofascism and its anti-Nazi component, see Julie Thore, "Austrofascism: Revisiting the 'Authoritarian State' 40 Years On," *Journal of Contemporary History* 45, no. 2 (2010): 315–43.

93. Hart, "Intellectuals in Spain"; Hart, *America, Look at Spain*, 9–10.

94. Edward Nik-Khah, "George Stigler, the Graduate School of Business, and the Pillars of the Chicago School," in *Building Chicago Economics: New Perspectives on the History of America's Most Powerful Economics Program,* ed. Robert van Horn, Philip Mirowski, and Thomas A. Stapleford (New York: Cambridge University Press, 2011), 116–51.

95. Adam Laats, *The Other School Reformers: Conservative Activism in American Education* (Cambridge, MA: Harvard University Press, 2015), 73–122.

96. "Social Science Textbooks Used in City Schools Part of Plan to Teach Socialism, Says Hart," *Binghamton Press,* December 13, 1939, 1.

97. *Economic Council Letter,* no. 78, April 15, 1940.

98. *Economic Council Letter,* no. 80, May 15, 1940.

99. *Economic Council Letter,* no. 82, October 1, 1940.

100. John S. Radota, "Scored by Hart, Rugg Upholds His Textbooks," *New York Herald Tribune,* February 23, 1941, 27.

101. Laats, *Other School Reformers,* 75.

102. Freda Kirchwey, "Hart on Democracy," *Nation,* September 28, 1940, 261–62.

103. W.E.B. Du Bois, *A World Search for Democracy,* ca. 1937, W.E.B. Du Bois Papers (MS 312), Special Collections and University Archives, University of Massachusetts, Amherst Libraries, http://credo.library.umass.edu/view/full/mums312-b225-i044.

CHAPTER 2. "THE SUPER SUPERPATRIOTIC TYPE"

1. See Justus D. Doenecke, *Storm on the Horizon: The Challenge to American Intervention, 1939–1941* (Lanham, MD: Rowman & Littlefield, 2000); Daniel Bessner, *Democracy in Exile: Hans Speier and the Rise of the Defense Intellectual* (Ithaca, NY: Cornell University Press, 2018); and Stephen Wertheim, *Tomorrow, the World: The Birth of U.S. Global Supremacy* (Cambridge, MA: Harvard University Press, 2020).

2. *Economic Council Letter,* no. 64, September 15, 1939; no. 65, October 1, 1939.

3. Westbrook Pegler, "Throw Them Out!" *Washington Post,* September 29, 1939, 15; Dorothy Thompson, "On the Record: Comrade Browder and Gauleiter Kuhn," *Washington Post,* October 27, 1939, 13; Benjamin Stolberg, "Exit on the Left: The End of the Communist Party," *Washington Post,* December 5, 1939, 9; Christopher Phelps, "Heywood Broun, Benjamin Stolberg, and the Politics of American Labor Journalism in the 1920s and 1930s," *Labor* 14, no. 1 (2018): 25–51. For the evolution of communism and fascism in political discourse under the umbrella term *totalitarianism,* see Benjamin Alpers, *Dictators, Democracy, and American Public Culture: Envisioning the Totalitarian Enemy, 1920s–1950s* (Chapel Hill: University of North Carolina Press, 2003).

4. "Dies at Rally Here Warns U.S. to Stop Its 'Aping' of Europe," *New York Times,* November 30, 1939, 1; "Dies Demands New Deal Tell Inquiry View," *New York Herald Tribune,* November 30, 1939, 1B.

5. William G. Rivers, "Military Expert Expects Long War," *Los Angeles Times,* September 8, 1939, 12.

6. *Economic Council Letter,* no. 81, June 15, 1940.

7. Public opinion had been shifting toward a more interventionist stance since the mid-1930s. A Gallup poll in 1935 showed that 75 percent of those surveyed favored a constitutional amendment requiring a national referendum before Congress could declare war; after the Munich Pact in 1938, support for such an amendment dipped to 61 percent, and after the outbreak of war in Europe support fell further to only 51 percent. A survey of newspapers' editorial stances in September 1939 conducted by the *Christian Science Monitor* showed 4-1 support for the partial repeal of the Neutrality Acts. Editorial, "Guideposts to Neutrality," *Minneapolis Star-Journal,* September 13, 1939, 12; "U.S. Press for Embargo Repeal by 4-1," *Christian Science Monitor,* September 20, 1939, 1.

8. Justus D. Doenecke, *Storm on the Horizon: The Challenge to American Intervention, 1939–1941* (Lanham, MD: Rowman & Littlefield, 2000), 117. See also Wayne S. Cole, *America First: The Battle against Intervention, 1940–1941* (Madison: University of Wisconsin Press, 1953), the major institutional history of the America First Committee.

9. Michele Flynn Stenehjem, *An American First: John T. Flynn and the America First Committee* (New Rochelle, NY: Arlington House, 1976), 42. See also John E. Moser, *Right Turn: John T. Flynn and the Transformation of American Liberalism* (New York: New York University Press, 2005), 118.

10. John T. Flynn, "Other People's Money," *New Republic,* November 22, 1933, 45–46.

11. Flynn, "Other People's Money—Hearst and the Spanish Rebels," *New Republic,* September 9, 1936, 129.

12. Flynn, "Other People's Money—Peace, It's Wonderful," *New Republic,* October 19, 1938, 305–6; Flynn, "Other People's Money—We're All for Cash-and-Carry," *New Republic,* October 11, 1939, 270. At least some opposed cash-and-carry on the grounds that Nazi Germany could *also* purchase U.S. arms, which could be shipped to Vladivostok on Japanese vessels and transported through Germany's new Soviet ally for final delivery in the Reich. "Denies Repeal of Arms Ban Would Hit Nazis," *Chicago Tribune,* September 28, 1939, 7. The scenario was fanciful, but given that American corporations sold war material to the Franco regime before the Neutrality Act of 1937 went into effect and that German automobile manufacturer Opel was a wholly owned subsidiary of General Motors before it was nationalized in 1939, the anti-fascist bona fides of the American corporation were suspect, to say the least. See Dominic Tierney, *FDR and the Spanish Civil War: Neutrality and the Commitment in the Struggle That Divided America* (Durham, NC: Duke University Press, 2007), 68–69; and Adam Tooze, *The Wages of Destruction: The Making and Breaking of the Nazi Economy* (New York: Penguin, 2006), 133, 152.

13. Stenehjem, *An American First,* 42; Moser, *Right Turn,* 118.

14. American Jewish Committee, "The Anti-Jewish Propaganda Front," 1937, https://www.ajcarchives.org/AJC_DATA/Files/TH-1.PDF.

15. Cole, *America First,* 85–90.

16. Ibid, 85–86.

17. Charles A. Lindbergh, *The Wartime Journals of Charles A. Lindbergh* (New York: Harcourt Brace Jovanovich, 1970), 415. Hart and Lindbergh maintained a lengthy correspondence throughout 1940, with Hart frequently sending Lindbergh speeches and papers for comment. See, for example, Merwin Hart to Charles Lindbergh, May 10, 1940, Charles Augustus Lindbergh Papers (MS 325), box 16, Manuscripts and Archives, Yale University Library, New Haven, CT.

18. "Marshall Dares Hostile Debate Crowd to Fight," *New York Herald Tribune*, January 10, 1941, 1; Justus D. Doenecke, "Verne Marshall's Leadership of the No Foreign War Committee, 1940," *Annals of Iowa* 41, no. 7 (Winter 1973): 1153–72.

19. "Reds Slated to Dominate, Solons Hear," Associated Press, February 10, 1941; "Lend-Lease Bill Means War, Foes Tell Senate Committee," *Christian Science Monitor*, February 10, 1941, 7; "N.M.U. Now Backs Britain," *New York Times*, July 3, 1941, 3.

20. "Seizure of Plants Fought at Hearing," *New York Times*, July 1, 1941, 38.

21. "Draft Extension Backed by Authors," *New York Times*, July 22, 1941, 7.

22. *Economic Council Letter*, no. 96, November 1, 1941.

23. Merwin K. Hart to Senator Robert A. Taft, July 11, 1941, Charles Augustus Lindbergh Papers, box 16.

24. James T. Patterson, *Mr. Republican: A Biography of Robert A. Taft* (Boston: Houghton Mifflin, 1972), 217; Eliot A. Rosen, *The Republican Party in the Age of Roosevelt: Sources of Anti-Government Conservatism in the United States* (Charlottesville: University of Virginia Press, 2015), 114–28.

25. "Economic Council Held Un-American," *New York Times*, April 11, 1941, 23; "State Economic Council Hears Baldwin Attack It," *New York Herald Tribune*, April 11, 1941, 19.

26. "Near Riot Greets Lindbergh N.Y. Speech," *Christian Science Monitor*, April 24, 1941, 7; "Crowds Battle Before Lindbergh Speech in N.Y.," Associated Press, April 23, 1941; "Lindbergh's Anti-War Plea Draws 25,000," *New York Herald Tribune*, April 24, 1941, 1; Merwin K. Hart to *New York Herald Tribune*, April 25, 1941, Charles Augustus Lindbergh Papers, box 16; "F.D.R. Places Lindbergh with the Appeasers," Associated Press, April 26, 1941; "Warburg Calls Col. Lindbergh a Help to Hitler," *New York Herald Tribune*, April 25, 1941, 9; "Mayor Attacks Lindbergh Stand," *New York Times*, April 25, 1941, 12.

27. "Lindbergh Quits Air Corps," Associated Press, April 28, 1941.

28. "Lindbergh Praised in Nazi Newspaper," *New York Times*, April 25, 1941, 13.

29. "Nazi Aid Charged to Anti-War Group," *New York Times*, March 12, 1941, 15; Friends of Democracy, Inc., *The America First Committee: The Nazi Transmission Belt* (Kansas City, MO: Friends of Democracy, 1941).

30. "Lindbergh's Anti-War Plea Draws 25,000."

31. "Lindbergh Says Jews, New Deal Strive for War," *New York Herald Tribune*, September 12, 1941, 3.

32. "Nye Denies Slamming Bankers," *Jewish Advocate*, August 29, 1941, 1; "Willkie to Head Film Defense in Senate Inquiry," *New York Herald Tribune*, September 2, 1941, 10; Chesly Manly, "War Oligarchy Rules Movies, Senate Is Told," *Chicago Tribune*, September 11, 1941, 1; "Isolationist Leaders Face Charges of

Anti-Semitism," *Christian Science Monitor*, September 15, 1941, 3; "Nye Attacks Willkie in Talk," Associated Press, September 23, 1941; Cole, *America First*, 136–40; Susan Dunn, *1940: FDR, Willkie, Lindbergh, Hitler—The Election amid the Storm* (New Haven, CT: Yale University Press, 2013), 65–67. See also Jennifer Frost, "Dissent and Consent in the 'Good War': Hedda Hopper, Hollywood Gossip, and World War II Isolationism," *Film History* 22, no. 2 (June 2010): 170–81 for a discussion of Nye's allies in Hollywood.

33. Hart to Lindbergh, September 15, 1941, and Hart to Lindbergh, December 4, 1941, Charles Augustus Lindbergh Papers, box 16.

34. A. Scott Berg, *Lindbergh* (New York: G. P. Putnam's, 1998), 429–31.

35. Lindbergh, *Wartime Journals*, 245.

36. Ibid., 541

37. *Aspects of Jewish Power in the United States* (Dearborn, MI: Dearborn Publishing, 1920), 223–33.

38. U.S. House, Special Committee on Un-American Activities, *Hearings before a Special Committee on Un-American Activities*, 76th Cong., 3rd sess. (1941), 7218, 7238, 7333.

39. Leo Ribuffo, *The Old Christian Right: The Protestant Far Right from the Great Depression to the Cold War* (Philadelphia: Temple University Press, 1983), 74.

40. *Economic Council Letter*, no. 99, January 1, 1942; Lindbergh, *Wartime Journals*, 565.

41. The most comprehensive biography of Dennis—who was, remarkably, a mixed-race man "passing" as white, is Gerald Horne, *The Color of Fascism: Lawrence Dennis, Racial Passing, and the Rise of Right-Wing Extremism in the United States* (New York: New York University Press, 2006).

42. "Pro-Fascists Hit War Bill," *Daily Worker*, December 10, 1941, 1.

43. Dillard Stokes, "Hill, Aide to Fish, Convicted on Two Charges of Perjury," *Washington Post*, January 16, 1942, 1.

44. "Victim of Smear Files Suit for a Million Dollars," *Chicago Tribune*, November 7, 1942, 13; "Hart Sues Democracy Friends," *New York Times*, November 7, 1942, 9; *Hart v. Friends of Democracy, Inc.*, 266 App. Div. 941 (N.Y. App. Div., 1943).

45. "Merwin K. Hart Loses Plea in $1,000,000 Suit," *New York Herald Tribune*, June 19, 1943, 12.

46. John Roy Carlson, *Under Cover: My Four Years in the Nazi Underworld of America—The Amazing Revelation of How Axis Agents and Our Enemies within Are Now Plotting to Destroy the United States* (New York: E. P. Dutton, 1943), 456.

47. Ibid., 461.

48. Ibid., 457.

49. Ribuffo, *Old Christian Right*, 190–93; Alpers, *Dictators, Democracy, and American Public Culture*.

50. *Economic Council Letter*, no. 120, January 1, 1944.

51. See, for example, Greg Robinson, *A Tragedy of Democracy: Japanese Confinement in North America* (New York: Columbia University Press, 2009).

52. Lt. Gen. J. L. DeWitt to the Chief of Staff, U.S. Army, June 5, 1943, in *U.S. Army, Western Defense Command and Fourth Army, Final Report; Japanese*

Evacuation from the West Coast 1942 (Washington, DC: Government Printing Office, 1943), vii–x.

53. Carlson, *Under Cover,* 156–57; Gerald L. K. Smith, "Hoarding Food in Japanese Camps," *The Cross and the Flag,* May 1943, 195–96.

54. Moser, *Right Turn,* 162–63.

55. Edward Weeks to W.E.B. Du Bois, January 26, 1942, W.E.B. Du Bois Papers (MS 312), Special Collections and University Archives, University of Massachusetts, Amherst Libraries.

56. Hy Berman, "Political Antisemitism in Minnesota during the Great Depression," *Jewish Social Studies* 34 nos. 3/4 (1976): 247–64; Ira Katznelson, *Fear Itself: The New Deal and the Origins of Our Time* (New York: Norton, 2013), 216–17.

57. *Economic Council Letter,* no. 118, November 1, 1943; *Economic Council Letter,* no. 119, December 1, 1943.

58. The administration, for its part, found it politically useful to attack anti–New Deal businessmen like Sloan as heartless robber barons. Secretary of the Treasury Henry Morgenthau famously compared Alfred Sloan to Al Capone in 1944 for attempting to evade paying his income taxes by incorporating his yacht. James T. Sparrow, *Warfare State: World War II Americans and the Age of Big Government* (New York: Oxford University Press, 2011), 28.

59. "Wills of Vermont Champions Willkie," *New York Times,* January 9, 1944, 14.

60. William Manchester, *American Caesar: Douglas MacArthur, 1880–1964* (Boston: Little & Brown, 1978).

61. "America First Party to Convene," *New York Times,* March 4, 1944, 9.

62. "Delegates Pray Smith May Recant," *Baltimore Sun,* March 11, 1944, 11. Smith later wrote to the House of Delegates chiding the members for having been taken in by "Communist propaganda." "Smith Writes to Delegates," *Baltimore Sun,* April 7, 1944, 5.

63. James A. Hagerty, "Willkie Condemns Isolationist Views," *New York Times,* March 22, 1941, 1. Smith, ever the provocateur, claimed the next day that Willkie had tried to bribe him for his support earlier in the year. "Claims Willkie Aid Sought to Buy His Support," *Chicago Tribune,* March 23, 1944, 2.

64. "America First Victory," *Baltimore Sun,* April 6, 1944, 1.

65. "Bennett Denies Ford Backs 'America Firster,' " *Louisville-Courier Journal,* April 9, 1944, 43.

66. Thomas Morrow, "Smithites Take over Ballroom a la Squatters," *Chicago Tribune,* June 26, 1944, 4.

67. Ralph McGill, "Gerald Smith Warbles Tune Familiar to South," *Atlanta Constitution,* July 19, 1944, 10.

68. "Bricker Is Put on Smith Ticket," *New York Times,* August 1, 1944, 7; "Bricker Rips Gerald L. Smith and His Party," *Chicago Tribune,* August 2, 1944, 8; "America First Party Picks New Running Mate for Smith," *Baltimore Sun,* August 3, 1944, 1.

69. "Ickes Won't Let Park Bison Go to GLK Smith," *New York Herald Tribune,* August 17, 1944, 12; "G.L.K. Smith Ejects Author at Meeting," *New York Times,* September 30, 1944, 11.

70. "Bars Gas for G.L.K. Smith," *New York Times,* October 3, 1944, 14.

71. "Ickes Claims Isolationists Back Dewey," *Christian Science Monitor,* October 9, 1944, 3.

72. "Asks Americans to Redeclare Independence," *Chicago Tribune,* July 3, 1943, 3; "In Empire State Building," *New York Times,* July 14, 1943, 33.

73. John T. Flynn, *The Smear Terror* (self-published, 1947).

CHAPTER 3. THE ROLE OF THE CRACKPOT

1. "Biographical Sketch," Benjamin Freedman subject file, Anti-Defamation League archives, New York.

2. *Economic Council Letter,* no. 177, October 15, 1947.

3. The literature on American Jewish anti-Zionism in the 1930s and 1940s is relatively small, but highlights include Thomas A. Kolsky, *Jews against Zionism: The American Council for Judaism, 1942–1948* (Philadelphia: Temple University Press, 1990); and Jack Ross, *Rabbi Outcast: Elmer Berger and American Jewish Anti-Zionism* (Washington, DC: Potomac Books, 2011). Among the best resources for the evolving state of American Jewish politics in the 1930s and 1940s are Menahem Kaufman, *An Ambiguous Partnership: Non-Zionists and Zionists in America, 1939–1948* (Detroit: Wayne State University Press, 1991); Rafael Medoff, *Zionism and the Arabs: An American Jewish Dilemma, 1898–1948* (Westport, CT: Praeger, 1997); Naomi W. Cohen, *The Americanization of Zionism* (London: Brandeis University Press, 2003).

4. *Economic Council Letter,* no. 177, October 15, 1947.

5. "Palestine—Chapter II," *Economic Council Letter,* no. 179, December 15, 1947, 181.

6. "The Fortune Survey," *Fortune,* February 1946, 257; "The Fortune Survey," *Fortune,* October 1947, 5.

7. Leonard Dinnerstein, *Anti-Semitism in America* (New York: Oxford University Press, 1994), 152–53; Bruce Bliven, "U.S. Antisemitism Today," *New Republic,* November 3, 1947, 16–19; Bliven, "Prejudice Is Curable," *New Republic,* December 29, 1947, 22–25.

8. Daniel Geary, "Carey McWilliams and Antifascism, 1934–1943," *Journal of American History* 90, no. 3 (December 2003): 912–34.

9. Carey McWilliams, *A Mask for Privilege: Anti-Semitism in America* (Boston: Little & Brown, 1948), 82.

10. Ibid., 101.

11. Ibid., 151. On Henry Ford and antisemitism, see Leo Ribuffo, "Henry Ford and 'The International Jew,'" *American Jewish History* 69, no. 4 (1980): 437–77; and Victoria Saker Woeste, *Henry Ford's War on Jews and the Legal Battle against Hate Speech* (Palo Alto, CA: Stanford University Press, 2012).

12. The literature on antisemitism as both a term and a concept is vast and varied. Useful recent introductions are David Nirenberg, *Anti-Judaism: The Western*

Tradition (New York: Norton, 2013); and David Feldman, "Toward a History of the Term 'Anti-Semitism,'" *American Historical Review* 123, no. 4 (October 2018): 1139–50.

13. Richard Hofstadter, *The Age of Reform: From Bryan to F.D.R.* (New York: Knopf, 1955), 77–82.

14. See, for example, Walter Nugent, *The Tolerant Populists: Kansas Populism and Nativism* (Chicago: University of Chicago Press, 1963).

15. Leo Ribuffo, *The Old Christian Right: The Protestant Far Right from the Great Depression to the Cold War* (Philadelphia: Temple University Press, 1983), xxii–xxv.

16. McWilliams, *A Mask for Privilege*, 185.

17. Ibid., 194.

18. On CIO-PAC, see James Caldwell Foster, *The Union Politic: The CIO Political Action Committee* (Columbia: University of Missouri Press, 1975).

19. Gail Q. Unruh, "Ultraconservative Distortion: Merwin K. Hart and the National Economic Council" (MA thesis, University of Oregon, 1981), 53.

20. "Upton Close's 'Offensive Tirades' on Britain Answered," *Los Angeles Times*, April 22, 1942, 6; "Upton Close Says N.B.C. Insists Sponsor Drop Him," *New York Herald Tribune*, November 15, 1944, 17; McWilliams, *A Mask for Privilege*, 201.

21. Philip Dodd, "FCC Concludes Hearing on CIO Radio Charges," *Chicago Tribune*, August 25, 1944, 25; letter to the editor, "Is the Gag Being Applied?" *Hartford Courant*, November 18, 1944, 6; Paul W. Ward, "FCC Unable to Act in Ouster of Upton Close from the Air," *Baltimore Sun*, November 16, 1944, 1; Roscoe Peacock, "'Liberals' and Free Speech," *Chicago Tribune*, February 24, 1945, 8.

22. Robert E. Segal, "Upton Close Finds a Cause: It's Upton Close Personally," *American Israelite*, March 7, 1946, 1.

23. McWilliams, *A Mask for Privilege*, 197–98; Robert McCormick to Merwin Hart, January 5, 1946, Papers of Colonel Robert R. McCormick, First Division Museum at Cantigny Park, box 38, folder "Hart, Merwin," Wheaton, IL.

24. McWilliams, *A Mask for Privilege*, 201–2. See also Art Shields, "I Saw the Big Business Fascists Spread Hate-the-Jew Propaganda," *Daily Worker*, November 17, 1946, 1–2. While the *Daily Worker's* coverage of the gala was over the top, the claims in the piece were substantiated by photographs showing Close, Hart, Raskob, and du Pont together at the dais.

25. McWilliams, *A Mask for Privilege*, 202–4.

26. Unruh, "Ultraconservative Distortion," 54–55; Gertrude Coogan, *Money Creators: Who Creates Money? Who Should Create It?* (Chicago: Sound Money, 1935). Coogan was also a member of the America First Committee in 1941.

27. Unruh, "Ultraconservative Distortion," 55; Gerald L. K. Smith, "Smear, the Fate of the Righteous," *The Cross and the Flag*, April 1946, 731.

28. Wood to Flynn, March 1, 1946, McCormick Papers, box 138.

29. De Lacy was allegedly a member of the Communist Party in the 1930s. Harvey Klehr, *The Heyday of American Communism: The Depression Decade* (New York: Basic Books, 1984), 256.

30. "Tells American Action, Inc., AIM: Saving U.S. Way," *Chicago Tribune*, October 16, 1946, 30; U.S. House, Special Committee to Investigate Campaign Expenditures, *Hearings before the Committee to Investigate Campaign Expenditures*, 79th Cong., 2nd sess. (1946), 231–32.

31. "Bare American Action Work in Illinois Races," *Chicago Tribune*, October 17, 1946, 8; "Action Group's 'Purge' List Will Be Kept Secret," *New York Herald Tribune*, October 17, 1946, 26A; U.S. House, Special Committee to Investigate Campaign Expenditures, *Hearings before the Committee to Investigate Campaign Expenditures*, 228–29.

32. " 'Action' Group's Campaign Gifts Total $100,000." *New York Herald Tribune*, October 16, 1946, 6A; "House Committee Acts," *New York Herald Tribune*, October 19, 1946, 12; Mary Spargo, "Political Expenditures Smash Record for Off-Year Election," *Washington Post*, November 5, 1946, 9.

33. Robert E. Segal, "As We Were Saying: Gerald Smith, Hamilton Fish, Two Minds with One Thought," *American Israelite*, April 18, 1946, 1; Segal, "As We Were Saying: American Action, Inc., Is Now a Million Dollar Business," *American Israelite*, October 10, 1946, 1. See also " 'America First' Takes Up Again under New Guise," *Jewish Advocate*, October 10, 1946, 3.

34. "New America Firsters Form Undercover Group," *Chicago Defender*, October 12, 1946, 1; "Powell Hits FEPC Haters," *Chicago Defender*, October 19, 1946, 2; "Communistic Opportunism," *Economic Council Letter*, no. 143, May 15, 1946.

35. "Marcantonio Re-elected to Sixth Term in House," *New York Herald Tribune*, November 6, 1946, 3A.

36. "Polls Victory of American Action Hailed," *Chicago Tribune*, November 18, 1946, 5. On the 1946 election, see Meg Jacobs, *Pocketbook Politics: Economic Citizenship in Twentieth-Century America* (Princeton, NJ: Princeton University Press, 2005), 222–31.

37. See, for instance, Benjamin Waterhouse, *Lobbying America: The Politics of Business from Nixon to NAFTA* (Princeton, NJ: Princeton University Press, 2013), 25–28.

38. McWilliams, *A Mask for Privilege*, 204.

39. Jacobs, *Pocketbook Politics*, 231–242.

40. "The Record of the Eightieth Congress," *Economic Council Letter*, no. 190, May 1, 1948.

41. The Jewish population of the United States was, in 1920, over 3.3 million, making the United States the country with the largest Jewish population outside of Europe and by far the most popular destination for Jewish migrants; by contrast, Palestine—until 1918 under Ottoman rule—had a Jewish population of only 85,000 in 1920. Harry Schneiderman, ed., *The American Jewish Year Book, September 13, 1920 to October 2, 1921* (Philadelphia: Jewish Publication Society of America, 1920), 361–62.

42. Mai Ngai, *Impossible Subjects: Illegal Aliens and the Making of Modern America* (Princeton, NJ: Princeton University Press, 2004), 22–24; Joseph W. Bendersky, *The "Jewish Threat": Anti-Semitic Politics of the U.S. Army* (New York: Basic Books, 2000); "Oppose Authority to Suspend Tariffs," *New York Times*, December 10,

1942, 16. On the history of the Judeo-Bolshevik conspiracy theory in European politics, see Paul Hanebrink, *A Specter Haunting Europe: The Myth of Judeo-Bolshevism* (Cambridge, MA: Harvard University Press, 2018).

43. Brian Burgoon, Janice Fine, Wade Jacoby, and Daniel Tichenor, "Immigration and the Transformation of American Unionism," *International Migration Review* 44, no. 4 (Winter 2010): 933–73.

44. "Urges Admission of Jewish Refugees," *New York Times*, November 30, 1933, 24.

45. David Brody, "American Jewry, the Refugees, and Immigration Restriction (1932–1942)," *Publications of the American Jewish Historical Society* 45 no. 4 (June 1956): 219–47.

46. Richard Breitman and Allan J. Lichtman, *FDR and the Jews* (Cambridge, MA: Belknap, 2013), 77–80, 92.

47. *Economic Council Newsletter*, no. 107, December 1, 1942.

48. Hadley Cantril, *Gauging Public Opinion* (Princeton, NJ: Princeton University Press, 1944), 307; Madeline Y. Hsu, *The Good Immigrants: How the Yellow Peril Became the Model Minority* (Princeton, NJ: Princeton University Press, 2015), 81–103; U.S. Office of Facts and Figures, "This Man Is Your Friend: Chinese: He Fights for Freedom," poster, Washington, DC, 1942, University of North Texas Digital Library, Government Documents Department, https://digital.library.unt.edu/ark:/67531/metadc233/m1/1/.

49. James T. Sparrow, *Warfare State: World War II Americans and the Age of Big Government* (New York: Oxford University Press, 2011), 110.

50. David Hyman, *The Abandonment of the Jews: America and the Holocaust, 1941–1945* (New York: Pantheon Books, 1984), 285–87. On the geographical boundaries of the Holocaust, see Timothy Snyder, *Bloodlands: Europe between Hitler and Stalin* (New York: Basic Books, 2010).

51. Westbrook Pegler, "1,000 Refugee Plan Doesn't Please Pegler," *Green Bay Gazette*, June 14, 1944, 5.

52. Leonard Dinnerstein, *America and Survivors of the Holocaust* (New York: Columbia University Press, 1982) 9–38; "U.S. Neglect of Jews Bared as Truman Orders Cleanup," *Atlanta Journal-Constitution*, September 30, 1945, 1A; Ann Cottrell, "Senators Hear Britain Reject Palestine Plea," *New York Herald Tribune*, October 3, 1945, 4A.

53. *Economic Council Letter*, no. 177, October 15, 1947.

54. Brian Kennedy, "The Surprising Zionist: Senator Robert A. Taft and the Creation of Israel," *Historian* 73, no. 4 (2011): 747–67.

55. "Senate Report Condemns Poll Tax Laws of South," *Chicago Defender*, January 1, 1944, 18; Harry McAlpin, "Dixie, GOP for States Rights," *Chicago Defender*, August 12, 1944, 3.

56. Quoted in Dinnerstein, *America and the Survivors of the Holocaust*, 140.

57. Kennedy, "The Surprising Zionist."

58. Gerald L. K. Smith, "Taft and the Jews," *The Cross and the Flag*, July 1948, 11.

59. Felix Morley, "Pointing towards Imperialism," *Human Events*, January 1, 1944, 2.

60. Frank C. Hanighen, "Not Merely Gossip," *Human Events*, December 18, 1946, 5

61. See, for instance, *The Cross and the Flag*, May 1949, which included the article "Is Communism Jewish?" along with "Jew Congressman Promotes Hate," "Jews Would Censor Mail," and "Jew Censorship of School Books." "Palestine—Chapter III: The Conquest of Zion," *Economic Council Letter*, no. 186, March 1, 1948.

62. U.S. Congress, *Proceedings and Debates of the 80th Congress, Vol. 91, Part 11*, 80th Cong., 2nd sess. (1948), A3787.

63. Harry S. Truman, *Public Papers of the Presidents of the United States; Containing the Public Messages, Speeches, and Statements of the President, 1948* (Washington, DC: Office of the Federal Register, National Archives and Records Service, 1964), 382–84. See also Mell Schiff, "President Truman and the Jewish DPs, 1945–1945: The Untold Story," *American Jewish History* 99, no. 4 (2015): 327–52.

64. Dinnerstein, *America and the Survivors of the Holocaust*, 285–87.

CHAPTER 4. MCCARTHYISM AND THE FAR RIGHT

1. There are a number of studies of the Malmedy massacre trial, the most definitive of which is Steven P. Remy, *The Malmedy Massacre: The War Crimes Trial Controversy* (Cambridge, MA: Harvard University Press, 2017). The biography of Peiper is found on 22–28. For additional historiographical views, see James J. Weingartner, *A Peculiar Crusade: Willis M. Everett and the Malmedy Massacre* (New York: New York University Press, 2000).

2. Remy, *Malmedy*, 28–32.

3. For Kiev massacre figures, see Karel C. Berkhoff, "The Corpses in the Ravine Were Women, Men and Children: Written Testimonies from 1941 on the Babi Yar Massacre," *Holocaust and Genocide Studies* 29, no. 2 (Fall 2015): 251–74. For Operation Meetinghouse figures and a largely apologetic account of the of the American bombing operation, see Thomas R. Searle, " 'It Made a Lot of Sense to Kill Skilled Workers': The Firebombing of Tokyo in March 1945," *Journal of Military History* 66, no. 1 (January 2002): 103–33. See also Yuki Tanaka, Toshiyuki Tanaka, and Marilyn B. Young, eds., *Bombing Civilians: A Twentieth-Century History* (New York: New Press, 2009), 85 for discussion of casualty estimates for the Tokyo bombing.

4. "Nazis Throw in Second Powerful Wave in Wake of Initial 200,000-Man Assault," *Washington Post*, December 21, 1944, 1.

5. Remy, *Malmedy*, 134–36.

6. Ibid., 140–42.

7. Ibid., 120–21, 93–94.

8. Ibid., 121–23.

9. "WAR CRIMES: Clemency," *Time*, January 17, 1949, 19; William R. Conklin, "Protests Increase on Malmedy Trail," *New York Times*, March 2, 1949, 1; Remy, *Malmedy*, 231–32; "Senators Open Probe of War Trials Monday," *Chicago Tribune*, April 16, 1949, A4.

10. Remy, *Malmedy*, 233. See also Dieter Berninger, "Milwaukee's German-American Community and the Nazi Challenge of the 1930's," *Wisconsin Magazine of History* 72, no. 2 (Winter 1987–1988): 118–42.

11. "Negroes Claim Discrimination," *Green Bay Press-Gazette*, January 21, 1942, 2; "Ten Firms Told to End Worker Discrimination," *Chicago Tribune*, April 13, 1942, 23; David Oshinsky, *A Conspiracy So Immense: The World of Joe McCarthy* (New York: Oxford University Press, 2005), 75.

12. John Wyngaard, "Mrs. Luce Asks GOP for Strong Foreign Policy," *Green Bay Press-Gazette*, June 28, 1943, 1–2.

13. "Political Groups Report Expenses for Primary Contests," *Rhinelander Daily News*, August 5, 1946, 1.

14. Oshinsky, *A Conspiracy So Immense*, 75.

15. Jack Anderson and Ronald W. May, *McCarthy: The Man, the Senator, the "Ism,"* (Boston: Beacon, 1952), 141–43; Robert Griffin, *Politics of Fear: Joseph R. McCarthy and the Senate* (Lexington: University Press of Kentucky, 1970), 18.

16. "McCarthy States His Position on 'American Action,' " *Wisconsin Jewish Chronicle*, October 25, 1946, 3.

17. U.S. House, House Select Committee on Lobbying Activities, *Lobbying, Direct and Indirect: Hearings*, 81st Cong., 2nd sess. (June 20, 1950), 69; *Economic Council Letter*, no. 449, February 15, 1959; Eric Pace, "Conservative Group Gives Prizes to Senator Byrd and William Loeb," *New York Times*, May 11, 1972, 28.

18. U.S. Senate, Subcommittee of the Committee on Armed Services, United States Senate, *Malmedy Massacre Investigation: Hearings*, 81st Cong., 1st sess. (May 4, 1950), 263; (September 5, 1949), 1303.

19. "Jewish Groups Assail McCarthy for False 'Anti-Semitic Issue,' " Jewish Telegraphic Agency, July 24, 1953.

20. On McCarthy and antisemitism, see, for example, Charles R. Allen Jr. and Arthur J. Dlugoff, "McCarthy and Anti-Semitism: A Documented Exposé," *Jewish Life*, July 1953, 4–15.

21. Remy, *Malmedy*, 283.

22. "Loyalty Oath at U. of California Ordered for All 4,000 on Staff," *New York Herald Tribune*, June 13, 1949, 1; "Revision of Oath Asked at UC," *Los Angeles Times*, June 15, 1949, 12; "Faculty Members Decry Coast Oath," *New York Times*, June 15, 1949, 32.

23. Jack B. Tenney, *Zion's Trojan Horse: A Tenney Report on World Zionism* (Hollywood: Standard, 1954). John Beaty, the author of the antisemitic book *Iron Curtain over America* discussed in chapter 5, wrote the introduction to Tenney's book. Holmes Alexander, "Collecting Local Color Make Friends," *Fort Myers News-Press*, September 10, 1952, 4.

24. On the chilling effect of McCarthyism in the academy, see Ellen Schrecker, *No Ivory Tower: McCarthyism and the Universities* (New York: Oxford University Press, 1986). On the effects of McCarthyism in government administration— particularly with regard to gender dynamics, see Landon R. Y. Storrs, *The Second Red Scare and the Unmaking of the New Deal Left* (Princeton, NJ: Princeton University Press, 2012).

25. William F. Buckley Jr. and L. Brent Bozell, *McCarthy and His Enemies: The Record and Its Meaning* (Chicago: Regnery, 1954); William F. Buckley Jr., *The Redhunter: A Novel Based on the Life of Senator Joseph McCarthy* (Boston: Little & Brown,

1999); Ann Coulter, *Treason: Liberal Treachery from the Cold War to the War on Terrorism* (New York: Crown Forum, 2003); M. Stanton Evans, *Blacklisted by History: The Untold Story of Senator Joe McCarthy and His Fight against America's Enemies* (New York: Crown Forum, 2007), 11–12.

26. There are innumerable books and articles on the Rosenberg case, which vary tremendously in scope, quality, and political interventions. Some of the strongest work has been on specific cultural and political dimensions of the case. See, for example, Virginia Carmichael, *Framing History: The Rosenberg Story and the Cold War* (Minneapolis: University of Minnesota Press, 1993) for a cultural history of the Rosenbergs; and Lori Clune, *Executing the Rosenbergs: Death and Diplomacy in a Cold War World* (New York: Oxford University Press, 2016) for an international history.

27. Austin Stevens, "Manpower Views Given by New Aide," *New York Times*, November 11, 1950, 5. Although in many respects dated, Arthur M. Schlesinger Jr., *The Coming of the New Deal, 1933–1935* (New York: Houghton Mifflin, 1958) provides useful biographical information on the businesspeople who formed the ranks of moderate New Dealers in the 1930s. For the debates over manpower utilization, particularly universal military training, see Michael J. Hogan, *A Cross of Iron: Harry S. Truman and the Origins of the National Security State* (New York: Cambridge University Press, 2000).

28. Nicole Hemmer, *Messengers of the Right: Media and the Modern Conservative Movement* (Philadelphia: University of Pennsylvania Press, 2016), 66–67.

29. J. B. Matthews to Fulton Lewis, November 27, 1950, Fulton Lewis Jr. Papers, box 233, Syracuse University Libraries Special Collections Research Center, Syracuse, NY. The original petition in question, ironically enough, was a protest "against the imprisonment of men and women for expressing their political opinions" warning that a " 'Red scare' was sweeping the country and threatening the complete destruction of civil liberties" and included the names of Franz Boas, Carl Van Doren, John Dos Passos, Upton Sinclair, and H. L. Mencken in addition to that of Anna Rosenberg. " 'Red Scare' Protest Issued by Liberals," *New York Times*, May 19, 1950, 18. The FBI later confirmed that this Anna Rosenberg was a different person than Anna M. Rosenberg. Mike Wallace, interview with Fulton Lewis Jr. *The Mike Wallace Interview*, February 1, 1958.

30. Senate Armed Services Committee, *Nomination of Anna M. Rosenberg to Be Assistant Secretary of Defense: Hearings before the United States Senate Committee on Armed Services*, 81st Congress, 2nd sess. (Washington, DC: Government Publishing Office, 1950), 1–24.

31. Ira Katznelson, *Fear Itself: The New Deal and the Origins of Our Time* (New York: Norton, 2013), 207–22; "Will Soldiers Vote?" *Time*, February 14, 1944, 19; David E. Rowe and Robert Schulmann, ed. *Einstein on Politics: His Private Thoughts and Public Stands on Nationalism, Zionism, War, Peace, and the Bomb* (Princeton, NJ: Princeton University Press, 2007), 47.

32. U.S. Congress, *Congressional Record*, 81st Cong., 2nd sess. (1950), vol. 96, pt. 12, p. 991; Arnold Forster and Benjamin R. Epstein, *The Trouble-Makers: An Anti-Defamation League Report* (Garden City, NJ: Doubleday, 1952), 53–59.

33. Forster and Epstein, *The Trouble-Makers*, 55–57; Senate Armed Services Committee, *Nomination of Anna M. Rosenberg to Be Assistant Secretary of Defense*, 318–32.

34. Senate Armed Services Committee, *Nomination of Anna M. Rosenberg to Be Assistant Secretary of Defense*, 37–122. Forster and Epstein's *The Trouble-Makers* has an abridged and editorialized transcript of De Sola's testimony, 31–39.

35. For Nellor's testimony, see Senate Armed Services Committee, *Nomination of Anna M. Rosenberg to Be Assistant Secretary of Defense*, 318–32.

36. Storrs, *The Second Red Scare*.

37. *Economic Council Letter*, no. 417, October 15, 1957.

38. Radio Reports Inc. to Fulton Lewis, January 7, 1951, Fulton Lewis Jr. Papers, box 233.

39. Upton Close to Fulton Lewis Jr., January 7, 1951, Fulton Lewis Jr. Papers, box 233; National Blue Star Mothers of America to Fulton Lewis, February 21, 1951, Fulton Lewis Jr. Papers, box 233.

40. U.S. Congress, *Congressional Record*, 81st Cong., 2nd sess. (1950), vol. 96, pt. 12, p. 1162; Wallace, interview with Lewis; "The Question of Robert Welch," *National Review*, February 13, 1962, 83; Gerald L. K. Smith, "The Truth about Anna M. Rosenberg," *The Cross and the Flag*, January 1951, 9.

41. Lewis was cited repeatedly as an anti-communist source by Merwin Hart into the 1960s. See, for example, *Economic Council Letter*, no. 476, April 1, 1960.

42. Forster and Epstein, *The Trouble-Makers*, 201.

43. John J. Sirica, *To Set the Record Straight: The Break-In, the Tapes, the Conspirators* (New York: Norton, 1979), 38–39; Renata Adler, *Gone: The Last Days of the New Yorker* (New York: Simon & Schuster, 1999); and Renata Adler, "A Court of No Appeal," *Harper's Magazine*, August 2000, 65–76.

44. Forster and Epstein, *The Trouble-Makers*, 60; Oshinsky, *A Conspiracy So Immense*, 204–5, 256; Glen Jeansonne, *Gerald L. K. Smith: Minister of Hate* (New Haven, CT: Yale University Press, 1988), 163. Smith reserved particular ire for President Eisenhower for having played a role in McCarthy's downfall. He spread wild rumors about Eisenhower throughout the 1950s—that he "fraternized in drunken brawls with Georgi Zhukov" after World War II, that he had been promoted to general because he had provided sexual services to Anna Rosenberg, and that he was (of course) secretly a Jew. Unlike John Birch Society founder Robert Welch, however, Smith refrained from alleging that Eisenhower was a member of the Communist Party. Gerald L. K. Smith, *Is Eisenhower a Communist? No! But—* (Los Angeles: Christian National Crusade, ca. 1961).

45. "70 Walk Out on Consumers' Research Staff," *New York Herald Tribune*, September 5, 1935, 15.

46. "Strikers Beat Official's Son at Jersey Plant," *New York Herald Tribune*, September 11, 1935, 4.

47. Josephine Danzel, "Consumers Research Board Refuses Strike Arbitration," *Daily Worker*, September 25, 1935, 5.

48. "Research Strikers Stone Jersey Plant," *New York Times*, October 15, 1935, 18; "Union Official Held in Strike," *New York Times*, October 22, 1935, 2.

49. Storrs, *The Second Red Scare,* 54–56; "Firm Blamed in Consumers' Research Strike," *New York Herald Tribune,* November 20, 1935, 14.

50. Lawrence Glickman, "The Strike in the Temple of Consumption: Consumer Activism and Twentieth-Century American Political Culture," *Journal of American History* 88, no. 1 (June 2001): 99–128.

51. J. B. Matthews, *Odyssey of a Fellow Traveler* (New York: Mount Vernon, 1938), 256–69, 275.

52. Storr, *Second Red Scare;* Robert M. Lichtman, "J. B. Matthews and the 'Counter-Subversives': Names as a Political and Financial Resource in the McCarthy Era," *American Communist History* 5, no. 1 (2006): 1–36.

53. Richard Gid Powers, *Not without Honor: The History of American Anticommunism* (New York: Free Press, 1995), 231; Lichtman, "J. B. Matthews and the 'Counter-Subversives.' "

54. "Testimonial Dinner to J. B. Matthews by His Friends," Sert Room, Waldorf-Astoria, February 13, 1953, J. B. Matthews Papers, box 700, David M. Rubenstein Rare Book & Manuscript Library, Duke University, Durham, NC.

55. Lichtman, "J. B. Matthews and the 'Counter-Subversives," 22; Roy Cohn to George Sokolsky, February 9, 1953, Ludwig von Mises to George Sokolsky, December 26, 1952, William F. Buckley Jr. to George Sokolsky, January 26, 1953, Ayn Rand to George Sokolsky, February 3, 1953, William Schlamm to George Sokolsky, December 19, 1952, all in J. B. Matthews Papers, box 700.

56. Shirley Feinberg to George Sokolsky, January 19, 1953, John B. Trevor to George Sokolsky, January 16, 1953, J. B. Matthews to Rabbi Benjamin Schultz, February 23, 1953, all in J. B. Matthews Papers, box 700.

57. Merwin Hart to George Sokolsky, February 3, 1953, National Council for American Education to George Sokolsky, February 3, 1953, J. B. Matthews to Harry Jung, February 19, 1959, Harry Jung to J. B. Matthews, February 24, 1953, all in J. B. Matthews Papers, box 700; Drew Pearson, "Washington Merry-Go-Round," *Bakersfield Californian,* July 11, 1953, 26; Lichtman, "J. B. Matthews and the 'Counter-Subversives," 22.

58. Victor Riesel to George Sokolsky, February 9, 1953, George Sokolsky to Victor Riesel, February 9, 1953, J. B. Matthews Papers, box 700.

59. Even Sokolsky, however, had his limits. He condemned Jack Tenney in 1952 as one who "made a splendid record as an anti-Communist and who now wallows in the intellectual and spiritual sty prepared for him by Gerald L. K. Smith." George Sokolsky, "Ghost Still Walks," *Burlington Free Press,* October 23, 1952, 6.

60. Many European antisemites, too, had their so-called "good Jews." Karl Lueger, the antisemitic mayor of Vienna before World War I whom Adolf Hitler cited as an influence, once famously declared—with regard to his circle of Jewish friends—"I decide who is a Jew!" Richard S. Geehr, ed., *"I Decide Who Is a Jew!" The Papers of Dr. Karl Lueger* (Washington, DC: University Press of America, 1982).

61. "The Man in the Middle," *Time,* May 24, 1954, 44–46.

62. Isaac Don Levine, "The Strange Case of Merwin K. Hart," *Plain Talk,* February 1950, 1–9.

63. *Economic Council Letter,* no. 229, December 15, 1949.

64. Thomas A. Kolsky, *Jews against Zionism: The American Council for Judaism, 1942–1948* (Philadelphia: Temple University Press, 1990), 134.

65. *Economic Council Letter,* no. 229, December 15, 1949.

66. Levine, "Strange Case of Merwin K. Hart," 2–3.

67. Ibid., 9.

68. *Economic Council Letter,* no. 233, February 15, 1950.

69. Ibid.; Levine, "Strange Case of Merwin K. Hart," 2.

70. See, for example, *Economic Council Letter,* no. 220, August 1, 1949; and *Economic Council Letter,* no. 256, February 1, 1951.

71. *Economic Council Letter,* no. 473, February 15, 1960.

72. Russell Maguire to George Sokolsky, February 12, 1953, J. B. Matthews Papers, box 700; Drew Pearson, "Tragedy of the Matthews Case," *Washington Post,* July 11, 1953, 27.

CHAPTER 5. MAGAZINE WARS

A version of this chapter was previously published in the *Journal of American History.* David Austin Walsh, "The Right-Wing Popular Front: The Far Right and American Conservatism in the 1950s," *Journal of American History* 107, no. 2 (September 2020): 411–32. By permission of Oxford University Press, Organization of American Historians.

1. "A Call for Revolt on the Campus," *American Mercury,* October 1951, 24–29; William Bradford Huie, "Why a Republican Can't Be a Liberal," *American Mercury,* December 1951, 55–61; William F. Buckley Jr. "The Treason of the Professors," *American Mercury,* March 1952, 29–37; John B. Judis, *William F. Buckley, Jr., Patron Saint of the Conservatives* (New York: Simon & Schuster, 1988); 103–4.

2. "Maguire of the *Mercury,*" *Newsweek,* August 25, 1952, 49.

3. "Biographical Sketch," Russell Maguire subject file, 6, Anti-Defamation League archives, New York.

4. Kaiden Kazanjian, "Willis Resign from CBS to Join Thompson Automatic Arms Corp.," *New York Times,* June 18, 1940, 35.

5. Auto-Ordnance was modestly sized compared to Connecticut's other major arms manufacturers because Auto-Ordnance focused primarily on the production of the weapon itself, not ammunition. In January 1941, Connecticut arms manufacturers had contracts worth $113 million with the U.S. government. Winchester alone, headed by future right-wing philanthropist John W. Olin, accounted for $65 million and employed a workforce of over seven thousand compared to Auto-Ordnance's five hundred workers. "Arms, Ammunition Plants Run at Full Speed Ahead," *Hartford Courant,* January 5, 1941, D14; "More Defense Contracts Announced; Total $18,848,038," *Wall Street Journal,* February 15, 1941, 3. "Biographical Sketch," Russell Maguire subject file, 6.

6. Drew Pearson, "The Merry-Go-Round," *Louisville Courier-Journal,* November 2, 1942, 7.

7. "Thompson Estate Fights Dividend," *New York Times,* December 3, 1940, 48; "Thompson Suit Dropped," *New York Times,* March 5, 1941, 31; "Biographical Sketch," Russell Maguire subject file, 4–10.

8. Robert Tompkins, "He's a Millionaire by Intuition," *Hartford Courant,* September 2, 1945, 4.

9. "Miss Boissevan, Elizabeth Maguire Presented Together," *New York Herald Tribune,* November 24, 1950, 23; "The Young, in the Clouds," *Vogue,* December 1, 1950, 93.

10. "J. Russell Maguire, 67, Is Dead; an Industrialist and Financier," *New York Times,* November 11, 1966, 43.

11. Lawrence Dennis to Harry A. Jung, July 4, 1953, Lawrence Dennis Papers, box 2, Hoover Institution Library and Archives, Stanford, CA.

12. U.S. House, Select Committee on Lobbying Activities, *Hearings before the Select Committee on Lobbying Activities,* 81st Cong., 2nd sess. (1950), 257, 270, 299, 363; "Biographical Sketch," Russell Maguire subject file, 11.

13. Adam Laats, *The Other School Reformers: Conservative Activism in American Education* (Cambridge, MA: Harvard University Press, 2015), 123–84.

14. William Bradford Huie to Irving Lieberman and Malcolm Logan, June 9, 1953, Russell Maguire subject file. Lieberman and Logan were both reporters for the *New York Post,* which had interviewed Huie for a series of articles on Maguire's antisemitic connections that ran in that newspaper from June 4 through June 8. Huie confirmed Zoll's connections to the *Mercury*—his deputy editor Martin Greenberg had approached him with concerns that Zoll was selling subscriptions for the magazine. Zoll in the early 1950s was roughly analogous to Fred Schwarz (who occasionally wrote for the *Mercury* from 1953 through 1957) in the mid-1960s—a "professional anticommunist" condemned as an extremist by the left and liberals but tolerated, even accepted, as part of the right's anti-communist popular front. See Heather Hendershot, *Open to Debate: How William F. Buckley Put Liberal America on the Firing Line* (New York: Broadside Books, 2016), 3–7. On Schwarz's *Mercury* output, see, for instance, Dr. Fred Schwarz, "Five Basic Steps to Communism," *American Mercury,* February 1957, 1.

15. On military intelligence as a hotbed of antisemitism, see Joseph W. Bendersky, *The "Jewish Threat": Anti-Semitic Politics of the U.S. Army* (New York: Basic Books, 2000). Throughout the 1950s Beaty taught at SMU, where he repeatedly clashed with faculty and the administration. See Paul F. Boller, *Memoirs of an Obscure Professor* (Fort Worth: Texas Christian University Press, 1992), 1–9; "S.M.U. Professor Accused by Board of Anti-Semitism," *Harvard Crimson,* June 17, 1954; Harold Lord Varney, "S.M.U. Papers Leftism," *American Mercury,* January 1960, 16–22.

16. MacArthur himself used the term "iron curtain over America" to describe the "socialist" tendencies of the Truman administration. "MacArthur Cites Threat of 'Creeping Sabotage,'" *Christian Science Monitor,* November 14, 1951, 7; John O. Beaty, *The Iron Curtain over America* (Dallas: Wilkinson, 1951).

17. Henry Edward Schultz to Lt. Gen. George E. Stratemeyer, October 4, 1955, William F. Buckley Jr. Papers (MS 576), box 2, Manuscripts and Archives, Yale University Library, New Haven, CT.

18. Henry Regnery to William F. Buckley Sr., December 30, 1952, Henry Regnery Papers, box 2, Hoover Institution Archives.

19. Allen Lesser, "Cross Section U.S.A.: Foot-Noted Hate," *Jewish Advocate*, October 9, 1952, 14; Milton Friedman, "National Spotlight: Echoes of 'Mein Kampf,' " *Jewish Advocate*, April 24, 1952, 8; James Rorty, "The Native Anti-Semite's 'New Look,' " *Commentary*, January 1954, 413–21. Note that Friedman was a staff journalist for the *Jewish Advocate* and was unrelated to the economist of the same name.

20. "Trouble for the *Mercury*," *Time*, December 8, 1952, 44; "Number Three for *Mercury*," *Time*, December 15, 1952, 61; "Shakeup at *Mercury* Follows *Exposé* Story," *Exposé*, January 1953, 1.

21. William F. Buckley Jr. to Dr. John O. Beaty, December 17, 1954, William F. Buckley Jr. to Russell Maguire, July 13, 1955, William F. Buckley Jr. Papers, box 1–2.

22. Smith was one of the right-wing activists who were *not* a part of the right-wing popular front, even behind the scenes, due both to his extreme antisemitism and—equally important—his image as an antiquated country bumpkin. This was the major theme of Smith's press coverage as early as his 1944 third-party presidential campaign, with even southern reporters ridiculing his flamboyant display of his suspenders during his stump speeches. Ralph McGill, "Gerald Smith Warbles Tune Familiar to South," *Atlanta Constitution*, July 19, 1944, 10; William F. Buckley Jr. to Mrs. Mary Driscoll (secretary to Senator Jos. R. McCarthy), December 29, 1954, William F. Buckley Jr. Papers, box 2; "Col. Lindbergh on Ickes List of 5th Columnists," *New York Herald Tribune*, November 21, 1940, 24.

23. "Thunder on Both Sides," *Newsweek*, February 2, 1953, 76.

24. *N. W. Ayer and Son's Directory of Newspapers and Periodicals* (Philadelphia: N. W. Ayer, 1954), 667; *N. W. Ayer and Son's Directory of Newspapers and Periodicals* (Philadelphia: N. W. Ayer, 1959), 722.

25. Alice Widener, "Who's Running the Ford Foundation? *American Mercury*, June 1953, 3–7.

26. Harold Lord Varney, "Can a Socialist Be an Anti-Communist?" *American Mercury*, March 1954, 89–94. On the Americans for Democratic Action, see Steven M. Gillon, *Politics and Vision: ADA and American Liberalism, 1947–1985* (New York: Oxford University Press, 1987).

27. Chesly Manly, "Sulzbergism," *American Mercury*, July 1954, 17–22.

28. William F. Buckley Jr. and L. Brent Bozell, *McCarthy and His Enemies: The Record and Its Meaning* (Chicago: Regnery, 1954), 333. Buckley would occasionally lapse into rhetoric about the "Communist-Socialist-Liberal movement" when writing privately to others on the right. William F. Buckley Jr. to Marcella M. du Pont, November 17, 1954; William F. Buckley Jr. to Walter E. Ditmars, January 12, 1956, William F. Buckley Jr. Papers, box 2.

29. Robert E. Vahey, "Anti-Anti-Communism," *American Mercury*, August 1954, 103–106.

30. W. G. Libsett, "The Mystery of Zimbabwe," *American Mercury*, December 1954, 111–15; Manning Johnson, "Negro Rebellion Is Still the Aim of Reds," *American Mercury*, February 1955, 97–102; A. Desmond Burridge, "Some Racial Truths

about South Africa," *American Mercury,* December 1956, 5–14; "Hitler's 'My Fight' Seven Times," *Atlanta Daily World,* August 30, 1936, 4; Harold Lord Varney, "Meet Senator Talmadge," *American Mercury,* February 1958, 7–17.

31. Gayle B. Montgomery, *One Step from the White House: The Rise and Fall of Senator William F. Knowland* (Berkeley: University of California Press, 1998), 194; "Senator Knowland Answers Twenty Questions on Foreign Policy," *American Mercury,* October 1955, 5–11.

32. J. B. Matthews, "Reds and Our Churches," *American Mercury,* July 1953, 3–14.

33. Robert Griffin, *Politics of Fear: Joseph R. McCarthy and the Senate* (Lexington: University Press of Kentucky, 1970), 231.

34. "J. B. Matthews Quits Post as Red Prober," *Chicago Tribune,* July 10, 1953, 1.

35. Daniel Williams, *God's Own Party: The Making of the Christian Right* (New York: Oxford University Press, 2010), 38–43; Markku Ruotsila, "Carl McIntire and the Fundamentalist Origins of the Christian Right," *Church History* 81, no. 2 (June 2012): 378–407. See also Neil J. Young, *We Gather Together: The Religious Right and the Problem of Interfaith Politics* (New York: Oxford University Press, 2015), which traces the development of the development of a common anti-secular identity among Catholics, Mormons, and evangelical Protestants.

36. Rabbi Benjamin Schultz, "Is Everybody Anti-Semitic?" *American Mercury,* July 1954, 137–42.

37. Russell Maguire, "In the *Mercury's* Opinion," *American Mercury,* June 1956, 97.

38. Matthew Avery Sutton, *American Apocalypse: A History of Modern Evangelicalism* (Cambridge, MA: Belknap, 2014), 207–31, 293–325.

39. Marshall Frady, *Billy Graham: A Parable of American Righteousness* (New York: Little, Brown, 1979), 229–31; "Heads Graham Fund," *New York Herald Tribune,* July 25, 1953, 20.

40. Billy Graham, "Satan's Religion," *American Mercury,* August 1954, 41–46. *Graham's* association with Maguire is all the more remarkable given that he cultivated a reputation as a moderate on racial integration, drawing a deliberate contrast with fundamentalist ministers like Carl McIntire and Billy James Hargis. See Stephen Miller, *Billy Graham and the Rise of the Republican South* (Philadelphia: University of Pennsylvania Press, 2009); and Williams, *God's Own Party.*

41. Publisher's Statement, *National Review,* November 11, 1955, 5; Heather Hendershot, *What's Fair on the Air? Cold War Right-Wing Broadcasting and the Public Interest* (Chicago: University of Chicago Press, 2011), 26–28.

42. Carl T. Bogus, *Buckley: William F. Buckley, Jr. and the Rise of American Conservatism* (New York: Bloomsbury, 2011), 61.

43. William F. Buckley Jr., "In Search of Anti-Semitism," *National Review,* December 30, 1991, 20–62.

44. Nock was a frequent luncheon guest at the Buckley household in the early 1940s. Bogus, *Buckley,* 67–69; William F. Buckley Sr. to Albert J. Nock, May 15, 1941, William F. Buckley Jr. Papers, box 118.

45. William F. Buckley Jr. to Robert H. W. Welch Jr., July 4, 1955, William F. Buckley Jr. Papers, box 2.

46. William F. Buckley Jr. to Ed Gossett, December 13, 1954, William F. Buckley Jr. Papers, box 2.

47. Ralph de Toledano to William F. Buckley Jr., September 19, 1955, William F. Buckley Jr. Papers, box 2; "Blowup at the *Mercury*," *Time*, October 3, 1955, 72.

48. "Jenner Sees Fight on Reds Flagging," *New York Herald Tribune*, September 24, 1955, 5; "Top Editors of *Mercury* Staff Quit in Reported Dispute over Policies," *Hartford Courant*, September 24, 1955, 7A.

49. "Memoirs of William LaVarre as Editor-in-Chief of the *American Mercury Magazine*, 1957–1958," 1977, William LaVarre Papers, box 3, 98, Hoover Institution Archives.

50. Theodore Peterson, *Magazines in the Twentieth Century* (Urbana: University of Illinois Press, 1956), 90–93; "New Distributors for Time, Inc., List," *New York Times*, June 15, 1955, 50.

51. William F. Buckley Jr. to Roy M. Cohn, August 19, 1957, William F. Buckley Jr. Papers, box 1.

52. Cohn was Jewish, but according to those in his orbit he had no problem associating with antisemites. Nicholas von Hoffman, *Citizen Cohn* (New York: Doubleday, 1988), 333, 369–70.

53. "Charges *American Mercury* with Bias," *Jewish Advocate*, June 13, 1957, 1.

54. LaVarre, "Memoirs," 32; "Money Made Mysterious," written by Paul Stevens (likely a pseudonym of Maguire), first began appearing in the *Mercury* in November 1956 and continued intermittently through 1958.

55. LaVarre, "Memoirs," 40–51.

56. Ibid., 43.

57. Ibid., 101.

58. Russell Maguire, "The Gravestones of 1913," *American Mercury*, August 1957, 103–04.

59. C. F. Hood to Russell Maguire, December 19, 1957, C. M. White to Russell Maguire, December 24, 1957, E. S. Bowerfind to Russell Maguire, December 24, 1957, E. E. Moore to Russell Maguire, March 21, 1958, all in LaVarre Papers, box 6.

60. Maguire, "In the *Mercury's* Opinion," *American Mercury*, February 195885–86.

61. Joseph Fronczak, "The Fascist Game: Transnational Political Transmissions and the Genesis of the U.S. Modern Right," *Journal of American History* 105, no. 3 (December 2018), 587.

62. W. H. Lawrence, "Knowland Backers in East Pay for Anti-Reuther Tract," *New York Times*, September 14, 1958, 1.

63. For biographical information on Charles White, see Irving Bernstein, *The Turbulent Years: A History of the American Worker, 1933–1941* (Boston: Houghton Mifflin, 1970), 516. For a discussion of corporate support for the American right, see Kim Phillips-Fein, *Invisible Hands: The Businessmen's Crusade against the New Deal* (New York: Norton, 2010), especially 26–53. Interestingly, Jasper Crane, a former vice president at DuPont and the major backer of the Mont Pelerin Society, initially expressed misgivings about backing the venture under the impression that founder Friedrich Hayek was Jewish.

64. Ralph de Toledano, "The Walter Reuther Story," *American Mercury*, May 1953, 3–13. LaVarre discusses the "labor issue" in his "Memoirs," 264–66. Senator William F. Knowland, "Labor Should Be Free," *American Mercury*, March 1958, 5–9.

65. Frederick James Simonelli, *American Fuehrer: George Lincoln Rockwell and the American Nazi Party* (Urbana: University of Illinois Press, 1999), 24; Donna Alvah, *Unofficial Ambassadors: American Military Families Overseas and the Cold War, 1946–1956* (New York: New York University Press, 2007), 94–98.

66. LaVarre, "Memoirs," 73–74.

67. Roslyn South, "Pity the Childless Couple," *American Mercury*, June 1957, 76–78; Murray T. Pringle, "Tried Walking Lately?" *American Mercury*, May 1958, 35–38.

68. George Lincoln Rockwell, "No Wonder Iceland Hates Us!" *American Mercury*, January 1957, 7–13; Rockwell, "Who Wants Panty-Waisted Marines?" *American Mercury*, April 1957, 117–22; Rockwell, "Miracle at Parris Island," *American Mercury*, May 1957, 132–38.

69. Irene Corbally Kuhn, "Women Don't Belong in Politics," *American Mercury*, August 1953, 3–6; Beryl Kent, "Is Democracy Making Japanese Women Neurotic?" *American Mercury*, June 1954, 139–40; Kuhn, "Twelve Senate Wives," *American Mercury*, August 1955, 52–58; Jessica Wyatt Payne, "Women—Man Your Stations," *American Mercury*, January 1954, 83–86.

70. George Lincoln Rockwell, *This Time the World*, 2nd ed. (New York: Parliament House, 1963), 226–27.

71. Ibid., 227–28.

72. Presumably Rockwell is referring to George Schulyer, a conservative African American who made frequent contributions to the magazine, usually suggesting that African Americans will "vote according to their economic and social interests," meaning that there is an opening for conservatives to appeal to Black voters. George S. Schuyler, "The Negro Voter Comes of Age," *American Mercury*, March 1957, 99–104.

73. Rockwell, *This Time the World*, 229–30.

74. LaVarre, "Memoirs," 366–67.

75. Russell Maguire, "The Forces of Darkness," *American Mercury*, January 1959, 110–11.

76. William F. Buckley Jr. to Karl Hess, January 9, 1957, William F. Buckley Jr. Papers, box 2.

77. William F. Buckley Jr. to L. Brent Bozell, December 15, 1959, William F. Buckley Jr. Papers, box 9; William F. Buckley Jr. to Senator William F. Knowland, February 26, 1958, William F. Buckley Jr. Papers, box 5.

78. "Racketeer & Communist Dominated Unions," *American Mercury*, April 1959, 78–112; Ralph de Toledano, "Nixon," *American Mercury*, May 1959, 5–16.

79. William F. Buckley Jr., Confidential Memorandum to Writers for *National Review*, April 1, 1959, William F. Buckley Jr. Papers, box 7.

80. Charles Willoughby to American Jewish Committee, August 15, 1960, Papers of Major General Charles A. Willoughby, USA, 1947–1973, series 1, box 1, RG-23, MacArthur Memorial Archives, Norfolk, VA.

81. "The *National Review* Scolds MERCURY WRITERS," AMERICAN MERCURY, JULY 1959, 151–52.

82. T. M. Morse to William F. Buckley Jr., June 5, 1959, Ethel M. Morse to William F. Buckley Jr., June 7, 1959, Father Thomas Murphy to William F. Buckley, Jr., June 4, 1959, John Hoar to William F. Buckley Jr., June 4, 1959, all in William F. Buckley Jr. Papers, box 7.

83. Chain letter, William F. Buckley Jr. Papers, box 7; Buckley, "In Search of Anti-Semitism," 37.

84. D. J. Mulloy, *The World of the John Birch Society: Conspiracy, Conservatism, and the Cold War* (Nashville, TN: Vanderbilt University Press, 2014), 8–9; Gail Q. Unruh, "Ultraconservative Distortion: Merwin K. Hart and the National Economic Council" (MA thesis, University of Oregon, 1981), iv.

85. Buckley, "The Question of Robert Welch," *National Review*, February 13, 1962, 83–88. See also, for example, "Republican Mayor Says Goldwater Is a 'Fascist,' " *New York Times*, July 19, 1964.

86. William F. Buckley Jr. to Revilo Oliver, February 10, 1960, William F. Buckley Jr. Papers, box 11.

87. For Buckley's personal reminiscences on the *l'affaire* Bircher, see William F. Buckley Jr., "Goldwater, the John Birch Society, and Me," *Commentary*, March 2008, https://www.commentarymagazine.com/articles/goldwater-the-john-birch-society-and-me/. See also Rick Perlstein, *Before the Storm: Barry Goldwater and the Unmaking of the American Consensus* (New York: Hill & Wang, 2001), 154–56, 476–77; and Alvin S. Felzenberg, *A Man and His Presidents: The Political Odyssey of William F. Buckley, Jr.* (New Haven, CT: Yale University Press, 2017), 131–55.

88. Rockwell, *This Time the World*, 102–7.

89. Bernard Nath to Arnold Forster, July 11, 1961, Arnold Forster to Russell Maguire, July 5, 1961, Russell Maguire subject file.

CHAPTER 6. THE JOHN BIRCH SOCIETY AND THE SECOND BROWN SCARE

1. Welch's letter, which was continually revised after its initial circulation in 1954, was eventually published in book format as *The Politician* in 1963. Among Welch's innumerable charges against Eisenhower was that Eisenhower's criticism of J. B. Matthews's 1953 *American Mercury* article on alleged communist infiltration of the Protestant churches in America showed Ike's latent hostility to Joseph McCarthy and his affinity for communism. Robert Welch, "The Politician," n.d. (after 1956), https://ia902709.us.archive.org/2/items/foia_Welch_Robert_The_Politician_manuscript.PDF, 83, 267. See also Edward H. Miller, *A Conspiratorial Life: Robert Welch, the John Birch Society, and the Revolution of American Conservatism* (Chicago: University of Chicago Press, 2022), 160–65.

2. "Ohio Senator Raps Welch as 'Little Hitler,' " *Los Angeles Times*, April 4, 1961, 2; "Birch Group Stirs Dispute on Coast," *New York Times*, March 26, 1961, 60.

3. Barry Goldwater, "A Look at Some Birch Critics," *Los Angeles Times,* December 19, 1961, B4; James Oviatt, "Enough of Anti-Anti Reds," *Los Angeles Times,* February 17, 1962, B4.

4. Rick Perlstein, "Retrospective Roundtable on Leo Ribuffo's *Old Christian Right:* Entry 2 from Perlstein," USIH blog, December 6, 2018, https://s-usih. org/2018/12/retrospective-roundtable-on-leo-ribuffos-old-christian-right-entry-2-from-perlstein/.

5. See, for instance, John A. Andrew, *The Other Side of the Sixties: Young Americans for Freedom and the Rise of Conservative Politics* (New Brunswick, NJ: Rutgers University Press, 1997), which characterized counter-right-wing efforts by the Kennedy administration and the AFL-CIO under Walter Reuther as "lumping together anyone on the Right who challenged mainstream thinking" and suggested that the Kennedy administration's attempts to arrest the growth of right-wing political organizations—among them Buckley's Young Americans for Freedom—through a combination of administrative and legal pressures, including politically motivated audits of conservative groups by the IRS, were an overreach. See also D. J. Mulloy, *The World of the John Birch Society: Conspiracy, Conservatism, and the Cold War* (Nashville, TN: Vanderbilt University Press, 2014), 59–61, which likewise characterizes the anxieties of some Cold War liberals and social democrats about the potential of a "fascist revival" as potentially as conspiratorial as Bircher beliefs about the international communist conspiracy. But even other conservatives admitted that Robert Welch's group was the largest and most successful organization on the right in the early 1960s— Martin Liebman described it as the "conservative-anti-communist apparat that we have all hoped for." Andrew, *Other Side of the Sixties,* 164.

6. Gene Grove, *Inside the John Birch Society* (New York: Gold Medal Books, 1961), 147–60. See also Mike Newberry, *The Fascist Revival: The Inside Story of the John Birch Society* (New York: New Century, 1961) for another example, which combines a somewhat distorted reading of Welch's published writing with astute observations about the popularity of the *John Franklin Letters*—a 1959 anonymously published novel positively depicting an armed uprising by "patriots" against a tyrannical U.S. government—among Birch Society members.

7. Grove, *Birch,* 148.

8. Ibid., 158–60.

9. Mulloy, *World of the John Birch Society,* 2; Peter Kihss, "Politicians Eye Rightist Power," *New York Times,* March 12, 1962, 22.

10. Robert Welch to William S. Schlamm, June 30, 1955, William F. Buckley Jr. Papers (MS 576), box 2. Manuscripts and Archives, Yale University Library, New Haven, CT; William F. Buckley Jr. to Robert Welch, October 21, 1960, William F. Buckley Jr. Papers (MS 576), box 12.

11. Robert Welch to Gerald L. K. Smith, April 24, 1962, https://archive.org/details/ RobertWelchToGeraldL.K.Smith.

12. On the social composition of the John Birch Society, see Lisa McGirr, *Suburban Warriors: The Origins of the New American Right* (Princeton, NJ: Princeton

University Press, 2001), 75–87, which emphasizes the professional and middle-class nature of the Birchers in Orange County, California. For a useful and nuanced definition and history of producerism as both a populist ethic and a means of excluding "parasitical" groups from full political citizenship, see Michael Kazin, *The Populist Persuasion: An American History* (Ithaca, NY: Cornell University Press, 1998).

13. On Welch's upbringing see Miller, *A Conspiratorial Life*, 23–43. Meany was described in the 1960 *American Opinion* "Scoreboard"—a review of supposed communist influence in every country around the globe—as having traveled to Ghana in 1957 to "extort the blacks everywhere to smash 'colonialism.' " Most of the opprobrium for labor leadership in *American Opinion*, however, was reserved for Meany's rival Walter Reuther, who was characterized by the magazine as a communist in all but name. "A World Gone Crazy," *American Opinion*, September 1960, 40; Jere Real, "This Is Walter Reuther," *American Opinion*, January 1963, 5–12.

14. On Kohlberg, a prominent member of the China lobby, and his influence on Welch and the John Birch Society, see Joyce Mao, *Asia First: China and the Making of Modern American Conservatism* (Chicago: University of Chicago Press, 2015), especially 105–35.

15. Carl T. Bogus, *Buckley: William F. Buckley, Jr. and the Rise of American Conservatism* (New York: Bloomsbury, 2011), 182–84; Mulloy, *World of the John Birch Society*, 143–51; chain letter, "Committee against Summit Entanglements," May 28, 1959, Buckley to Oliver, June 23, 1959, William F. Buckley Jr. Papers, box 9.

16. Oliver to Buckley, June 26, 1959, William F. Buckley Jr. Papers, box 9.

17. Claire Connor, *Wrapped in the Flag: What I Learned Growing Up in America's Radical Right, How I Escaped, and Why My Story Matters Today* (Boston: Beacon, 2013), 40.

18. Revilo P. Oliver, *The Jewish Strategy* (Earlysville, VA: Kevin Alfred Strom, 2002).

19. William F. Friedman to Revilo P. Oliver, June 23, 195,. National Security Archive, https://archive.org/details/41787919082692/mode/1up.

20. Oliver, *The Jewish Strategy*.

21. Revilo P. Oliver, *America's Decline: The Education of a Conservative* (London: Londinium, 1981), 54–55.

22. Bogus, *Buckley*, 183; Oliver, *America's Decline*, 57.

23. Masthead, *National Review*, April 4, 1956, 7.

24. Revilo Oliver to William F. Buckley, March 23, 1955, William F. Buckley Jr. Papers, box 2.

25. Oliver to Willmoore Kendall, March 30, 1956, Buckley to Oliver, April 18, 1956, William F. Buckley Jr. Papers, box 2.

26. Buckley to Oliver, April 18, 1956,

27. Revilo Oliver, review of Ashley Montagu, *Man: His First Million Years*, *National Review*, November 2, 1957, 405.

28. William F. Buckley Jr., "Why the South Must Prevail," *National Review*, August 24, 1957, 148–49.

29. Garry Wills, *Outside Looking In: Adventures of an Observer* (New York: Viking, 2010), 169–70.

30. "Meeting Set by Congress of Freedom," *Chicago Tribune*, March 29, 1959, 4; Buckley to Oliver, September 3, 1959, William F. Buckley Jr. Papers, box 9.

31. Oliver to Buckley, September 6, 1959, William F. Buckley Jr. Papers, box 9.

32. Buckley to Brent Bozell, December 15, 1959, William F. Buckley Jr. Papers, box 9.

33. M. S. Lurio to Buckley, December 3, 1959, Buckley to Oliver, December 16, 1959, Buckley to Lurio, December 16, 1959, William F. Buckley Jr. Papers, box 9. Oliver to Buckley, December 22, 1959, Oliver to Buckley, January 25, 1960, Buckley to Oliver, February 10, 1960, Oliver to Buckley, February 15, 1960, Oliver to Buckley, February 22, 1960, Oliver to Buckley, March 12, 1960, Buckley to Oliver, May 16, 1960, William F. Buckley Jr. Papers, box 11.

34. Buckley to Robert Welch, October 21, 1960. The primary source for Oliver's personal correspondence comes from files uploaded on the internet by Oliver's neo-Nazi disciple Kevin Alfred Strom shortly after his arrest on charges of child pornography and witness tampering in 2007. They are, at the time of this writing, still available on Strom's personal website dedicated to Oliver and his thought. According to Strom, "Due to a tragic theft aided and abetted by the FBI's 'Joint Terrorism Task Force,' only about half of Dr. Oliver's alphabetical files are available." Strom's website has not been updated since 2015. A considerable portion of the correspondence is of an academic nature. See The Revilo P. Oliver Papers, https://www.revilo-oliver.com/papers/.

35. Oliver to Buckley, December 24, 1960, William F. Buckley Jr. Papers, box 11.

36. Arnold Forster to National Civil Rights Committee, December 24, 1963, Anti-Defamation League, John Birch Society Collection, box 8, folder 11, Center for Jewish History, New York; Revilo P. Oliver, "Marxmanship in Dallas," *American Opinion*, February 1964, 13–28. The original "unedited" version of the manuscript can be found at http://www.revilo-oliver.com/rpo/Marxmanship1.html.

37. Peter Kihss, "Kennedy Target of Birch Writer," *New York Times*, February 11, 1964, 11; "L'assassinat du President Kennedy vu par la John Birch Society," *Le Monde*, February 13, 1964, 2; "Dean Defends Teacher's Right to Own Views," *Los Angeles Times*, February 13, 1964, 11; Illinois AAUP statement, February 20, 1964, box 26, folder 2, "Oliver, Revilo, Controversy, 1964," Samuel K. Gove Papers, University of Illinois Archives, Urbana; Thomas Buck, "U of I Board Hits Profs Article: Decides against Disciplinary Action," *Chicago Tribune*, March 19, 1964, 8.

38. "Birchite Backs U of I Teacher," *Chicago Tribune*, February 26, 1964, 8; "Birch Head Disputes Attack on Kennedy," *New York Times*, May 14, 1964, 42.

39. William F. Buckley Jr., "Two Who Were Smeared," *Boston Globe*, February 28, 1964, 15.

40. Peter Braestrup, "Now Birch Society Polarizes the Right," *New York Times*, April 9, 1961, E10; William F. Buckley Jr., "National Review's Position," *New York Times*, April 14, 1961, E10.

41. George Lincoln Rockwell to William F. Buckley, December 6, 1958, Buckley to Rockwell, December 23, 1958, Rockwell to Buckley, December 29, 1958, William F. Buckley Jr. Papers, box 2.

42. G. E. Voight to Fridtjef-Kara Press, May 17, 1961, William F. Buckley Jr. Papers, box 149.

43. George Lincoln Rockwell, *This Time the World* (New York: Parliament House, 1963), 199.

44. Rockwell to Buckley, August 13, 1961, William F. Buckley Jr. Papers, box 149.

45. Rockwell to Buckley, July 3, 1962, William F. Buckley Jr. Papers, box 149.

46. "Buckley, Welch, Fields, and Rockwell on TV! An Hypothesized Panel Show," *Rockwell Report* 3, no. 7 (January 1964).

47. William F. Buckley Jr., "The Conscience of George Lincoln Rockwell," *National Review,* September 19, 1967, 1011.

48. Rockwell to Buckley, May 6, 1964, William F. Buckley Jr. Papers, box 149; Buckley, "Conscience of George Lincoln Rockwell."

49. Rockwell to Buckley, May 6, 1964.

50. William F. Buckley Jr., "Public Order Ranks above the Right to Assemble in Birmingham," *Richmond News-Leader,* May 11, 1963, 8.

51. William F. Buckley to Robert Hoyt, March 18, 1963, Papers of James J. Kilpatrick, Accession #6626-b, box 6, Special Collections, University of Virginia Library, Charlottesville; Buckley to Kilpatrick, February 25, 1964, Kilpatrick Papers, Accession #6626-b, box 6; Miller, *A Conspiratorial Life,* 256–57.

52. ADL report, n.d. (post-1964), Anti-Defamation League, John Birch Society Collection, Center for Jewish History, box 1 folder 10; Russell Freeburg, "Senator Heckled by U.S. Nazis in Capital," *Chicago Tribune,* July 21, 1964, 1.

53. Charles Mohr, "Goldwater Bars Klan Aid; Confers with Eisenhower," *New York Times,* August 7, 1964, 1.

54. "Text of Goldwater Speech on Rights," *New York Times,* June 19, 1964, 18.

55. "Goldwater and Fascism," *Chicago Defender,* July 20, 1964, 11; "Says Goldwaterites Are Like Hitler Fanatics," *Chicago Defender,* October 27, 1964, 10.

56. Leah Wright Rigueur, *The Loneliness of the Black Republican: Pragmatic Politics and the Pursuit of Power* (Princeton, NJ: Princeton University Press, 2015), 47.

57. David Binder, "Khrushchev and Gomulka Assail Goldwater's Views," *New York Times,* July 22, 1964, 1.

58. Michał Kalecki, "The Fascism of Our Times (1964)," in *The Last Phase in the Transformation of Capital* (New York: Monthly Review, 1972), 99–105.

59. Frank S. Meyer, "The Birch Malady," *National Review,* October 19, 1965, 919–20; Neal Freeman, "How to Beat a Good Congressman," *National Review,* June 29, 1965, 547–50; James Burnham, "Get US Out!" *National Review,* October 19, 1965, 925–27; Barry Goldwater, letter to the editor, *National Review,* October 19, 1965, 928–29.

60. Richard F. Plechner Oral History Interview, January 16, 2008, by Sandra Stewart Holyoak and Mary Lou Strahlendorff, Page #, Rutgers Oral History Archives, https://oralhistory.rutgers.edu/alphabetical-index/interviewees/30-interview-html-text/318-plechner-richard-f-part-2; "Anti-Semitic Charges Stir Up Storm for

Young GOP," *Central Jersey Home News,* January 28, 1966, 8; David Schmerler, "Rightist Says Song Spoofed Liberals," *Hackensack Record,* February 2, 1966, 1.

61. Jerry Bakst to Arnold Forster, September 2, 1965, box 5, folder 14, Anti-Defamation League, John Birch Society Collection, box 8, folder 11.

CHAPTER 7. THE BIRTH OF THE WHITE POWER MOVEMENT

1. On the history of *Firing Line,* see Heather Hendershot, *Open to Debate: How William F. Buckley Put Liberal America on the Firing Line* (New York: Broadside Books, 2016), especially 105–8. James J. Kilpatrick, "What Makes Wallace Run?" *National Review,* April 18, 1967, 400–409; "The Wallace Movement," *Firing Line with William F. Buckley Jr* (New Orleans, LA, April 15, 1968), Hoover Institution, Firing Line broadcast records, https://digitalcollections.hoover.org/objects/6029.

2. "The Wallace Crusade," *Firing Line with William F. Buckley Jr* (St. Louis, MO, January 24, 1968), Hoover Institution, Firing Line broadcast records, https://digitalcollections.hoover.org/objects/6022. On grassroots conservative support for Wallace, see John H. Huntington, *Far-Right Vanguard: The Radical Roots of Modern Conservatism* (Philadelphia: University of Pennsylvania Press, 2021), 194–99

3. On the international dimensions of conservative and far-right politics in the United States, see Kyle Burke, *Revolutionaries for the Right: Anticommunist Internationalism and Paramilitary Warfare in the Cold War* (Chapel Hill: University of North Carolina Press, 2018); and on the origins of the white power movement, see Kathleen Belew, *Bring the War Home: The White Power Movement and Paramilitary America* (Cambridge, MA: Harvard University Press, 2018).

4. "The Wallace Crusade."

5. This scholarship is too vast to cite. For a primer, see, for instance, the 1619 Project in the *New York Times.*

6. Hendershot, *Open to Debate.* For a recent example of *National Review* embracing race/IQ science, see, for instance, Robert Verbruggen, "Why I Write about Race and IQ," *National Review,* July 5, 2017. See also John P. Jackson and Andrew S. Winston, "The Mythical Taboo on Race and Intelligence," *Review of General Psychology* 25, no. 1 (2021): 3–26.

7. On the social composition of the John Birch Society, see Lisa McGirr, *Suburban Warriors: The Origins of the New American Right* (Princeton, NJ: Princeton University Press, 2001).On the attitudes of the John Birch Society toward the civil rights movement, see D. J. Mulloy, *The World of the John Birch Society: Conspiracy, Conservatism, and the Cold War* (Nashville, TN: Vanderbilt University Press, 2014), 107–37.

8. Mulloy, *World of the John Birch Society,* 107.

9. Ibid., 109.

10. *Anarchy U.S.A.,* filmstrip (John Birch Society, 1966), https://www.c-span.org/video/?420311-1/anarchy-usa; Mulloy, *World of the John Birch Society,* 133.

11. U.S. House, Committee on Un-American Activities, *Investigation of Communist Activities in the New York City Area,* 81st Cong., 1st sess. (May 4, 1953), 2136–38;

U.S. House, Committee on Un-American Activities, *Investigation of Communist Activities in the Baltimore Area*, 83rd Cong., 2nd sess. (March 25, 1954), 4121–24; State of Louisiana, *Subversion in Racial Unrest: An Outline of a Strategic Weapon to Destroy the Governments of Louisiana and the United States*, Public Hearings of the State of Louisiana Joint Legislative Committee, March 6–9, 1957 (Baton Rouge), 107–9.

12. Meredith L. Roman, *Opposing Jim Crow: African Americans and the Soviet Indictment of U.S. Racism, 1928–1937* (Lincoln: University of Nebraska Press, 2012), 155–57.

13. Ibid., 162.

14. Louisiana, *Subversion in Racial Unrest*, 112.

15. Louis Lisman to Isadore Zack, January 25, 1965, Anti-Defamation League, John Birch Society Collection, box 5, folder 11, Center for Jewish History, New York; "Former FBI 'Agent' Calls Dr. King Patsy for Reds," *Burlington Free Press*, January 20, 1965; Justin F. Finger to ADL Regional Offices, July 5, 1967, Anti-Defamation League, John Birch Society Collection, box 5, folder 11.

16. Report on Lola Belle Holmes, April 3, 1967; Sol Rabkin to Robert Carter, April 11, 1967, Anti-Defamation League, John Birch Society Collection, box 7, folder 46, characterized some of Holmes's remarks about the civil rights movement as close to slander and raised the possibility (which was dismissed) of legal action against her.

17. Arnold Forster and Benjamin R. Epstein, *Danger on the Right* (New York: Random House, 1964); Samuel Blumenfeld profile, February 1966, box 5, folder 6, Anti-Defamation League, John Birch Society Collection; Jewish Society of Americanists Statement of Principles, n.d., box 18, folder 19, Anti-Defamation League, John Birch Society Collection; Irwin Suall to Arnold Forster, December 8, 1968, box 18, folder 22, Anti-Defamation League, John Birch Society Collection.

18. Revilo P. Oliver, *Conspiracy or Degeneracy? The Complete Text of an Address Given at the New England Rally for God, Family, and Country in Boston, Massachusetts, July 2, 1966, Together with Documentary and Supplemental Notes* (Nedrow, NY: Power Products, 1967); William F. Buckley Jr. to Brent Bozell, December 15, 1959, William F. Buckley Jr. Papers (MS 576), box 9, Manuscripts and Archives, Yale University Library, New Haven, CT.

19. Benjamin R. Epstein to Arnold Forster, August 22, 1966, box 9, folder 33, Anti-Defamation League, John Birch Society Collection.

20. Oliver to Donna Allegro, June 14 1970, The Revilo P. Oliver Papers, https://www.revilo-oliver.com/papers/.

21. *The John Franklin Letters* (New York: Bookmailer, 1959).

22. Revilo Oliver, "A Review of Reviews," *American Opinion*, February 1960, 44.

23. Daniel Levitas, *The Terrorist Next Door: The Militia Movement and the Radical Right* (New York: St. Martin's Press, 2002), 66–73.

24. Art Spiegel to Isadore Zack, January 7, 1966, Anti-Defamation League, John Birch Society Collection, box 2, folder 14.

25. Donna Allegro to Oliver, June 8 1970, Revilo P. Oliver Papers.

26. Rick Perlstein, *Nixonland: The Rise of a President and the Fracturing of America* (New York: Simon & Schuster, 2008), 282. Carl T. Bogus, *Buckley: William F. Buckley, Jr. and the Rise of American Conservatism* (New York: Bloomsbury, 2011), 337.

27. Garry Allen, "Mr. Nixon: A Hard Look at the Candidate," *American Opinion*, September 1968, 1–23; Susan L. M. Huck, "Mr. Wallace: A Hard Look at the Candidate," *American Opinion*, September 1968, 25–40.

28. Hunter S. Thompson, *Fear and Loathing on the Campaign Trail '72* (San Francisco: Straight Arrow, 1973), 139.

29. Dan T. Carter, *The Politics of Rage: George Wallace, the Origins of the New Conservatism, and the Transformation of American Politics* (New York: Simon & Schuster, 1995), 301, 310; "Tom Turnipseed," *The Times* [UK], March 26, 2020, https://www.thetimes.co.uk/article/tom-turnipseed-obituary-v6odgvmtb.

30. Harald Friedrich to Curtis LeMay, October 22, 1968, box D2, Curtis E. LeMay Papers, 1918–1969, Library of Congress, Washington DC.

31. Richard G. Thomas, "U.S. Pressure Scuttled Africa Trip, Group Says," *Dayton Journal Herald*, February 3, 1968, 13.

32. Barrett told reporters that Genovese had "knifed every American soldier in the back by his acts." C. M. Howard, "Loyal Son of Rutgers Hands Back His Sheepskin," *Central New Jersey Home News*, June 23, 1966, 4.

33. Ironically, the Klan's attitude toward Barrett is known only because of the rampant FBI infiltration of the Klan in the late 1960s—the attitudes of the various Klan groups in the state toward Barrett, based on these informant reports, is contained in Barrett's FBI file. Notably, the file also indicates that Barrett was uncooperative with the bureau, which he considered to be a proto-Gestapo. Federal Bureau of Investigation, "Richard Barrett," n.d., https://archive.org/details/RichardBarrett/Richard%20Barrett%2001/.

34. "Wallace Group Head Hits GOP," *Birmingham Post-Herald*, August 9, 1968, 4.

35. "Conservative Angels Back 'Youth for Wallace' Drive," *Oregonian*, September 3, 1968, 12.

36. Susan Gainen, "Wallace Captures Youth," *Diamondback*, October 22, 1968, 2; Frank Coots, "Kentucky Youth for Wallace Map Strategy," *Kentucky Kernel*, October 23, 1968, 2.

37. Charles Hopkins, "Blacks for Wallace?" *Duke Chronicle*, October 10, 1968, 6–7. For more on Hopkins and Black student activism at Duke in the 1960s, see Theodore D. Segal, *Point of Reckoning: The Fight for Racial Justice at Duke University* (Durham, NC: Duke University Press, 2021).

38. Bob Ashley, "Wallace Visits Durham, Lashes out at Academia," *Duke Chronicle*, October 25, 1968, 1; editorial, "The Wallace Threat," ibid., 4.

39. Richard Smirthwaite, "Campus Political Leaders React to Bombing Pause," *Duke Chronicle*, November 2, 1968, 1.

40. Federal Bureau of Investigation, "National Youth Alliance, File No. 157 3447," "National Youth Alliance," March 31, 1970, 1, https://archive.org/details/NationalYouthAllianceNYC15734471. Note that Acord's name is redacted but his identity as the FBI's primary source for the report is easily discernable because

he was identified as an agent of the American Southern African Council, Acord's Rhodesia organization, in an unredacted portion of the text.

41. On the development of the National Youth Alliance and the Pittsburgh conference, see George Michael, *Willis Carto and the American Far Right* (Gainesville: University Press of Florida, 2008), 95–98. See also FBI, "National Youth Alliance," March 31, 1970, 1–6.

42. FBI, "National Youth Alliance, File No. 157 3447," National Youth Alliance NEWS [Acord faction newsletter], no. 2, June 1969; National Youth Alliance [Acord faction] press release, June 17, 1969, https://ia801002.us.archive.org/27/items/nationalyouthalliancenyc1573447_201908/National%20Youth%20Alliance%20-%20NYC%20157-3447.pdf.

43. FBI, "National Youth Alliance, File No. 157 3447," "National Youth Alliance," March 31, 1970, 8, https://ia801002.us.archive.org/27/items/nationalyouthalliancenyc1573447_201908/National%20Youth%20Alliance%20-%20NYC%20157-3447.pdf.

44. Ibid., 18.

45. Ibid., 15.

46. James Parker Faris to William Luther Pierce, November 9, 1968, Faris to Revilo Oliver, November 21, 1968, Oliver Papers.

47. FBI, "National Youth Alliance, File No. 157 3447," "National Youth Alliance," March 31, 1970, 23.

48. Ibid.; *Downtowner*, September 23, 1970.

49. Michael, *Carto*, 97.

50. FBI, "National Youth Alliance, File No. 157 3447," https://ia801002.us.archive.org/27/items/nationalyouthalliancenyc1573447_201908/National%20Youth%20Alliance%20-%20NYC%20157-3447.pdf; "Why Revolution?" *Attack!* Summer 1971.

51. FBI, "National Youth Alliance, File No. 157 3447," "Revolutionary Notes," *Attack!*, Summer 1971; Abbie Hoffman, *Steal This Book* (New York: Pirate Editions, 1971); William Powell, *The Anarchist Cookbook* (New York: Lyle Stuart, 1971).

52. Robert S. Griffin, *The Fame of a Dead Man's Deeds: An Up-Close Portrait of White Nationalist William Pierce* (Bloomington, IN: Book Library, 2001).

53. On the YAF's political fissures in the late 1960s, see Gregory L. Schneider, *Cadres for Conservatism: Young Americans for Freedom and the Rise of the Contemporary Right* (New York: New York University Press, 1999), 127–45.

54. FBI, "National Youth Alliance, File No. 157 3447," "National Youth Alliance/Racial Matters," May 20, 1969, 5, https://ia801002.us.archive.org/27/items/nationalyouthalliancenyc1573447_201908/National%20Youth%20Alliance%20-%20NYC%20157-3447.pdf. Given the heavy redaction in this file, it is impossible to determine the FBI's source for this information.

55. D. Frank Andrews to Revilo P. Oliver, November 4, 1970, Oliver to Andrews, December 11, 1970, Oliver Papers; *The Right Angle*, Stuart A. Rose Manuscript, Archives, and Rare Book Library, Emory University, Atlanta.

56. C. H. Simonds, "The Strange Story of Willis Carto," *National Review*, September 10, 1971, 978–89; Michael, *Carto*, 98.

CHAPTER 8. WHO OWNS CONSERVATISM?

1. Eric Pace, "National Review Losing Buckley as Chief Editor," *New York Times*, October 6, 1990, 28.
2. Rick Hampson, "Verbal Battle Wages over Mideast," *Fort Worth Star-Telegram*, September 20, 1990, 6.
3. Randall Rothenberg, "Thunder on the Right," September 6, 1990, A21.
4. A. M. Rosenthal, "Forgive Them Not," *New York Times*, September 14, 1990, A33.
5. Eleanor Randolph and Howard Kurtz, "Rosenthal Attacks Buchanan," *Washington Post*, September 15, 1990, D1.
6. Richard Cohen, "Buchanan Had It Coming," *Washington Post*, September 25, 1990, A23;
7. Debra Nussbaum, "Jews Repudiate Buchanan's 'Anti-Semitic' Remarks," *American Israelite*, October 11, 1990, 20; Edward Alexander, "Buchanan's Abhorrent Record Mirrors His Long-Standing Anti-Semitism," *Jewish Exponent*, October 19, 1990, 37.
8. William F. Buckley Jr., "Patrick Buchanan and the Antisemitism Flap," *Washington Post*, September 19, 1990, A23.
9. William F. Buckley Jr., "In Search of Anti-Semitism," *National Review*, December 30, 1991, 20–62; William F. Buckley Jr., *In Search of Anti-Semitism* (New York, Continuum, 1992).
10. Kathleen Belew, *Bring the War Home: The White Power Movement and Paramilitary America* (Cambridge, MA: Harvard University Press, 2018).
11. "And, from the Fever Swamps," *National Review*, August 9, 1985, 20.
12. Michael, *Willis Carto and the American Far Right*.
13. The offending article was Gregory F. Rose, "The Swarmy Life and Times of the NCLC," *National Review*, March 30, 1979, 409.
14. Suzanne Garment, "Capital Chronicle," *Wall Street Journal*, October 11, 1985, 28.
15. Lawrence Feinberg, "Lawyer Puts Buckley on the Firing Line in D.C. Libel Trial," *Washington Post*, October 11, 1985, C7.
16. Joyce Hens Green, interview by Jennifer M. Porter, March 11, 2001, in Washington, DC, transcript, Historical Society of the District of Columbia Circuit, Washington, DC, https://dcchs.org/sb_pdf/interview-6-joyce-hens-green/;Francis X. Clines, "A $160,000 Riposte Wins $1,001," *New York Times*, October 28, 1985, A12.
17. Lawrence Feinberg, "*National Review* Wins $1,001 in Libel Suit against Liberty Lobby," *Washington Post*, October 26, 1985, C3.
18. Green interview.
19. On Rothbard, see Daniel Bessner, "Murray Rothbard, Political Strategy, and the Making of Modern Libertarianism," *Intellectual History Review* 24, no. 4 (December 2014): 441–56; and John P. Jackson, "The Pre-History of Holocaust Denial," *American Jewish History* 105, nos. 1/2 (January/April 2021): 25–48. See also Murray Rothbard, "Right-Wing Populism: A Strategy for the Paleo Movement," *Rothbard-Rockwell Report*, January 1992, 5–14.
20. George H. Nash, "The Historical Roots of Contemporary American Conservatism," *Modern Age*, Summer 1982, 303. On the racial anxieties see,

most infamously, Norman Podhoretz, the author of a 1963 cover story in *Commentary* entitled "My Negro Problem—and Ours."

21. Susanne Klingenstein, " 'It's Splendid When the Town Whore Gets Religion and Joins the Church': The Rise of the Jewish Neoconservatives as Observed by the Paleoconservatives in the 1980s," *Shofar* 21, no. 3 (Spring 2003): 83–98.

22. M. J. Sobran Jr., "The Printed Word: Opening Questions," *National Review*, September 12, 1975, 996–97.

23. "Come on in, the Water's Fine," *National Review*, March 9, 1971, 249.

24. See Peter Steinfels, *The Neoconservatives: The Origins of a Movement* (New York: Simon & Schuster, 1979); and Murray Friedman, *The Neoconservative Revolution: Jewish Intellectuals and the Shaping of Public Policy* (New York: Cambridge University Press, 2005).

25. Russell Kirk, "Some Predictions for 1970," *Human Events*, January 10, 1970, 12; Nathan Glazer, "The New Left and Its Limits," *Commentary*, July 1968, https://www.commentary.org/articles/nathan-glazer-2/the-new-left-and-its-limits/; Thomas Jeffers, *Norman Podhoretz: A Biography* (New York: Cambridge University Press, 2011), 77–79.

26. Paul Gottfried, "A View of Contemporary Conservatism," *Intercollegiate Review*, Spring 1986, 18–21.

27. See, for example, Daniel Patrick Moynihan, "The Schism in Black America," *Public Interest*, spring 1972, and Daniel Patrick Moynihan "How the Great Society 'Destroyed the American Family,' " *Public Interest*, Summer 1992. See also R. J. Herrnstein, "Still an American Dilemma," *Public Interest*, Winter 1990; and Arthur R. Jensen, "IQ and Science: The Mysterious Burt Affair," *Public Interest*, Fall 1991.

28. "McDonald's Last Words," *American Opinion*, October 1983, 1; "Reagan vs. the New Right," *Newsweek*, September 19, 1983, 37; Lou Cannon, "Reagan Seeks Limits on Soviet Airliners," *Washington Post*, September 5, 1983, A1; "Conservatives Dismayed by Limp Response to Soviets," *Human Events*, September 17, 1983, 796–97.

29. "Humanities Dept. Bankrolling Leftist Democratic Network," *Human Events*, October 31, 1981, 965.

30. Carla Hall, "Bradford's Boosters: 16 GOP Senators Push Texan for NEH Chair," *Washington Post*, October 20, 1981, D1.

31. Don Irwin, "Top Choice for Humanities Post in Doubt," *Los Angeles Times*, October 31, 1981, A11.

32. Bradford also bragged that Eugene Genovese, at the time still widely identified as a Marxist, supported his nomination. Carla Hall, "Bradford Speaks Out," *Washington Post*, October 28, 1981, B1.

33. "Humanities Dept. Bankrolling Leftist Democratic Network."

34. Hall, "Bradford Speaks Out."

35. George F. Will, "A Shrill Assault on Mr. Lincoln," *Washington Post*, November 29, 1981, C7; "Helms Wants Assurance on NEH," *Washington Post*, December 25, 1981, E2.

36. Eric Foner, "Lincoln, Bradford, and the Conservatives," *New York Times,* February 13, 1982, 25.

37. M. J. Sobran Jr., "Lay-Deez and Gen-Tle-Mennn: Pree-Zen-Ting . . . the Orgulous . . . Supersubtle . . . Garry . . . Wills!!!" *National Review,* June 22, 1973, 676–81; M. J. Sobran Jr., "The Sage and Serious Doctrine of Hugh Hefner," *National Review,* February 1, 1974, 133–36.

38. M. J. Sobran Jr., "Of Ms. and Men," *National Review,* May 24, 1974, 579–81; M. J. Sobran Jr., "Having It Both Ways," *National Review,* November 8, 1974, 1302; Joseph Sobran, "Pensées: Notes for the Reactionary of Tomorrow," *National Review,* December 31, 1985, 24–58.

39. Joseph Sobran, "Israel's World Is Reality, Not Fantasy," *Detroit Free Press,* July 20, 1981, 7.

40. Joseph Sobran, ". . . We Can't Take Mondale on Faith," *Detroit Free Press,* September 13, 1984, 11.

41. Joseph Sobran, "Race, Realism, and Reality," *Chico Enterprise-Record,* May 12, 1986, 24.

42. Norman Podhoretz, "The Hate That Dare Not Speak Its Name," *Commentary* 82, no. 5 (November 1986): 21; John S. Friedman, "Culture War II," *Nation,* April 18, 1981, 452–53.

43. John B. Judis, *William F. Buckley, Jr., Patron Saint of the Conservatives* (New York: Simon & Schuster, 1988), 458–60.

44. Stephen Chapman, "A Conservative Thinker and the Racist Right," *Chicago Tribune,* June 22, 1986, D2; Richard Cohen, "Conservatism and Anti-Semitism," *Washington Post,* June 25, 1986, A25; Jonathan Alter, "A Columnist under Fire: Charge: Anti-Semitism," *Newsweek,* July 7, 1986, 64–67; Alexander Cockburn, "The Likes of Sobran," *Nation,* June 7, 1986, 785.

45. William F. Buckley Jr., "In Re Joe Sobran and Anti-Semitism," *National Review,* July 4, 1986, 20.

46. Brian Lamb, *The Sobran Scandal,* C-SPAN video, 58 minutes, July 14, 1986, https://www.c-span.org/video/?123711–1/sobran-scandal.

47. Nicholas Lemann, *The Promised Land: The Great Black Migration and How It Changed America* (New York: Knopf, 1991), 210; Patrick J. Buchanan, *Right from the Beginning* (Washington, DC: Regnery, 1998).

48. Michael Koncewicz, *They Said No to Nixon: Republicans Who Stood Up to the President's Abuse of Power* (Berkeley: University of California Press, 2018), 164.

49. Rowland Evans and Robert Novak, "Haig Crisis in White House," *Orlando Sentinel,* September 8, 1974, 30; William V. Shannon, "The Good Ship Lollipop," *New York Times,* September 18, 1974, 41; Pat Buchanan, interview by Richard Norton Smith, October 4, 2010, in Ann Arbor, Michigan, transcript, Gerald R. Ford Oral History Project, Ann Arbor, MI, https://geraldrfordfoundation.org/centennial/oralhistory/pat-buchanan/.

50. Patrick J. Buchanan, *Conservative Votes, Liberal Victories: Why the Right Has Failed* (New York: New York Times Book Co., 1975), 138; William A. Rusher, *The Making of the New Majority Party* (New York: Sheed & Ward, 1975), 107; Jeane Kirkpatrick, "Why the New Right Lost," *Commentary,* February 1, 1977, 34–39;

Julilly Kohler-Hausmann, "Welfare Crises, Penal Solutions, and the Origins of the 'Welfare Queen,' " *Journal of Urban History* 41, no. 5 (September 2015): 756–71.

51. Patrick J. Buchanan, "Politicians, Blacks out of Touch," *Chicago Tribune*, March 6, 1980, B4.

52. "House Critic Buchanan Joins Reagan's Team," *Time*, February 18, 1985; "The New Staff, Continued," *National Review*, March 8, 1985, 17.

53. William F. Buckley Jr., "Pat Buchanan's Gutsy Way," *National Review*, April 5, 1985, 62.

54. Rowland Evans and Robert Novak, "Man for the Cause," *Washington Post*, February 8, 1985, A19; "Liberal Media Stung by Buchanan Choice," *Human Events*, February 16, 1985, 3; Elizabeth Kastor, "The Popular Front: Cheering Buchanan at the CPAC Bash," *Washington Post*, March 2, 1985, G1.

55. Dave Walter, "Antigay Conservative Named to White House Communications Post," *Advocate*, March 19, 1985, 15.

56. Lou Cannon, "Buchanan Seen Hurting President," *Washington Post*, April 27, 1985, A1.

57. Jacob S. Eder, *Holocaust Angst: The Federal Republic of Germany and American Holocaust Memory since the 1970s* (New York: Oxford University Press, 2016), 63–64.

58. "Group Criticizes Buchanan over Views on Nazi-Hunting," *Washington Post*, April 10, 1985, A5; Licette Lagnado, "Pat Buchanan and the Émigré Nazis," *Nation*, May 4, 1985, 525.

59. "Jews Are Angry at Pat Buchanan," *Jewish Exponent*, April 19, 1985, 8.

60. Lou Cannon, "Reagan Team Falters on Damage Control," *Washington Post*, April 20, 1985, A1.

61. Eleanor Randolph, "Buchanan's Jottings Cited 'Pressure' of Jews, NBC Says," *Washington Post*, May 3, 1985, A13.

62. James R. Dickenson, "Buchanan Says Story on His Note-Taking is 'Silly,' " *Washington Post*, May 4, 1985, A5.

63. There have been any number of books and articles written about the Demjanjuk case in English, German, and Hebrew—the trial in Jerusalem even inspired a 2005 cabaret show satirizing the political circus of the case. By far the most comprehensive and nuanced is the legal history by Lawrence Douglas, *The Right Wrong Man: John Demjanjuk and the Last Great Nazi War Crimes Trial* (Princeton, NJ: Princeton University Press, 2016). See also " 'Holocaust Cabaret' about Demjanjuk Case Plays Heidelberg," *Local DE*, March 29, 2010, https://www.thelocal.de/20100329/26191/.

64. Patrick J. Buchanan, "Nazi Butcher or Mistaken Identity?" *Washington Post*, September 28, 1986, C1.

65. L. A. Rollins, "The Holocaust as a Sacred Cow," *Journal of Historical Review* 4, no. 1 (Spring 1983).

66. Mark Weber, "The Japanese Camps in California," *Journal of Historical Review* 2, no. 1 (Spring 1981): 45–58.

67. Ted O'Keefe, review of *Quiet Neighbors: Prosecuting Nazi War Criminals in America, Journal of Historical Review* 6, no. 2 (Summer 1985): 231–37.

68. "White House Communications Chief Indicates Supporting Nazi Scientist," *Pacific Daily News,* October 18, 1985, 59.

69. "Buchanan Fighting Nazi's Deportation," *Tampa Tribune,* February 13, 1987, 86.

70. Jay Matthews, "Nazi Hunters Brace for Criticism in Linnas Case," *Washington Post,* July 14, 1986.

71. Pat Buchanan, "The Wrong Man May Be Hanged by Israeli Court," *Tennessean,* March 19, 1990, 10.

72. Alan Dershowitz, "Pat Buchanan's Heart Bleeds for Nazi War Criminals," *Rochester Democrat and Chronicle,* March 27, 1990, 8. Dershowitz had written intermittently about Buchanan and the Demjanjuk case throughout the late 1980s—a column a year earlier compared Buchanan's defense of Demjanjuk to white supremacist newspapers like *Thunderbolt* and the *National Socialist Bulletin.* Alan Dershowitz, "Pat Buchanan's Attacks on Jews Are Alarming," *Tampa Bay Times,* October 7, 1989, 14; Mark Lasswell, "Pat Buchanan's Gonna Punch You out, You Flag-Burnin,' Bleeding-Heart, Commie Simp . . . but Only if Your Back Is Turned," *GQ,* August 1, 1990, 147.

73. Rosenthal, "Forgive Them Not," A33.

74. Ibid., 24, 38.

75. Sam Tanenhaus, "Athwart History," *New Republic,* March 19, 2007,. 31–33.

76. William F. Buckley Jr., "In Search of Anti-Semitism," *National Review,* December 30, 1991, 21; John O'Sullivan, "A Note to Our Readers," 1–5.

77. Richard Brookhiser, "Waiting for Righty," *National Review,* January 20, 1992, 40–42; William McGurn, "Pat Buchanan and the Intellectuals," *National Review,* February 17, 1992, 41–43; "Mr. Buchanan's Choice," *National Review,* March 2, 1992, 12–15.

78. Peter Berger, Walter Berns, Robert H. Bork, Terry Eastland, Patrick Glynn, Michael Joyce, Harvey C. Mansfield Jr., Richard John Neuhaus, James Nuechterlein, Michael Novak, Thomas L. Pangle, R. Emmett Tyrrell Jr., and George Weigel, "Dissent on the Right," and William F. Buckley, letter to editor response, *National Review,* March 16, 1992, 5; John O'Sullivan, "First Word, Last Word," *National Review,* March 16, 1992, 6.

79. John O'Sullivan, "Mr. Buchanan and His Friends," *National Review,* March 16, 1992, 40.

80. "Divided We Fall," *National Review,* March 30, 1992, 11–13; William McGurn, "The Boys on the Bus," *National Review,* March 30, 1992, 18–20.

81. Michael Barone, "The New Face of American Politics," *National Review,* April 27, 1992, 38–39. On the political implications of Buchanan's speech and its influence on the subsequent "culture wars," see Andrew Hartman, *A War for the Soul of America: A History of the Culture Wars* (Chicago: University of Chicago Press, 2015).

82. Ramesh Ponnuru, "A Conservative No More," *National Review,* October 11, 1999, 34–38.

83. Joseph Sobran, "New Democrats Come to Town," *National Review,* February 1, 1993, 38–46; Joseph Sobran, "An Essay by Joseph Sobran," *National Review,* March 16, 1992, S4–S10; Joseph Sobran, "The Rise of Style," *National Review,* June 21, 1993, 30–31.

84. Joseph Sobran, "New Beginning," *Wanderer,* January 28, 1993, 5; Joseph Sobran, "Memories," *Wanderer,* May 13, 1993, 5; Joseph Sobran, "My Dinner with Bill," *Wanderer,* September 30, 1993, 5; William F. Buckley Jr., letter to the editor, *Wanderer,* October 14, 1993, 4; Joseph Sobran, "Firing Line," *Wanderer,* October 21, 1993, 5.

85. Matthew Scully, "Bard of the Right," *National Review,* November 1, 2010, 35–39.

86. Timothy Stanley, *The Crusader: The Life and Tumultuous Times of Pat Buchanan* (New York: St. Martin's, 2012), 359; John Lukacs, "Necessary Evil," *American Conservative,* June 2, 2008, https://www.theamericanconservative.com/articles/necessary-evil/.

EPILOGUE

1. Rick Perlstein, "I Thought I Understood the American Right. Trump Proved Me Wrong," *New York Times Magazine,* April 11, 2017, https://www.nytimes.com/2017/04/11/magazine/i-thought-i-understood-the-american-right-trump-proved-me-wrong.html.

2. John H. Huntington, *Far-Right Vanguard: The Radical Roots of Modern Conservatism* (Philadelphia: University of Pennsylvania Press, 2021); Julian Zelizer, *Burning Down the House: Newt Gingrich, the Fall of a Speaker, and the Rise of the New Republican Party* (New York: Penguin, 2020); Nicole Hemmer, *Partisans: The Conservative Revolutionaries Who Remade American Politics in the 1990s* (New York: Basic Books, 2022).

3. One of the earliest pieces speculating on Trump and fascism was an interview by Isaac Chotiner of Robert Paxton for *Slate* in February 2016. See Isaac Chotiner, "Is Donald Trump a Fascist?" *Slate,* February 10, 2016, https://slate.com/news-and-politics/2016/02/is-donald-trump-a-fascist-an-expert-on-fascism-weighs-in.html; and Isabel Best, "Should We Even Go There? Historians on Comparing Fascism to Trumpism," *Guardian,* December 1, 2016, https://www.theguardian.com/us-news/2016/dec/01/comparing-fascism-donald-trump-historians-trumpism. See also Udi Greenberg, "What Was the Fascism Debate?" *Dissent,* Summer 2021.

4. Robert O. Paxton, "I've Hesitated to Call Donald Trump a Fascist. Until Now," *Newsweek,* January 11, 2021, https://www.newsweek.com/robert-paxton-trump-fascist-1560652.

5. Probably the most influential argument about the dangers of liberal anti-fascism is articulated in Daniel Bessner and Matthew Sparke, "Nazism, Neoliberalism, and the Trumpist Challenge to Democracy," *Environment and Planning A: Economy and Space* 49, no. 6 (2017): 1214–23. See also Samuel Moyn, "The Trouble with Comparisons," *New York Review of Books,* May 19, 2020, https://www.nybooks.com/daily/2020/05/19/the-trouble-with-comparisons/; Dylan Riley, "What Is Trump?" *New Left Review,* November/December 2018, 5–31.

6. Adolph Reed, "The Whole Country Is the *Reichstag*," *Nonsite.org*, August 23, 2021, https://nonsite.org/the-whole-country-is-the-reichstag/; Christopher Cadelago and Olivia Olander, "Biden Calls Trump's Philosophy 'Semi-Fascism,' " *Politico*, August 25, 2022, https://www.politico.com/news/2022/08/25/biden-trump-philosophy-semi-fascism-00053831. On the broader question of fascism in American history, see Olivier Burtin, "Fascism Has an American History, Too," *Reviews in American History* 49, no. 3 (September 2021): 494–520.

7. Jonah Goldberg, *Liberal Fascism: The Secret History of the American Left, from Mussolini to the Politics of Meaning* (New York: Doubleday, 2007).

8. Aimé Césaire, *Discourse on Colonialism* (1951; repr., New York: Monthly Review,2000); Kathleen Cleaver, "Racism, Fascism, and Political Murder," *Black Panther*, September 14, 1968, in Bill V. Mulklen and Christopher Vials, eds., *The U.S. Antifascism Reader* (New York: Verso, 2020), 260–67.

9. Robert Paxton, "The Scholarly Flaws of 'Liberal Fascism,' " *History News Network*, 2010, https://historynewsnetwork.org/article/122231.

10. Eric Hananoki, "Glenn Beck's New Book Club Pick: Nazi Sympathizer Who Praised Hitler and Denounced the Allies," *Media Matters*, June 4, 2010, https://www.mediamatters.org/glenn-beck/glenn-becks-new-book-club-pick-nazi-sympathizer-who-praised-hitler-and-denounced-allies.

11. Paul E. Gottfried and Richard B. Spencer, eds., *The Great Purge: The Deformation of the American Conservative Movement* (Arlington, VA: Washington Summit, 2015); Rich Lowry, "Parting Ways," *National Review*, April 7, 2012, https://www.nationalreview.com/corner/parting-ways-rich-lowry/.

12. "Against Trump," *National Review*, January 22, 2016, https://www.nationalreview.com/2016/01/donald-trump-conservative-movement-menace/; Robert P. Saldin and Steven M. Teles, *Never Trump: The Revolt of the Conservative Elites* (New York: Oxford University Press, 2020).

13. Jeet Heer, "*National Review*'s Sad Surrender to Trump," *New Republic*, January 31, 2017, https://newrepublic.com/article/140287/national-reviews-sad-surrender-trump.

America First Committee (AFC): and American Action, 83, 85; and anti-semitism, 77; and Carey McWilliams, 82; and Charles Lindbergh, 61–62; and Gerald L.K. Smith, 72; and history of, 253n8; and *Human Events*, 82, 95; and John T. Flynn, 56, 74; and Merwin K. Hart, 16, 53; operation of, 57; organization of, 55; reception of, 86; and Yale University, 55

America First movement: and accusations of fascism, 56–57; and American Action, 104; and Americanism, 73; and Avedis Derounian, 66; and Charles Lindbergh, 57; and Frank C. Hanighen, 95; and Franklin Delano Roosevelt, 64; and Gerald K. Smith, 73; and Gerald Nye, 61; and isolationism, 52; and John T. Flynn, 58; and Merwin K. Hart, 58; in New York City, 60–61; opposition to, 64–65; and politics, 55–58; and Robert Wood, 72, 85

America First Party, 53, 72–73

American Action, 10, 75, 78, 82–88, 98, 104, 158

American Catholics, 40–41, 136, 202, 216, 232

American Communist Party, 44, 67, 106

American conservatism: characteristics of, 250n71; and the conservative coalition, 5–6, 11, 55, 89, 98, 103, 105, 120, 127, 136, 139, 156, 159, 167, 178, 193–94, 201, 203–4, 206, 214–15, 218, 228–29, 231; and the conservative movement, 1–2, 5–6, 152, 159–60, 176, 178, 195, 205–7, 216, 223, 227, 229–31, 233, 235–38; and Donald Trump, 236, 238; evolution of, 6, 239, 242n9; and fascism, 2, 236; and the far right, 2, 17; and George W. Bush, 226; history of, 242n14; and the John Birch Society, 178; and the *National Review*, 5; and William F. Buckley Jr., 2, 5, 127, 181; and World War II, 5. *See also* American right

American Federation of Labor (AFL), 29–30, 34, 89, 160; and AFL–CIO, 160, 273n5

American left, 43, 107

American Legion, 48–49, 54, 83, 86, 139

American Liberty League, 30–33, 85